Pivotal Response Treatment for Autism Spectrum Disorders

Pivotal Response Treatment for Autism Spectrum Disorders

Second Edition

edited by

Robert L. Koegel, Ph.D.
Stanford University School of Medicine
Stanford, CA

and

Lynn Kern Koegel, Ph.D., CCC-SLP
Stanford University School of Medicine
Stanford, CA

with invited contributors

·PAUL·H·
BROOKES
PUBLISHING CO.®

Baltimore • London • Sydney

·P A U L·H·
BROOKES
PUBLISHING CO.®

Paul H. Brookes Publishing Co.
Post Office Box 10624
Baltimore, Maryland 21285-0624
USA

www.brookespublishing.com

Typeset by Progressive Publishing Services, York, Pennsylvania.
Manufactured in the United States of America by Sheridan Books, Inc., Chelsea, Michigan.

The individuals described in this book are composites or real people whose situations are masked and are based on the authors' experiences. In all instances, names and identifying details have been changed to protect confidentiality.

Case studies are real people or composites based on the authors' experiences. Pseudonyms have been used and identifying details are altered to preserve confidentiality.

Library of Congress Cataloging-in-Publication Data

Names: Koegel, Robert L., 1944– author. | Koegel, Lynn Kern, author.
Title: Pivotal response treatment for autism spectrum disorders / by Robert L. Koegel, Ph.D., Stanford University School of Medicine, Stanford, CA, and Lynn Kern Koegel, Ph.D., CCC-SLP, Stanford University School of Medicine, Stanford, CA, with invited contributors.
Other titles: Pivotal response treatments for autism
Description: Second edition. | Baltimore, Maryland : Paul H. Brookes Publishing Co., [2019] | "Previous edition copyright 2006"—T.p. verso. | Includes bibliographical references and index.
Identifiers: LCCN 2018014550 (print) | LCCN 2018025920 (ebook) | ISBN 9781681252971 (epub) | ISBN 9781681252988 (pdf) | ISBN 9781681252964 (Paper)
Subjects: LCSH: Autism.
Classification: LCC RC553.A88 (ebook) | LCC RC553.A88 K64 2018 (print) | DDC 616.85/882—dc23
LC record available at https://lccn.loc.gov/2018014550

British Library Cataloguing in Publication data are available from the British Library.

2022 2021 2020 2019 2018

10 9 8 7 6 5 4 3 2 1

Table of Contents

About the Downloads xi
About the Authors xiii
About the Contributors xv
For the Reader xvii
Acknowledgments xix
Introduction xxi

Section I **Overview: Pivotal Response Treatment in Context**

Chapter 1 The History and Basic Components of Pivotal Response Treatment 3
Robert L. Koegel and Lynn Kern Koegel

Chapter Goals 3
History: Applied Behavior Analysis and Children With ASD 3
The Role of Motivation in Learning 5
Learned Helplessness, Motivation, and Children With ASD 5
Motivational Components of PRT 7
The Overall Motivational Package 10
Key Insights: Components of PRT 14
Summary 15
Study Questions 15
References 16

Chapter 2 Assessment, Feedback, and Treatment Planning 19
Lynn Kern Koegel

Chapter Goals 19
Challenges Facing Parents of Children Diagnosed With ASD 20
Testing Individuals With ASD: The Limits of Standardized Testing 22
Getting a More Complete Picture: Behavioral Assessments 24
The Value of Strength-Based Assessment 26
Assessment Leading to Treatment Goals 29
Putting It all Together: Assessment, Diagnosis, and Treatment 30
Key Insights: Working With Parents During Assessment, Diagnosis, and Early Intervention 32
Summary 33
Study Questions 33
References 34

Chapter 3 Ecocultural Theory and Cultural Diversity 35
Sunny Kim, Lynn Kern Koegel, and Robert L. Koegel

Chapter Goals 35
Tenets of Ecocultural Theory 36
Cultural Considerations and Sensitivity 36
Embedding Cultural Beliefs and Values Into Treatment 40
Matching Culturally Competent Service Providers With Families 41
Key Insights: Addressing Cultural and Linguistic Diversity 43
Summary 44
Study Questions 44
References 45

Section II Beginning Stages: Early Intervention

Chapter 4 Intervention for Infants and Young Toddlers 49
Jessica Bradshaw and Lynn Kern Koegel

Chapter Goals 49
Guidelines for Early Diagnosis 49
Intervention With Infants and Toddlers 53
Key Insights: Working Effectively With Infants, Toddlers, and Their Families 60
Summary 61
Study Questions 62
References 62

Chapter 5 Teaching First Words 65
Lynn Kern Koegel and Daina Tagavi

Chapter Goals 65
Understanding Early Language Development 66
Early Communication and First Words in Children With ASD 67
Interventions to Elicit First Words: A Brief History 68
Using PRT to Elicit First Words: Specific Components 69
Research Support for Including Motivational Components 72
Creating Ample Opportunities for Verbal Communication 73
Working With Nonresponsive Children 74
Using PRT With Infants 76
Key Insights: Working to Produce a Child's First Words 77
Summary 78
Study Questions 78
References 79

Chapter 6 Expanding Friendship Opportunities for Children With ASD 81
Grace W. Gengoux and Laurie A. Vismara

Chapter Goals 81
Background: Potential Benefits of Intervention 82

Assessing a Child's Social Opportunities 85
Field-Tested Strategies for Expanding Friendship Opportunities During Play Dates 87
Beyond Play Dates: Expanding Friendship Opportunities Across Settings 97
Key Insights: Expanding Friendship Opportunities 100
Summary 101
Study Questions 101
References 102

Section III Childhood: Treatment Options at Home and at School

Chapter 7 Parent Education in Pivotal Response Treatment 107
Lynn Kern Koegel, Kelsey Oliver, and Robert L. Koegel

Chapter Goals 107
The Importance of Parent Education 108
Fidelity of Implementation of PRT 111
Models of Parent Education 112
Key Insights: Helping Parents Effectively Teach Their Children With ASD 119
Summary 120
Study Questions 120
References 120

Chapter 8 Inclusive Education 123
Robert L. Koegel and Kelsey Oliver

Chapter Goals 123
Making Education a Top Priority for Children With ASD 124
Inclusion of Children With ASD 127
Revisiting the Debate Over Full Inclusion 136
Key Insights: Providing Inclusive Education for Children With ASD 139
Summary 140
Study Questions 140
References 141

Chapter 9 Motivational Academics 147
Lynn Kern Koegel and Samantha K. Poyser

Chapter Goals 147
Background: The Relationship Between Behavior and Academics 148
Incorporating Motivational Variables to Improve Academic Engagement and Behavior 150
Parent Involvement 154
Key Insights: Improving Academics and Behavior Through Motivational Strategies 155
Summary 156
Study Questions 156
References 157

Section IV Adolescence and Young Adulthood: Moving Toward Independence

Chapter 10 Functional Behavior Assessment and Self-Management 161
Brittany Lynn Koegel And Lynn Kern Koegel

Chapter Goals 161
The History of Behavioral Interventions 162
Self-Management as a Behavioral Intervention 169
How to Develop a Self-Management Program 174
Key Insights: Using Positive Behavioral Interventions and Fostering Independence 179
Summary 180
Study Questions 180
References 181

Chapter 11 Improving Communication Skills in Adolescents and Adults With ASD 185
Lynn Kern Koegel and Shereen J. Cohen

Chapter Goals 185
Visual Frameworks 186
Video Modeling in PRT 187
Instruction in Empathy 191
Question Asking and Question Banks 195
Self-Management 196
Key Insights: Improving Young Adults' Communication Skills 198
Summary 198
Study Questions 199
References 199

Chapter 12 Improving Socialization in Adolescents and Adults With ASD 203
Lynn Kern Koegel, Kristen Ashbaugh, and Daina Tagavi

Chapter Goals 203
The Impact of Social Difficulties 204
Interventions for Improving Socialization 205
Foundational Studies Using Restricted and Preferred Interests to Improve Socialization 206
Developing Interest-Based Social Opportunities for Adolescents and Young Adults 207
Training Paraprofessionals to Implement Social Programs 209
Structured Social Planning: Improving Opportunities for Adults 210
Key Insights: Targeting Socialization 215
Summary 216
Study Questions 216
References 218

Section V Adulthood: Higher Education and Employment

Chapter 13 Improving Outcomes in Higher Education for Adults With ASD 223

Kristen Ashbaugh, Erin Engstrom, Lynn Kern Koegel, and Katarina Ford

Chapter Goals 223
Supporting Individuals With ASD in Higher Education 224
Common Challenges 225
Methods for Addressing Challenges 227
Key Insights: Helping College Students With ASD Succeed 242
Summary 243
Study Questions 243
References 244

Chapter 14 Supporting Individuals With ASD in Employment Settings 247

Erin Engstrom, Kristen Ashbaugh, Lynn Kern Koegel, and Katarina Ford

Chapter Goals 247
Barriers to Employment 249
Vocational Rehabilitation and Related Programs 250
Behavioral Interventions That Support Employment 251
Integrating Strengths Into the Workplace 259
Supported Employment 260
Key Insights: Fostering Successful Employment 262
Summary 263
Study Questions 264
References 265

Index 269

About the Downloads

Purchasers of this book may download, print, and/or photocopy the following chapter materials for educational use: Chapter Goals, Key Insights, and Study Questions. These materials are also available at www.brookespublishing.com/koegel/materials for both print and e-book buyers.

About the Authors

Robert L. Koegel, Ph.D., Senior Researcher, Stanford University School of Medicine, 401 Quarry Road, Stanford, CA 94305

Dr. Robert Koegel's research is in the area of autism, specializing in language intervention, family support, and school integration. He has published more than 200 articles and papers relating to the treatment of autism as well as several books on the treatment of autism and positive behavioral support. He is the Founding Editor of the *Journal of Positive Behavior Interventions.* Models of his procedures are used in public schools and in parent education programs throughout the world. He has trained many health care and special education leaders in the United States and abroad.

Lynn Kern Koegel, Ph.D., CCC-SLP, Clinical Professor, Stanford University School of Medicine, 401 Quarry Road, Stanford, CA 94305

Dr. Lynn Kern Koegel has been active in the development of programs to improve communication in children with autism, including the development of first words, grammatical structures, pragmatics, and social conversation. In addition to her published books and articles in the area of communication and language development, she has developed and published procedures and field manuals in the area of self-management and functional analysis that are used in school districts and by parents throughout the United States and have been translated in other major languages. Dr. Lynn Koegel is the author of *Overcoming Autism* and *Growing Up on the Spectrum* with parent Claire LaZebnik, published by Viking/Penguin and available in most bookstores. In addition, she appeared on ABC's hit show "Supernanny" working with a child with autism.

The Koegels are the developers of Pivotal Response Treatment, an empirically supported treatment for autism that focuses on improving motivation. The Koegels have been the recipients of many awards, including the first annual Children's Television Workshop Sesame Street Award for "Brightening the Lives of Children," the first annual Autism Speaks award for "Science and Research," and the International Association for Behavior Analysis (ABA) award for "enduring programmatic contributions in behavior analysis." Their work has also been showcased on ABC, CBS, NBC, PBS, and the Discovery Channel. The Koegels are current and past recipients of many federal, state, and private foundation grants and gifts for developing interventions and helping families with ASD.

About the Contributors

Kristen Ashbaugh, Ph.D.
Stanford School of Medicine, Autism and Developmental Disabilities Clinic
Stanford University
Stanford, CA 94305

Jessica Bradshaw, Ph.D.
Department of Psychology
University of South Carolina
Columbia, SC 29208

Shereen J. Cohen, M.A.
UCSB Koegel Autism Center
University of California, Santa Barbara
Santa Barbara, CA 93106

Erin Engstrom, M.A.
UCSB Koegel Autism Center
University of California, Santa Barbara
Santa Barbara, CA 93106

Katarina Ford, M.A.
UCSB Koegel Autism Center
University of California, Santa Barbara
Santa Barbara, CA 93106

Grace W. Gengoux, Ph.D.
Department of Psychiatry and Behavioral Sciences
Division of Child and Adolescent Psychiatry
Stanford University, School of Medicine
Stanford, CA 94305

Sunny Kim, Ph.D.
UCSB Koegel Autism Center
University of California, Santa Barbara
Santa Barbara, CA 93106

Brittany Lynn Koegel, Ph.D.
CEO, Koegel Autism Consultants
Goleta, CA 93111
Research Coordinator
Stanford University School of Medicine
Stanford, CA 94305

Kelsey Oliver, M.A.
UCSB Koegel Autism Center
University of California, Santa Barbara
Santa Barbara, CA 93106

Samantha K. Poyser, B.A.
UCSB Koegel Autism Center
University of California, Santa Barbara
Santa Barbara, CA 93106

Daina Tagavi, M.A.
UCSB Koegel Autism Center
University of California, Santa Barbara
Santa Barbara, CA 93106

Laurie A. Vismara, Ph.D., BCBA-D
Early Emory Center for Child Development and Enrichment
Emory University School of Medicine
Atlanta, GA 30322

For the Reader

If you're interested in learning more about PRT®, the authors and their team offer a range of resources, services, and training. Please see their web site, http://www.koegelautism.com, for more information or to schedule an event. Also note that PRT®, Pivotal Response Teaching®, Pivotal Response Training®, and Pivotal Response Treatment® are registered service marks with the U.S. Patent and Trademark Office, registered as marks of Koegel Autism Consultants, LLC, in association with educational conferences and workshops the authors provide in the field of non-aversive treatment interventions for children with autism and with the authors' learning center.

Other good resources for detailed information include the authors' first edition of this book, *Pivotal Response Treatments for Autism: Communication, Social, & Academic Development,* as well as *The PRT Pocket Guide: Pivotal Response Treatment for Autism Spectrum Disorders,* both published by Paul H. Brookes Publishing Co.

Acknowledgments

We are grateful for the assistance of the funding agencies that made possible much of the research described in this book. A great deal of the research was funded by the National Institutes of Health, National Institute of Mental Health, National Institute on Deafness and Other Communication Disorders; U.S. Department of Education; the Eli and Edythe L. Broad Foundation; Autism Speaks; the Kelly Family Foundation; the Kind World Foundation; the Weitz Family Foundation; and the Douglas Foundation.

Introduction

Pivotal Response Treatment for Autism Spectrum Disorders, Second Edition, describes intervention procedures and outcome data for Pivotal Response Treatment (PRT), a groundbreaking approach to working with individuals with autism spectrum disorders (ASD). Supported by decades of research conducted by the authors and others, PRT addresses core areas of autism and related disorders, resulting in especially rapid and broad-ranging intervention outcomes. Intervention in infancy and early childhood can result in especially significant gains by setting children on a more typical course of development; however, it is also possible for individuals with ASD to benefit from interventions later in childhood, in adolescence, or in adulthood. At any age, treating the following core areas of ASD seems to produce especially large intervention gains:

- Motivation to engage in social-communicative interactions
- Social initiations (interactions initiated by the individual), especially those involving shared enjoyment and joint attention
- Self-regulation of behavior

These areas are *pivotal,* meaning that targeting them often results in improvements in other areas as well. This book explains how practitioners who work with individuals with ASD can address these pivotal areas from infancy through early adulthood. At any stage of development, intervention should 1) involve the family—and when possible the individual—in designing and delivering the intervention, 2) provide treatment in the natural environment, 3) focus primarily on treating key pivotal behaviors and only secondarily on modifying other behaviors, and 4) be implemented across multiple contexts (e.g., home and school).

A brief note on terminology: Although the terms *autism* and *autism spectrum disorders* are sometimes used interchangeably, *autism spectrum disorders* or *ASD* covers a wide range of subcategories, such as Asperger syndrome and pervasive developmental disorder–not otherwise specified (PDD-NOS). The term *autism* refers to children who demonstrate symptoms in social communication and exhibit restricted and repetitive behaviors. Throughout this book, we generally use the broader term *autism spectrum disorders* or *ASD*; however, many of the examples we present relate to the symptom areas of autism.

WHAT IS PIVOTAL RESPONSE TREATMENT?

Pivotal Response Treatment is a comprehensive service delivery model that uses a developmental approach and applied behavior analysis procedures. PRT aims to provide opportunities for learning within the context of the individual's natural environments (Koegel & Koegel, 2012; Koegel, Koegel, Harrower, & Carter, 1999; Koegel, Koegel, Shoshan, & McNerney, 1999). Pivotal areas, also referred to in the research literature as pivotal responses or pivotal behaviors, are areas that, when targeted, lead to large collateral changes in other (often untargeted) areas of functioning and responding (Koegel & Koegel, 2012; Koegel & Koegel, 1995; Koegel, Koegel, Harrower, & Carter, 1999; Koegel, Koegel, Shoshan, & McNerney, 1999; Koegel & Frea, 1993; Matson, Benavidez, Compton, Paclawskyj, & Baglo, 1996; Mundy, Sigman, & Kasari, 1990; Mundy & Stella, 2000; Schreibman, Stahmer, & Pierce, 1996). Pivotal responses, once acquired, result in widespread and generalized improvements in individuals with ASD.

Thus far, five pivotal areas have been studied: motivation, responsivity to multiple cues, self-management, self-initiations, and empathy (Koegel, Koegel, & Carter, 1999; Koegel, Koegel, Harrower, & Carter, 1999; Koegel, Koegel, & McNerney, 2001; Koegel, Koegel, Shoshan, & McNerney, 1999). It is important to note that treatment consists of a coordinated effort by all relevant stakeholders (Carr et al., 2002) so that a consistent and ongoing intervention is implemented across people, settings, and environments. The PRT model emphasizes the importance of parents as primary intervention agents when treating children with ASD. However, to ensure a well-coordinated and comprehensive delivery of the model, other people who interact with the individual receiving treatment are also included as intervention agents. These people might include siblings, teachers and other school personnel, consultants, psychologists, speech therapists, special educators, and peers—and for young adults, their professors, college administrators and staff, roommates, employers, and co-workers, as well.

The primary goals of PRT are to 1) help individuals with ASD move toward a typical developmental trajectory by targeting a broad range of behaviors and 2) increase their opportunities to lead meaningful and fulfilling lives in natural, inclusive settings. To achieve these goals, PRT focuses upon pivotal areas using the core principles of intervention.

Core Principles of PRT Intervention

PRT is based on the fundamental principle that people learn better when their motivation to learn is high. This is true for all individuals but is particularly important for individuals with autism. This principle applies to learning within any domain—academic, behavioral, or social-communicative—and at any stage of development. Extensive research on PRT has yielded a great deal of evidence supporting the use of five motivational components to improve learning:

1. Providing individuals with choices related to the learning activities
2. Interspersing tasks (e.g., difficult tasks with easy ones; previously learned tasks with new ones)
3. Varying tasks to avoid monotony
4. Using natural rewards (e.g., giving a child a cookie for saying the word *cookie*)
5. Rewarding individuals for their attempts to perform desired behaviors or skills, even when these attempts are imperfect

Astute readers will notice that these five motivational components recur again and again throughout this book as we discuss working with individuals with ASD in different contexts. Whether a practitioner is working with a family to teach an infant to say his first word, with an adult college student to help her build fulfilling social relationships, or with individuals at any stage in between, using motivational components is crucial. These five components will be explained in depth in Chapter 1, *The History and Basic Components of Pivotal Response Treatment.* They are highly effective in reducing disruptive behaviors; they function effectively as an antecedent or preventive intervention; they can be used in tandem with the restricted interests associated with ASD; and they can even help educators, families, and practitioners create social environments where individuals with ASD are highly valued and included.

Several other principles of PRT are broadly applicable across many different learning contexts and stages of development:

1. Early intervention is associated with the most positive outcomes.
2. Intervention that can be delivered in the natural environment (e.g., home, classroom, workplace) is associated with better generalization and maintenance of the behaviors or skills the individual learns.
3. Relatedly, it is helpful to get other people within those environments involved in implementing the intervention: family members, peers, teachers and school personnel, classmates—and later, professors, co-workers, and the like. For children and adolescents, family involvement is particularly important in ensuring that interventions are implemented consistently. Adolescents and adults can learn self-management strategies that help them take control of their own intervention and learning.

These core principles do not substantially differ from the foundational principles discussed in the first edition of this book, *Pivotal Response Treatments for Autism: Communication, Social, and Academic Development* (2006) or its companion text, *The PRT Pocket Guide: Pivotal Response Treatment for Autism Spectrum Disorders* (2012). In other respects, however, this second edition has undergone significant changes.

Significant Changes to This Edition

Throughout this edition, supporting research has been updated to reflect the insights and evidence gained from the authors' and others' studies of PRT interventions and related topics. In particular, we include additional research supporting PRT, including randomized clinical trials. We also discuss additional studies that have been conducted in the area of initiations. This edition also addresses issues relating to improving socialization for adolescents and adults, as well as interventions for making experiences at college and the job site more successful.

In some respects, this book might be viewed as written primarily for clinicians and other practitioners whose work centers on treatment and intervention for people with autism or other disorders on the autism spectrum. However, it is our hope that anyone involved in implementing interventions will be able to glean valuable information and insights from the book. Thus, we've revised this edition to be user friendly and accessible to parents; teachers and other educational professionals; and, indeed, any reader who cares about someone with ASD and wants to learn about PRT. New features include Chapter Goals for the reader; a list of Key Insights at the end of each chapter, followed by a brief chapter summary and Study Questions; and extensive case examples that illustrate how

PRT works with children and young adults. The Chapter Goals, Key Insights, and Study Questions are also provided in the downloadable materials available online to purchasers of this book.

This second edition also includes new or heavily reworked chapters on a number of key topics: Chapter 2, *Assessment, Feedback, and Treatment Planning;* Chapter 4, *Intervention for Infants and Young Toddlers;* Chapter 10, *Functional Behavior Assessment and Self-Management;* and several chapters on working with young adults: Chapter 11, *Improving Communication Skills in Adolescents and Adults With ASD;* Chapter 12, *Improving Socialization in Adolescents and Adults With ASD;* Chapter 13, *Improving Outcomes in Higher Education for Adults With ASD,* and Chapter 14, *Supporting Individuals With ASD in Employment Settings.*

In addition, we have organized this edition to follow a developmental trajectory. Chapters are grouped in four sections. *Section I, Overview: Pivotal Response Treatment in Context,* contains the foundational understandings the reader needs to apply PRT effectively. This section includes Chapter 1, which presents *The History and Basic Components of Pivotal Response Treatment;* Chapter 2, which introduces *Assessment, Feedback, and Treatment Planning;* and Chapter 3, which situates PRT in the context of *Ecocultural Theory and Cultural Diversity.*

Section II, Beginning Stages: Early Intervention, guides practitioners through the issues that arise when working with very young children and their families. This section begins with the overview presented in Chapter 4, *Intervention for Infants and Young Toddlers.* Chapter 5 addresses the crucial social-communication goal of *Teaching First Words,* which has profound implications for lifelong outcomes for individuals with ASD. Chapter 6, *Expanding Friendship Opportunities for Children With ASD,* helps practitioners work with families to begin to broaden their child's social world.

Section III, Childhood: Treatment Options at Home and at School, focuses on how practitioners, educators, and families can work together effectively to foster positive outcomes for children academically, behaviorally, and socially. It begins with Chapter 7, *Parent Education in Pivotal Response Treatment,* which discusses parents' crucial role in intervention and effective practices and models for teaching parents to implement PRT with fidelity. Chapter 8, *Inclusive Education,* argues for educating children with ASD in an inclusive setting with their typically developing peers and discusses effective interventions for inclusion. Chapter 9, *Motivational Academics,* explains how to use motivational components to foster academic engagement and reduce disruptive or avoidant behaviors.

Given that many individuals with autism are adolescents and adults, we have included in this edition a significant amount of material on areas relevant to these stages of development. *Section IV, Adolescence and Young Adulthood: Moving Toward Independence,* is designed to show practitioners how to help individuals with ASD learn the behavioral, communicative, and social skills that will enable them to transition out of secondary school and into adulthood successfully. This section begins with Chapter 10, which explores how to use *Functional Behavior Assessment and Self-Management* to foster adaptive, prosocial behaviors. Chapter 11, *Improving Communication Skills in Adolescents and Adults With ASD,* and Chapter 12, *Improving Socialization in Adolescents and Adults With ASD,* guide practitioners as they work to help teens and young adults with ASD navigate their ever-expanding social world and increasing responsibilities.

Section V, Adulthood: Higher Education and Employment, explores ways practitioners can work with young adults with ASD to help them live a rewarding and productive adult life that includes fulfilling work and meaningful relationships. Young adults encounter many new challenges at college and in the workplace, topics addressed in Chapter 13, *Improving Outcomes in Higher Education for Adults With ASD,* and Chapter 14, *Supporting Individuals With ASD in Employment Settings.*

A final note: the very powerful PRT interventions described in this book were developed and refined by the authors and their colleagues through decades of research. Strategies for addressing communication, behavior, and socialization are described in relation to each other and in relation to research conducted by many programs worldwide. Throughout this book, our purpose is to describe an integrated and comprehensive approach to intervention, with the goal of profoundly improving the lives of individuals with ASD and their families; to help these individuals participate fully in their communities; and to focus on their strengths, so that they may be viewed as valued, contributing members of society.

REFERENCES

Carr, E. G., Dunlap, G., Horner, R. H., Koegel, R. L., Turnbull, A. P., Sailor, W., Anderson, J. L., Albin, R. W., Koegel, L. K., & Fox, L. (2002). Positive behavior support: Evolution of an applied science. *Journal of Positive Behavior Interventions, 4*(1), 4–16, 20.

Koegel, R. L., & Frea, W. D. (1993). Treatment of social behavior in autism through the modification of pivotal social skills. *Journal of Applied Behavior Analysis, 26*(3), 369–377.

Koegel, L. K., & Koegel, R. L. (1995). Motivating communication in children with autism. In E. Schopler & G. B. Mesibov (Eds.), *Learning and cognition in autism* (pp. 73–87). New York, NY: Springer.

Koegel, R. L., & Koegel, L. K. (2012). *The PRT pocket guide: Pivotal Response Treatment for autism spectrum disorders.* Baltimore, MD: Paul H. Brookes Publishing Co.

Koegel, L. K., Koegel, R. L., Harrower, J. K., & Carter, C. M. (1999). Pivotal response intervention I: Overview of approach. *Journal of the Association for Persons with Severe Handicaps, 24*(3), 174–185.

Koegel, L. K., Koegel, R. L., Shoshan, Y., & McNerney, E. (1999). Pivotal response intervention II: Preliminary long-term outcome data. *Research and Practice for Persons with Severe Disabilities, 24*(3), 186–198.

Koegel, R. L., Koegel, L. K., & Carter, C. M. (1999). Pivotal teaching interactions for children with autism. *School Psychology Review, 28*(4). 576–594.

Koegel, R. L., Koegel, L. K., & McNerney, E. K. (2001). Pivotal areas in intervention for autism. *Journal of Clinical Child Psychology, 30*(1), 19–32.

Matson, J. L., Benavidez, D. A., Compton, L. S., Paclawskyj, T., & Baglo, C. S. (1996). Behavioral treatment of autistic persons: A review of research from 1980 to the present. *Research in Developmental Disabilities, 17,* 433–465.

Mundy, P., Sigman, M., & Kasari, C. (1990). A longitudinal study of joint attention and language development in autistic children. *Journal of Autism and Developmental Disorders, 20*(1), 115–128.

Mundy, P., & Stella, J. (2000). Joint attention, social orienting, and communication in autism. In S. F., Warren & J. Reichle (Series Eds.) & A. M. Wetherby, S. F. Warren, & J. Reichle (Vol. Eds.), *Communication and language intervention series: Vol. 7. Transitions in prelinguistic communications* (pp. 111–133). Baltimore: Paul H. Brookes Publishing Co.

Schreibman, L., Stahmer, A. C., & Pierce, K. L. (1996). Alternative applications of pivotal response training: Teaching symbolic play and social interaction skills. In L. K. Koegel, R. L. Koegel, & G. Dunlap (Eds.), *Positive behavior support: Including people with difficult behavior in the community* (pp. 353–371). Baltimore, MD: Paul H. Brookes Publishing Co.

I

Overview

Pivotal Response Treatment in Context

1

The History and Basic Components of Pivotal Response Treatment

Robert L. Koegel and Lynn Kern Koegel

CHAPTER GOALS

Goal 1. The reader will learn about early applied behavior analysis (ABA) procedures and how they led to the development of Pivotal Response Treatment (PRT).

Goal 2. The reader will learn about specific motivational variables in PRT.

Goal 3. The reader will learn how PRT positively affects family interactions.

Goal 4. The reader will be able to discuss learned helplessness and how it relates to autism spectrum disorders (ASD).

This chapter describes how PRT emerged as an especially powerful yet child- and family-friendly approach for working with children with ASD. First, we trace PRT's roots in the principles and techniques of ABA used to treat children with ASD in the 1960s and 1970s. Next, we explore several core motivational variables within PRT—variables revisited throughout this book in discussions of how to implement interventions with children and young adults with ASD—and how PRT affects family interactions. Finally, to understand the role of motivation in PRT, it is crucial to understand how learned helplessness can impact the lives of people with ASD. We explore this topic at the end of the chapter.

HISTORY: APPLIED BEHAVIOR ANALYSIS AND CHILDREN WITH ASD

PRT is a treatment that addresses core, or *pivotal,* areas of autism and related disorders. Addressing these areas early and systematically appears to result in large and rapid gains, thereby helping children with ASD make significant improvements in behavior, communication, and social interactions. To understand PRT and the role of motivation within this approach, it is necessary first to discuss PRT's roots in ABA.

In the 1960s and 1970s, treatments based on principles of ABA began to emerge as viable and effective for improving the behaviors of children with ASD (Lovaas, 1977). Prior to that time, the parents were wrongly believed to be the cause of the disorder, and interventions largely separated the parents from their children (Bettelheim, 1967). During that period, almost all children with ASD were institutionalized by adolescence, many at much younger ages. There were few interventions available that effectively changed the children's behaviors, and, thus, challenging behaviors worsened over time.

Fortunately, ABA techniques used the field's established stimulus–response–consequence paradigm (Skinner, 1953), in which an instruction is given (stimulus), the individual responds (response), and a consequence is provided (either a reward or punisher). This paradigm was applied to behaviors of children with autism to teach new skills, decrease problem areas, and increase appropriate behaviors. Clinical trials using these procedures became known as discrete trials, wherein a clinician would present an instruction, or stimulus, such as "Touch your nose," wait for a child's response, and then provide a consequence. For example, if the child touched his nose, the clinician might say "Good job," and give the child a small treat. If the child responded incorrectly, the clinician might say "No!" and present a new trial. This stimulus–response–consequence teaching paradigm became known as discrete trial teaching, or DTT.

Throughout the 1960s and 1970s, ABA treatment studies primarily focused on developing interventions—which were heavily based on positive and negative consequences—to create behavior changes. Many relied on very salient reinforcement and punishment, as the children did not generally respond well to social consequences. For example, consequences such as electric shock, yelling "No," and isolation were used to reduce dangerous behavior, severe tantrums, and self-injurious behavior (Risley, 1968). Treats, meals, and positive feedback were used to teach and reinforce positive behaviors (Wolf, Risley, & Mees, 1963). Shaping and chaining procedures were used to teach behaviors as well as communication (Wolf et al., 1963). Shaping procedures are those in which successively more correct responses are reinforced; chaining procedures are those in which a complex or multistep behavior or skill is broken down into discrete steps. These early procedures resulted in decreases in self-stimulation and echolalia and improved communication, play, and socialization (Lovaas, Koegel, Simmons, & Long, 1973). In the meantime, research was emerging showing that parents of children with autism were not the cause of the disorder (Koegel, Schreibman, O'Neill, & Burke, 1983). The results of ABA treatment studies were inconsistent with the parental causation theory, because generalization and maintenance of gains was only evidenced in the children whose parents received training in the ABA procedures (Lovaas et al., 1973; Koegel, Glahn, & Nieminen, 1978).

While these ABA procedures resulted in significant improvements in the children, the intervention was tedious and required many trials to teach each behavior. For example, Lovaas (1977), who developed the early shaping procedures for teaching speech to children who were nonverbal, reported that it might take as many as 90,000 trials to teach a single word. Further, children did not appear to enjoy the intervention, despite the fact that they were improving. Often the children tried to avoid or escape the intervention sessions, and much of a therapist's time was devoted to procedures designed to decrease challenging behaviors. These limitations of ABA drew the authors' attention to the potential role of motivation in ABA-based interventions and DTT.

THE ROLE OF MOTIVATION IN LEARNING

As researchers involved in those early ABA treatment studies, we were cognizant of the idea that learning is more likely to occur when a child is motivated. We began to explore whether the concept of motivation could be behaviorally measured and whether procedures to improve a child with autism's motivation could be developed. We were also concerned that the children did not appear to be happy when engaged in the intervention. Thus, our goal was twofold:

1. To improve the intervention so that children would not want to exhibit disruptive avoidance and escape behaviors
2. To be able to measure improved affect as a behavioral representation of improved motivation

In regard to motivated learning, we have measured responsiveness, latency of responding, and rate of correct responding, as well as behaviors that are incompatible with active learning, such as disruptive and off-task behaviors. In regard to affect, we have measured variables such as interest, happiness, enthusiasm, and engagement, using Likert scales. Thus far, in many single subject design studies and in randomized clinical trials (Mohammadzaheri, Koegel, Rezaei, & Bakhshi, 2015; Mohammadzaheri, Koegel, Rezaee, & Rafiee, 2014), our clinics and others have found that PRT results in greater gains and the children exhibit higher levels of positive affect and lower levels of disruptive behavior when the motivational components are incorporated into the intervention. Thus, the PRT motivational components appear to be an important iteration of the ABA interventions.

LEARNED HELPLESSNESS, MOTIVATION, AND CHILDREN WITH ASD

Before we discuss the motivational components of PRT, let's discuss theory so you can understand how a *lack* of motivation may have developed in children with autism. Since the 1970s, researchers have examined the effects of repeated exposure to events that cannot be controlled or avoided (Maier & Seligman, 1976; Schwartz, 1981). This research led to the theory of learned helplessness. These environmental circumstances teach individuals that they are helpless because they are unable to escape a negative situation. The theory of learned helplessness is that exposure to events that are uncontrollable leads individuals to believe that their behaviors and the outcomes of these behaviors are independent, which produces an effect on the individual's motivation, cognition, and emotion (Maier & Seligman, 1976). For example, studies have found that when participants are repeatedly exposed to uncontrollable events (e.g., shocks, noise), they often exhibit a subsequent disruption in attempts to escape the aversive events (Abramson, Seligman, &

Teasdale, 1978). This generally involves lethargy and a lack of trying. More concerning is that learned helplessness can lead to depression, and individuals with depression perform even worse than nondepressed groups in learned helplessness situations. For example, if students are given unsolvable problems, they perform worse on later tasks; if they also show depressive symptoms, they will perform even more poorly (Klein, Fencil-Morse, & Seligman, 1976).

An additional factor in learned helplessness is attribution—the source to which the individual attributes the difficulty. Individuals who attribute the difficulty to causes within themselves (internal attribution), such as feeling that they are not intelligent enough to get a good grade on a test or to solve a problem, exhibit greater symptoms of learned helplessness than those who attribute the difficulty to outside factors (external attribution), such as the test or problem being too hard (Alloy & Seligman, 1979). Furthermore, learned helplessness can be influenced by whether an individual attributes difficulties or lack of control over the environment to global, all-pervasive factors or more limited factors (e.g., "I am unintelligent" versus "I have trouble with math"), and to stable, unchanging factors or temporary ones (e.g., "I am clumsy and uncoordinated" versus "I never learned how to do this dance step").

Now, ponder how this theory may pertain to ASD as you read the case history of Thomas.

CASE HISTORY
Learned Helplessness in Thomas, Age 4

Consider Thomas, a 4-year-old child with ASD, who is having difficulties in many areas. His communication is significantly delayed, although he has learned to use about 30 words, primarily words naming his favorite items, which he requests. He has restricted and repetitive behaviors that interfere with daily living activities, and he shows little interest in others. Major tantrums or "meltdowns" occur regularly, especially when he has to transition away from the television or iPad. Life is a challenge for the family. Preschool starts at 8:00, and Thomas's parents need to be at work shortly after. To avoid meltdowns, Thomas's family dresses him in the morning so he won't be late to school and they'll be on time for work. Sometimes he engages in meltdowns, so they carry him to the car with his iPad to avoid delays while he tantrums. Because he has difficulty communicating, his parents—who usually know what he wants—let others know what he wants. Overall, Thomas engages in little social-verbal communication and engages in very few self-help skills throughout the day. Consequently, he is very lethargic and just waits for others to dress him and help with daily living skills. He is able to communicate verbally but does so infrequently because he usually gets what he wants if he becomes disruptive or just waits.

Thomas is exhibiting what appears to be learned helplessness. Compare the impact of learned helplessness on Thomas's daily life to its impact on the daily life of Sarah.

CASE HISTORY
Learned Helplessness in Sarah, Age 13

Sarah is a middle schooler who has a diagnosis of Asperger syndrome. Her parents both hold graduate degrees. She has no siblings and is bright but performs poorly in school because of inattentiveness during class. She often does not turn in homework and engages in elaborate avoidance behavior when her parents try to help her with homework, such as telling jokes, making faces, joking about the homework, guessing at answers until her parents tell her she is correct, lying down, asking for water, and so on. Her parents are wonderful and caring people and bend over backwards to respond to her every need. In fact, they even help her get dressed and undressed, serve her dinner on a tray while she watches TV, and sit with her every evening to help her with homework. They are exhausted but feel like there is no other way. Sarah has reached a point where she does little for herself and expects to be waited on. Sometimes she even snaps her fingers with a demand for her parents.

Developing learned helplessness can be complex, depending on the extent to which uncontrollable environmental conditions occur and can be exacerbated by other issues. However, if the individual attributes his or her failure to control the environmental conditions to a global attribute, such as being a poor communicator or not being smart enough, this may cause an individual to feel helpless. Because well-meaning adults often "help" individuals with ASD, they can create learned helplessness. The negative effects of the lack of contingent consequences can worsen over time if the situation continues and is present across environments (stable attribution). The antidote to learned helplessness is to create situations in which individuals with ASD experience success on their own and can link their behaviors to the consequences. To do this, we must motivate individuals with learned helplessness to respond.

MOTIVATIONAL COMPONENTS OF PRT

In order to improve motivation during teaching sessions, several specific, evidence-based procedures have been developed: giving individuals a choice of materials used, interspersing previously learned tasks with new tasks, varying tasks, using natural rewards, and rewarding attempts at the task.

Provide Choice

Simply stated, if an individual has some choice over the instructional materials used during the teaching sessions, he will perform better. Many studies have found that choice is important in improving performance in many areas, including (but not limited to) learning first words (Koegel & Koegel, 1995), acquisition of language structures (Carter, 2001), engagement with toys (Reinhartsen, Garfinkle, & Wolery, 2002), and articulation and speech intelligibility (Koegel, Camarata, Koegel, Ben-Tall, & Smith, 1998). Child choice is also helpful in reducing challenging behaviors, such as repetitive behaviors (Morrison & Rosales-Ruiz, 1997) and disruption (Moes, 1998). For example, all too often teachers and therapists predetermine their teaching materials without considering the interests of the child. Or, if parents find a cool toy, they may try and redirect the child to it, regardless of whether the child shows interest in that toy or is actively engaged with another toy. Choice can be determined by watching what the child plays with, asking the child what she'd like to play with, and/or being vigilant when a child approaches an activity.

It is important to remember that preference is different than choice. You may have a plethora of toys the child prefers, but because choice can vary from day to day and even minute to minute, you'll need to provide constant choices among the preferred items (Carter, 2001). There are times when choice may not seem possible. For example, if a child is fully included and the teacher gives a homework assignment, such as a printed math sheet, it has to get done. In this situation, however, the child can still choose where he wants to sit to complete the homework, what type of writing utensil he wants to use, what problems he wants to do first, what color paper he'd like to use, and so on (Moes, 1998). Choice can also be provided for social activities for adolescents and adults (Koegel, Ashbaugh, Koegel, Detar, & Regester, 2013) and can improve social conversation (Koegel, Dyer, & Bell, 1987).

Choice is important. Follow the child's lead. Be attentive and observant. Teach adolescents and adults with ASD how to self-direct a conversation that may appropriately include their interests and develop social activities around their favorite themes. It will make a difference in regard to engagement, learning, appropriate behavior, and enjoyment.

Intersperse Tasks

No one likes to be drilled, drilled, drilled, especially on hard stuff. In the past, we developed goals and then worked repetitively and repeatedly on those goals. But research shows that interspersing previously mastered, or maintenance, tasks with the target, or acquisition, tasks results in faster learning, decreased disruptive behavior, and improved affect (Dunlap, 1984). It might seem counterintuitive. One might expect learning to be slower when using maintenance tasks as there are potentially fewer trials in which to teach the acquisition task. However, the opposite is true. When most of students' academic tasks are easy, the students show greater progress on the rest of the tasks that are challenging and the children exhibit lower levels of disruptive behavior. It may be that this situation creates behavioral momentum or simply that we all perform better when we are having some success.

Vary Tasks

Doing the same task over and over again can be frustrating, monotonous, and boring. Oftentimes as special educators, we feel that we have to focus on getting the most done in the least amount of time, and therefore we focus on the same task over and over again. However, better outcomes result when the task is varied. That is, when a target task is presented less frequently, the children exhibit better behavior and learn faster. For example, the clinician may choose five activities to work on and present each new task no more than two times in a row, rather than working repetitively on a single target behavior (Winterling, Dunlap, & O'Neill, 1987).

Again, while one might expect this procedure to result in slower learning, it actually accelerates the acquisition of learning. So, as a whole, when interspersal and task variation are included in the teaching sessions, individuals with ASD are observed to be more interested, enthusiastic, and happier. As well, they acquire the target behavior faster and demonstrate lower levels of repetitive and disruptive behaviors.

Use Natural Rewards

Not long ago, many of the research studies in this field focused on how to administer rewards. For example, studies conducted at the authors' autism center showed that mixing up the rewards was more effective than keeping the reward constant (Egel, 1980, 1981). During the time when these studies were conducted, we used flash cards to teach the children and rewarded them with food treats. Rather than giving the children a piece of candy each time they responded correctly, we found that changing it up and alternately giving them a chip, drink, or piece of candy instead of giving them the same reward every time improved responding. Later, we found that tying the reward more directly to the child's response resulted in even greater improved learning (Williams, Koegel, & Egel, 1981). For example, if we are teaching a child to open a lunch box, placing the candy inside of the lunch box not only provides a reward that is temporally closer to the behavior, but also allows the child to be rewarded directly for his or her actions. The reward follows naturally from the child's actions.

You can apply these types of natural rewards to just about any behavior. For example, with self-help skills, if the child is working on learning how to get dressed, having him put on a jacket in a chilly room will result in a natural reward. Similarly, setting the table with the end reward of getting to eat dinner would be an example of a natural reward. In the area of communication, having a child produce a word for a desirable item to gain access to that item would be a natural reward. Natural rewards can even be used with teaching academic skills. For example, when teaching literacy skills, having a child write or read clues to a scavenger hunt or write a letter to a favorite relative has natural rewards and is more meaningful and fun than drill-type instruction. Because we provide natural rewards, we don't need to worry about what special items or activities we will use as rewards and how we will implement the administration of the reward. By paying attention to child choice, then providing that favorite item or activity in a natural way, we have a much more enthusiastic and active learner.

Reward Attempts

Finally, rewarding all true attempts is important for improving motivation. Early on in the history of interventions for ASD, researchers and clinicians believed children with autism needed very clear and unambiguous feedback. Intervention was implemented within the context of a strict shaping paradigm. Therefore, if a child's attempt was not as good as, or better than, the previous response, a reward was not provided. Worse, we often told the child "No" when the response wasn't good enough, even when the child was trying. Most of that early work focused on teaching first words to the children, and at that time, very few learned how to talk. In fact, even with the best interventions, only about half learned to use expressive verbal communication (Prizant, 1983). Then, we found that if we rewarded the children for any clear attempt, even if their pronunciation wasn't perfect or a response wasn't as good as the previous one, they acquired verbal communication faster (Koegel, O'Dell, & Dunlap, 1988). This research demonstrated the importance of making sure each and every attempt is rewarded along with the correct responses. So, in our own practice, you won't hear any of our clinicians say "Wrong!" or "No!" when the child is engaged and trying. Even if the response isn't correct, if the child makes an effort, we'll say "Good try" or "Great try!"

However, we have one important warning: Don't confuse attempts with correct responding. If a child is engaging in off-task or disruptive behaviors and responds correctly, but isn't trying, he should not be rewarded. Because our target goal is focusing on motivation, we need to make sure that all rewards are given for attempts or correct responses only when the individual with ASD is truly making an effort and trying.

THE OVERALL MOTIVATIONAL PACKAGE

Now that we have described the five motivational components of PRT, let's talk a bit about putting them altogether. When implemented together, the components become especially powerful.

Combining the Motivational Components to Teach Expressive Communication Skills

In a first study of motivational components, we targeted expressive communication with older preschool and kindergarten children with autism to whom it had been especially difficult to teach expressive communication (Koegel, O'Dell, & Koegel, 1987). During the baseline, we used a traditional ABA approach that did not include the motivational variables. During this type of teaching, the children remained relatively nonverbal. That is, they may have imitated a word or word approximation on occasion but very rarely, even over a period of many months. However, once the motivational components were incorporated into the teaching paradigm, the children began to show improvements in their imitative utterances and their deferred imitation, meaning they would use the words even when they did not have a verbal model prompt. We also examined spontaneous utterances in this study. When the motivational components were incorporated into the intervention, the children began to emit a large number of spontaneous utterances outside of the clinical setting, with a huge variety in the words they were using. This study focused on communication was the first systematic implementation using all of the motivational variables combined as a package.

At that time, in the 1980s, it was unheard of to implement behavioral intervention in a nonstructured manner. Then, effective interventions were implemented in a very clinical, drill-type format in a room free from distractions. We typically used flash cards for teaching first words. With children who were nonverbal, we would often start by getting their eye contact (e.g., "Look at me!"), sometimes working on eye contact alone for a period of time. For children who were completely nonverbal, we generally started with sounds in isolation first—for example, prompting them, "Say *mmmm,*" then rewarding the imitation. Eventually we added a second sound, for example, "Say *ah.*" Once they were able to imitate and discriminate between the two sounds we added them together, using prompts such as "Say *ma*" and eventually "Say *mama*." Of course, many of the words we were teaching these children did not name their desired items, and when we got past the eye contact and imitation phases, we started with the flash cards. So, it wasn't much fun, and it was pretty common for the kids to exhibit lots of avoidance and escape-motivated disruptive behavior. Yet, they did learn. It was slow—painfully slow—but the kids did progress. Unfortunately, it was difficult to find people in the field who were willing to work with the children. Most professionals felt that the amount of effort the intervention took, coupled with the small gains, made the intervention undesirable. However, that was before the epidemic in autism diagnoses, and before we had developed the specific motivational procedures.

So, let's go back to the 1987 study where we focused on communication using motivational components. It was amazing. Children who had never talked before started rapidly learning words. Some learned quickly and some learned more slowly, but most learned to talk. Up until that time, it was not unusual for 50% of children with autism to remain nonverbal for their whole lives (Prizant, 1983), so this was a huge improvement. Read on for just one example of the gains children in this study made.

CASE HISTORY
Charlie and His First Word

I (Lynn) remember one day when I was working with little 5-year-old Charlie. He had never said a word in his life. We had drilled him with flash cards for a year, with little success. Then, focusing on the motivational procedures, I brought his favorite cookie to the session—chocolate chip. Instead of the flash cards, I held up the cookie and modeled the word "cookie." In a very labored but effortful way, he slowly, but surely, said "coo - kie"—a little slow, but perfectly pronounced. It was his first word. And, of course, I immediately broke off a piece of the cookie and gave it to him as a natural reward. We did this over and over, and he had no trouble coming up with the word "cookie." The next day, I brought another one of his favorite foods, an apple. Again, he slowly but surely said the word "apple." We were on our way! Some kids will use the same word or same sounds until they have learned about 10 words and get the idea that each item has its own label. Not Charlie. He started coming out with word after word after word. And again, it wasn't that we hadn't tried to teach him to talk. It was just that we hadn't done it the right way. He wasn't able to make that connection between using a word and having that communicative behavior lead to a positive consequence. What a difference the motivational components made for him.

What's also interesting are the statistics for children older versus younger than 5. The number of children who are nonverbal and begin talking after the age of 5 is low, even with the motivational components. If we begin intervention before the age of 3, approximately 95% will learn to use verbal communication; for children who begin receiving intervention between ages 3 and 5, it's slightly lower, about 85%–95%; but after age 5, if the children are completely nonverbal (meaning they have not even made any word attempts), only about 20% will learn to use expressive verbal communication (Koegel, 2000). Thus, early intervention is extremely important. But keep two things in mind: 1) a small percentage of children do not learn to talk even when intervention is provided before the age of 5; and 2) some children learn to talk even after the age of 5.

The Natural Language Paradigm and the Development of PRT

Because the motivational intervention for teaching communication looked so natural and similar to the way in which typical language learners acquire communication, we called it "The Natural Language Paradigm" or "NLP." Soon after, we learned that the motivational components could be applied to a wide variety of other behaviors, so we re-named the procedures "PRT" or "Pivotal Response Treatment." (PRT can also stand for "Pivotal Response Teaching" or "Pivotal Response Training"; these three terms can be used interchangeably.) We use the word *pivotal* for an important reason. When the motivational components are incorporated, we see wide positive improvements in a number of other untreated behaviors. For individuals with ASD, who have a number of behavioral and social concerns that need to be addressed, this is particularly important, especially if we want to get them on a more typical developmental trajectory.

Now, back to our research. Incorporating the motivational components seemed to make such a difference for the children's expressive communication that we decided to document how they affected other behavior. In a subsequent study, we worked with preschool children between 3 and 4 years of age (Koegel, Koegel, & Surratt, 1992). We targeted first words for nonverbal children or language for the verbal children. We used a repeated reversals design, alternating the treatments between a standard ABA communication therapy, without the motivational components incorporated, and the PRT intervention. We assessed the preschoolers' disruptive behaviors that interfered with the teaching of communication skills, including turning away from the teacher, screaming, crying, yelling, loud repetitive behaviors that masked the teacher's instructions, slapping, grabbing, knocking the materials off the table, climbing under the table or chair, lying down on the floor, and so on. We found that when we implemented the ABA sessions without the motivational components, the incidence of these behaviors was very high. In contrast, every time we incorporated the motivational components, these behaviors were low. One detail that did not appear in the publication, but that we remember so clearly, was the teachers' behavior. Because the teachers were naïve to the experimental hypothesis, we just told them what to do during each session. After we had completed several sessions, the teachers began to moan and groan every time we told them to use the standard ABA procedures. Without even being aware of the experimental design, they were visibly bothered when they had to teach without the motivational components.

PRT and Parental Stress During Family Interactions

The response of these teachers wasn't unique. In a later study, we examined parental stress during family interactions (Koegel, Bimbela, & Schreibman, 1996). In one trial, we taught the parents of children who were between 3 and 9 years old how to implement ABA intervention without the motivational components; we taught another group to incorporate motivational components. Videotapes of their home interactions were scored for happiness, interest, stress, and communication style. The results of this study showed participants scoring at similar levels in all areas prior to intervention. Following the ABA intervention without the motivational components, all of the parents remained similar in all areas during family interactions. In contrast, when the PRT intervention was taught, the parents' happiness, interest, and communication styles improved and their stress decreased. In fact, all of the parents went from neutral to positive family interactions following the PRT parent education. This finding is especially important as parents of children with ASD often exhibit very high levels of persistent stress. This underscores the importance of interventions that have a positive effect on the child while also reducing parent stress. Children with ASD need to be provided with a constant therapeutic environment throughout their waking hours. For most parents, providing this environment can be a very difficult experience or a neutral experience at best. However, including the motivational components in the intervention can make this a pleasant experience. These collateral gains are critically important for family systems.

Applying PRT to Other Target Behaviors: Academic and Social Skills

Following this initial work in the area of communication, we focused on applying PRT to other target behaviors. For example, we found that the motivational components can easily be incorporated into academic activities (Koegel, Singh, & Koegel, 2010). These techniques are discussed in detail in Chapter 9.

We also found that motivational components can be incorporated into social activities (Baker, Koegel, & Koegel, 1998). In this study, we selected elementary school children with ASD who tended to spend all or most of their lunch and recess periods in social isolation. We interviewed each child's teacher and parents to understand if they had any restricted interests—interests that we might use to provide the motivational variable of choice. Then, we developed a social game to be played with a group of typical children with the theme of the game based on the restricted interest. Once the restricted interest was incorporated, the children with ASD actively engaged in the social activity. What's more, the children's social interactions with typical peers also increased during other times of the day. Read on for an example.

CASE HISTORY
David and His States

David was a second grader who spent his entire recess and lunch periods perched on the top of the slide watching the cars pass by. He never uttered a word to a peer, nor did he express any interest in participating in any other activities, even when suggested. However, he was deeply interested in the United States. He had learned every state and its geographic location on a map; every state capital, state flag, flower, and animal; and the governor of each state (including family information). His interest had begun to develop in kindergarten when he could rapidly put together puzzles of the U.S., even when the puzzle pieces were flipped over with only the shape of each state as a cue. Fortuitously, his elementary school had a map of the U.S. painted on the playground. To take advantage of his restricted interest, we developed a "States Game" wherein one person called out the name of a state and a mode of movement (e.g., hop, skip, run, walk). When the caller said, "Run to Florida," all the children scurried along to the state. The last student to arrive on the state was the caller for the next round.

Most second graders don't know where 90% of the states are located, so David proved to be the valued player of the game. The children looked toward him when they didn't know the location of a state. David enthusiastically played the game and also engaged in peer interactions more frequently throughout the day. In a questionnaire given to his classmates, they made comments such as "We didn't know David was so smart" and "David is really fun to play with." |||

From a practical point of view, we know that restricted interests are very challenging, as individuals with ASD are often extremely driven to engage in the restricted interest and often engage in challenging behaviors if redirected away from that interest. However, by designing social activities based on restricted interests, which are often at the pinnacle of these individuals' reinforcer hierarchies, adults can help to make socialization pleasant and enjoyable for children with ASD. Further, because of their accumulation of detail and vast knowledge of the topic, these children are often viewed as the most valued members of their peer cliques.

Other research labs have shown that PRT can be used to improve additional areas of social behavior. For example, typically developing peers can be taught to use PRT strategies during play, which results in improved engagement, more initiated play, longer play interactions, and more social conversation between the children with ASD and the typical peers (Pierce & Schreibman, 1995). Similarly, PRT procedures were used to improve the symbolic play complexity of children between the ages of 4 and 9 (Stahmer, 1995). In addition, the children's creative symbolic play and interaction skills also improved with the improvement of symbolic play, which was targeted through PRT.

As a whole, the positive improvements of the PRT motivational components have been shown with first words, language, play, socialization, self-help, and academics. One important consideration of PRT is its use as an antecedent positive behavioral support strategy. That is, when the intervention is implemented in a motivational way, this can be conceptualized as an antecedent intervention to create an environment where behavior problems are reduced or eliminated. Using such strategies reduces the need for reactive behavior intervention plans.

The motivational components of PRT were the first pivotal area we researched. Following this research, we discovered additional areas, including child initiations, self-management, responsiveness to multiple cues, and empathy, that also appear to have a widespread positive effect on other untreated areas. These are discussed in subsequent chapters.

Key Insights ||| Components of PRT

Motivation is crucial within PRT and involves the following variables:

- **Child choice:** Carefully observing the child to assess his or her interests and using preferred items and activities as stimulus materials in the sessions is critical.
- **Interspersal:** Incorporating previously learned (maintenance) activities with newly targeted (acquisition) tasks improves motivation.

- **Task variation:** Varying the activities, instead of drilling the child on target behaviors, results in faster learning.
- **Natural rewards:** When the consequences of a behavior are inherently linked to the behavior itself, a faster learning curve is achieved.
- **Rewarding attempts:** When all clear attempts are rewarded, regardless of whether they are perfect responses, individuals with ASD learn faster.

Motivation is central to the following strategies for working with students with ASD:

- **Reduce disruptive behavior:** When motivational components are incorporated into the intervention, disruptive behaviors decrease or vanish.
- **Use antecedent interventions:** Incorporating motivational components into the intervention reduces escape and avoidance behaviors and thereby functions as an antecedent intervention, which is a positive behavior support strategy.
- **Use perseverative interests:** Selecting an individual with ASD's perseverative interest and using that as the theme of a club or activity improves socialization during the activity and during other times of the day.
- **Create valued member environments:** When the strengths of an individual with ASD are chosen for the social context of an activity, the individual with ASD is often considered the valued member of the peer clique.

SUMMARY

PRT emerged from the principles and techniques of ABA used to treat children with ASD in the 1960s and 1970s. PRT built upon seminal behavioral research that relied upon the stimulus-response-consequence paradigm; at that time, DTT was the method used to help individuals with ASD learn targeted behaviors. Early PRT research considered the role of motivation in learning and the negative effects of learned helplessness upon learning and affect. Multiple early studies ultimately identified five critical motivational variables: choice, interspersal, task variation, use of natural rewards, and the importance of rewarding attempts to perform a target behavior. These variables, central to PRT interventions, can help practitioners working with children with ASD to reduce disruptive behavior, use antecedent interventions, work in a positive way with restricted interests, and create environments in which individuals with ASD are valued members.

STUDY QUESTIONS

1. What are the behavioral measures of a "motivated" individual?
2. List five treatment variables that have been empirically shown to improve motivation.
3. What are the collateral benefits of incorporating motivational aspects into the intervention?

4. Describe the effect of motivational variables on the stress of parents.
5. Discuss the changes that occur during family interactions when motivational components are incorporated into the intervention.
6. Provide an example of how a natural reinforcer can be incorporated into intervention for communication, self-help, and language intervention.
7. List some specific methods of creating an environment wherein the individual with ASD may be considered the valued member of the peer group.
8. List at least five skill areas that have been shown to result in improved performance when motivational procedures are incorporated.
9. Provide an example of how to teach first words using motivational procedures.
10. Discuss variables that may make perseverative interests difficult to treat.
11. Describe the theory of learned helplessness and how learned helplessness may be created in a child with ASD.

REFERENCES

Abramson, L. Y., Seligman, M. E., & Teasdale, J. D. (1978). Learned helplessness in humans: Critique and reformulation. *Journal of Abnormal Psychology, 87*(1), 49.

Alloy, L. B., & Seligman, M. E. (1979). On the cognitive component of learned helplessness and depression. *Psychology of Learning and Motivation, 13*, 219–276.

Baker, M. J., Koegel, R. L., & Koegel, L. K. (1998). Increasing the social behavior of young children with autism using their obsessive behaviors. *Research and Practice for Persons with Severe Disabilities, 23*(4), 300–308.

Bettelheim, B. (1967). *Empty fortress*. New York, NY: Simon and Schuster.

Carter, C. M. (2001). Using choice with game play to increase language skills and interactive behaviors in children with autism. *Journal of Positive Behavior Interventions, 3*(3), 131–151.

Dunlap, G. (1984). The influence of task variation and maintenance tasks on the learning and affect of autistic children. *Journal of Experimental Child Psychology, 37*(1), 41–64.

Egel, A. L. (1980). The effects of constant vs varied reinforcer presentation on responding by autistic children. *Journal of Experimental Child Psychology, 30*(3), 455–463.

Egel, A. L. (1981). Reinforcer variation: Implications for motivating developmentally disabled children. *Journal of Applied Behavior Analysis, 14*(3), 345–350.

Klein, D. C., Fencil-Morse, E., & Seligman, M. E. (1976). Learned helplessness, depression, and the attribution of failure. *Journal of Personality and Social Psychology, 33*(5), 508.

Koegel, L. K. (2000). Interventions to facilitate communication in autism. *Journal of Autism and Developmental Disorders, 30*(5), 383–391.

Koegel, L. K., Ashbaugh, K., Koegel, R. L., Detar, W. J., & Regester, A. (2013). Increasing socialization in adults with Asperger's syndrome. *Psychology in the Schools, 50*(9), 899–909.

Koegel, R. L., Bimbela, A., & Schreibman, L. (1996). Collateral effects of parent training on family interactions. *Journal of Autism and Developmental Disorders, 26*(3), 347–359.

Koegel, R. L., Camarata, S., Koegel, L. K., Ben-Tall, A., & Smith, A. E. (1998). Increasing speech intelligibility in children with autism. *Journal of Autism and Developmental Disorders, 28*(3), 241–251.

Koegel, R. L., Dyer, K., & Bell, L. K. (1987). The influence of child-preferred activities on autistic children's social behavior. *Journal of Applied Behavior Analysis, 20*(3), 243–252.

Koegel, R. L., Glahn, T. J., & Nieminen, G. S. (1978). Generalization of parent-training results. *Journal of Applied Behavior Analysis, 11*(1), 95–109.

Koegel, L. K., & Koegel, R. L. (1995). Motivating communication in children with autism. In E. Schopler & G. B. Mesibov (Eds.), *Learning and cognition in autism* (pp. 73–87). New York, NY: Springer US.

Koegel, R. L., Koegel, L. K., & Surratt, A. (1992). Language intervention and disruptive behavior in preschool children with autism. *Journal of Autism and Developmental Disorders, 22*(2), 141–153.
Koegel, R. L., O'Dell, M., & Dunlap, G. (1988). Producing speech use in nonverbal autistic children by reinforcing attempts. *Journal of Autism and Developmental Disorders, 18*(4), 525–538.
Koegel, R. L., O'Dell, M. C., & Koegel, L. K. (1987). A natural language teaching paradigm for nonverbal autistic children. *Journal of Autism and Developmental Disorders, 17*(2), 187–200.
Koegel, R. L., Schreibman, L., O'Neill, R. E., & Burke, J. C. (1983). The personality and family-interaction characteristics of parents of autistic children. *Journal of Consulting and Clinical Psychology, 51*(5), 683.
Koegel, L. K., Singh, A., & Koegel, R. (2010). Improving motivation for academics in children with autism. *Journal of Autism and Developmental Disorders, 40*(9), 1057–1066.
Lovaas, O. I. (1977). *The autistic child: Language development through behavior modification.* New York, NY: Irvington.
Lovaas, O. I. (1987). Behavioral treatment and normal educational and intellectual functioning in young autistic children. *Journal of Consulting and Clinical Psychology, 55*(1), 3.
Lovaas, O. I., Koegel, R., Simmons, J. Q., & Long, J. S. (1973). Some generalization and follow-up measures on autistic children in behavior therapy. *Journal of Applied Behavior Analysis, 6*(1), 131–165.
Maier, S. F., & Seligman, M. E. (1976). Learned helplessness: Theory and evidence. *Journal of Experimental Psychology: General, 105*(1), 3.
Moes, D. R. (1998). Integrating choice-making opportunities within teacher-assigned academic tasks to facilitate the performance of children with autism. *Research and Practice for Persons with Severe Disabilities, 23*(4), 319–328.
Mohammadzaheri, F., Koegel, L. K., Rezaei, M., & Bakhshi, E. (2015). A randomized clinical trial comparison between Pivotal Response Treatment (PRT) and adult-driven Applied Behavior Analysis (ABA) intervention on disruptive behaviors in public school children with autism. *Journal of Autism and Developmental Disorders,* 45(9), 2899–2907.
Mohammadzaheri, F., Koegel, L. K., Rezaee, M., & Rafiee, S. M. (2014). A randomized clinical trial comparison between Pivotal Response Treatment (PRT) and Structured Applied Behavior Analysis (ABA) intervention for children with autism. *Journal of Autism and Developmental Disorders, 44*(11), 2769–2777.
Morrison, K., & Rosales-Ruiz, J. (1997). The effect of object preferences on task performance and stereotypy in a child with autism. *Research in Developmental Disabilities, 18*(2), 127–137.
Pierce, K., & Schreibman, L. (1995). Increasing complex social behaviors in children with autism: Effects of peer-implemented pivotal response training. *Journal of Applied Behavior Analysis, 28*(3), 285–295.
Prizant, B. M. (1983). Language acquisition and communicative behavior in autism: Toward an understanding of the "whole" of it. *Journal of Speech and Hearing Disorders, 48*(3), 296–307.
Reinhartsen, D. B., Garfinkle, A. N., & Wolery, M. (2002). Engagement with toys in two-year-old children with autism: Teacher selection versus child choice. *Research and Practice for Persons with Severe Disabilities, 27*(3), 175–187.
Risley, T. R. (1968). The effects and side effects of punishing the autistic behaviors of a deviant child. *Journal of Applied Behavior Analysis, 1*(1), 21–34.
Schwartz, S. (1981) Language disabilities in infantile autism: A brief review and comment. *Applied Psycholinguistices, 2*(1), 25–31.
Skinner, B. F. (1953). *Science and human behavior*. Simon and Schuster.
Stahmer, A. C. (1995). Teaching symbolic play skills to children with autism using pivotal response training. *Journal of Autism and Developmental Disorders, 25*(2), 123–141.
Williams, J. A., Koegel, R. L., & Egel, A. L. (1981). Response-reinforcer relationships and improved learning in autistic children. *Journal of Applied Behavior Analysis, 14*(1), 53–60.
Winterling, V., Dunlap, G., & O'Neill, R. E. (1987). The influence of task variation on the aberrant behaviors of autistic students. *Education and Treatment of Children,* 105–119.
Wolf, M., Risley, T., & Mees, H. (1963). Application of operant conditioning procedures to the behaviour problems of an autistic child. *Behaviour Research and Therapy, 1*(2), 305–312.

2

Assessment, Feedback, and Treatment Planning

Lynn Kern Koegel

CHAPTER GOALS

Goal 1. The reader will understand issues associated with assessment of autism spectrum disorders (ASD).

Goal 2. The reader will understand issues related to standardized testing.

Goal 3. The reader will describe a strength-based approach to assessment.

Goal 4. The reader will be able to discuss issues related to providing feedback on diagnosis to parents.

Goal 5. The reader will be able to discuss methods for linking assessment to treatment options.

This chapter discusses several concerns related to assessing children with ASD, including considerations in making an initial diagnosis and sharing this information with a child's family. First, I discuss the emotional and practical stressors parents typically experience when a child is diagnosed with ASD—crucial for any effective practitioner to understand in working with families. Next, I explore different types of assessment (standardized testing, naturalistic observation), their advantages and limitations, and specific issues for practitioners to be aware of when assessing children. This chapter recommends a strength-based approach to assessment and discusses the rationale for, and elements of, this approach. Throughout, the chapter draws connections between assessment, treatment planning, and providing effective feedback and support to families.

A note on the relationship between assessment and treatment: You might be asking yourself why treatment is discussed in this chapter. It is because too many reports only tell parents, educators, and care providers what's wrong, but not how to fix the problem. A good assessment should lead to treatment goals and should provide suggestions as to how to accomplish those goals. Whenever possible, the assessment should include multiple ways to address the issues at hand. For example, most behavior problems do not evaporate with one intervention. Generally, families need a number of programs implemented simultaneously. Similarly, for social difficulties, a group of interventions implemented synchronously is important, as no single intervention technique will result in complete amelioration of social challenges. Good assessments should identify target behaviors and suggest interventions. Assessments should provide comprehensive information on present levels of behaviors against which changes during interventions can be compared. This is critical for evaluating the effectiveness of an intervention.

CHALLENGES FACING PARENTS OF CHILDREN DIAGNOSED WITH ASD

Parents of individuals with autism report that receiving the diagnosis is one of life's major events. They remember the exact moment, location, and words that were uttered: "Your child has autism." Too often these words are accompanied by pessimism about the future. Many parents report that the diagnostician declared that their child has a lifelong disability; will be unlikely to have friends, marry, or have a job; and may be dependent on them throughout life. This is far from the truth. Parents should know that interventions have steadily evolved, and almost all children with ASD will improve significantly. Many may overcome their symptoms with the right interventions. There is no doubt that it will take immense effort on the part of the parents and the child's larger community, but for most individuals, this effort does pay off. Despite the fact that there is great hope for families, we know that parents of individuals with ASD experience much stress. Society hasn't come up with support mechanisms to lessen the burden on families. Let's begin by discussing some of the issues families face when their child is diagnosed with ASD.

Difficult Emotions: Stress, Fear, Guilt

Although all parents feel some stress, the challenges and life changes of having a child with autism are associated with significantly higher levels of stress (Koegel et al., 1992). Further, it appears that higher levels of autism symptoms are related to higher levels of stress (Hastings & Johnson, 2001). That is, parents who cannot connect and interact easily with their children will show greater levels of stress. The level of child social competency and the presence of repetitive disruptive behavior can also significantly elevate parents' stress (Davis & Carter, 2008). In addition, delays and deficits in a child with ASD's social skills also produce significant stress for both mothers and fathers (Davis & Carter, 2008).

Families also face the fear of the unknown. There is wide heterogeneity among children diagnosed with ASDs; parents often search the Internet for information on the diagnosis and are confronted with worst-case scenarios that may not apply to their child. Every child is different, and no one can read the future, but we do know that interventions are constantly improving. Parents need to have hope in order to work with their child effectively. Stresses and depression can interfere with effective parenting.

Finally, parents blame and question themselves when a child is diagnosed. Common questions are, "Did I do anything wrong when I was pregnant?" "Are the behaviors a result of something I did?" "Am I a bad parent?" "I have some symptoms of autism—did my child inherit those from me?" Although we know that having a child with autism can happen to anyone, regardless of ethnicity, socioeconomic status, and so on, it doesn't stop parents from questioning themselves. However, we do know that autism is likely genetic. It occurs more frequently with identical twins and in boys. We also absolutely know that it isn't the parents' fault, and parents are a necessary part of the habilitation process.

Practical Challenges: Behavioral Concerns and Limited Supports

Parents note specific concerns about the ways in which their children behave. These concerns can be related to language development, sleep difficulties, lack of social behavior including a lack of pointing and eye contact, and disruptive behavior (Midence & O'Neill, 1999). It is important to listen to parents and address their concerns immediately. Given the importance of early intervention, their child's issues need to be addressed as early as possible. A "wait and see" approach may waste months or even years in a child's life. Moreover, parental concerns about a child's behavior can be exacerbated by a lack of available social support and by difficulties in promptly obtaining the services the child needs.

Lack of Social Support Social support is multidimensional and can include a variety of methods that provide assistance and comfort that help people cope with problems. We all have a friend or relative who is a "go-to" person when we are feeling down or stressed. However, the diagnosis of autism and accompanying child behavior may create unique types of stress with a paucity of social support (Boyd, 2002). Social support is critical. For example, mothers who receive less social support experience more stress and anger (Gray & Holden, 1992). Social support can be provided by a spouse, by a relative, by other parents with a similar child, and—in particular—by interventionists. Rejoicing in small accomplishments, providing optimism for the parent, teaching independence, and providing other effective, evidence-based direct services that result in improvements in the child can help reduce parental stress.

Wait Lists and Lack of Services Following a diagnosis, many parents are faced with a lack of services and long wait lists. For many geographically remote families, no services at all are available. Parents are aware of the numerous advantages of early intensive intervention, but may not have access to services, thereby creating even more anxiety and frustration.

The Role of Assessment: What Parents Need to Know

Given the many stressors facing families of children with ASD, you are likely wondering how you can help parents as they begin to navigate the complicated process of seeking out assessment and treatment for their child.

First, there isn't a genetic test for ASD. Currently the symptoms are identified according to the fifth edition of the American Psychiatric Association's *Diagnostic and Statistical Manual of Mental Disorders*, commonly referred to as the DSM-5 (American Psychiatric Association, 2013). ASD is considered when an individual demonstrates persistent deficits in social communication and social interaction across multiple contexts. These include deficits in social-emotional reciprocity; nonverbal communication used for social interaction; and developing, maintaining, and understanding relationships. In addition, the individual must demonstrate restricted and repetitive patterns of behavior, interests, or activities (often referred to as RRBs). This category consists of *stereotypy*, insistence on sameness/inflexible adherence to routines/ritualized patterns of behavior, and restricted or fixated interests. It's important to note that all children and adults demonstrate some of these behaviors. When they interfere with everyday functioning or are stigmatizing, however, it is important to get an assessment. Research is beginning to suggest that it may be helpful to address pre-linguistic symptoms of autism, so early asocial behaviors, pragmatic difficulties, or repetitive patterns of behavior should be assessed. In addition, assessment should address the level of support the individual with ASD is expected to need, a point we revisit later in this chapter. Once a diagnosis is possible, consider the fact that a parent may be surprised, shocked, and stressed with a diagnosis of ASD. It may be especially difficult when it is a parent's first child and the parent does not have another child with whom to compare those developmental milestones.

In sum, learning that their child has been diagnosed with autism or a related disorder is often a stressful and difficult situation for parents. A clinician's approach to assessment, diagnosis, and feedback can affect how parents experience and cope with this stress. With that in mind, we now discuss specific approaches to assessment and diagnosis.

TESTING INDIVIDUALS WITH ASD: THE LIMITS OF STANDARDIZED TESTING

Now that you understand how hard it is for a parent to hear a diagnosis of autism, let's talk about testing children with autism. Some diagnostic centers and interventionists rely only, or primarily, upon standardized testing during the diagnostic process and observations in a clinical setting. The authors of this book published a study showing that for many children with ASD, standardized testing may not be accurate and may underestimate the child's true abilities (Koegel, Koegel, & Smith, 1997).

Specifically, we selected six pre- and elementary school age children to assess during 44 separate testing sessions. We had two conditions in this study: a standardized testing condition, and a condition in which we implemented a motivational/attentional intervention during the testing. In the standardized testing condition, we administered language and intelligence tests according to the instructions in the test manuals. That is, test materials were set up at a small table with a chair on each side, and each child was asked to sit at the table. The preliminary trial items were presented with feedback, as suggested by the manual, and then the children were tested. Verbal praise and candy treats were given to the children for appropriate sitting and appropriate test-taking behavior.

In the other condition, motivational and attentional variables were identified that might interfere with accurate test taking. The testing situation was then modified to address these variables. Of course, these variables differed across children. Therefore, we observed each child and interviewed each child's parents to determine behaviors that were likely to interfere during the testing. With this information in hand, we modified the standardized testing situation in relation to each child's needs. Please note that no test questions were changed or delivered in a non-standardized manner that would influence the child's correct or incorrect responses. The modification only targeted behavior problems that might interfere with appropriate test taking. For example, one child engaged in repetitive talk using cartoon characters' voices during standardized tests. Thus, to improve his motivation, we provided him with predictable breaks contingent upon his responding to the test stimuli, at which time he could engage in repeating cartoon lines in the cartoon character voices. Another child did not attend to the test stimuli or task instructions. Therefore, we had him repeat the test instructions. For example, on the vocabulary test, instead of having the examiner say, "Point to the ball," we would say "Can you say 'ball'?" After the child repeated the word "ball" we would say, "Now point to it." A third child engaged in repetitive, interfering stereotypic behavior, so he was permitted to engage in this behavior contingent upon on-task responding. A fourth child engaged in disruptive behavior any time she was asked to come to the table and sit down. Therefore, we provided her with the choice of where she wanted to sit and brought the test materials to her. Another child brought books with him that he repetitively flipped through, and he threw a tantrum when the books were taken away. Thus, contingent on his responding to the test questions, we provided breaks when he could flip through the pages of his books. A final preschool child engaged in disruptive behavior when his mother left the room; therefore, we invited his mother to sit in the room (but not interact in a way that might change his responses) while he was being tested.

The results of this study showed that all 44 test scores were higher when the motivational/attentional variables were considered, regardless of the order in which the child was given the different testing conditions. Specifically, during all of the language and IQ tests, scores were lower during the standardized testing condition. In some cases, the children performed in the severely disabled range on tests during the standardized testing condition, but scored within the average range when the motivational and attentional techniques were included.

This study was important for several reasons. First, it suggests that many children with ASD may have behaviors that negatively influence their test performance. Without ensuring that the child's motivation and attention are addressed, the child's abilities may be underestimated. Second, a child's educational programs are often based on the results of standardized testing. If programs are developed based on inaccurate scores, the curriculum may be below the child's actual level. Therefore, incorporating idiosyncratic reinforcement into the test-taking situation appears to be especially important for children with ASD, particularly those who demonstrate challenging or off-task behaviors. Such steps are likely to reduce avoidance and escape behaviors that commonly occur when these children are presented with tasks that do not have natural reinforcers and to improve the accuracy of assessments.

GETTING A MORE COMPLETE PICTURE: BEHAVIORAL ASSESSMENTS

It is important to assess a child in a variety of situations, including how he or she functions in everyday settings. If a tester has implemented standardized tests only, without any direct observations in natural environments, he or she probably has not done a good job. We can learn so many things from observing in natural environments that just cannot be tested. For example, I have had parents bring their child to me demonstrating play behaviors in my office that look completely average, but sometimes these parents tell me that their child is so rigid and engages in repetitive behaviors at home. When I have then observed the child in the home setting, this is completely true. For example, I have cool new toys the child has not seen before, and during our hour-long play session the child plays appropriately, At home, however, the child picks one toy to play with repetitively, and taking that single toy away causes a complete meltdown. The opposite can also be true—some children come to my office and engage in disruptive behavior for a full hour but engage in perfectly fine behavior when they are in their regular routines at school and home.

Advising Parents

The bottom line is this: Advise parents to make sure their child is observed in natural settings. If the family lives a distance away from an assessment center, parents can bring or send representative video clips of their child's behavior in natural settings. Next, parents should make sure the tester observes their child with similarly aged peers. ASD involves social communication, so the child needs to be observed with peers to assess areas of need. Some children with ASD are much better (or even fine) socially with adults, but not with peers. It is important to understand that peer–peer relationships are much different than adult–child relationships. The authors of this book have witnessed many children with ASD who interact well with adults yet have difficulty playing with peers, engaging in social conversation, and engage in different sets of rules than their peers. Again, if the tester cannot go to the child's school or a playground or other location where there are peers, parents should be advised to get sample video and/or audio recordings for the evaluator. If there is no opportunity to observe the child with peers because he or she never interacts at all, the tester should know this. Also, advise parents to please make sure the samples are *representative*. It is always helpful if the evaluator can see the best behaviors as well as the most challenging behaviors. For example, we once had a young adult come to our center. The family had sent videotapes and the adult looked like a perfect angel, but when he arrived he had major meltdowns and broke almost every item we had in our center—televisions, lamps, anything breakable. The videotapes we had viewed were not representative, which limited their usefulness. So, parents should make sure to gather samples to create a representative recording so the staff can accurately evaluate the child and be prepared.

Specific Recommendations for Naturalistic Observations of Behavior

Now that we've established the importance of naturalistic observations, let's discuss specifics. Live observations of behavior, or recordings, should meet the following criteria:

1. They should be long enough to convey how the child typically behaves.
2. They should include a sample of the child's social language use.
3. They should include assessment of the child's affect.

These criteria are discussed further in the sections below.

Accurately Convey How the Child Typically Behaves First, make sure that observations or clips are long enough to accurately convey the child's typical behavior. I have had parents send me short clips showing *solely* times when the child is on his best behavior, only later to find out that much of the day the child was engaging in considerable disruptive behavior. The opposite is also true. I have had parents send me clips of their child's disruptive behavior, which appeared pretty severe and constant, then found upon meeting the child that he or she is relatively well-behaved and rarely engages in disruptive behavior. Therefore, it is important to document the duration of any inappropriate behavior, including repetitive behavior, disruptive behaviors, and any other area that may need intervention.

Second, observe when inappropriate behaviors are occurring and when they are not occurring. I recently observed a child in school who engaged in disruptive repetitive behaviors, such as humming and making noises, whenever he was bored (which was much of the time). However, when reading or engaged in an interesting task, he was completely quiet. The teacher was so annoyed by him, but actually her teaching style was so slow and highly verbal that he was bored silly, despite being far above the other students in the class in most academic areas. The revelation that good behavior was common during interesting tasks helped the teacher understand that she needed to use more engaging teaching strategies, which helped all of her students.

Thorough and detailed observations ensure that the right intervention plan can be put in place. We often discuss a functional assessment for disruptive behavior, in which the cause of the challenging behavior is assessed to understand why it is occurring and to provide functionally equivalent replacement behaviors. This process can be implemented for any number of behaviors, not just disruptive behaviors. In summary, carefully describe each behavior, gather information on the frequency and duration of behaviors that need to be addressed, and figure out if any environmental variables are influencing the behaviors. Then an intervention plan can be developed to address those behaviors.

Include a Language Sample Next, get a language sample from a speech-language pathologist (SLP) who is trained in methods to analyze natural conversational interactions so the child's articulation, language structures, prosody, social interaction, pragmatics, and many other areas can be analyzed. Because it is somewhat tedious to do a language sample, SLPs may not automatically offer to do so, but for children with ASD it can be very helpful. It is important to make sure at least 50 child utterances are collected. If a child does not make 50 utterances in a reasonable period of time, the sample can be shorter, but that information is also important for the team to have.

Include Assessment of the Child's Affect Another important, and often ignored, area to assess is the child's affect. Questions to consider are, "During what activities does the child seem happy and interested? During what activities is the child bored and disinterested?" Dunlap (1984) developed a six-point rating scale addressing affect that has been used in many articles. Specifically, he had raters score the child's enthusiasm, interest, happiness, and general behavior. Three general categories were developed that can be scored for negative, neutral, and positive affect, which help provide an evaluation of the individual with ASD's level of affect during various tasks and activities. For example, consider how a rater might score one component of affect, the child's enthusiasm for a particular in-seat activity or task. *Negative enthusiasm* (scored as 0) would entail the child trying to leave the room, having a tantrum, kicking, screaming, throwing items, pushing tasks away, or crying. The rater would assign a score of 1 if the child remains in the chair but does not engage in the task and exhibits stereotypic behavior, yawning or making vocalizations or motor behaviors unrelated to the task. The next category, *neutral enthusiasm,* is scored with a 2 if the child generally complies with the instructions but gets fidgety, is inattentive, plays with the materials, and wiggles. A 3 is scored if the child complies but does not perform the task readily and occasionally focuses on the task or teacher. *Positive enthusiasm* is scored with a 4 if the child performs the task readily and frequently and is attentive. A 5 is scored if the child attends to the task and also smiles and laughs appropriately while attending and performs extra behaviors related to the task. Similar scales can be used for rating teachers' and parents' affect. Developing teaching activities around desired activities, measured by high affect, is important for both the child and the adult working with that child. If parents or teachers do not like the activities and are not enthusiastically working with the child, it may influence the child's responsiveness. The scales can also give us an idea of how to assist with parent and teacher education. In contrast, if parents and teachers are having fun with an activity, they are likely to engage in that activity more frequently.

THE VALUE OF STRENGTH-BASED ASSESSMENT

Traditional assessments tend to focus on deficits in social, cognitive, self-help, communication, and behavioral areas. In fact, most clinical training programs teach students to assess for areas of weakness to target during intervention. The result of this approach is that all of the individual's weaknesses are identified and described. This can be devastating to parents who love and see the positives in their child. In fact, research has shown that most parents report that they receive a very negative prognosis when their children are diagnosed with ASD (Nissenbaum, Tollefson, & Reese, 2002). Strength-based assessment (SBA) has been discussed as a viable option for individuals with ASD (Cosden, Koegel, Koegel, Greenwell, & Klein, 2006).

The goal of a SBA is to identify strengths within in the individual being tested, as well as within the individual's family and his or her broader environmental context. In doing so, the related goal is to provide a positive attitude that will improve the parents', educators', and care providers' perceptions of the individual's abilities, as well as create hope regarding the child's future and potential. After all, depressed parents and educators who focus on the child's limitations and pathology will not be as effective as those who believe the child can learn and succeed. The field, often described in the literature as positive psychology, aims to focus on hope and optimism and on building positive qualities, rather than a preoccupation with repairing deficits (Seligman & Csikszentmihalyi, 2014). This positive attitude may be especially important for children with ASD given the stress and uncertainty associated with the condition (Koegel, Bimbela, & Schreibman, 1996).

Specific Applications of Strength-Based Assessments

Cosden et al. (2006) describe four ways in which SBA has been used in regard to individuals with autism. First, positive characteristics of the individual with ASD and his or her family can be used to assist in developing and implementing intervention plans. For example, consistent with PRT, adults implementing the intervention plan can use preferred items and activities to motivate the child to engage in less preferred activities. As noted in Chapter 1, this can also lead to decreases in unwanted behavior and improvements in desired behaviors. Second, SBA can address individual and contextual assets in a systematic manner. For example, family interests and involvement, school strengths, and community resources can be explored by the examiner during an assessment. Third, the findings of SBA can change the attitude of the family, assessor, educators, and the individual with ASD by providing a sense of hope, creating a positive collaborative environment, and fostering a sense of optimism. Fourth, and equally important, is that SBA can encourage educators and interventionists to establish goals and recommend interventions that go beyond focusing on repairing deficits and instead address socially significant meaningful goals that will lead to a higher life quality and long-term outcome for the individual with ASD.

Preference Assessments as a Component of Strength-Based Assessment

SBA should also include a preference assessment. Every individual has likes and dislikes, but because individuals with ASD frequently lack the motivation to socially engage, many seemingly desirable rewards (e.g., social praise, smiles, stickers) may not be rewarding. To that end, assessments should include individualized recommendations for preferences, which can be utilized in the treatment plan. Several methods can be used to conduct a preference assessment, including direct observation, interviews, and surveys.

Assessing Preferences Through Direct Observation Preference assessments can be accomplished by direct or in-vivo observations focusing on activities and items toward which the individual gravitates. On rare occasions, it will appear that the individual is uninterested in any item or activity and wants only to leave the room. This is also important information, as escape can be used as a reinforcer. Some children's first word is "bye" or "done" because they want to terminate the session. That's fine, a word is a word! When conducting a preference assessment, it is important to document the most motivating activities, and sometimes those activities may be avoiding or escaping any type of demand. The nice thing about using direct observations for a preference assessment is that it is independent of language level. Even if the individual cannot communicate his or her most reinforcing items and activities, direct observations will help you figure this out.

Assessing Preferences Through Interviews Interviews are also helpful for preference assessments. We worked with one older elementary school child who did not appear to have any strong reinforcers; when we interviewed her mother, the mother indicated that her child watched old movies from the time she got home from school until bedtime. With that information in hand, we were able to develop a social intervention plan that included her highly preferred topic of old movies. Interviews can be done with anyone who is familiar with the child—a parent, caregiver, teacher, or even a babysitter. One preschooler we assessed, who was nonverbal, had nonstop tantrums and appeared uninterested in anything. However, his babysitter mentioned that he loved water and bath time and always calmed down and behaved when in the tub. So, we started his intervention program using water activities. The main point here is to get everyone's input. Sometimes it's a team effort to really understand what motivates someone.

If the individual with ASD is verbal, he or she may be able to help you with the preference assessment. Sometimes they will come up with things we never would have guessed. For instance, the authors of this book worked with a brilliant graduate student with Asperger syndrome whose favorite subject was physics. He had poor hygiene, which was an issue addressed within his self-management goals. As a reward for completing his self-management goals, he chose to tutor his therapist in physics. While this wasn't the therapist's favorite activity, it was what the individual chose and what encouraged him to work on the target behavior.

Assessing Preferences Through Surveys A third way of assessing preference is through a survey. For example, the Reinforcer Assessment for Individuals with Severe Disability (RAISD) (Fisher, Piazza, Bowman, & Amari, 1996) is available online and can be given to a teacher, parent, or caregiver. In addition to foods and other activities, this assessment suggests various areas that may be idiosyncratic to people with autism, such as sounds, smells, and visual objects (e.g., mirrors, spinning objects, shiny objects). It is always important to remember that preferences can change from day to day and over time. Regular reassessments are important. Also, as mentioned in Chapter 1 and throughout the book, task variation is an important part of PRT. It is important to vary preferred items so that the child does not satiate on one preference and the activity does not become drill-like.

ASSESSMENT LEADING TO TREATMENT GOALS

Now that we have discussed assessment, let's talk about where we go from there. Parents of children with ASD are often faced with a bewildering array of recommendations when it comes to treatment and intervention. Clinicians, educators, and care providers can help guide parents in evaluating potential interventions and choosing the right treatment plan for their child.

An article published in *Pediatrics* (Johnson & Meyers, 2007) warns parents that they should seek additional information if any of the following circumstances is true:

1. Treatments are based on overly simplified scientific theories.
2. Therapies claim to be effective for multiple different unrelated conditions or symptoms.
3. There is a claim that children will be cured or will respond dramatically to the intervention.
4. The intervention is based on case reports or anecdotal data rather than carefully designed scientific studies.
5. There is a lack of peer-reviewed studies to support the intervention, or an interventionist denies that there is a need for controlled studies.
6. The treatment is said to have no potential or adverse side effects. This is particularly important with nonstandard and therapies that do not have a research base of support.

Let's examine each of these points. First, treatments based on overly simplified scientific theories do not adequately address children's behavioral issues. Behaviors are complex and often developed over time. In fact, I recently saw a highly verbal, bright child who was told by a therapist that the reason she was noncompliant, aggressive, and refused to urinate or defecate in the toilet was because she didn't like anything having to do with her "self." This couldn't have been further from the truth. Her behavior was complex and there were many functions for the behavior issues. Similarly, no "one" therapy will resolve all behavior issues. If someone promises parents that one intervention will solve all of their child's issues, the child with ASD probably won't improve. Also, when advising parents about available interventions, emphasize that they should make sure the interventions are empirically based. This means that studies have been published in peer-reviewed journals. Parents should feel free to ask you, or other practitioners working with their child, for articles to make sure the participants in the studies are similar to their child. In addition, parents should make sure the interventions are safe and that the assessor advises them of the potential side effects. For example, many medications have side effects that may be worse than the original behavior. Other non–scientifically documented interventions may have potential consequences for the individual's health; for example, the casein-free diet (often recommended with gluten-free diets) has been found to result in low bone density and a number of studies are showing that the diet has no positive effects on autism symptoms or behavior (cf., Elder, Shankar, Shuster, Theriaque, Burns, & Sherrill, 2006; Hyman, Stewart, Foley, Peck, Morris, Wang, & Smith, 2016).

PUTTING IT ALL TOGETHER: ASSESSMENT, DIAGNOSIS, AND TREATMENT

This chapter describes the complex, interrelated factors involved in assessing and diagnosing children who exhibit symptoms of ASD, beginning to develop a treatment plan for these children, and working effectively with their parents throughout the process. Let's conclude by reviewing your role in that process—and theirs.

Your Input as an Assessor

As noted, the DSM-5 characterizes ASD as a condition involving persistent deficits in social communication and social interaction across multiple contexts, as well as restricted and repetitive patterns of behavior, interests, or activities (RRBs). When these characteristics and behaviors are significant enough to interfere with a child's day-to-day functioning or cause a child to be stigmatized, it is appropriate to assess for ASD. Early signs of ASD—such as early asocial behaviors, pragmatic difficulties, and repetitive patterns of behavior—should be assessed and addressed, as research suggests that addressing these pre-linguistic symptoms of autism can be helpful.

Next, the severity level of these symptoms should be assessed. Currently, the DSM-5 offers suggestions for three levels (American Psychiatric Association, 2013). At Level 1 the individual requires support; at Level 2 the individual requires substantial support; and at Level 3 the individual requires very substantial support. We recommend that each of these areas be behaviorally defined and quantified. For example, if a child turns a toy truck upside down and spins the wheel, rather than playing appropriately with the toy, you will want to report that behavior and measure the amount of time he or she does it. Is it 100% of the time or 5% of the time? If it is 5% of the time, how does he or she play the remaining 95% of the time? If it is 100% of the time, how does he or she respond when you interrupt this activity or try to direct him or her to play appropriately? Make sure you specify a time period and settings for these analyses. Behavior varies across settings. Some children yak away to teachers but never utter a word with a peer. This needs to be documented. Similarly, some children engage in all sorts of repetitive behaviors when they are bored or when the task is difficult, but their behavior looks totally appropriate when they are engaged in fun activities. Make sure these differences are noted in your assessment. Also, careful behavioral observations and recordings will be helpful for later assessing the effectiveness of the intervention plans. Often programs need to be tweaked, changed, or intensified, and your baselines will provide important information regarding the behaviors in everyday settings. These types of analyses can be accomplished with any of the symptoms of ASD.

The DSM-5 also suggests that the assessor should indicate whether the ASD is accompanied by intellectual impairment and language impairment (American Psychiatric Association, 2013). Remember, it is imperative that the person being tested is adequately motivated. Do not rely solely on standardized testing, as these tests may underestimate the intellectual and linguistic abilities of a child, particularly if the individual has challenging behaviors (Koegel, Koegel, & Smith, 1997).

Another category recently added to the DSM-5 is Social (Pragmatic) Communication Disorder (American Psychiatric Association, 2013). This disorder is diagnosed when an individual has deficits in using communication for social purposes, exhibits an inability to change communication to match the context, has difficulties following the rules for conversation and storytelling, and has difficulties understanding what is not explicitly stated. Generally, an SLP, especially one who specializes in ASD, can provide important information regarding speech, language, pragmatics, and prosody, and other communicative areas.

In regard to very early diagnosis, challenges exist in the accuracy and stability of the diagnosis. Therefore, it is recommended that the diagnostic assessment include a developmental history, parents' descriptions of the child's behavior and activities in everyday settings, and direct assessment of social interaction with peers, as well as assessments of communication, cognitive functioning, and adaptive functioning (Charman & Baird, 2002). Because many children in the very young age group are nonverbal, attention to behaviors such as social orienting, joint attention, imitation, play, and affect is also important (Charman & Baird, 2002).

Parent Input and Strength-Based Reporting

Although early diagnosis and intervention can make a significant difference in lifetime outcomes, families of children with ASD may experience frustrating delays. A survey based on more than 700 replies from families indicated that about 15% of parents of children later diagnosed with autism became concerned about their child before their child's first birthday, and more than half became concerned before their child's second birthday (Howlin & Asgharian, 1999). Almost a third reported that they were told "no problem" or "not to worry" by the pediatrician, child psychiatrist, psychologist, or another professional. Those parents made repeated efforts to try to understand their child's behavior, and most were given a diagnosis by the second or third consultation 1–3 years later. Thus, a significant time period may elapse before a diagnosis is given (Howlin & Asgharian, 1999). Parents of children with Asperger syndrome report even being more frustrated and generally do not get a diagnosis until the third diagnostic visit (Howlin & Asgharian, 1999). Consequently, parents experience frustration and delays during the evaluation process and waste time seeking further consultation, when intervention could be commencing. Even if a preliminary evaluation is not possible, it is the obligation of professionals to carefully observe the child and address any reported parental concerns, comparing the child's development to what is typically expected at that age, and then to provide intervention programs that address the parental concerns. Parents need to know that there is hope, and providing them with appropriate interventions is helpful, especially if they can immediately begin to use the interventions.

Families may also receive insufficient information once their child has been diagnosed with ASD. Another survey by Mansell and Morris (2004) suggested that more than half of the parents receiving the diagnosis of ASD felt that sources of information and treatment, coping strategies, and future outcomes were greatly lacking during the assessment. Parents do not want a bleak prognosis and they should not get one, as many children diagnosed with ASD improve tremendously. Although it is fair to tell parents that no one can predict the future, it is also fair to let the parents know that, with the right interventions, many children with ASD progress steadily and quickly. This especially important because, although many parents report feeling relieved after getting a diagnosis, they also report increased worries. More than 40% of parents are "shocked," "upset," and "devastated" by the diagnosis despite having suspected their child had a disability (Mansell & Morris, 2004). Again, this suggests that as a society we have a long way to go in supporting parents during and following the diagnosis of ASD.

Key Insights ||| Working With Parents During Assessment, Diagnosis, and Early Intervention

To work effectively with parents whose child has been, or may soon be, diagnosed with ASD, it is important to understand the stressors they are experiencing:

- **Feeling concerned before anyone else is; feeling dismissed:** Parents are often the first to express a concern over their child's development. These concerns should be addressed immediately and taken seriously. Early intervention is critical, and too many parents report that their first concerns were dismissed.
- **Experiencing stress, fear, and guilt:** All are common emotions parents experience after their child is diagnosed with ASD.
- **Feeling "alone" after the diagnosis:** Many parents feel isolated. Friends, family, and professionals may not understand or empathize with the stress a parent feels after receiving the diagnosis of ASD. Surrounding the parent with social support after the diagnosis is important.
- **Being put on a wait list:** Wait lists are common. Most parents want to get started with intervention as quickly as possible, but often they are confronted with long wait lists. Providing some initial suggestions along with the diagnosis is helpful.

It is also important to understand the benefits and limitations of different types of assessment and to be able to explain these to parents:

- **ASDs are currently diagnosed by behavioral characteristics.** There is no genetic or medical test to confirm ASD. Behavioral characteristics need to be measured across settings.
- **Standardized language and intelligence tests may underestimate a child.** Be cautious and understand that if a child has any behaviors that may interfere with the testing, the score is likely to be inaccurate.
- **Include behavioral assessments.** To get a true idea of the individual's functioning level, it is important to conduct observations in the natural environment. This data will also be helpful when assessing changes during the subsequent intervention program.

- **Look for and report strengths in the individual with ASD.** Strengths help us to build a treatment program that focuses on the individual's existing skills. These should be assessed and discussed in the evaluation.
- **For many, signs of ASD can be observed in the first year of life.** Early detection is helpful so that intervention can be implemented at the earliest point in time.

SUMMARY

The diagnosis of ASD requires a differential diagnosis and is confirmed by the presence of social communication difficulties as well as restricted and repetitive behavior patterns. These may present in a variety of different ways and can vary in severity. Behavioral assessments in the child's natural environments are important to assess the stability (or lack thereof) across environments, the intensity of the behavior, and the duration of each behavior. Although all individuals exhibit some symptoms of ASD, a diagnosis is given when the symptoms interfere with everyday engagement. It is important to note that almost all parents who receive a diagnosis of ASD for their child immediately experience high levels of stress. The greater community has not yet developed ways to support families so that this stress can be eliminated.

STUDY QUESTIONS

1. Discuss some of the emotions a parent of a child with autism may experience after diagnosis.
2. Describe some of the early symptoms a child who is later diagnosed with ASD may present.
3. Describe some of the behavioral challenges or issues often seen in individuals with ASD.
4. List some of the behavioral challenges that may interfere with standardized testing of a child with ASD.
5. Discuss interventions that may improve the responsiveness of a child with ASD during standardized testing.
6. List ways that behavioral assessments can be implemented and discuss the importance of behavioral assessment.
7. What is a strength-based assessment, and why is it important?
8. List ways that assessments can lead to treatment goals.
9. Describe methods of collecting data on symptoms of ASD.
10. Describe a comprehensive assessment plan.
11. Discuss ways in which the evaluation and diagnosis of ASD can be reported to parents (hint: Strength-based).

REFERENCES

American Psychiatric Association. (2013). *Diagnostic and statistical manual of mental disorders, 5th edition (DSM-5)*. Washington, DC: Author.

Boyd, B. A. (2002). Examining the relationship between stress and lack of social support in mothers of children with autism. *Focus on Autism and Other Developmental Disabilities, 17*(4), 208–215.

Charman, T., & Baird, G. (2002). Practitioner review: Diagnosis of autism spectrum disorder in 2-and 3-year-old children. *Journal of Child Psychology and Psychiatry, 43*(3), 289–305.

Cosden, M. Koegel, L. K., Koegel, R. L., Greenwell, A., & Klein, E. (2006). Strength-based assessment for children with autism spectrum disorders. *Research and Practice for Persons with Severe Disabilities, 31*(2), 134–143.

Davis, N. O., & Carter, A. S. (2008). Parenting stress in mothers and fathers of toddlers with autism spectrum disorders: Associations with child characteristics. *Journal of Autism and Developmental Disorders, 38*(7), 1278–1291.

Dunlap, G. (1984). The influence of task variation and maintenance tasks on the learning and affect of autistic children. *Journal of Experimental Child Psychology, 37*(1), 41–64.

Elder, J. H., Shankar, M., Shuster, J., Theriaque, D., Burns, S., & Sherrill, L. (2006). The gluten-free, casein-free diet in autism: results of a preliminary double blind clinical trial. *Journal of Autism and Developmental Disorders, 36*(3), 413–420.

Fisher, W. W., Piazza, C. C., Bowman, L. G., & Amari, A. (1996). Integrating caregiver report with systematic choice assessment to enhance reinforcer identification. *American Journal of Mental Retardation, AJMR, 101*(1), 15–25.

Gray, D. E., & Holden, W. J. (1992). Psycho-social well-being among the parents of children with autism. *Australia and New Zealand Journal of Developmental Disabilities, 18*, 83–93.

Hastings, R. P., & Johnson, E. (2001). Stress in UK families conducting intensive home based behavioral intervention for their young child with autism. *Journal of Autism and Developmental Disorders, 31*, 327–336.

Howlin, P., & Asgharian, A. (1999). The diagnosis of autism and Asperger syndrome: Findings from a survey of 770 families. *Developmental Medicine & Child Neurology, 41*(12), 834–839.

Hyman, S. L., Stewart, P. A., Foley, J., Peck, R., Morris, D. D., Wang, H., & Smith, T. (2016). The gluten-free/casein-free diet: a double-blind challenge trial in children with autism. *Journal of Autism and Developmental Disorders, 46*(1), 205–220.

Johnson, C. P., & Myers, S. M. (2007). Management of children with autism spectrum disorders. *Pediatrics, 120*(5), 1162–1182.

Koegel, R. L., Bimbela, A., & Schreibman, L. (1996). Collateral effects of parent training on family interactions. *Journal of Autism and Developmental Disorders, 26*(3), 347–359.

Koegel, L. K., Koegel, R. L., & Smith, A. (1997). Variables related to differences in standardized test outcomes for children with autism. *Journal of Autism and Developmental Disorders, 27*(3), 233–243.

Koegel, R. L., Schreibman, L., Loos, L. M., Dirlich-Wilhelm, H., Dunlap, G., Robbins, F. R., & Plienis, A. J. (1992). Consistent stress profiles in mothers of children with autism. *Journal of Autism and Developmental Disorders, 22*, 205–216.

Mansell, W., & Morris, K. (2004). A survey of parents' reactions to the diagnosis of an autistic spectrum disorder by a local service: Access to information and use of services. *Autism, 8*(4), 387–407.

Midence, K., & O'Neill, M. (1999). The experience of parents in the diagnosis of autism. *Autism, 3*, 273–285.

Seligman, M. E., & Csikszentmihalyi, M. (2014). *Positive psychology: An introduction* (pp. 279–298). Dordrecht, Netherlands: Springer.

3

Ecocultural Theory and Cultural Diversity

Sunny Kim, Lynn Kern Koegel, and Robert L. Koegel

CHAPTER GOALS

Goal 1. The reader will understand the basic tenets of the ecocultural theory.

Goal 2. The reader will understand cultural considerations and sensitivity.

Goal 3. The reader will learn about the differences between individualistic and collectivistic cultures.

Goal 4. The reader will understand the importance of embedding cultural beliefs and values into treatment and will provide examples of how treatment can be developed using ecocultural considerations.

Goal 5. The reader will discuss advantages and disadvantages that families may experience related to ecocultural variables.

Goal 6. The reader will understand the benefits of matching service providers who share the same cultural and linguistic background as the families and children with disabilities with whom they work.

This chapter discusses issues that are relevant to working with individuals with autism spectrum disorders (ASD) and their families who are culturally and linguistically diverse (CLD). We begin by introducing the tenets of ecocultural theory as a framework for this discussion. Next, we discuss general cultural considerations to keep in mind when working with culturally diverse individuals with ASD as well as ways to be culturally sensitive to these individuals and their families. This section includes discussion of the differences between individualistic and collectivistic cultures, especially insofar as these differences affect attitudes toward disability, education, and treatment. Next, we discuss ways practitioners can embed cultural values into treatment, balancing sensitivity to cultural differences with a commitment to using effective, evidence-based interventions. We conclude by addressing the advantages and disadvantages that cultural and linguistic diversity may create for families of children with ASD and discussing the benefits of matching service providers and families who share the same cultural background.

TENETS OF ECOCULTURAL THEORY

From an ecocultural perspective, culture plays a pivotal role in a child's development (Weisner, 2002). Ecocultural theory states that it is important to take the family's perspective (i.e., their goals, values, and needs) into account when developing goals and interventions for individuals with ASD (Bernheimer, Gallimore, & Weisner, 1990; Gallimore, Weisner, Kaufman, & Bernheimer, 1989). According to Bernheimer et al. (1990), there are three key components to ecocultural theory:

1. It requires understanding the child's disability as it is perceived by the family (in terms of the family's goals, values, and needs).
2. It incorporates the family's daily routines, as these routines mediate the ecocultural effects of interactions with other pertinent individuals.
3. It ensures the applicability and provision of services to families in all cultures.

Ecocultural theory also posits that a child's outcomes should be meaningful as they relate to the family's values and beliefs, congruent to the student's characteristics, and sustainable across conditions (Bernheimer et al., 1990).

To make the educational and treatment experience meaningful for individuals with ASD who come from diverse cultural backgrounds, it is important to incorporate these key aspects of ecocultural theory. Assessing general cultural profiles can provide helpful information for all families and may include understanding the family's work cycle and financial base as well as the domestic workload and child care tasks, which can further be broken into division of labor by sex, age, and other variables. In addition, it is helpful to understand the family's health and demographic characteristics; safety issues, both at home and the community; and the parents' marital roles and relationship. Also, understanding the child's peer and play groups can be helpful. Finally, the community's influence on the child in regard to networks, supports, cultural influence, sources of parental information, and the degree of community heterogeneity influencing the family are all important areas that constitute the "ecocultural niche" of the child and family (Bernheimer et al., 1990).

CULTURAL CONSIDERATIONS AND SENSITIVITY

There is a paucity of research focusing on culturally and ethnically diverse individuals with ASD (Starr, Martini, & Kuo, 2016; West et al., 2016) and access to services for ASD remains suboptimal for linguistically and ethnically diverse groups (Amant, Schrager, Peña-Ricardo, Williams, & Vanderbilt, 2017; Khanlou et al., 2017). For example, Wilder, Dyches, Obiakor, and Algozzine (2004) thoroughly examined the still commonly used Executive Summary from the National Research Council (2001), a document that identifies scientifically based intervention approaches for educating individuals with ASD. They found no recommendations on addressing multiculturalism. The document, however, urged service providers to be culturally sensitive and suggested a need for further research investigating how diversity affects services for culturally and ethnically diverse individuals with ASD. The limited research on the matter suggests that the problems experienced by multicultural individuals with ASD could be tri-fold, as many of these individuals are culturally diverse, linguistically different, and exhibit many challenging behaviors (Wilder et al., 2004).

Recognition of ASD Across Cultures

Wilder et al. (2004) pointed out that while the symptoms of ASD are universal, the recognition of ASD can differ across cultures. For example, in many Asian cultures, it is common for all individuals to avoid making eye contact with an adult and to silently respond to an adult's question (Lian, 1996). In the Navajo culture, self-stimulatory behavior is commonly practiced among young children (Connors & Donnellan, 1998); and in the Indian culture, language delays are considered typical for boys because of the belief that boys speak at a later age than girls (Daley & Sigman, 2002). Although these behaviors may be considered red flags for symptoms of ASD in our Western culture, they are considered to be culturally normal in their respective cultures. Therefore, the authors stress the importance of having service providers consider cultural variables when classifying, and developing treatment goals for, ethnically and culturally diverse individuals with ASD.

Individualistic and Collectivistic Cultures

It is especially important to understand the various ways that individualistic cultures differ from collectivistic cultures. These differences, reflected in core cultural values, can affect areas such as communication, educational methods and goals, attitudes toward disability, academic motivation, and responses to stress.

Differences in Core Values The individualistic culture values and emphasizes independence, an individual's success, and personal achievements (Greenfield et al., 2006). In general, independent learning, active participation, and praise are the common methodologies for educating children from an individualistic culture. In regard to communication, children from an individualistic culture are taught to ask questions and verbalize their thoughts and feelings. Competition among members of individualistic cultures is also common.

In contrast, the collectivistic culture values and emphasizes the success of the group as a whole. Individuals from a collectivistic culture tend to align their goals with other members in their group (e.g., extended family, religion, other valued group). In general, working in a group, observing other members, and receiving constructive feedback are the common methodologies for educating children from a collectivistic culture. In regard to communication, children from a collectivistic culture are taught to follow directives and rely on nonverbal communication skills (Greenfield et al., 2006). Competition among members of the group is relatively de-emphasized in favor of focusing on the success of the group as a whole.

Farver, Kim, and Lee (1995) conducted a study to investigate the different educational goals and values between Western culture (individualistic values) and Korean culture (collectivistic values). The authors found that the Korean teacher emphasized academic skills, task perseverance, and passive involvement in learning, while the American teacher emphasized independent thinking, problem solving, and active involvement in learning.

Differences in Approaches to Disability, Education, and Treatment Every student with ASD has unique needs. However, these students and their families may face additional challenges and stressors when dealing with a different language in addition to different cultural values and belief systems that may conflict with Western values and educational priorities. These challenges may be exacerbated when formal and informal support is not available for families (Starr et al., 2016). Meyer (2010) suggested that although both individualistic and collectivistic cultures value providing assistance to a child with a disability, the Western individualistic culture produces a rights-based approach to disabilities. For example, Park and Turnbull (2001) conducted a study to investigate the perceptions, levels of satisfaction, and concerns of Korean-American parents of children with disabilities in regard to special education services their child was receiving in America. On the one hand, although Korean-American parents were satisfied with certain aspects of the special education services their child was receiving, they were reluctant to place their child in the general education classroom. This is because in the collectivistic Korean culture, teachers are highly respected and trusted, considered the experts in a child's education. The parents in this study, therefore, were concerned that if they placed their child in an inclusive classroom setting, their child would not receive enough attention from the teacher (Giangreco, Edelman, Luiselli, & MacFarland, 1997; Marks, Schrader, & Levine, 1999). On the other hand, the families in Park and Turnbull's study were pleased with the idea of being equal team members when developing educational goals for their child—a Western individualistic cultural perspective of providing rights to families and children with a disability.

To further illustrate how different cultures have different strengths, Cho, Singer, and Brenner (2003) compared parental views and adaptation to childhood disability between Korean immigrant mothers residing in the United States (individualistic culture) and Korean mothers residing in South Korea (collectivistic culture). The authors found that in general, Korean mothers with a child with a disability living in Korea exhibited higher levels of depression, stress, and suicidal thoughts than Korean immigrant mothers with a child with a disability. Overall, Korean mothers in South Korea had more negative experiences raising a child with a disability, which can be attributed to the fact that the Korean culture is less accepting of children with a disability than the American culture. One report of a Korean immigrant mother in the study clearly illustrates the positive perception of disability in America. This mother reported that the American society provides free services such as transportation to school, education, and behavioral services. The mother also expressed how she was grateful for raising her child with a disability in a society where she perceived that people are less likely to discriminate against individuals with disabilities. For the most part, the Korean immigrant mothers were satisfied with the free educational services for their children, whereas in

Korea these services are not free and many Korean parents bear the responsibility of privately funding their child's education, causing considerable strain to these mothers (Cho et al., 2003).

Other factors have been correlated with motivation for academic areas in Hispanic families (Arzubiaga, Rueda, & Monzó, 2002). Although this study was not implemented with children with ASD, findings indicated that as the families' domestic workload increases (e.g., increases in number of younger siblings, domestic work, child care needs), motivation decreases. Also, the amount of time the family spends together seemed to be related to motivation for academics. As well, gaps in social competence of young children may be greater among poor Latino families (Galindo & Fuller, 2010). From a theoretical point of view, such ecocultural features related to socioeconomic status, workload, and nurturance may need to be addressed for optimal outcomes in Latino children with ASD. That is, families who face financial and child care challenges may need to have these areas addressed for more successful outcomes. Other cultural variables that may affect access to services among Latino families relate to language barriers, access to transportation, perception of "disability," and willingness to question "authoritarian figures" (Santarelli, Koegel, Casas, & Koegel, 2001). In this publication, the authors found that Latino families were often concerned about the lack of services available in Spanish, particularly parents who were monolingual Spanish speakers. Other families found that transportation to a treatment center was a barrier, particularly when the family did not own a car; therefore, providing services in the home may be necessary. In regard to perception of "disability," many Latino families of children with ASD and/or their extended families experienced less stress related to their child's symptoms and did not always feel an urgency about addressing deficits. Therefore, it is helpful to coordinate goals and interventions with the entire extended families. Finally, many Latino families were not comfortable questioning "authoritarian figures" such as third-party payers, school teams, and special educators. They were therefore likely to receive fewer or less intensive services. All of these cultural and ethnic areas contribute to disparities and are important to address.

In contrast, in Western cultures, having a child with a disability can cause great stress to many families, and stressors are considered negative life events (Connors & Donnellan, 1998). This often leads families to actively and forcefully seek services. Dyches, Wilder, Sudweeks, Obiakor, and Algozzine (2004) suggested, however, that different subcultures do not necessarily regard having a child with ASD as a negative, stressful life event. For example, in some cultures, families positively appraise having a child with ASD, and the child is considered to be a valued member of the community. Similarly, some cultures believe a child with ASD is a gift from God and view it as a challenge from God to become a better person. Still other cultures regard ASD as a curse that may result in families needing to cope with high levels of stigma (Fong & Lee, 2017). Dyches et al. also suggested that many families from diverse cultures (e.g., Native Hawaiian, African American, and Hispanic) can rely on extended family and community members for extra social support in raising their child with ASD, which can help reduce the stress levels for these families. Depending on one's perspective, these variables may provide social support for families; however, they may also place the child at a disadvantage if services are not provided.

EMBEDDING CULTURAL BELIEFS AND VALUES INTO TREATMENT

All cultures have their strengths and weaknesses. Using the strengths from different cultures can lead to very positive blended approaches to intervention. Different cultures emphasize different educational and treatment goals for children, based on the dominant culture's values and beliefs (Rosenthal, 1999). Therefore, as a child's development is viewed as a cultural invention (Kessen, 1979), integrating positive aspects of different cultural values can lead to the development of more appropriate and meaningful educational and treatment goals for these children.

Welterlin and LaRue (2007) published an article about the importance of embedding key aspects of ecocultural theory when developing intervention treatment plans for immigrant families of children with ASD. Because the educational and treatment approaches used in America mainly reflect individualistic ideologies, the authors suggested that when educators and service providers work with culturally and ethnically diverse individuals with ASD, they need to be culturally sensitive, as different cultures have different ideologies and beliefs about effective intervention approaches. For example, some cultures may use alternative treatments (e.g., plants, animals, massage, sacrifice, prayer, herbal remedies) that are regarded as having limited empirical support in America (Welterlin & LaRue, 2007).

Addressing Cultural Differences in Disciplinary Practices

Different cultures may also have different ways of disciplining children. In some Asian cultures, physical punishment is viewed as acceptable (Ho, 1990), while this type of discipline is viewed as abusive and is generally discouraged in American cultures. Telling a family from such a culture that they cannot use punishment can place the family under considerable stress; yet allowing the family to use strong forms of physical punishment can place the family at risk for being reported for child abuse.

At first glance, this seems like an unsolvable dilemma. However, preliminary research has suggested that this issue may be solvable (Wang, McCart, &Turnbull, 2007). That is, regardless of the alternative treatments and discipline methods used among culturally and ethnically diverse families, it is imperative to educate families about treatment approaches that have strong empirical validation and explain that some of the alternative intervention approaches (i.e., the ones that lack empirical validation) can be more harmful than helpful for these students. Almost all families will opt for the most effective approach, and this typically solves the dilemma.

Using Positive Behavior Support With Culturally Diverse Families

There is very strong empirical support for using nonaversive interventions in the field of positive behavior intervention and support (PBIS; Koegel, Dunlap, & Koegel, 1996). Wang et al., (2007) published an article demonstrating that PBIS, a commonly used intervention approach in America, is rooted in American cultural values; professionals can make PBIS work for culturally and ethnically diverse families. For example, one key tenet of PBIS is to conduct a functional assessment in order to identify the cause of a behavior. In regard to functional assessment, values embedded within PBIS include scientific rationale in viewing disability/challenging behavior, individualism, change and progress for the future, and action and achievement. In contrast, the traditional Chinese culture values spiritual rationale in viewing disability, promotion of the family unit, no need for change, and suspicion of the usefulness of intervention. Wang et al. suggested that professionals should have the following to be culturally responsive:

- A clear understanding of the embedded cultural values of PBIS
- Culture-specific knowledge, without stereotyping another culture's values
- A clear acknowledgement that there are variations in cultural beliefs and values

The authors suggested that when these variables are taken into consideration, PBIS can become a valued and effective intervention for Chinese families who otherwise would have been unlikely to be interested in the approach.

MATCHING CULTURALLY COMPETENT SERVICE PROVIDERS WITH FAMILIES

As more CLD children are being diagnosed with ASD (NAEYC, 2009), there is a corresponding increase in the need for culturally competent service providers (Delgado & Strawn, 2014; Welterlin & LaRue, 2007). The literature suggests that service providers who share families' cultural and linguistic background are in a unique position to help develop more culturally meaningful goals for CLD children with ASD.

For example, Chopra et al. (2004) conducted a qualitative study to investigate the role of primary and secondary school paraprofessionals and their ability to serve as connectors between the home and school environment. A total of 49 paraprofessionals volunteered to participate in the focus group interviews, with nearly half being bilingual (primarily English and Spanish) and with 34 living in the same communities as the students with whom they worked. During the focus groups, the protocol included asking paraprofessionals about their relationships with children and their families and about their roles in representing their community to the school and vice versa. The researchers noticed a common theme among them: paraprofessionals were reporting that they had closer relationships with students and their families than the case managers and teachers did. The researchers also noted that in most cases, the paraprofessionals reported that parents felt more comfortable communicating with them because they often spoke the same language, lived in the same neighborhood, and were generally more available. Several paraprofessionals explained that many parents would rely on them for help outside of the school setting, often to obtain information about the community and other resources that might be available to their child.

Similarly, Ernst-Slavit and Wenger (2006) investigated the role of bilingual paraprofessionals in educating minority students. The authors found that because these bilingual paraprofessionals had ethnic and linguistic backgrounds similar to those of the minority students, they were better able to understand the educational difficulties these students encountered. For example, one paraprofessional in the study noted how minority students sought advice from her about various problems such as dealing with racist comments or getting an absence excused. Another paraprofessional worked with the school librarian on getting multicultural books so that minority students would be more motivated to read because the books featured characters and authors from the same cultural and ethnic background as themselves. The authors suggest that because the paraprofessionals and the minority students shared similar ecocultural and linguistic backgrounds, these school personnel were in a position to make the education more meaningful and were perhaps more capable of incorporating culturally relevant pedagogy.

Although these studies illustrate the many benefits of employing service providers who share similar ethnic and cultural backgrounds, there has been a paucity of research that specifically focuses on service providers who work with children with ASD from diverse cultural and ethnic backgrounds (Wilder et al., 2004). However, from an ecocultural perspective, service providers who share the same cultural and linguistic background as the families they serve may better assist children and their families to access appropriate services, as well as provide valuable insight about the learning patterns of these children (Miramontes, 1991).

CASE HISTORY
Cultural Considerations in Working With Jake, Age 11

Jake was an 11-year-old boy diagnosed with autism who had limited expressive language. He was born in South Korea and moved to America when he was 7 years old. He was placed in a special day program in Korea prior to moving to the United States but was not diagnosed with ASD until he was evaluated in the U.S. In addition, because he was their first son, the parents reported that they had hoped he was just delayed and would catch up; therefore, they hadn't wanted to rush to get a diagnosis. They also reported that disabilities were a stigma in South Korea—another reason for not getting a thorough diagnosis. Although Jake's ability to speak in complete sentences in the English language was limited, he was able to communicate in complete sentences (i.e., five- to six-word utterances) in the Korean language.

During home therapy sessions, Jake's mom cleared the living room area so that Jake and the therapist could work in a one-to-one setting. At the end of the session, the therapist checked in with Jake's mom and reviewed the goals that were targeted during the session. Note that in the Korean culture, it is very common for parents to insist for sessions to be solely led by the teacher/therapist (Cho et al., 2003). This is because teachers/therapists are viewed as experts in regard to the child's education. Anecdotally, Jake's mom shared personal information with her Korean-American therapist and oftentimes confided in the Korean therapist and sought guidance on school and health information. This may have been due to the fact that Jake's mom was able to communicate freely with the Korean therapist about culturally sensitive issues and in her native language (i.e., Korean). For example, when Jake was sick, his mother insisted that Jake take Korean herbal medication (i.e., han-yak) to help his immune system. The Korean therapist was able to relate, as she had taken "han-yak" growing up in a traditional Korean household.

When it came to school services, Jake's mom preferred to attend Jake's individualized education program (IEP) meetings with the support from the Korean home therapist. She always consulted with the Korean therapist before signing any legal documents. As the Korean culture places great emphasis on the school system to focus primarily on academics, Jake's mom wanted to ensure that Jake's school program provided a well-rounded academic program (i.e., one with math, reading, and writing goals). Although Jake's mom viewed social skills as an important area for development, this area was not a priority for her. During home sessions, Jake's mom never requested or attempted to facilitate play-dates with same-age peers, as she viewed Jake's younger brother and cousins to be adequate peer models.

In regard to developing behavioral goals, Jake's mom's first priority was to target academics. Recall that one motivational component of PRT focuses on task variation. However, consistent with the Korean culture, Jake's mom preferred that academics be targeted in a repetitive, drill-like manner. For example, she insisted that Jake memorize math facts by repeatedly solving problems that he answered incorrectly. The Korean therapist was able to incorporate motivational components of PRT while respecting Jake's mom's request, by interspersing easy math facts with difficult math problems. The therapist also varied the task by using different math concepts such as solving arithmetic problems, identifying shapes, reading word problems, and writing numbers. As such, the mother's cultural values were respected while the therapist still incorporated the evidence-based PRT procedures. Eventually, Jake was able to apply his math skills in natural settings as his mother and therapist developed a program that allowed him to purchase his favorite food items at a local grocery store.

Key Insights ||| Addressing Cultural and Linguistic Diversity

Keep the following principles and practices in mind when working with individuals with ASD and their families who are from culturally and linguistically diverse backgrounds.

- **Consider culture:** Sensitivity to a family's culture, including their goals, values, and needs, is an important consideration during assessment and intervention.
- **Understand important ecocultural issues:** It is critical to view the student's disability as it is perceived by the family, with their unique cultural perspectives. Understanding the family's daily routines is important, as they mediate the ecocultural effects of interactions with other pertinent individuals. In addition, a student's outcomes should be meaningful in relation to the family's values and beliefs and the student's unique characteristics, and these outcomes should be sustainable across conditions (Bernheimer et al., 1990).
- **Understand general cultural profiles:** General cultural profiles may include the work patterns of the family, economic issues, division of domestic and child care tasks, health issues, marital roles, peer networks, and so on. These profiles can provide helpful information when developing an intervention program for the child and family.
- **Understand the differences between individualistic and collectivistic cultures:** Individualistic cultures value and emphasize independence, an individual's success, and personal achievements (Greenfield et al., 2006). In contrast, collectivistic cultures value and emphasize the success of the group as a whole.

Various goals need to be developed that respect the culture of the family, are useful and acceptable within the culture, and place the child at an advantage within his or her own culture.

- **Coordinate and educate:** Some cultural interventions may not be compatible with Western values. When differences arise, it is important to educate and coordinate with the family so as to create a mutually acceptable intervention.
- **Match families and treatment providers:** Improved outcomes and consumer satisfaction result when families are matched with treatment providers of the same cultural background. This provides the family with an opportunity to communicate in their own language and to work with someone who has an understanding of cultural values that may be important to the family.

SUMMARY

From an ecocultural perspective, accumulating research shows that it is imperative to understand, be sensitive to, and integrate key components of families' social and cultural environments, beliefs, and values when designing and implementing intervention. By embedding the unique beliefs and values of CLD individuals with ASD, service providers are more likely to make meaningful progress with that family. Thus, it is important that future research investigates how service providers can be trained to integrate key aspects of cultural values.

STUDY QUESTIONS

1. List examples of ecocultural areas that may need to be considered when working with diverse populations.
2. Describe cultural differences that may lead to different understanding of the symptoms of ASD.
3. Discuss the differences between individualistic and collectivistic cultures and provide examples of how these differences may affect goals and intervention.
4. List examples of intervention procedures that may need to be addressed to meet the needs of culturally diverse families.
5. Provide examples of situations in which families may need to be educated in regard to interventions that are compatible with living in Western culture.
6. Describe some examples of cultural differences that may exist between Western values and those of other cultures.
7. Why may it be important to match culturally and linguistically similar clinicians with families?
8. Provide an overview of the importance of sensitivity to and consideration of a family's cultural heritage and values.

REFERENCES

Amant, H. G. S., Schrager, S. M., Peña-Ricardo, C., Williams, M. E., & Vanderbilt, D. L. (2017). Language barriers impact access to services for children with autism spectrum disorders. *Journal of Autism and Developmental Disorders, 48*(2), 333–340.

Arzubiaga, A., Rueda, R., & Monzó, L. (2002). Family matters related to the reading engagement of Latino children. *Journal of Latinos and Education, 1*(4), 231–243.

Bernheimer, L. P., Gallimore, R., & Weisner, T. S. (1990). Ecocultural theory as a context for the individual family service plan. *Journal of Early Intervention, 14*(3), 219–233.

Cho, S-J., Singer, G. H. S., & Brenner, B. M. (2003). A comparison of adaptation to childhood disability in Korean immigrant and Korean mothers. *Focus on Autism and Other Developmental Disabilities, 18*(1), 9–19.

Chopra, R. V., Sandoval-Lucero, E., Aragon, L., Bernal, C., De Balderas, H. B., & Carroll, D. (2004). The paraprofessional role as connector. *Remedial and Special Education, 25*(4), 219–231.

Connors, J. L., & Donnellan, A. M. (1998). Walk in beauty: Western perspectives on disability and Navajo family/cultural resilience. In H. I. McCubbin, E. A. Thompson, A. I. Thompson, & J. E. Fromer (Eds.), *Resiliency in Native American and immigrant families* (pp. 159–182). Thousand Oaks, CA: Sage.

Daley, T. C., & Sigman, M. D. (2002). Diagnostic conceptualization of autism among Indian psychiatrists, psychologists, and pediatricians. *Journal of Autism and Developmental Disorders, 32*(1), 13–23.

Delgado, S. V., & Strawn, J. R. (2014). *Difficult psychiatric consultations: An integrated approach.* Heidelberg: Springer.

Dyches, T. T., Wilder, L. K., Sudweeks, R. R., Obkiakor, F. E., & Algozzine, B. (2004).
Multicultural issues in autism. *Journal of Autism and Developmental Disorders, 34*(2), 211–222.

Ernst-Slavit, G., & Wenger, K.J. (2006). Teaching in the margins: The multifaceted work and struggles of bilingual paraeducators. *Anthropology and Education, 37*(1), 62–82.

Farver, J. M., Kim, Y. K., & Lee, Y. (1995). Cultural differences in Korean- and Anglo-American preschoolers' social interaction and play behavior. *Child Development, 66*(4), 1088–1099.

Fong, E. H., & Lee, H. (2017). Sociocultural perspective on autism intervention. In M. Fitzgerald and J. Yip (Eds.), *Autism paradigms, recent research and clinical applications* (pp. 291–300). London: England: InTech Open.

Gallimore, R., Weisner, T. S., Kaufman, S. Z., & Bernheimer, L. P. (1989). The social construct of ecocultural niches: Family accommodation of developmentally delayed children. *American Journal on Mental Retardation, 94*(3), 216–230.

Galindo, C., & Fuller, B. (2010). The social competence of Latino kindergartners and growth in mathematical understanding. *Developmental Psychology, 46*(3), 579.

Giangreco, M. F., Edelman, S. W., Luiselli, T. E., & MacFarland, S. Z. (1997). Helping or hovering? Effects of instructional assistant proximity on students with disabilities. *Exceptional Children, 64*(1), 7–18.

Greenfield, P. M., Trumbull, E., Keller, H., Rothstein-Fisch, C., Suzuki, L., & Quiroz, B. (2006). Cultural conceptions of learning and development. In P. Winne & P. Alexander (Eds.), *Handbook of Educational Psychology* (2nd ed., pp. 675–692). Mahwah, NJ: Erlbaum.

Ho, C. K. (1990). An analysis of domestic violence in Asian American communities: A cultural approach to counseling. *Women & Therapy, 9*, 129–150.

Kessen, W. (1979). The American child and other cultural inventions. *American Psychologist, 34*(10), 815–820.

Khanlou, N., Haque, N., Mustafa, N., Vazquez, L. M., Mantini, A., & Weiss, J. (2017). Access barriers to services by immigrant mothers of children with autism in Canada. *International Journal of Mental Health and Addiction, 15*(2), 239–259.

Koegel, L. K., Dunlap, G., & Koegel, R. L (1996). *Positive behavioral support.* Baltimore, MD: Paul H. Brookes Publishing Co.

Lian, M. J. (1996). Teaching Asian American children. In E. Duran (Ed.), *Teaching students with moderate/severe disabilities, including autism: Strategies for second language learners in inclusive settings* (pp. 239–253). Springfield, IL: Charles C. Thomas.

Marks, S. U., Schrader, C., & Levine, M. (1999). Paraeducator experiences in inclusive settings: Helping, hovering, or holding their own? *Exceptional Children, 65*(3), 315–328.
Meyer, H. D. (2010). Culture and disability: Advancing comparative research. *Comparative sociology, 9*(2), 157–164.
Miramontes, O.B. (1991). Organizing for effective paraprofessional services in special education: A multilingual/multiethnic instructional service team model. *Remedial and Special Education, 12*(1), 29–36.
NAEYC (2009). Position Statement: *Developmentally Appropriate Practice in Early Childhood Programs Serving Children from Birth through Age 8*. Retrieved April 20, 2009 from: https://www.naeyc.org/sites/default/files/globally-shared/downloads/PDFs/resources/position-statements/PSDAP.pdf
National Research Council. (2001). *Educating children with autism. Committee on Educational Interventions for Children with Autism. Division of Behavioral and Social Sciences and Education*. Washington, DC: National Academy Press.
Park, J., & Turnbull, A. P. (2001). Cross cultural competency and special education: Perceptions and experiences of Korean parents of children with special needs. *Education and Training in Mental Retardation and Developmental Disabilities, 36*(2), 133–147.
Rosenthal, M. K. (1999). Out-of-home child care research: A cultural perspective. *International Journal of Behavioral Development, 23*(2), 477–518.
Rueda, R., & Monzo, L. (2002). Apprenticeship for teaching: Professional development issues surrounding the collaborative relationship between teachers and paraeducators. *Teaching & Teacher Education, 18*(5), 503–521.
Santarelli, G., Koegel, R. L., Casas, J. M., & Koegel, L. K. (2001). Culturally diverse families participating in behavior therapy parent education programs for children with developmental disabilities. *Journal of Positive Behavior Interventions, 3*(2), 120–123.
Starr, E. M., Martini, T. S., & Kuo, B. C. (2016). Transition to kindergarten for children with autism spectrum disorder: A focus group study with ethnically diverse parents, teachers, and early intervention service providers. *Focus on Autism and Other Developmental Disabilities, 31*(2), 115–128.
Wang, M., McCart, A., & Turnbull, A.P. (2007). Implementing positive behavior support with Chinese American families: Enhancing cultural competence. *Journal of Positive Behavior Intervention, 9*(1), 38–51.
Weisner, T. S. (2002). Ecocultural understanding of children's developmental pathways. *Human Development, 45*(4), 275–281.
Welterlin, A., & LaRue, R.H. (2007). Serving the needs of immigrant families of children with autism. *Disability & Society, 22*(7), 747–760.
West, E. A., Travers, J. C., Kemper, T. D., Liberty, L. M., Cote, D. L., McCollow, M. M., & Stansberry Brusnahan, L. L. (2016). Racial and ethnic diversity of participants in research supporting evidence-based practices for learners with autism spectrum disorder. *The Journal of Special Education, 50*(3), 151–163.
Wilder, L. K., Dyches, T. T., Obiakor, F. E., & Algozzine, B. (2004). Multicultural perspectives on teaching students with autism. *Focus on Autism and Other Developmental Disabilities, 19*(2), 105–113.

II

Beginning Stages

Early Intervention

4

Intervention for Infants and Young Toddlers

Jessica Bradshaw and Lynn Kern Koegel

CHAPTER GOALS

Goal 1. The reader will understand early symptoms of autism spectrum disorders (ASD) and red flags exhibited by at-risk infants and toddlers.

Goal 2. The reader will become familiar with adaptations and strategies used with pre-linguistic infants during intervention.

Goal 3. The reader will learn strategies to teach parents how to implement an adapted Pivotal Response Treatment (PRT) intervention for infants and toddlers.

Goal 4. The reader will become familiar with positive outcomes associated with providing parents with education in PRT for infants and toddlers.

Goal 5. The reader will learn how to use motivational strategies with infants and young toddlers.

This chapter describes the symptoms and red flags for ASD that appear in earliest childhood and discusses ways to work effectively with at-risk infants and toddlers and with their families. Early intervention can positively impact long-term outcomes for children with ASD; parents, who spend a great deal of time with their children in the infant and toddler years, can be taught to implement intervention strategies adapted from PRT interventions.

GUIDELINES FOR EARLY DIAGNOSIS

ASD is considered to be a neurodevelopmental disorder that typically unfolds over the first few years of life. As mentioned in Chapter 2, the diagnostic characteristics of ASD are classified into two categories: 1) deficits in social communication and social interaction and 2) restricted, repetitive patterns of behavior, interests, or activities (American Psychiatric Association, 2013). In infancy, these characteristics can be evaluated by a psychologist, speech-language pathologist, and/or other qualified individuals using direct diagnostic assessment; parent interviews about behavior; and standardized measures of development, language, and social communication (Saulnier & Ventola, 2012). Social communication and restricted interests/repetitive behaviors in infancy can also be assessed by a clinician using behavioral assessments, such as the Autism Observation Scale for Infants (Bryson, Zwaigenbaum, McDermott, Rombough, & Brian, 2008), the Infant Autism Diagnostic Observation Schedule (Lord et al., 2012), and Communication and Symbolic Behavior Scales (Wetherby & Prizant, 2002). In addition, a cognitive assessment such as the Mullen Scales of Early Learning (Mullen, 1995) or the Bayley Scales of Infant and Toddler Development (Bayley, 2005) can be helpful in evaluating the infant's or child's overall developmental level compared with peers of the same age, including his or her nonverbal problem solving, gross and fine motor skills, and expressive and receptive language. It is critical to conduct a comprehensive evaluation and to directly observe the infant or child in all relevant settings to assess the impact of concerns on everyday life. Although a diagnosis of ASD in infants younger than 24 months is not always possible or warranted, a comprehensive evaluation by experienced clinicians with expertise in ASD can provide insight into a child's strengths and show areas of vulnerability, which can be addressed using PRT strategies. Awareness of how social communication skills emerge in typically developing children, as well as of early social communication behaviors and other behaviors associated with ASD, is important in diagnosing and treating infants and toddlers who may be at risk for ASD.

Emerging Social Communication in Typically Developing Infants and Toddlers

The median age of diagnosis of ASD remains around 4–5 years of age in the United States (Autism Developmental Disabilities Monitoring Network Surveillence Year 2010 Principal Investigators, 2014), yet the beginnings of social communication abilities may emerge as early as 2 months of age (Malatesta, Culver, Tesman, JShepard, Fogel, Reimers, & Zivin, 1989). Social communication is broadly defined as an individual's ability to interact with others using verbal and nonverbal strategies. Social smiling, which emerges at around 2 months of age, is one of the first developmental milestones related to social communication. By age 6 months, infants consistently engage in mutually shared positive affect and back-and-forth social smiling during dyadic interactions with adults (Parlade et al., 2009). During parent–infant interactions, infant affect is high, and they spend at least 20% of the time smiling at their parents (Fogel, Hsu, Shapiro, Nelson-Goens, & Secrist, 2006; Messinger, Cassel, Acosta, Ambadar, & Cohn, 2008). After about 9 months of age, infants begin to communicate using babbling, coordinated eye contact with gestures, and social smiling. Infants at this age reach for what they want while coordinating eye contact, and they look and smile at caregivers during social interactions. Babbling at this stage is not only an important precursor for language development but also allows for increased social interaction, such as back-and-forth imitative activities. At 12 months, infant communication is characterized by coordinated gestures, eye contact, and the emergence of first words.

Common gestures at this age include the infant's giving an object to a caregiver to ask for help or to share, showing an object to a caregiver to share his or her attention, and reaching for or pointing to an object while looking at a caregiver. Infants also begin to understand and respond to adult gestures, such as following points and giving an object when an adult extends his or her hand. They also respond to language, such as turning to the sound of their name being called and recognizing familiar words.

Between 1 and 2 years of age, infant social communication and play skills increase at an amazing rate. In regard to language development, infants typically say approximately 10 words meaningfully by 18 months; combine words by 21 months; and say simple three-word sentences, using a repertoire of at least 50 words, by 24 months of age. Within their first lexicon, social questions emerge in a primitive manner, such as asking "Dat?" which elicits a parent to label items so that the child learns vocabulary words. Infant play will also undergo a dramatic expansion during this period. Play will transition from simple back-and-forth social interaction games at 6 months of age, such as Peek-a-boo and songs, to complex pretend play with objects, such as feeding a baby doll, during the second year of life.

Early Social Communication Characteristics Associated With ASD

Prospective research investigating infants who are at high risk for developing ASD has identified several possible early markers of ASD in infants between 12 and 24 months of age. During social interactions, infants with ASD tend to make less eye contact, show fewer smiles, exhibit less pleasure, and show less social interest than their typically developing peers (Bryson et al., 2008; Ozonoff et al. 2010; Rozga et al., 2011; Wan et al., 2013; Zwaigenbaum et al., 2005). Infants with ASD between 12 and 24 months of age also attend less to social aspects of the environment, such as people, and instead direct their attention to objects.

Social communication is typically the first and largest area of concern for parents of infants with ASD when expressive language milestones, such as babbling, first words, and word combinations, are not being met on time (Turygin, Matson, Williams, & Belva, 2014). Gestures, such as giving or pointing with an index finger, may also not have emerged by 24 months. Some infants with ASD do communicate using words and gestures, but they seem to communicate for nonsocial purposes, such as requesting a desired object, rather than to initiate a social interaction. Immediate repetition of language, also known as echolalia, or repetitive reciting of previously heard phrases, also known as scripted speech, are atypical language features of infants and are sometimes seen in children with ASD. Signs of receptive language delay are also common and include not responding to one's name and not following the points of a caregiver.

Early Signs of Restricted Interests and Repetitive Behaviors

The second diagnostic category of ASD, restricted interests and repetitive behaviors, often manifests more robustly in the early childhood years but can still be observed in infants with ASD. Infants may exhibit intense or "sticky" attention to objects at 12 months, show close visual inspection of objects, or engage in repetitive behaviors with toys and objects.

However, it is also important to note that some features of ASD in infancy that we have just described can also be part of normative development. For example, infants learn language by repeating what an adult has said. Similarly, infants explore objects through repetitive actions, such as banging and dropping. Even hand-flapping is a common behavior of typically developing infants. Therefore, it is important for parents with concerns about their infant to seek guidance from professionals who have expertise in ASD.

Figure 4.1 lists the characteristics and behaviors children may exhibit during the first 2 years of life that are generally considered red flags indicating that the child is not developing on a typical trajectory and may be at high risk of being diagnosed with ASD.

The Importance of Early Diagnosis and Intervention

Early diagnosis of ASD is important for recognizing areas of vulnerability and beginning early intervention as soon as possible. Figure 4.2 depicts the ways in which the developmental trajectory of young children who are later diagnosed with ASD differs from that of their typically developing age-peers.

Red flags for autism spectrum disorders (ASD)	
6 Months	• Reduced social smiling • Infrequent vocalizations
9 Months	All of the above, plus: • No or low back-and-forth babbling • Lack or depressed positive affect during dyadic interactions • No or low response to name
12 Months	All of the above, plus (some of the following may also be noted earlier): • Difficulty making eye contact • Interest in objects over people • "Sticky" attention to objects • No or low imitation (e.g., clapping hands) • Less positive affect during communication • No or low levels of responding to name • Reduced responsivity to language • Few or no vocalizations or babbling • Infrequent use of gestures, such as giving, pointing, and showing • No initiating or responding to joint attention
24 Months	All of the above, plus (some of the following may also be noted earlier): • No pretend play • Reduced responsivity to language and gestures • Language delay • Reduced overall communication, especially for social purposes • Echolalia • Repetitive behaviors (e.g., hand flapping) • Interest in small parts of objects rather than the whole object (e.g., spinning wheels on a car)

Figure 4.1. Red flags for ASD in the first 2 years of life.

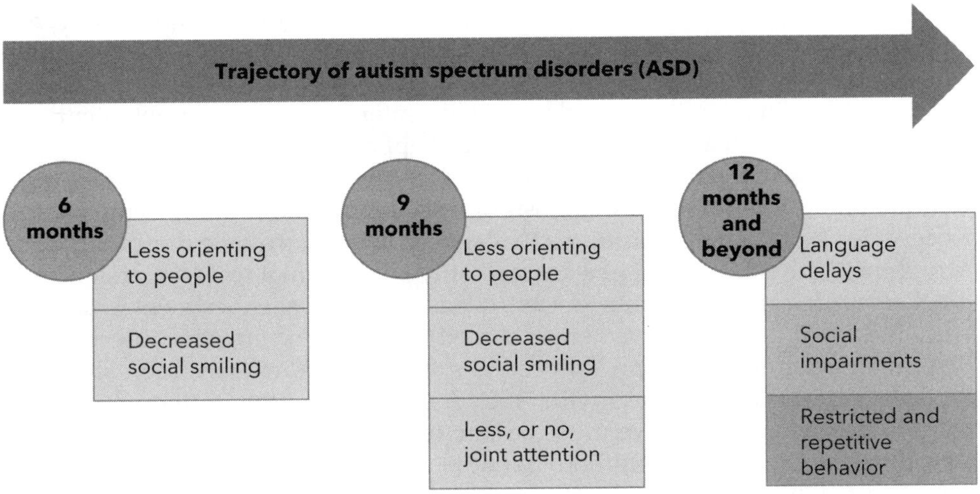

Figure 4.2. The usual developmental trajectory during the first 2 years of life for children who are later diagnosed with ASD.

Earlier intervention leads to better prognosis for children with ASD; those who receive a diagnosis by 24 months have significantly improved outcomes by age 4 (Chawarska, Klin, Paul, Macari, & Volkmar, 2009). For these reasons, we have developed several modifications of PRT to address the needs of our youngest infants who exhibit characteristics and behaviors of ASD. The PRT motivational strategies are beneficial for all children—those with and without ASD—and so we recommend using these for any young infant who may be at risk for ASD or has difficulty with social engagement or social communication, even without a diagnosis of ASD.

INTERVENTION WITH INFANTS AND TODDLERS

Emerging studies suggest the feasibility and effectiveness of early intervention during the first and second years of life. Theoretically, if practitioners can target atypical behaviors early on, we may be able to help the infant get on a better developmental trajectory at a younger age. It should be noted that this type of research is preliminary. There is wide variability in infants' temperaments and behavior, so we generally focus on those infants who show early red flags of ASD that are stable during repeated assessments over a period of time. Our research has shown that overall low levels of positive social engagement during parent–infant interactions for 6-month-old infants are not by themselves a predictor of ASD but are associated with overall low social responsivity (Bradshaw, 2015). If social responsivity is low over a period of time, it can be a red flag for ASD. Thus, repeated observation of early infant social behavior, in addition to standardized assessment, can help to differentiate infants who exhibit red flags for ASD from typically developing infants (Bradshaw, Koegel, & Koegel, 2017).

Another issue to consider is that first words do not generally emerge in typical language developers before the first year. Therefore, interventions during the first year of life should focus on pre-linguistic skills rather than expressive verbal communication per se. That is, intervention might focus on improving social interaction, positive engagement, joint attention, and other important pre-linguistic behaviors. Beginning in the second year of life, interventions can target intentional communication such as first words and word approximations.

In a review of the literature of interventions for infants 24 months or younger who are at risk for, or with, a diagnosis of ASD, Bradshaw, Steiner, Gengoux, and Koegel (2015) described procedures that appear to be effective in improving early symptoms. Only studies that had a systematic, experimental research design, (e.g., single-case designs, randomized controlled trials, quasi-experimental designs) were included (case histories were excluded). Most of the effective interventions were adapted from behavioral procedures that had previously been shown to be effective for older children with ASD. As we make clear in the sections that follow, these effective interventions adhere to the overarching principles of PRT introduced in Chapters 1–3, although the specific strategies have been adapted or modified for this age group. Note also that parents' role in interventions can be especially influential during these early years.

Benefits of Parent-Mediated Intervention in Infants' Natural Environments

Interestingly, effective interventions for children younger than 24 months tend to be *parent-mediated* (Bradshaw et al., 2017). That is, parents were taught the intervention procedures and encouraged to implement them outside of the treatment sessions. Further, most of the parent education sessions were implemented in the infants' natural environments and most used a "practice-with-feedback" model, wherein the parents implemented the intervention and received feedback from a professional specializing in ASD. This parent–professional partnership had the important benefit of teaching the child naturalistic skills that could be readily used in their everyday environments, eliminating the need for difficult and time-consuming generalization strategies, such as needing to teach the target behaviors in multiple environments. In addition, the parent-mediated approach can be made readily available because it usually is efficient in terms of professional time and intervention costs. That is, in the first few years there are fewer behavioral differences between children with ASD and their peers. The goal is to address those needs at a young age, so they don't multiply or magnify, and related behavior problems don't develop. Much of the intervention literature is based upon recommendations that many hours of intervention are necessary for children with autism, with interventions often requiring 25–40 hours per week (see recommendations by Lovass, 1987; Scheinkopf & Siegel, 1998). The resulting cost can be prohibitive for many families. However, through a parent education model, the parents can implement the intervention throughout the child's waking hours. As a result, this type of intervention can effectively generalize gains and reduce costs. For the most part, the parent education sessions are implemented for 1–2 hours per week for infants. This type of model—with active parent participation—reduces problems related to generalization and provides a continuous therapeutic environment for the infant.

Benefits of Using Modified PRT With Pre-Linguistic Infants

Several studies have shown the effectiveness of modified PRT interventions with very young infants. One such study used a modified PRT intervention with prelinguistic infants between 4 and 9 months of age who exhibited consistently low or erratic levels of engagement, failure to respond to name, low levels of eye contact, and flat/neutral affect during parent–infant interactions (Koegel, Singh, Koegel, Hollingsworth, & Bradshaw, 2013). The study included the following components:

1. A strength-based approach assessing activities that evoked positive affect in the infants, so as to determine which activities were child-preferred
2. Parents' engaging their infants in child-preferred activities, with task variation, during initial sessions
3. Interspersal of child-preferred activities with activities that evoked neutral responses, with the intent of improving the infants' affect and engagement during these activities

The study components and results are described in the sections that follow.

A Strength-Based Approach to Assessment The PRT intervention used a strength-based positive behavior approach by assessing areas that evoked positive affect in the infants (Koegel et al., 2013). In this study, we first videotaped the parents playing with their children and later scored the times when the parents were able to evoke positive affect. For the most part, the infants responded with neutral affect to most of the activities. However, a few activities raised positive emotion from the infants, such as smiles. The particular activities that elicited either positive or neutral affect varied across children. For example, one child's mother played games like Peek-a-boo, kissed and rubbed her infant, and made animal noises and other sounds, all of which the infant did not react to positively, remaining neutral or uninterested. However, three activities evoked smiles and eye contact. These were when the mom said, "I'm gonna get you," when she made silly faces, and when she gently nibbled on her infant's toes and fingers. Another infant responded with neutral affect when the mother sang to him, played Pattycake and Peek-a-boo, and made silly faces. However, this infant responded with eye contact and smiles when his mother lifted him up and said "Whee," tickled him, made raspberry lips, and bounced him in her lap while saying, "Giddy-up, horsie!" So, as you can see, the activities that elicit high affect were quite variable across infants and therefore had to be individually determined. Once we determined the three or four activities to which each infant responded, we considered those "child preferred."

Parent-Child Engagement in Child-Preferred Activities With Task Variation We began the intervention by having the parents only engage in child-preferred activities. A second aspect shown to improve motivation—task variation—was also incorporated. We asked the parents to engage in each of the preferred activities for brief periods of time (approximately 10 seconds) and to rotate through the activities for 5–7 minutes before carrying the children on a short walk. Because the infants tended to fixate their attention on objects (e.g., the ceiling fan) when they were not engaged, this walk gave us an opportunity to provide feedback to parents without extended periods of time for the infant to engage in attention to objects. We did not want the non-engagement break periods to provide the child with an opportunity to fixate on an inanimate object, which could be interpreted as a non-social reward. Instead, the walk with a parent provided a social break for the infants after each round of intervention. Further, we wanted to be sensitive to the length of time in which parent–infant dyads could remain in a positive affective and highly aroused state. This entire process was repeated for an hour once weekly during clinic sessions and it was suggested that parents engage in these activities throughout the day.

After just one week of the parent education, the infants showed markedly increased positive affect throughout the sessions. That is, they showed more interest and happiness during and after intervention. Specifically, they were more engaged in the activities, more alert, and more involved. In addition, the data showed that they smiled and laughed more during intervention and follow-up.

Interspersal of Child-Preferred Activities With Neutral Activities After the infants were demonstrating high affect during three consecutive sets of play routines, we began to intersperse the neutral activities. The goal of the interspersal was to classically condition the infants to expand their repertoires of activities during which they emitted positive affect. Gradually and systematically, more neutral activities were included, until the infants were engaging in improved affect throughout the sessions. The results of this study showed that, following intervention, the infants engaged in higher levels of responsiveness, attention to the activity, and engagement. As well, the infants smiled and laughed more frequently during these parent–child interactions. The infants also showed improved eye contact and responsiveness to their names being called. The positive effects of the intervention continued to be seen when follow-up data were collected 2–6 months after completion of the parent education sessions. This study provides promise for the validity and success of interventions implemented during the first year of life.

Benefits of Using Modified PRT With Young Toddlers

Other studies have focused on PRT intervention for 12-month-olds. For example, Steiner, Gengoux, Klin, and Chawarska (2013) selected toddlers who had early symptoms associated with ASD, such as lack of a pointing response, low eye contact, few vocalizations, repetitive behavior, and so on. The toddlers' scores on the Autism Diagnostic Observation Schedule–Toddler Module (ADOS-T) ranged from moderate/severe to little/no concern. All had siblings diagnosed with ASD. This study focused on teaching intentional and functional communicative attempts such as eye contact, gestures (e.g., showing, giving), and vocalizations. The PRT consisted of the following components:

1. Following the child's choice of stimulus materials
2. Providing clear prompts for communication
3. Interspersing maintenance and acquisition tasks
4. Using natural rewards delivered immediately
5. Rewarding goal-directed communicative attempts

Parents participated in weekly practice-with-feedback sessions wherein they would provide their toddlers with opportunities for communication and provide the preferred objects when the toddler used functional communication. Again, the goal was for the parents to implement the procedures between the sessions. The results of this study showed that all toddlers improved in their levels of eye contact, vocalizations, and gestures, as indicated by the data graphed in Figure 4.3.

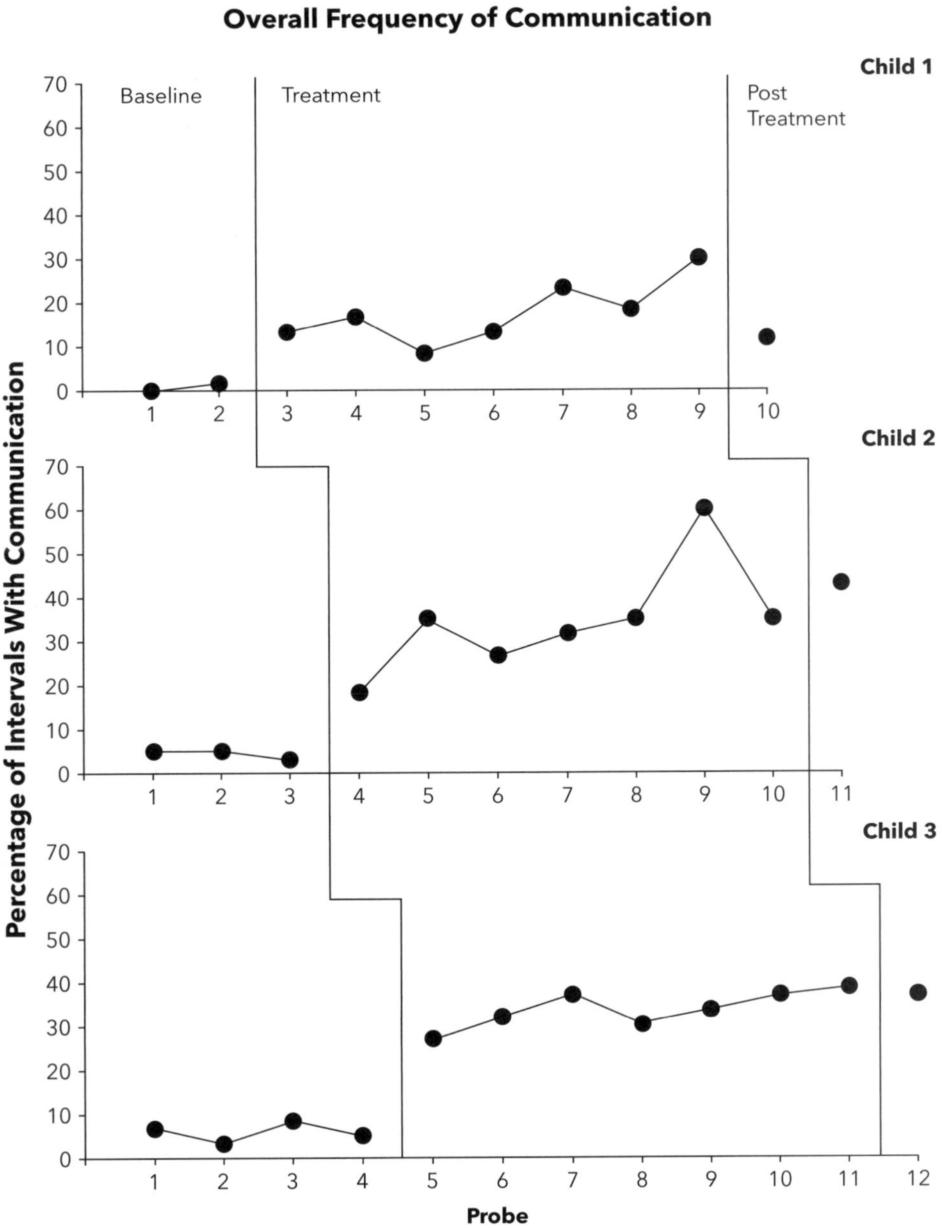

Figure 4.3 Percentage of intervals with child communication across baseline, treatment, and post-treatment probes. (From Steiner, A. M., Gengoux, G. W., Klin, A., & Chawarska, K. [2013]. Pivotal response treatment for infants at-risk for autism spectrum disorders: A pilot study. *Journal of Autism and Developmental Disorders, 43*[1], 91–102. Reprinted by permission.)

As well, the parents reported high levels of satisfaction with the intervention. They also reported that the program was helpful in learning how to get their toddlers to play and respond. This was important because many interventions for ASD are demanding for families to implement and can produce increased stress for parents.

Benefits of Using Modified PRT With Older Toddlers

Another PRT study focused on teaching expressive first words to toddlers ages 15–21 months (Bradshaw, Koegel, & Koegel, 2017). The toddlers all demonstrated significant delays in communication, only using two to four expressive words. In addition, the children engaged in repetitive behaviors, tantrums, and difficulties with socialization. This study also implemented 1-hour weekly coaching sessions with the parents over a 12-week period. During these sessions, which were implemented in natural settings such as the child's home or neighborhood parks, the parents were taught the core motivational components of PRT. That is, they were taught to

1. Follow the child's lead
2. Gain the child's attention
3. Provide clear and concise prompts for expressive words
4. Intersperse the few words the child already used (maintenance tasks) with the prompting for new words (acquisition tasks)
5. Reward the child for any verbal attempt or clear word with natural reinforcers

In this study, parents used child-preferred items; parents were taught to model verbally by labeling the child-preferred item and then to wait for a response from the child before giving the child the item. A similar approach was used for maintenance words, but for these words, adults did not initially provide a verbal model. Instead they just held the desired object and provided a delay of around 10 seconds, waiting for the child to respond to the object without a prompt. If the child did not respond, the word was modeled.

Following the PRT intervention, all of the parents showed large increases in the number of times they prompted new verbal communication. Simultaneously, the children demonstrated a dramatic increase in the number of times they used words or word approximations to request their preferred items. In fact, during 10-minute sample probes during baseline, all of the children used 10 or fewer words or word approximations while interacting with their parents. After intervention, the toddlers regularly used more than 50 words or word approximations during the 10-minute sample probes. In addition, their spontaneous verbalizations of words increased following intervention.

However, the parents who participated in this study still exhibited stress related to their children's diagnosis of autism. (It seems likely to us that such stress will not be significantly reduced until the interfering symptoms of autism can be eliminated.) Nevertheless, the parents all reported that they experienced some decreased stress during the times the intervention was being implemented, that the intervention was easy to implement, that they were able to use the PRT strategies outside of the sessions, and that the PRT training improved their day-to-day interactions with their child. They also reported increased confidence in being able to help their child to engage socially and communicate with him or her. The fact that these early gains can be seen suggests an advantage when adults address children's symptoms in the first 2 years of life.

CASE HISTORY
Using Motivation to Improve Danny's Social Engagement and Affect

When Danny was 5 months old, his mother became concerned about his failure to engage with her. He was her second child, and she noticed a huge difference between him and his older brother. His brother smiled, laughed, cooed, and craved attention. But Danny was different. He was content staring at the ceiling fan or a mobile attached to his crib. When she called his name, he rarely disengaged, preferring to stare at his chosen items. When the dog walked by, he paid little attention. Tickles and hugs resulted in little emotion. Although he was an easy baby, requiring little attention, she knew something was wrong.

Danny came to our clinic at 6 months. We engaged him in several tasks on the Autism Observation Scale for Infants (AOSI). We tried to get his attention, but he preferred to look at nonhuman items. When we smiled at him, he failed to smile back. He didn't look at us when we called his name, and repeated efforts to play simple games like Peek-a-boo seemed completely uninteresting to him. He appeared completely oblivious when we tickled his tummy, and when we placed items on the table he grabbed each item and put it in his mouth. In general, his affect and social engagement were consistently low. His mother was extremely concerned and asked if we could provide any early intervention.

We collected several weeks of video and analyzed the clips. Our goal was to find any activity that produced some high, positive affect. We were looking for any instances of smiles or laughs and eye contact. Of the dozens of activities with his mother, we were able to find three that elicited a modicum of excitement. The first was when his mother nibbled on his toes. The second was when she bounced him on her knee. And third, when she made silly noises, he tended to pay attention and laugh. We selected these activities as child preferred.

Our modified PRT intervention consisted of having her engage in the three activities with Danny for brief periods of time (about 10 seconds for each activity), rotating through them to provide him with some task variation. In this way, we were able to engage him for longer periods of time with high affect and good eye contact.

We had noticed that after Danny's mom engaged with him, she laid him on the floor, where he would resume his staring at the ceiling fan. To be assured that staring at the fan was not serving as a reinforcer for him, we began having her take him on brief walks after the child-preferred play sessions. During these breaks, we talked about his behavior, his affect, her implementation of the procedures, and so on. Shortly thereafter, Danny began to show higher affect during the child-preferred activities for several minutes at a time, so we began gradually and systematically adding activities that appeared to be neutral for him, as evidenced by his showing little affect. In other words, we considered the activities that he did not react to with smiles, laughs, or eye contact as acquisition tasks. We interspersed these for brief periods of time and noted that he began to show higher affect with these paired neutral activities. Over time, we gradually added more and more neutral activities, and over time he gradually began to smile, giggle, and use eye contact more frequently, even with the previously neutral activities. We encouraged Danny's mom to engage in these activities throughout the day, and she reported that she also taught Danny's child care staff how to implement the procedures.

Within a few months, Danny was regularly demonstrating high affect during a variety of activities. As he grew up, he showed fewer and fewer red flags for ASD. At a follow-up meeting, we didn't see any concerning behaviors. Although Danny did not have a diagnosis of autism, he had clearly been showing early symptoms that appeared to lessen after the onset of intervention. From a theoretical point of view, it is likely that the intervention caused the neutral activities to be classically conditioned to be positive. While preliminary, the ease and effectiveness of this type of brief parent education program may be helpful in reducing early social communicative symptoms that may worsen if not addressed.

Key Insights ||| Working Effectively With Infants, Toddlers, and Their Families

To use adapted PRT strategies with infants and toddlers and work most effectively with their families, keep the following principles in mind:

- **Include parents:** Parents are the first natural social partners for infants and toddlers, making them the best possible candidates for implementing the naturalistic strategies of PRT. Furthermore, parents are with their infants and toddlers much of the time and can be great change agents during these early years. They can also help others learn procedures to encourage improved affect and appropriate verbal and nonverbal communication. Because many children with ASD demonstrate disruptive behavior when they cannot communicate, learning alternative means early on may reduce these challenging behaviors.
- **Babies are variable:** There is considerable variability in the temperaments of infants. When assessing babies, repeated measures by expert clinicians are important. If the infant or toddler demonstrates red flags during repeated assessments, intervention may be warranted.
- **Use child-preferred activities:** Effective intervention studies focus on the child's strengths. When working with infants and toddlers, assessing for preferred activities that maximize social interaction is an important first step.
- **Use natural rewards:** Choosing child-preferred items and activities creates opportunities to provide the child with access to those items and activities contingent upon desired behaviors. For example, studies show that PRT for first words and nonverbal intentional communication can be evoked using preferred items that are contingently provided to the child.
- **Vary the task:** Repeated attempts to engage in activities that typically developing children appear to enjoy may not be successful with infants and toddlers who exhibit red flags. Make sure to vary the task so the infant or toddler

does not satiate, which can lead to reduced responding or disruptive behavior. Breaks from social interaction are also important to promote arousal regulation.

- **Intersperse maintenance and acquisition tasks:** It is especially important to ensure that infants and toddlers experience success. As many as seven easy tasks ("maintenance tasks") can be used before one more challenging task ("acquisition task") is provided.

Figure 4.4 summarizes principles and goals of using PRT with infants and toddlers.

Pivotal Response Treatment for Infants

Intervention Goal

- Increase positive affect and social interest during parent-infant interactions

Intervention Method

- Parent education
- Practice with feedback
- 60 minutes per week with follow through outside of the session

PRT Strategies

- Child choice
- Task variation
- Interspersed neutral and preferred activities
- Reinforcement

Figure 4.4. Summary of PRT goals, interventions, and strategies for working with infants.

SUMMARY

In summary, red flags may be apparent in the first and second year of life for most infants and toddlers who later receive a diagnosis of ASD. Although temperament is quite variable across infants and some may appear at times to exhibit early social challenges, concern about ASD may be valid when the symptoms are constant over time. More research in this area is warranted. However, if symptomology is present, emerging PRT interventions can be helpful with improving affect and acquiring first words and communicative gestures.

Most interventions in the infant and early toddler years rely significantly on parent involvement to help provide intervention on a regular basis throughout the high-risk infants' or toddlers' waking hours. Generally, weekly parent–professional collaboration with parents following through on the procedures throughout the week seems to be helpful in improving social engagement, affect, and early communication. It is important to use an intervention that is both effective for the infant/toddler and a stress reducer for the parents. As more studies emerge, best practices for this very young age group will continue to evolve.

STUDY QUESTIONS

1. Why is it important to recognize early red flags of ASD in the infant and toddler years?
2. What are some of the red flags indicating an infant who is high risk for a later diagnosis of ASD?
3. As a practitioner, how do you differentiate an early red flag from a temperamental difference or part of normative development?
4. What are potential intervention targets for at-risk infants younger than 12 months? Older than 12 months?
5. What PRT points can be used with pre-linguistic infants?
6. How can child-preferred activities be assessed in infants?
7. How is task variation used with infants?
8. How is the concept of interspersal of maintenance and acquisition tasks implemented during infant interventions?
9. Why is it important to teach the parents how to implement the intervention(s) with infants and toddlers?

REFERENCES

American Psychiatric Association. (2013). *Diagnostic and statistical manual of mental disorders.* 5th Edition. Arlington, VA: American Psychiatric Association.

Autism Developmental Disabilities Monitoring Network Surveillance Year 2010 Principal Investigators. (2014). *Prevalence of Autism Spectrum Disorder Among Children Aged 8 Years—Autism and Developmental Disabilities Monitoring Network, 11 Sites, United States, 2010.* CDC Morbidity and Mortality Weekly Report Surveillance Summaries, 63(SS02), 1–21.

Bayley, N. (2005). *Bayley Scales of Infant and Toddler Development, Third Edition (Bayley-III).* San Antonio, TX: Pearson.

Bradshaw, J. (2015). Clinical correlates of social smiling in early infancy: Implications for early identification of autism spectrum disorder. (Unpublished Doctoral Dissertation). The University of California, Santa Barbara.

Bradshaw, J., Koegel, L. K., & Koegel, R. L. (2017). Improving functional language and social motivation with a parent-mediated intervention for toddlers with autism spectrum disorder. *Journal of Autism and Developmental Disorders, 47*(8), 2443–2458.

Bradshaw, J., Koegel, L., Koegel, R. (2012). Assessment and Improvement of Social Engagement in Communication in Infancy. Presented at the proceedings of the International Meeting for Autism Research. Toronto, ON.

Bradshaw, J., Steiner, A. M., Gengoux, G., & Koegel, L. K. (2015). Feasibility and effectiveness of very early intervention for infants at-risk for autism spectrum disorder: A systematic review. *Journal of Autism and Developmental Disorders, 45*(3), 778–794.

Bryson, S. E., Zwaigenbaum, L., McDermott, C., Rombough, V., & Brian, J. (2008). The Autism Observation Scale for Infants: scale development and reliability data. *Journal of Autism and Developmental Disorders, 38*(4), 731–738.

Chawarska, K., Klin, A., Paul, R., Macari, S., & Volkmar, F. (2009). A prospective study of toddlers with ASD: Short-term diagnostic and cognitive outcomes. *Journal of Child Psychology and Psychiatry, 50*(10), 1235–1245.

Fogel, A., Hsu, H. C., Shapiro, A. F., Nelson-Goens, G. C., & Secrist, C. (2006). Effects of normal and perturbed social play on the duration and amplitude of different types of infant smiles. *Developmental Psychology, 42*(3), 459.

Koegel, L. K., Singh, A. K., Koegel, R. L., Hollingsworth, J. R., & Bradshaw, J. (2013). Assessing and improving early social engagement in infants. *Journal of Positive Behavior Interventions, 16*(2), 69–80.

Lord, C., Rutter, M., DiLavore, P., Risi, S., Gotham, K., & Bishop, S. (2012). *Autism Diagnostic Observation Schedule: ADOS-2.* Torrance, CA: Western Psychological Services.

Malatesta, C. Z., Culver, C., Tesman, J. R., Shepard, B., Fogel, A., Reimers, M., & Zivin, G. (1989). The development of emotion expression during the first two years of life. *Monographs of the Society for Research in Child Development*, i–136.

Messinger, D. S., Cassel, T. D., Acosta, S. I., Ambadar, Z., & Cohn, J. F. (2008). Infant smiling dynamics and perceived positive emotion. *Journal of Nonverbal Behavior, 32*(3), 133.

Mullen, E. M. (1995). *Mullen Scales of Early Learning,* AGS Edition. Circle Pines, MN: American Guidance Service. Inc.

Ozonoff, S., Iosif, A.M., Baguio, F., Cook, I.C., Hill, M.M., Hutman, T., Rogers, S.J., Rozga, A., Sangha, S., Sigman, M. & Steinfeld, M.B. (2010). A prospective study of the Emergence of early behavioral signs of autism. *Journal of the American Academy of Child & Adolescent Psychiatry, 49*(3), pp. 256–266.

Parlade, M. V., Messinger, D. S., Delgado, C. E., Kaiser, M. Y., Van Hecke, A. V., & Mundy, P. C. (2009). Anticipatory smiling: Linking early affective communication and social outcome. *Infant Behavior and Development, 32*(1), 33–43.

Rozga, A., Hutman, T., Young, G. S., Rogers, S. J., Ozonoff, S., Dapretto, M., & Sigman, M. (2011). Behavioral profiles of affected and unaffected siblings of children with autism: Contribution of measures of mother–infant interaction and nonverbal communication. *Journal of Autism and Developmental Disorders, 41*(3), 287–301.

Saulnier, C. A., & Ventola, P. E. (2012). *Essentials of autism spectrum disorders evaluation and assessment*. Hoboken, NJ: John Wiley & Sons.

Scheinkopf, S. J., & Siegel, B. (1998). Home based behavioral treatment for young autistic children. *Journal of Autism and Developmental Disorders, 28*(1), 15–23.

Steiner, A. M., Gengoux, G. W., Klin, A., & Chawarska, K. (2013). Pivotal response treatment for infants at-risk for autism spectrum disorders: A pilot study. *Journal of Autism and Developmental Disorders, 43*(1), 91–102.

Turygin, N., Matson, J. L., Williams, L. W., & Belva, B. C. (2014). The relationship of parental first concerns and autism spectrum disorder in an early intervention sample. *Research in Autism Spectrum Disorders, 8*(2), 53–60.

Wan, M. W., Green, J., Elsabbagh, M., Johnson, M., Charman, T., Plummer, F., & Basis Team. (2013). Quality of interaction between at-risk infants and caregiver at 12–15 months is associated with 3-year autism outcome. *Journal of Child Psychology and Psychiatry, 54*(7), 763–771.

Wetherby, A. M., & Prizant, B. M. (2002). *Communication and symbolic behavior scales: Developmental profile.* Baltimore, MD: Paul H. Brookes Publishing Co.

Zwaigenbaum, L., Bryson, S., Rogers, T., Roberts, W., Brian, J., & Szatmari, P. (2005). Behavioral manifestations of autism in the first year of life. *International Journal of Developmental Neuroscience, 23*(2-3), 143–152.

5

Teaching First Words

Lynn Kern Koegel and Daina Tagavi

CHAPTER GOALS

Goal 1. The reader will learn about language development and word acquisition in typically developing children.

Goal 2. The reader will understand the unique delays in language understanding and production among children with autism spectrum disorders (ASD).

Goal 3. The reader will understand the importance of language development in children with ASD in terms of future adolescent and adult outcomes.

Goal 4. The reader will become familiar with Pivotal Response Treatment (PRT) evidence-based treatments for teaching first words to children with ASD.

Goal 5. The reader will learn specific strategies to teach first words to nonverbal children with ASD.

This chapter discusses differences in the development of communication between children with ASD and typical language learners. We focus on red flags that appear early on and are indicators that communicative milestones may not be appearing as they should. We also describe potential issues that may arise later in life if early communicative milestones are not reached. Finally, we describe PRT interventions for targeting first words and the expected outcomes of intervention. Although not every child with ASD will learn to use verbal communication as a primary mode of communication, the majority should if intervention begins in the preschool years. The motivational components of PRT that are greatly helpful in improving the numbers of children who learn to use first words and expressive verbal communication are described later in this chapter.

UNDERSTANDING EARLY LANGUAGE DEVELOPMENT

Early childhood is a critical period for the development of social and verbal communication. As each year passes, verbal communication becomes more challenging for children who do not learn first words, and after age 5, very few children who are completely nonverbal will learn to talk. Therefore, it is important to be aware of the early signs of ASD so that interventions targeting social communication and language production can be implemented as early as possible. In typically developing children, the earliest signs of language development and communicative behaviors begin to emerge well before their first birthday. At this age, typical language learners enjoy engaging in many nonverbal forms of communication, such as demonstrating understanding of words through social smiles or gesturing to get a parent's attention. These early bids for engagement, attention, communicating discomfort, and so on, are the same emotions, thoughts, and requests to which they will eventually attribute words (Carpenter, Nagell, & Tomasello, Butterworth, & Moore, 1998). After the first year of life, more functional receptive language acquisition generally emerges. Around 12 months, infants begin to understand simple phrases and will produce their first recognizable words. Boys sometimes develop communication slightly later than girls, but some type of verbal back-and-forth, even if it is babbling or cooing, should be evident. From 12 to 18 months, expressive vocabulary in typically developing children continues to develop gradually and aspects of social communication, such as the use of family members' names and greetings, begin to emerge.

By 18 months, children without language delays are usually able to use around a dozen or more expressive words, which they can say without prompting and coaxing. During this period, verbal learning begins to grow exponentially, in what is often referred to as a "vocabulary burst" or "word explosion" (Fenson et al., 1994, Tager-Flusberg et al., 2005). This stage of language development is unique and central, in that children are beginning to understand the symbolic and practical nature of words, and they are starting to use these words to gather information and make inferences and judgments about the world around them (Nazzi & Bertoninci, 2003). Around age 2, typical language learners will acquire a large vocabulary and begin to combine words into simple, one- to two-word sentences, with most verbal expressions revolving around objects and people and their actions and interactions (Tager-Flusberg et al., 2005).

This learning phenomenon establishes language development in early childhood as an exceptionally organized and adaptive process that parallels how young children think and the things they perceive as significant. The language learning process is therefore not random and contributes to development by forming a clear link between nonverbal and verbal communication and different functions that can help toddlers successfully propel through childhood. Without this pattern of development, children are at a severe disadvantage, which could continue to affect their development and functioning throughout the lifespan if not addressed.

EARLY COMMUNICATION AND FIRST WORDS IN CHILDREN WITH ASD

A delay in the onset of first words is among the most prevalent and noticeable presenting symptom of ASD to parents (Herlihy, Knoch Vibert, & Fein, 2015). Even children diagnosed with ASD whose nonverbal intelligence test scores are in the average range are typically late talkers, with a mean age of 38 months for first using words (Howlin, 2003). Although parents—especially those with older children—report behavioral abnormalities in many areas, including social interaction, repetitive behaviors, a lack of play, not understanding others, and so on, most pediatricians and professionals are reluctant to give a diagnosis during the first year of life (Oswald, Haworth, Mackenzie, & Willis, 2017). However, when expressive words do not emerge, referrals for intervention are generally made.

Until recently, it was difficult to systematically examine these early prelinguistic abnormalities in communication because most studies in this realm relied on retrospective reports from parents or inconsistent home videos of children. However, because about 20% of siblings of children with ASD will develop ASD, there has been an increase in research examining the trajectory of early language development in children in this population (Ozonoff et al., 2011). Through studying at-risk siblings, Mitchell et al. (2006) found that children who eventually went on to develop ASD showed significant delays in early language and communication compared with both controls and siblings who did not have ASD. Even at 12 months, the group of children who later developed ASD understood significantly fewer words and phrases, produced fewer nonverbal gestures, and strayed away from the typical trajectory of language development. Further, at 18 months, infants who eventually received an ASD diagnosis understood fewer phrases and words, produced fewer words, and made fewer representative gestures (Mitchell et al., 2006). Overall, this and other prospective studies affirm that delays in nonverbal communication, including pragmatics, a lack of understanding, low responsiveness, and the use of inappropriate gestures rather than pointing and other social gestures are observable particularly early in life in children who eventually develop ASD. (These factors are represented in Figure 5.1.) Thus, future research and practice could serve to highlight the importance of early, personalized screening that should inquire about delayed nonverbal social communication patterns and first words, which may be among the earliest, most apparent, and obvious signs of ASD.

Once young children are diagnosed with ASD, research has demonstrated that their linguistic and communicative development appears to be a factor directly associated with adult outcomes. It has been known for many years that individuals who fail to develop and progress in early nonverbal and verbal language are at significant risk of more severe impairments throughout life (Koegel, Koegel, Shoshan, & McNerney, 1999; Venter, Lord, & Schopler, 1992). In previous decades, it was reported that, even with intervention, approximately 50% of children diagnosed with ASD remained nonverbal (Prizant, 1983). In addition, children who are not using verbal communication regularly by school age have been shown to have poorer outcomes in terms of independence and integration at school and with peers (Howlin, 2005). More broadly, Howlin, Mawhood, and Rutter (2000) found

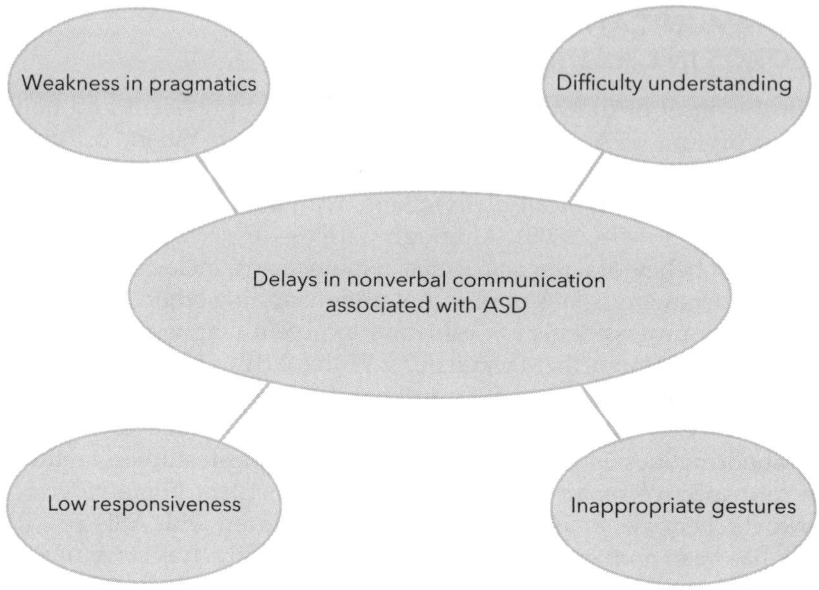

Figure 5.1. Delays in nonverbal communication associated with ASD.

that even when comparing children with a diagnosed receptive language disorder, early language development in children with ASD is significantly related to social functioning in adulthood, demonstrating the broad impact that these delays can have throughout the lifetime.

With advances in early screening, diagnosis, and intervention, it has been reported that most children diagnosed with ASD have the potential to use verbal expressive language as their primary mode of communicating if good (empirically validated) interventions are implemented before the age of 5 and preferably before the age of 3 (Koegel, 1995; Koegel & Koegel, 2006, 2012; Koegel, Koegel, Harrower, & Carter, 1999). It is, therefore, imperative for professionals to continue to develop and refine these interventions for early language development in infancy and focus on the widespread dissemination and implementation of these protocols so that the greatest number of children with early communicative delays can have improved chances for lifelong success.

INTERVENTIONS TO ELICIT FIRST WORDS: A BRIEF HISTORY

Since behavioral interventions for ASD were first established, many researchers focused on teaching verbal communication (Hewett, 1965; Lovaas, 1966, 1977). Since the 1970s, however, the nature of these interventions has changed. Historically, the earliest interventions centered on discrete trial training (DTT); these methods were initially very laborious to implement. They gradually evolved to become naturalistic and, eventually, to incorporate the very powerful motivational components of PRT, which can produce extremely rapid speech and language development.

Early Interventions: Discrete Trial Training

Early effective interventions used DTT, teaching children to attend to adults by responding to a series of step-like verbal instructions intended to help children imitate the speech of the provider (Lovaas, 1966, 1977, 2002). Steps included in this approach include prompting the child to imitate manual, oral motor, and vocal behavior (usually individual phonemes or consonant vowel combinations) and then finally to imitate full words. Despite the effectiveness of these protocols, it often took hundreds or even thousands of trials over an extended length of time to accomplish the acquisition of even a few words. Lovaas' (1977) early groundbreaking work in this area showed two things: first, that it was possible to teach verbal communication to these children—many of whom had previously been considered hopeless; and second, that it was very hard work, sometimes taking as many as 90,000 trials, to teach a first word.

Naturalistic Interventions as the Basis for PRT

Over time, research showed that adding specific motivational procedures to these early behavioral interventions created more rapid acquisition of communication and improved the child's affect during the teaching session as well as the interventionists. That is, the newer procedures have been able to produce more rapid speech acquisition while also resulting in happier children, parents, and clinicians.

For example, an early study used the traditional stimulus–response–consequence discrete trial format of applied behavior analysis (ABA) but differed from traditional ABA in that intervention took place in a natural, interactive setting and allowed for the use of specific motivational variables (e.g., child-chosen tasks) to help foster behavioral change (Koegel, O'Dell, & Koegel, 1987). Specifically, the treatment placed a unique emphasis on the personalization of the learning situation, through the use of the following:

- Child-directed interactions
- Natural and direct reinforcers
- Interspersal of new teaching interactions among previously acquired responses
- Reinforcing the children's attempts to communicate in addition to their perfectly correct words
- A focus on generalization and development of skills across settings, activities, and people (Koegel & Koegel, 2012; Rogers et al., 2006)

In that early study, we referred to the forerunner of the PRT intervention as the "natural language paradigm" or "NLP." The study and procedure became the basis of PRT.

USING PRT TO ELICIT FIRST WORDS: SPECIFIC COMPONENTS

These motivational procedures to target first words included the following components: 1) providing child choice, 2) modeling the verbal labels of the items, 3) varying the task, 4) using natural and direct rewards, and 5) rewarding attempts at verbal communication. These components, as shown in Figure 5.2, are further discussed in the sections that follow.

Provide Child Choice

Instead of using instructional materials that are pre-determined by the parent, teacher, therapist, or other provider, the child is able to choose from a pool of highly desired items or activities that are commonly found in the natural environment. Careful attention is paid to the interests of the child so that those items can be utilized in the intervention session. It is important to remember that preference may change from session to session or within a session. Therefore, it is critical for the interventionist to keep a close eye on the child, ensuring shifts are made when a child tires of an item or activity so that the child's preference is constantly being assessed.

Model the Label of the Item

As the interventionist determines the items and/or activities a child chooses, he or she should model the label of the desired item or activity. For example, you can hold up the item and say the label you would like the child to use (e.g.,"chip") or say the activity the child would like to engage in (e.g., "swing") as a model for the child to imitate before providing the child with the item or activity. Be sure to make it clear for the child by simply saying a single word. Sometimes adults may get caught up with adding many extra words—such as, "Look over here, look

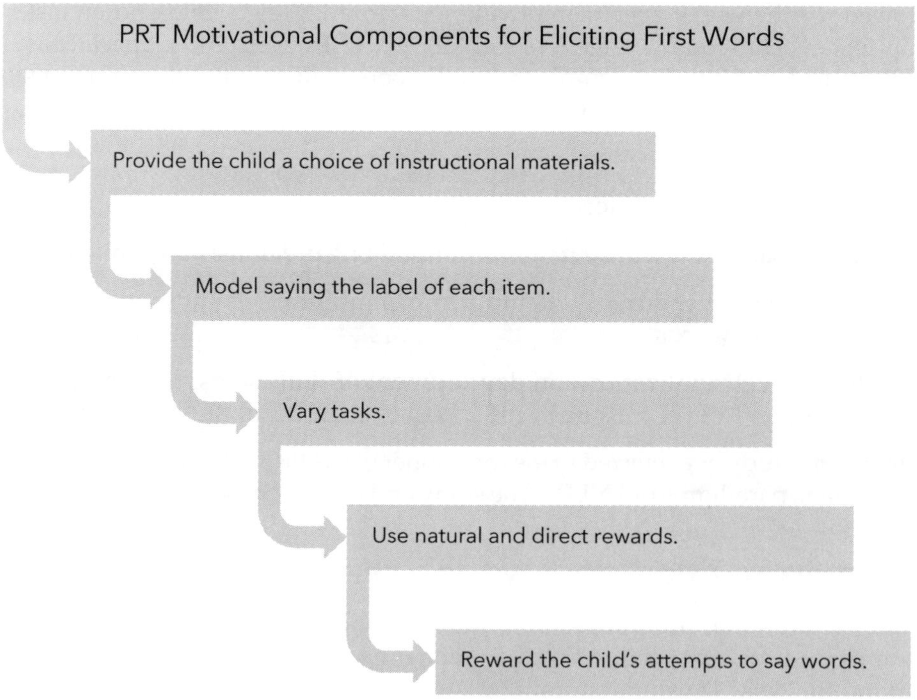

Figure 5.2. PRT motivational components for eliciting first words.

what I've got. It's something you really like. Can you say 'chip'? I know you can say it" —which may ultimately end up being confusing to a child with ASD who is learning first words. Also, in our clinical experience, we haven't had much luck with physical prompts for evoking first words. That is, trying to shape his or her articulators in the correct position hasn't seemed to help with the correct production of sounds. However, simply modeling the single word we want the child to learn appears to be the most helpful strategy initially. While doing this, it is important to be prepared for the child to go through her or his repertoire of communicative behaviors that have been effective in the past, which may include behaviors such as crying, grabbing, and screaming, before trying verbal communication. You may even see an extinction burst, with the child's inappropriate behavior getting worse before the child figures out that those behaviors won't work any longer. Eventually, the goal is for the child to learn that those inappropriate communicative behaviors are ineffective and that verbal expressive words *are* effective.

Vary Tasks

Mix it up. Anyone gets bored doing the same thing over and over again. This is especially important when learning first words, as it may be frustrating for the child with ASD who hasn't yet been able to get the connection between the power of a verbal word and the reward that ensues. This task variation can be done in conjunction with reinforcing attempts. Sometimes it's helpful to just focus on a small number of words instead of providing opportunities for each item the child wants. Be careful, however, not to reward the child for inappropriate behaviors, such as grabbing, in place of appropriately responding to a trial. The amount you can push a child will depend on keeping his or her motivation high while providing enough trials with favorite items so that the child learns that each item has its own label. Thus, varying the stimulus item, so as to parallel the child's shifting interests, will reduce the repetitiveness of the intervention and keep the child's motivation level high.

Use Natural and Direct Rewards

Make the response and the reinforcer directly related to each other. If you combine this practice with the use of child-choice items, then the items the child is choosing can be used as natural rewards. Most young children with ASD will make a verbal request (or attempted verbal request) for a desired item. When the child attempts to request the item verbally, give it to him or her immediately. That way, the connection between the verbal request and the positive result of getting the highly desired item or activity will motivate the child to use verbalizations again in the future. The goal here is to not only teach the specific task at hand, but to also teach the child that there is a connection between the child's responding and the outcome of those responses. This serves to increase the child's overall motivation to respond to the tasks.

Reward Attempts

Some children produce clearly articulated words on their first attempts, and others aren't so clear. The important thing is to reinforce the child for *any* verbal attempt to respond instead of requiring perfectly correct responses in this early stage of learning words. In the past, we systematically rewarded only perfectly correct advances toward the adult word through a strict shaping paradigm, but research has shown that these initial steps are fragile, and if the children are trying they should be rewarded for all attempts at verbal communication. (The effectiveness of rewarding attempts is illustrated by Koegel, O'Dell, & Dunlap's [1988] study, discussed in the following section.) When doing this, be sure to reward only purposeful attempts, and do not give a reward unless the child's response is clearly goal directed.

RESEARCH SUPPORT FOR INCLUDING MOTIVATIONAL COMPONENTS

During our initial studies relating to first words, we found that when we were using the traditional analogue teaching condition (without the aforementioned motivational variables), many of the children were not making any spontaneous utterances outside of the clinical sessions. That is, even if they were beginning to say words, they didn't use the learned words in any natural contexts. However, once the PRT components were introduced, with all the natural and motivational items, the children began to increase their spontaneous utterances in both number and frequency within and outside of the teaching sessions. Perhaps the most important aspect of these gains, and a unique one, is that they generalized to novel settings, pointing to the powerful and robust effects of the motivational variables on children's overall functioning and well-being. These findings highlight the importance of targeting the pivotal area of motivation to most efficiently and effectively produce first words in young nonverbal children. In fact, the gains took place not only with respect to the targeted speech, but also resulted in many collateral gains in speech, language, affect, social behavior, and reductions in disruptive behavior, the motivational aspect of the intervention seemed to be targeting a pivotal and core area of autism—thus producing very widespread improvement in both specific targeted behaviors as well as in general symptoms of autism. This is why we eventually named the procedure PRT!

As noted, it is important to reward verbal communicative attempts. Koegel et al. (1988) found that insisting on perfectly formed words, or word approximations that were at least as good as the child's previous attempt, may not be the best way to get children with ASD to use first words. In this intervention, clinicians reinforced any attempt by a child to produce sounds as long as it was purposeful and task-directed, regardless of whether the attempt was perfectly correct phonetically and regardless of whether the child had previously made a better attempt. For example, if a clinician prompted the child to say "swing" while sitting on a swing, the clinician would provide a natural reward (i.e., pushing the child on the swing) as long as the child 1) oriented his or her body or face toward the clinician, and 2) made any vocalization that was of normal loudness and appeared be purposeful with the intent of communicating a desire to swing. The clinician provided this reinforcement for the child's vocalization without requiring that it exactly resemble the target word or be an equal or better response as the previous. This unique use of reinforcing attempts to motivate the child not only increased word production and word approximations but also resulted in higher affect ratings for the children in the areas of happiness, interest, and enthusiasm. That is, during the sessions when all of the children's focused word attempts were rewarded (in addition to their correct words), the children showed higher levels of engagement, smiled more, were rated as more interested, and had better levels of appropriate behavior. It was as if most of the response was already in the child's repertoire, and our task was to bring the words out, rather than needing to tediously shape each motor response.

Most notably, at a follow-up 4 years later, the younger children (ages 3 years 3 months through 11 years 9 months) who received 4 years of treatment focused on reinforcing verbal attempts, were highly verbal. During short conversational probes lasting approximately 10–20 minutes, these children were speaking from 75 to 122 words. In contrast, a comparison child who received 4 years of traditional discrete trial motor speech intervention was still essentially nonverbal, speaking no words during the conversational probes. Again, the traditional discrete trial intervention worked to help the children use words during the intervention sessions, but they did not use the newly acquired words in natural conversational interactions outside of treatment, and were therefore functionally still nonverbal.

These findings speak to the necessity of rewarding the attempts of children with ASD in order to affect the core area of motivation—not only when targeting children's first words, but possibly when targeting any behavior. In fact, subsequent research has shown that the widespread speech and language gains resulting from PRT were just the tip of the iceberg, as you will see when you read other chapters of this book. Motivation has been so extremely pivotal in intervention that very large and widespread gains in speech, language, social behavior, and decreases in disruptive behavior have been evidenced when the children receive such intervention.

CREATING AMPLE OPPORTUNITIES FOR VERBAL COMMUNICATION

Once children with ASD begin using words, it is important to create ample opportunities for them to continue doing so. In addition to the specific motivational components already described, two factors are especially important to keep in mind: the role parents and caregivers play in treatment and the effect of behavioral momentum.

Parents and Caregivers as Treatment Mediators

A key aspect of treatment, in addition to the specific motivational components, is the use of parents or caregivers as mediators of treatment delivery. A study by Yoder and Warren (2002) found that combining a naturalistic communication approach with a parent-education element, which aimed to teach parents to provide their children with learning opportunities in the home, was highly effective in teaching children with ASD to speak their first words. This combination of professional intervention with parent follow-through even increased generalization, with children engaging in spontaneous verbal communication in novel settings.

The Power of Behavioral Momentum

Tsiouri, Simmons, and Paul (2012) attempted to expand on these findings by harnessing the concept of behavioral momentum to enhance a standard DTT intervention with motivational components already included. Behavioral momentum refers to the "resistance of behavior to a change or to reinforcement conditions" (Nevin, Mandell, & Atak, 1983). The first step in achieving first words is often imitation of words because children with ASD often have great difficulty imitating, which can be extremely challenging and frustrating (Rogers, Hayden, Hepburn, Charlifue-Smith, Hall, & Hayes, 2006). The principle of behavioral momentum asserts that teaching children a series of "easy" behaviors creates momentum, which can be used to improve their motivation to master a new, more difficult behavior. The incorporation of this concept into the beginning of treatment can be powerful in keeping children engaged and motivated, and therefore more likely to respond to and even enjoy the intervention even when parts of it become difficult.

Research furthering this area of study shows that, in young children with ASD who make the most gains, two components are correlated with these gains. The first is making sure that parents are correctly implementing the PRT motivational variables. The second is that the parents are providing enough opportunities for the child to practice the words (Hardan, 2017). Thus, for the best outcomes, parents need to learn the unique PRT strategies to help their child with ASD learn to use words and also provide lots of opportunities throughout the day.

The effectiveness and generalizability of the PRT treatment package speaks to the importance of including parents in the intervention process, teaching them to implement the procedures with fidelity and making sure they are providing lots of opportunities when targeting first words. Making parents "quasi-experts" on the treatment methods used with their children helps ensure that intervention will be applied more consistently and naturally and that the children will make more rapid and robust improvements in spoken language, ensuring the best possible prognosis for them in this domain.

WORKING WITH NONRESPONSIVE CHILDREN

Although the PRT treatment packages have been shown to be effective in many studies, findings have shown that a small group of children in this population still do not acquire spoken language even with intensive intervention (Koegel, Shirotova, & Koegel, 2009). For these children, we have found it helpful to work with the child's orientation to cues and to use carrier phrases and sounds already in the child's repertoire.

Orient the Child to Cues

It appears that in addition to the motivational problems, another pivotal area is also important: the child's orientation to cues. That is, some children do not pay attention or orient to the important and relevant cues during intervention for first words. To target this particularly resistant subgroup, the authors and their colleagues attempted to use antecedent, individualized orienting cues presented immediately before a verbal word model to help redirect the child's attention away from the irrelevant cue during the treatment sessions (Koegel et al., 2009). This intervention used PRT. However, less than 1 second before modeling the desired word, the clinician would orient the child to attend to the clinician with a personalized and motivating cue such as a high-five, hug, or modeled motor action. Consistent with the PRT motivational procedures, the clinician immediately provided the child with a natural reinforcer after any purposeful and task-directed vocalization or correct word. The addition of the orienting cues resulted in improvements in functional word acquisition directly following the intervention and continued improvement at 6-month follow-up, as evidenced by the following:

- One child who used no words during 29 weeks of baseline began using full sentences at follow-up.
- A second child who had made minimal progress during 17 weeks of baseline began using two- to three-word combinations.
- A third child who used no words during baseline began to use a few words.

For these children, who were previously not responding to the PRT even after many months of intervention, it appeared that once the children's attention was drawn to the relevant cues, they began making verbal responses. In addition, for most of the children, it was not necessary to continue using the orienting cues, as the children continued to make dramatic gains with the regular procedures after just a few months of intervention. It appears that once they learned that the relevant cues were coming from the teacher, they continued to orient to the teacher without additional prompting. These findings not only provide a promising technique to teach first words to nonresponders, but also point to important areas for understanding how to facilitate treatment responsivity as a whole for children with ASD.

Use Carrier Phrases and Sounds in the Child's Repertoire

For those children who are having difficulty learning first words using basic PRT, we have clinically found two other methods to be helpful: using a carrier phrase and using sounds already in the child's repertoire. Using a carrier phrase involves priming the child with a series of words:

- The clinician says "Ready, set, go" and then pushes the child on the swing, repeating this several times and then says "Ready, set ..." while waiting for the child to finish the phrase.
- The clinician says "One, two, three," then lets a car go down the child's favorite ramp toy, repeating this several times, and then says "One, two ..."

Following several trials using the complete carrier phrase, the clinician can then leave off the last word and pause, giving the child an opportunity to say the last word. Any carrier phrase can be used (even songs such as Old MacDonald Had a Farm, using EIEIO as the carrier phrase and leaving off the O). Often this practice and momentum are just what the child needs to finish off the phrase.

Another method involves connecting sounds that are already in the child's repertoire and attaching those sounds to meaningful words. For example, if the child randomly says "ka," the parent may give the child a bite of his favorite cookie right after saying the sound. With repeated practice, the child may learn that the vocalization can be used to communicate with intent.

USING PRT WITH INFANTS

PRT can also be adapted for younger children. For example, Steiner, Gengoux, Klin, and Chawarska (2013) showed that PRT could be used with preverbal infants with autism aged 12 months who had siblings with ASD (two of which scored in the moderate/severe concern on the Autism Diagnostic Observation Schedule – Toddler Module or ADOS-T) and were showing communication delays and behavioral symptoms of consistent with ASD. This study taught parents to implement PRT to target functional communication, including eye contact, gestures, showing, giving, and vocalizations to communicate. Ten weekly PRT parent education sessions were held. All of the parents improved in their use of the PRT strategies and reported high satisfaction with the program. Also, all of the children improved in their use of functional communication. Thus, adaptations of naturalistic interventions; including PRT (Bradshaw, Koegel, & Koegel, 2017; Coolican, Smith, & Bryson, 2010; Koegel, Singh, Koegel, Hollingsworth, & Bradshaw, 2013; Koegel & Koegel, 2012) have been found to be effective in a range of age groups, including those receiving very early intervention. Further, early on the parents may be successful change agents, reducing the need for many hours of treatment implemented by professionals—hours that can be expensive and difficult to obtain. As children are being diagnosed at younger ages, such early programs during the first year of life become important.

CASE HISTORY
Using PRT to Produce First Words

It wasn't long ago when we began teaching first words to children with ASD with sound production. Usually we combined a consonant, such as "mmmm," with a vowel, such as "ah." In the original early-developed discrete trial procedures, we prompted the child to say the sound we modeled ("Say *mmm*" or "Say *ah*") and reinforced the child for doing so. If the child responded correctly, we gave him or her a small treat; if not, we molded the child's lips into the right shape to produce the target sound, such as lightly pinching the lips together for "mmm." It was tedious; most of the children didn't learn to talk, and even those who did speak did not especially like the intervention. Some could imitate the sounds if we presented them over and over, but when we mixed the sequence up, they couldn't differentiate between the two sounds. Even for the small group of children who did learn the different sounds, we had to model how to string them together into a syllable, such as "ma," then a word, such as "mama," and then the child didn't know what the word meant. Not only did the children not connect the words with intent, they seemed totally uninterested in the sessions; some even engaged in disruptive avoidance or escape behaviors to get out of the sessions.

Then, we started experimenting with using fun toys and highly desired items. We still remember working with a cute little 5-year-old, red-headed boy who had never said a word despite years of traditional DTT intervention for sound imitation. For him, cookies were "to die for" and interventionists frequently used a cookie as a non-natural reward for this child. During one session, we tried using the cookie to prompt communication rather than using it for a reward. We held up the cookie and modeled the word *cookie*. To our amazement, he slowly uttered each syllable: "coo," then "kie." This rapid turnaround was shocking and exciting. He must have said "coo-kie" 20 times that first session. Although it was only a tiny tweak in the intervention, it made a world of difference for him. This little guy and the group of children in his cohort helped us break the mold of teaching first words through a strict and tedious motor shaping paradigm. Applying these naturalistic pivotal response procedures during the preschool years has dramatically improved the number of children who can use verbal communication.

Key Insights ||| Working to Produce a Child's First Words

When working with children who have not developed expressive verbal communication (yet), keep these key insights in mind.

- **Language skills vary in early childhood:** It is important to note that, although most children who eventually develop ASD have delayed language acquisition and abnormal language development, the trajectory of this development varies greatly from child to child. Because of this, it is important to develop and use personalized and individualized screeners, assessments, and interventions to capitalize upon each child's unique skills and target specific delays.
- **Use natural interactive environments and reinforcers:** Research has continually shown that the most effective interventions are implemented in the natural environment using natural rewards, which increase child motivation and, in turn, increase the generalizability of the target behavior.
- **Reinforce any purposeful attempt:** By reinforcing any purposeful attempt at producing speech, parents and professionals can begin to foster the development of early verbal skills and even further increase the effectiveness of natural language paradigms.
- **Capitalize on the pivotal area of motivation:** Research has shown that targeting the pivotal area of motivation through intervention is key in achieving optimal outcomes for children with ASD. This can be achieved through using child-preferred activities, natural reinforcers, reinforcing attempts, and varying the tasks used throughout session.
- **Use novel components in the procedures for nonresponders:** Even with intensive intervention, some children with ASD still fail to develop spoken language. Researchers have found that using novel methods, such as orienting cues, phonemes already in their repertoire, and carrier phrases to engage the child throughout treatment, can be effective in eliciting language in this subgroup.

- **Involve parents:** It is ideal, whenever possible, to actively involve parents (or other caregivers) in the treatment implementation to ensure the best prognosis for children with ASD. Teaching parents to elicit behavior change or produce symptom reduction at home helps ensure that intervention is applied more consistently and naturally, leading to rapid and robust improvements in spoken language.

SUMMARY

It is now widely accepted throughout the literature that one of the single most important prognostic indicators for young children with ASD is early language ability (Koegel, Koegel, et al., 1999; Schreibman, 1988). While typically developing children are beginning to use nonverbal language during the first year of life and acquiring a plethora of first words soon after, children who eventually develop ASD tend to have a delayed onset of first words and continue to struggle to develop verbal communication skills throughout childhood. Research has demonstrated that individuals who fail to develop and progress in early nonverbal communication and verbal language skills are at a significant risk of more severe impairments in all domains throughout the lifespan (Venter et al., 1992).

To address this, a number of interventions have been developed to help evoke and develop first words in preverbal children with ASD. These interventions initially taught children to attend to adults by responding to a series of step-like verbal instructions, intended to help children imitate the speech of the provider. These techniques have been expanded to incorporate a natural, interactive treatment setting and the use of child-preferred tasks, which has greatly increased the generalizability and maintenance of early language skills in young children. Because of the poor outcomes associated with early language delays, it is important for researchers and clinicians to not only continue to develop, test, and refine interventions to help teach first words, but also research ways to effectively disseminate and implement these powerful, evidence-based interventions so that young children with ASD have the greatest possible chance for optimal lifelong functioning and success.

Our clinical outcomes with large groups of children diagnosed with ASD who were nonverbal and participated in our nationally funded grants suggest that if we start intervention before age 3, as many as 95% of the children (approximately) can learn to use verbal communication as a primary mode of communication. Between ages 3 and 5 years, the number seems to decrease a bit to about 85%. After age 5, the percentage seems to decrease dramatically, with only about 20% of children who are completely nonverbal learning expressive verbal communication. Therefore, early intervention that includes motivational components will result in the most positive outcomes in children with ASD.

STUDY QUESTIONS

1. Describe the development of communication in the first year of life.
2. Discuss the acquisition of first words and word combinations for typical language development in the second year of life, including the vocabulary explosion.

3. What are the implications for children with ASD who do not develop verbal communication?
4. Describe early methods for teaching communication to children who are nonverbal.
5. Discuss motivational components that have been successfully used to teach first words.
6. Why is it important to focus on a child's motivation during the teaching of first words?
7. Describe procedures that can be used with nonresponders while teaching first words.
8. Discuss the importance of rewarding attempts during the teaching of first words.

REFERENCES

Bradshaw, J., Koegel, L. K., & Koegel, R. L. (2017). Improving functional language and social motivation with a parent-mediated intervention for toddlers with autism spectrum disorder. *Journal of Autism and Developmental Disorders, 47*(8), 2443–2458.

Coolican, J., Smith, I. M., & Bryson, S. E. (2010). Brief parent training in pivotal response treatment for preschoolers with autism. *Journal of Child Psychology and Psychiatry, 51*(12), 1321–1330.

Carpenter, M., Nagell, K., Tomasello, M., Butterworth, G., & Moore, C. (1998). Social cognition, joint attention, and communicative competence from 9 to 15 months of age. *Monographs of the Society for Research in Child Development*, i–174.

Fenson, L., Dale, P. S., Reznick, J. S., Bates, E., Thal, D. J., Pethick, S. J., & Stiles, J. (1994). Variability in early communicative development. *Monographs of the Society for Research in Child Development*, i–185.

Hardan, A. (2017). Keynote address at the Pivotal Response Treatment annual conference, Stanford University, Palo Alto, CA.

Herlihy, L., Knoch, K., Vibert, B., & Fein, D. (2015). Parents' first concerns about toddlers with autism spectrum disorder: Effect of sibling status. *Autism, 19*(1), 20–28.

Hewett, F. M. (1965). Teaching speech to an autistic child through operant conditioning. *American Journal of Orthopsychiatry, 35*(5), 927.

Howlin, P. (2003). Outcome in high-functioning adults with autism with and without early language delays: Implications for the differentiation between autism and Asperger syndrome. *Journal of Autism and Developmental Disorders, 33*(1), 3–13.

Howlin, P. (2005). Outcomes in autism spectrum disorders. In F. R. Volkmar, R. Paul, A. Klin, & D. Cohen (Eds.), *Handbook of autism and pervasive developmental disorders: Diagnosis, development, neurobiology, and behavior* (pp. 201–220). Hoboken, NJ: John Wiley & Sons Inc.

Howlin, P., Mawhood, L., & Rutter, M. (2000). Autism and developmental receptive language disorder—a follow-up comparison in early adult life. II: Social, behavioural, and psychiatric outcomes. *Journal of Child Psychology and Psychiatry, 41*(5), 561–578.

Koegel, L. K. (1995). Communication and language intervention. In R. L. Koegel & L. K. Koegel (Eds.), *Teaching children with autism: Strategies for initiating positive interactions and improving learning opportunities* (pp. 17–32). Baltimore, MD: Paul H. Brookes Publishing Co.

Koegel. R. L. & Koegel, L. K. (2006). *Pivotal response treatments*. Baltimore, MD: Paul H. Brookes Publishing Co.

Koegel, R. L., & Koegel, L. K. (2012). *The PRT pocket guide: Pivotal Response Treatment for autism spectrum disorders.* Baltimore, MD: Paul H. Brookes Publishing Co.

Koegel, L. K., Koegel, R. L., Harrower, J. K., & Carter, C. M. (1999). Pivotal response intervention I: Overview of approach. *Journal of the Association for Persons with Severe Handicaps, 24*(3), 174–185.

Koegel, L. K., Singh, A. K., Koegel, R. L., Hollingsworth, J. R., & Bradshaw, J. (2013). Assessing and improving early social engagement in infants. *Journal of Positive Behavior Interventions, 16*(2), 69–80.

Koegel, L. K., Koegel, R. L., Shoshan, Y., & McNerney, E. (1999). Pivotal response intervention II: Preliminary long-term outcome data. *Research and Practice for Persons with Severe Disabilities, 24*(3), 186–198.

Koegel, R. L., O'Dell, M., & Dunlap, G. (1988). Producing speech use in nonverbal autistic children by reinforcing attempts. *Journal of Autism and Developmental Disorders, 18*(4), 525–538.

Koegel, R. L., O'Dell, M. C., & Koegel, L. K. (1987). A natural language teaching paradigm for nonverbal autistic children. *Journal of Autism and Developmental Disorders, 17*(2), 187–200.

Koegel, R. L., Shirotova, L., & Koegel, L. K. (2009). Antecedent stimulus control: Using orienting cues to facilitate first-word acquisition for nonresponders with autism. *Behavior Analyst, 32*(2), 281.

Lovaas, O. I. (1966). A program for the establishment of speech in psychotic children. *Early childhood autism*, 115–144.

Lovaas, O. I. (1977). *The autistic child: Language development through behavior modification*. Irvington.

Lovaas, O. I. (2002). *Teaching individuals with developmental delays: Basic intervention techniques*. Austin, TX: PRO-ED.

Mitchell, S., Brian, J., Zwaigenbaum, L., Roberts, W., Szatmari, P., Smith, I., & Bryson, S. (2006). Early language and communication development of infants later diagnosed with autism spectrum disorder. *Journal of Developmental & Behavioral Pediatrics, 27*(2), S69–S78.

Nazzi, T., & Bertoncini, J. (2003). Before and after the vocabulary spurt: Two modes of word acquisition? *Developmental Science, 6*(2), 136–142.

Nevin, J. A., Mandell, C., & Atak, J. R. (1983). The analysis of behavioral momentum. *Journal of the Experimental Analysis of Behavior, 39*(1), 49–59.

Oswald, D. P., Haworth, S. M., Mackenzie, B. K., & Willis, J. H. (2017). Parental report of the diagnostic process and outcome: ASD compared with other developmental disabilities. *Focus on Autism and Other Developmental Disabilities, 32*(2), 152–160.

Ozonoff, S., Young, G. S., Carter, A., Messinger, D., Yirmiya, N., Zwaigenbaum, L., & Hutman, T. (2011). Recurrence risk for autism spectrum disorders: A Baby Siblings Research Consortium study. *Pediatrics, 128*(3), e488–e495.

Prizant, B. M. (1983). Language acquisition and communicative behavior in autism: Toward an understanding of the whole of it. *Journal of Speech and Hearing Disorders, 48*(3), 296–307.

Rogers, S. J., Hayden, D., Hepburn, S., Charlifue-Smith, R., Hall, T., & Hayes, A. (2006). Teaching young nonverbal children with autism useful speech: A pilot study of the Denver model and PROMPT interventions. *Journal of Autism and Developmental Disorders, 36*(8), 1007–1024.

Schreibman, L. (1988). *Autism.* Newbury Park, CA: Sage.

Steiner, A. M., Gengoux, G. W., Klin, A., & Chawarska, K. (2013). Pivotal response treatment for infants at-risk for autism spectrum disorders: A pilot study. *Journal of Autism and Developmental Disorders, 43*(1), 91–102.

Tager-Flusberg, H., Paul, R., Lord, C., Volkmar, F., Paul, R., & Klin, A. (2005). Language and communication in autism. *Handbook of Autism and Pervasive Developmental Disorders, 1,* 335–364.

Tsiouri, I., Simmons, E. S., & Paul, R. (2012). Enhancing the application and evaluation of a discrete trial intervention package for eliciting first words in preverbal preschoolers with ASD. *Journal of Autism and Developmental Disorders, 42*(7), 1281–1293.

Venter, A., Lord, C., & Schopler, E. (1992). A follow-up study of high-functioning autistic children. *Journal of Child Psychology and Psychiatry, 33*(3), 489–597.

Yoder, P. J., & Warren, S. F. (2002). Effects of prelinguistic milieu teaching and parent responsivity education on dyads involving children with intellectual disabilities. *Journal of Speech, Language, and Hearing Research, 45*(6), 1158–1174.

6

Expanding Friendship Opportunities for Children With ASD

Grace W. Gengoux and Laurie A. Vismara

CHAPTER GOALS

Goal 1. The reader will understand the potential benefits of stronger peer connections for children with autism spectrum disorders (ASD).

Goal 2. The reader will be able to discuss multiple contexts for peer interaction and ideas for parents and professionals to expand a child's social opportunities.

Goal 3. The reader will describe specific strategies to plan and carry out play dates between children with ASD and typically developing peers.

Goal 4. The reader will identify challenges that can occur when play dates are disorganized, last-minute, or unsupported.

Goal 5. The reader will discuss research outcomes from facilitating play dates between children with ASD and typically developing peers.

Goal 6. The reader will identify research questions for subsequent studies to improve friendship development between children with ASD and typically developing peers.

The purpose of this chapter is to guide the reader to work with parents, school personnel, and other providers to help them expand opportunities for children with ASD to develop peer relationships and make friends. We focus on concrete strategies that will lead to positive experiences with peers across contexts, with an emphasis on research-supported techniques. Parents of children with ASD are often concerned about their child's difficulties interacting and making friends with other children (Frankel, Gorospe, Chang, & Sugar, 2011). Most parents don't need their child to be a social butterfly or the center of attention at every occasion, but what they do want is for their child to be happy and to have friends. We recognize the individual differences that exist within the broad spectrum of autism and the natural variability that exists within different cultures, ethnic traditions, and family structures. For these reasons, the strategies discussed in this chapter have been used and tested with a wide variety of children and families to facilitate play dates and peer interactions. We also provide helpful recommendations through case examples, highlighting additional supports and resources for more difficult social situations. We hope readers use this chapter for information and suggestions for helping families to find new ways to arrange play dates and provide children with ASD with opportunities to engage and have fun with their peers. (Please note that although this chapter largely focuses on young children, many of the principles and strategies discussed are applicable through the elementary school years.)

BACKGROUND: POTENTIAL BENEFITS OF INTERVENTION

Why is it so important to expand friendship opportunities for children with ASD? Social relationships have long been recognized as a critical contributor to long-term well-being (Hartup & Stevens, 1997). For instance, relationships provide support and protection from the negative effects of stressful events (Burgess, Wojslawowicz, Rubin, Rose-Krasnor, & Booth-LaForce, 2006). As children grow, close friendships are also an important context for developing and refining various social skills (Buhrmester, 1990; Nelson & Aboud, 1985). However challenging this socialization may be, there are reasons parents of children with ASD can have great optimism for their children. First, research shows that interventions can both improve children's social skills and expand their social networks. Moreover, parents and service providers can play a significant role in helping children develop social skills, make friends, and develop a network of peers. Their early efforts can have a long-term impact.

The Impact of Intervention

The first reason for optimism is that new intervention strategies are remarkably effective at improving social skills and, more important, at creating opportunities for children to be more socially connected across contexts. One of the most exciting developments in social skills research is the evidence that brief interventions can change children's social networks. For example, several studies have shown the powerful effects when children with ASD participate in school contexts where providers (and importantly, peers) have been trained to support social development (e.g., Kasari, Rotheram-Fuller, Locke, & Gulsrud, 2012). An important randomized controlled trial demonstrated that by the end of a 6-week (12-session) peer-training program, many children with ASD had more central roles in classroom social networks, were more frequently nominated as friends by peers, and were less socially isolated on the playground. A related study, a "Remaking Recess" program, demonstrated that children with ASD showed greater peer engagement when paraprofessionals were provided with training to identify unengaged children on the playground, introduce motivating games and activities, and facilitate peer interactions (Kretzmann, Shih, & Kasari, 2015). Data such as these provide a great deal of hope that brief interventions provided in inclusive settings can have meaningful effects on relationships for children with ASD.

What Adults Can Do

Another reason for optimism is that parents and providers can actually do a lot to help a child who is struggling socially. Most typically developing children participate regularly in play dates outside of school, and these get-togethers are thought to be important for friendship development (Gottman, 1983). Parent involvement in setting up peer get-togethers is associated with children receiving more invitations from peers (Ladd, Hart, Wadsworth, & Golter, 1988). For children who struggle socially, parent involvement is an even more critical factor for successful relationship development (Frankel & Myatt, 2003). In fact, frequent hosting of play dates has even been associated with higher rates of peer interaction on the school playground (Frankel et al., 2011), and teacher prompting results in increased engagement between children with ASD and their peers (Chang, Shih, & Kasari, 2016). Additional important considerations for parents, care providers, and professionals are contained in the following sections.

Provide Inclusive Environments With Appropriate Support Parents and providers can facilitate peer network development and friendships by ensuring that children with ASD are around good potential friends. In 1999, Sigman and Ruskin found that children with ASD who have access to typically developing peers are more socially engaged than children in segregated settings. Inclusion has been shown to have many positive benefits for children with ASD (e.g., Grindle et al., 2012; Rafferty, Piscitelli & Boettcher, 2003; Strain & Bovey, 2011) and is critical for maximum social opportunities. In fact, even larger class size has also been associated with greater peer engagement on the playground, perhaps because of greater selection of peers and available activities (Locke, Williams, Shih, & Kasari, 2017).

However, inclusion alone is not enough to make sure children with ASD form meaningful relationships with peers (Kasari, Locke, Gulsrud, & Rotheram-Fuller, 2011; Koegel, Koegel, Frea, & Fredeen, 2001). Many show few peer-directed behaviors and are less socially engaged than other children in the same contexts (McConnell, 2002; McGee, Feldman, & Morrier, 1997). Creating opportunities for rewarding social interactions by well-trained facilitators is critical so that support enhances, rather than hinders, peer interaction (Anderson, Moore, Godfrey, & Fletcher-Flinn, 2004; Kasari et al., 2011; Koegel, Kim, & Koegel, 2014).

Distinguish Between Skill and Performance Deficits Another consideration when facilitating social interaction is the distinction between skill deficits and performance deficits (Gresham, 1981). A skill deficit is present when a child fails to perform the required behavior because a child doesn't have the behavior in his or her repertoire. A performance deficit, by contrast, is present when a child fails to perform the desired behavior for some other reason, such as lack of motivation, confidence, or interest, even though he or she is perfectly capable of using that skill in other contexts—for example, with adults or when playing his very favorite game. The basic PRT techniques described in other chapters of this book are great for teaching new skills, that is, fixing skills deficits. However, many children with ASD actually have substantial social skill *performance* deficits too, meaning they do not consistently use even those social skills they do have. A number of years ago, the authors of this book and colleagues completed a study comparing play date facilitation techniques, which showed clear benefit when mutually reinforcing activities and adult facilitation of cooperative arrangements were in place (Koegel, Werner, Vismara, & Koegel, 2005). In fact, we observed benefits in both reciprocal social interactions during play dates, as well as an overall increase in invitations from peers. Thus, with the right contextual supports, children with ASD can get practice engaging in appropriate social skills and become more comfortable and motivated during peer interactions.

Provide Contextually Supported Play Dates Readers might wonder what it means to provide "contextual supports" for social interactions. Put simply, these supports focus on two key principles:

1. Select mutually reinforcing activities, which must be activities that the child with ASD enjoys.
2. Structure play dates so that the completion or engagement in the activity requires the participation of both the child with ASD and his or her peer.

Textbox 6.1 describes a few simple examples of how adults might provide these contextual supports. More detailed examples are discussed in subsequent sections of this chapter.

Appeal to Children's Interests to Motivate Use of Social Skills Interest is essential for social development. That is, children with ASD learn and use social skills when they have a good reason for doing so. Without interest, the child's demonstration of a social skill is likely to depend indefinitely on adult prompts. Fun activities provide natural reinforcement for using social skills. Consider the difference between prompting a child to say "Hi" and prompting a child to ask for what he wants. The child may spontaneously demonstrate the first skill only rarely, due to minimal motivation, while the second skill may easily generalize because of the natural reinforcer he receives for the behavior. One of the most promising techniques for social facilitation comes from applying PRT naturalistic behavioral strategies of environmental arrangement and natural reinforcement. Just as adults can motivate children to request by maintaining shared control of desired items, social activities can be set up to motivate children to make requests from each other.

TEXTBOX 6.1. Examples of ways adults can provide contextual supports for children's social interactions

Providing Contextual Supports for Social Interaction

Example 1. The child with ASD enjoys making cookies, as does the peer. One child holds the cup, while the other child pours the sugar or other ingredients.

Example 2. The child with ASD and the peer enjoy swimming in the pool, but the former socially isolates himself. The children are taught to play the underwater telephone game.

Example 3. The child with ASD enjoys art, as does the peer. One child squeezes the glue, while the other child holds items for a collage.

In a pilot study of initiation training (Fredeen, 2005), these strategies were used to teach five children with ASD how to make requests (behavior regulation initiations) from peers during games. For instance, the clinician set up the game so the peer had control of the necessary pieces and then, if necessary, prompted the child with ASD to request a desired piece. The peers provided natural reinforcement within the game by giving the child what he asked for. The study showed that after 8 weeks, which included approximately 90 minutes of practice per week, children with ASD showed improvement in nontargeted initiations (social interaction and joint attention initiations). This is particularly exciting as these types of initiations have less tangible reinforcers and can be more difficult to teach. Thus research clearly suggests that behavioral contingencies can result in generalization of social interaction (Koegel, Kuriakose, Singh, & Koegel, 2012).

The gains evidenced when social initiations are taught using PRT strategies include the following:

- Increase in child-initiated play
- More verbal initiations to peers
- More sophisticated verbal initiations with peers
- Greater peer interest in the child with ASD
- More sophisticated verbal initiations from typically developing peers to the child with ASD

ASSESSING A CHILD'S SOCIAL OPPORTUNITIES

Before talking with parents about specific strategies for facilitating social development, encourage them to examine the settings where their child could practice social skills and to consider whether opportunities to improve social development could be provided. Use the following questions to help parents and other adults in the child's life identify ways to expand the child's social opportunities in different contexts:

- *School:* Does the child have regular opportunities to interact with typically developing children during the day? Are there adequate supports in place, especially during unstructured times like lunch and recess, to prompt and reinforce social interactions?
- *Community:* Does the child have ample opportunities to interact with other children and not just adults? If the child is participating in a social group, do peer models have strong social skills from which the child can learn? Is the child participating in extracurricular activities with competent peers?
- *Home:* Is the child having regular interaction with friends, neighbors, or classmates outside of school? Does the child get invited to birthday parties, get-togethers, or play dates? How often are you hosting other children for play dates at your home?

If the child needs more supports and opportunities in these settings, there are many procedures that families have found helpful in each type of context.

Expanding Social Opportunities at School

For children with ASD who are socially isolated even some of the time, it is important for the child's family to make sure that the educational team prioritizes social success. Children need strong social skills to be successful, and the skills they learn on the playground will help them be more successful during learning activities and in class. Much of classroom (and life) success relies on being able to interact effectively, problem-solve in a small group, and alternate between listening and speaking, leading and following. For parents whose child has significant social challenges, the first step is often to request an evaluation for eligibility for additional services; these can often be provided in the regular classroom with the child's peer group. Some schools may start the process with a student study team meeting or by considering a 504 plan, and many children with ASD will qualify for an individualized education program (IEP). Children age 3 and older may qualify for an IEP; children younger than age 3 who need specialized intervention may qualify for an individualized family services program or IFSP.

For a child who already has an IEP, make sure that the plan includes goals related to social development, including peer interaction. It is helpful to begin with data collection relating to how the child is actually interacting at school, especially during unstructured periods. For instance, many children with ASD need support to engage appropriately with peers during recess and lunchtime. Many times a child's paraprofessional needs specific training in how to facilitate peer interactions, and research shows such training can be quite effective and well accepted by school personnel (Kim, Koegel, & Koegel, 2017). Once motivation is assessed, the child can be prompted to appropriately request items and activities, ask questions, and engage in specialized activities developed around his interest or even a restricted interest.

The school setting is also a great place for identifying potential after-school friends. Teachers can often suggest compatible peers and families. In addition, parents may find it helpful to hang out in the parking lot before or after school to chat with other parents and learn about extracurricular activities their child may enjoy. It sometimes takes time to build friendships (even for adults), but these connections should help create more social opportunities. Eventually, as parents of a child with ASD build trust with fellow parents, they may be able to arrange carpools, spontaneous outings, and eventually regular play dates that will lead to friendships.

Expanding Social Opportunities in the Community

Another way families can enhance their child's chances of making peer connections is to involve the child in activities outside of school with similarly aged peers. This could be a music or gymnastics class, a Lego club, a sports team, or swim class. In accordance with PRT principles, it's best for parents to first consider the activities their child enjoys. An activity compatible with their child's interests will provide natural reinforcers. The child will be more likely to find compatible peers as well.

Sometimes children with ASD need extra adult support to participate in organized community or extracurricular activities, especially if the staff have minimal experience including children with special needs. When children are young, it may be appropriate for parents to accompany their children to these classes and help out. If that is not feasible, sometimes a babysitter or high school student helper can be taught the basic principles of social facilitation and can attend. If more support or programming is needed, families may choose to schedule these types of activities during times when a therapist with whom they are already working can attend. For the child who has primary deficits in peer social interaction, this can be quite a productive use of the therapist's time.

In your work with parents, encourage them to keep an eye out for children in the community who are getting along well with their child and for parents who look friendly and open to connecting, just as they would do at school. Many parents meet great potential friends (for themselves or for their children) by chatting on the sidelines while their children are taking a class, participating in a club, or playing a sport.

Expanding Social Opportunities at Home

A child's social opportunities may be expanded when parents host play dates for peers. Ideally, a play date would involve the children playing together, focusing on the same activity, and interacting back and forth—not just with the adult. A successful play date will have both children as valued members of the interaction and enjoying the time together. The problem is that without special planning, play dates are not always successful. Parents and providers need strategies for making play with peers more interactive, cooperative, and fun because this can make a big difference for a child's chances of making and keeping friends (Frankel, 2010). Remember, children who have friends see those friends outside of school; children who are still learning to make friends may not beg their parents for play dates as often as typically developing children do. Parents may need to encourage and assist with play dates at first (and make sure the play dates are so much fun that the child wants more and more)!

FIELD-TESTED STRATEGIES FOR EXPANDING FRIENDSHIP OPPORTUNITIES DURING PLAY DATES

Researchers at Stanford University explored group parent education in PRT (Minjarez, Williams, Mercier, & Hardan, 2011) to teach parents of children with ASD how to facilitate peer interactions and successful play dates. Eleven parents participated in a pilot project, which included approximately 10 parent education sessions focused on PRT strategies such as child choice, maintenance tasks, and natural reinforcement of attempts as they applied to play dates. We also taught specific step-by-step instructions.

Parents who completed a satisfaction survey after treatment reported finding the strategies useful, and all parents reported they would recommend the program to other parents of children with ASD. Many parents also felt more confidence setting up play dates and knowing how to make them fun and successful. When parents rated their children's social responsiveness after the program, there were improvements in social communication skills and social motivation. Of the eleven participating families in this program, nine reported at least some improvement in overall social responsiveness during the play dates. Though eight of the eleven parents rated their children's social responsiveness as severe at baseline, four of these parents reported their child's skills in the mild–moderate range following treatment. One parent who rated her child's skills in the mild–moderate range at baseline reported improvement into the normal range by post-treatment. These preliminary data show that parents can make a big difference at home in their child's social development and peer relationships. What follows are step-by step instructions based on our pilot studies and experience helping families set up successful play dates. These instructions explain in depth how to 1) pick compatible peers, 2) prepare by planning a fun activity in advance, 3) facilitate cooperative arrangements, and 4) learn from what worked (and what didn't) to troubleshoot and improve the next time.

Step 1: Pick the Right Peers

Many times, the trickiest part of planning a play date is figuring out who to invite. Some children with ASD have very few peer connections (Chang et al., 2016). Other children have peers who are potential friends, but those children are over-scheduled. We discuss common questions about the ideal playmate, but remember, some practice with socializing is probably better than no practice at all. Practitioners working with families on this issue should advise parents to start with what they can manage. When they review the child's first play date, they will be able to decide if that peer match was workable enough for next time or if they need to make a change.

If parents are struggling to figure out playmates for their child, recommend that they ask the child's teacher for ideas about children who get along well with their child at school. They should also consider children who attend extracurricular activities with their child, live in their neighborhood, or play at the park they typically visit. Parents just meeting another family for the first time may not be able to invite them over right away, but if the kids are having fun together, the families could plan another meet-up at the same park the following week. If parents find it too difficult or awkward to approach a stranger at first, they might consider whether their child has cousins who live nearby or an old friend with a son or daughter of the same age. Encourage parents to rely on their social networks, if necessary. Emphasize that children with ASD who have friends are often the ones with parents who helped a lot initially. Once the family can initiate some positive peer interactions, more opportunities tend to open up.

If a child already has several play partners, the family can arrange play dates with them, but parents will also want to evaluate how compatible these playmates are based on the following characteristics: social skills, age, gender, and interests.

Social Skills Our experience working with families tells us that children with ASD learn social skills best from other children who themselves are socially skilled, talkative, and flexible. Though children with ASD often enjoy friendships with other children who have social disabilities, it can be frustrating to try to practice new social skills with a partner who doesn't respond consistently. Even if families do not yet know any potential playmates for their child, they can make it a goal to find typically developing peers to invite for play dates so their child gets practice interacting with children who model appropriate social behaviors.

Age Sometimes families may want to consider the age of the potential playmate. Children with ASD may find it easier to interact with younger children who follow their agenda more readily or with older children who may lead the interaction more decisively. If their child already has a friend a few years older or younger, families may want to start with that friend but also make a point to plan some get-togethers with children closer to their child's age. That way, the child can improve the reciprocity skills required for same-age interactions.

Gender The family's goal in fostering their child's social development should be to give their child the skills to interact with both boys and girls. It is normal for young children to play with both. As children enter the elementary school years, many tend to play in same-gender groups. If parents notice their child plays exclusively with peers of one gender, they can try to figure out why that might be easier for him or her. For example, is it because a certain female classmate shows more patience and enjoys adult attention, which makes her a good match for their child's temperament and also makes it more likely the children will receive help from an adult facilitator? Or does the child's enjoyment of physical games make the male classmates who enjoy the same kind of play a better match for the child's high energy?

Interests Some children enjoy a wide variety of games and activities and like to try new things; others have more narrow interests or prefer familiarity. When parents are selecting peers, suggest that they find children who share some of their child's specific interests or at least are eager to try new things the child enjoys. If the child's interests are very narrow, parents may not be able to find a perfect match, but they can have success with children who share interests in the same general category (Koegel, Bradshaw, Ashbaugh, & Koegel, 2014). For instance, maybe their child loves trains. Children who like other vehicles, or enjoy constructing with Legos, manga tiles, or cardboard, may be compatible. Maybe a child loves playing with pretend food items; if so, children who enjoy fantasy play with dress-up clothes, tea sets, and doll houses may be compatible. If a child loves leaves and sticks, peers who like collecting bugs, building in the sand box, or climbing trees may be compatible.

"What If They Say 'No'?": Helping Families Address Potential Obstacles

If a family is not having much luck identifying available playmates for their child, it's time to try to understand what might be interfering. Try your best to help the parents understand what factors may be getting in the way, and develop a strategy to handle the issue.

First off, remind parents that many children these days have packed schedules. They may need to plan a play date a week or more in advance to get it on the other family's calendar. Families with working parents may not have time on weekdays for anything more than dinner and baths before bed. Encourage parents to consider planning weekend get-togethers or offering to pick the peer up from school so the other parent doesn't have to rush to leave work. Think of other ways parents can make play dates a convenience for the other family. This may result in more positive responses to invitations.

Some parents may say "no" to a play invitation because of uncertainty about the child with ASD's behaviors. Every family handles the question of how and when to disclose the ASD diagnosis differently, and there may be no one "right" way to handle this sensitive issue. Regardless of what parents decide is best for their own family, remind them that other parents will be most comfortable if obvious behaviors are acknowledged. If a child has atypical behaviors and his or her parents seem unaware of them, then other parents might be unsure of how to respond or wonder how conscientiously play dates will be supervised.

It is actually pretty easy for families of a child with ASD to show awareness of obvious behaviors without disclosing more than they want to about the child's diagnosis. For instance, suggest to parents that they acknowledge their child's behaviors with remarks such as, "It's okay, Mike just makes that noise sometimes when he gets really excited about something," or "Don't worry, sometimes Sarah doesn't hear kids talking the first time. You might need to go closer or say it again." Parents may direct these remarks to the other parents or directly to their child's peer if they are more comfortable with that approach. These comments help the other parent and peer understand the child's behavior and use strategies for successfully interacting.

Step 2: Prepare

The key to successful play dates is to find an activity or activities that all the participating children will enjoy. In choosing activities for play dates, we know of several active ingredients that have been shown to promote the likelihood of fun and success for children with ASD and their typical peers (Koegel et al., 2005; Werner, Vismara, Koegel, & Koegel, 2006). Play dates are more likely to maintain group attention, interest, and enthusiasm when activities are fun, structured, organized, cooperative, familiar, and short and sweet. These characteristics of successful play date activities are further explained below.

Choose Fun Activities When something is mutually reinforcing to the people involved, it means that everyone finds the experience rewarding, enjoyable, and satisfying to their needs. Such an outcome makes it highly likely that the people will repeat the activity or event in order to experience the positive consequences. The same logic can apply to play dates. When a play date is mutually reinforcing to both children, they are likely to want to see and play with each other again. For children with ASD, this motivation to participate is especially important so that they continue to feel excited and driven to engage and interact with their peers.

Research has shown that children demonstrate increased social engagement when activities incorporate their interests (Koegel, Vernon, Koegel, Koegel, & Paullin, 2012; Wolfberg, DeWitt, Young, & Nguyen, 2015). Select activities based on the interests of the child with ASD as well as the peer's. What does each like and do their respective lists include any common interests or areas for overlap? Families can gather this information by talking to the other child's parents, as well as asking teachers, aides or paraprofessionals, and the children themselves about the preferred activities they may share. Another idea is to search online for play date or activity ideas based on children's mutual interests, as well as options available in that city or neighborhood. Sometimes this uncovers new ideas. Here are some activity ideas that have made memorable play dates from our experience:

Cook something. If the children like cooking, the family can give the children a ball of pizza dough and toppings to have a pizza-making party; they can make and/or decorate cupcakes, cookies, a gingerbread house, muffins, or scones.

Mix something up. If the children like measuring, the parents can help them make play slime, play dough, or kid-friendly paint. If they run out of ideas, they can search online for "Do It Yourself" home and science experiments for kids.

Make art with recycled materials. If the children enjoy art, parents can try these activities:

- Cut one end of a cardboard toilet paper or paper towel roll into strips so that it is frayed, and dip it into different colors of paint to decorate a paper plate or paper (or with glue and glitter).
- Cut off one row of an egg carton all in one piece, paint each section (where an egg goes) the same or different color, and glue on googly eyes and pipe cleaners for antennas and legs to make a caterpillar.
- Cut an egg carton into individual sections; paint and glue a pom-pom for a head, along with googly eyes, and add pipe cleaners for legs to make a turtle.

Build something. If the children enjoy constructing, the family can try these activities:

- Connect Legos or PVC tubes and connectors in the backyard, then connect the tubes to the hose to see how the water flows and sprays in different directions.
- Fill a glass or clear plastic jar with water, dish soap, 1–2 drops of food coloring, and vinegar, then swirl ingredients around to make a "tornado in a bottle."
- Build a sensory ball in a few fun steps. First, add polymer beads to a bowl with water. After 15 minutes, transfer the mixture to a 16.9-ounce water bottle filled halfway with water. Blow up a balloon about halfway, and stretch the end of the balloon over the water bottle. Next, squeeze the water bottle to get the beads inside the balloon along with the water. Let some (not all) of the air and water out of the balloon until the sensory ball is the desired shape and size.

Get outside. If the children prefer the outdoors, the family can make a game of items or objects to find or collect while taking a walk, riding a bike, rollerblading, or doing any other outdoor physical activity. It can be a themed treasure hunt using the children's interests for extra incentive.

Go somewhere. Parents should consider their child's special interests when deciding on places to go (museums, botanical gardens, history centers, zoo). Many include interactive exhibits built specifically for children to explore and learn about the topics.

Keep Play Dates Structured and Organized It is important to resist the temptation to invite a child over and "just see how it goes." Parents are more likely to maximize success when they plan at least a few specific activities that differ from their child's everyday routine and are interesting to the peer(s). A well-defined activity teaches both children what is expected and how to participate fully in the play. Parents may have noticed on prior play dates how easily their child may get discouraged or lose motivation to engage when the activity is not clearly defined and the children are just "hanging out." Unstructured time can be the most difficult type of social context for most children with ASD (Gengoux, 2015). The more clarity, consistency, and predictability the activity can provide, the more likely a child with ASD can participate with independence and make meaningful contributions equal to those of his or her peer(s). The structure gives a theme or purpose to the activity to encourage back-and-forth participation between the child and peer(s).

When planning play activities, parents should keep in mind that some activities may require the children to wait before the next step can occur. Too much waiting can disrupt the social momentum the adults are trying to maintain between the children and can result in boredom or dissatisfaction with the interaction. Consider some suggestions to avoid or work through these situations. For example, baking can be a fun activity that children enjoy doing together, especially when it is time to eat the delicious treats! However, baking involves some period of waiting if ingredients need to refrigerate, cook, and/or cool off. For children who may have trouble waiting, parents might buy or bake the treats beforehand and have the children decorate them. Lots of interaction and conversation can still happen around what the child and peer will use to decorate as well as how they will decorate their treats. If the wait time cannot be avoided, a different technique is to stay busy with another activity until the first activity can resume. It might be something as simple as the child and peer playing a board game or completing the next set of tasks related to the current activity (e.g., washing the mixing bowls, setting out the decorations). This time can provide an opportunity for the child to practice newly learned specific skills (e.g., showing his room to the peer, asking questions to start conversation, responding on topic to keep conversation going).

Sometimes children naturally lose interest or finish an activity sooner than expected. It's always a good idea to prepare a few back-up activities in case problems occur with the first choice. Parents should make sure the child with ASD is familiar with, enjoys, and knows how to do these other activities.

Support Cooperative Activities The quality of interaction will be better if families can find ways to support cooperation during the play date (Werner et al., 2006). When children are cooperating, it means they are sharing materials and ideas. To enhance cooperation, parents will need to set up situations in which children can share materials (this is pretty easy to do) and, if possible, ideas. One way to do this is to prompt the child with ASD to initiate a request (Fredeen, 2005). The reason this distribution of materials works so well is that child will be motivated to ask for the item from the peer, and when the peer responds, the child receives natural reinforcement for initiating. This is ideal because, with minimal prompting, the child is getting practice with one of the most difficult social skills, initiations. Furthermore, if the initiation is effective, the child is likely to do it again even without an adult prompting him. In addition, when a child with ASD is taught to initiate requests, collateral gains such as improvements in social engagement and joint attention result (Fredeen, 2005). If your child feels more confidence in requesting items from peers, he will be more motivated to make other kinds of initiations and appropriately engage more frequently.

Through trial and error, we have found that certain activities lend themselves very well to cooperation. For instance, games with multiple pieces or rules related to turn-taking help a lot. We outline specific strategies for cooperative arrangements in Step 3, Keep It Cooperative.

Ensure Play Date Activities Are Familiar Many children with ASD have an easier time socializing when they are familiar with the activity. For this reason, it is often quite helpful for the family to introduce the selected activity to the child with ASD before the play date occurs. Priming familiarizes the child with what will happen inside the activity and gives the child the opportunity to practice the steps and actions involved in a nondemanding way (Zanolli, Daggett, & Adams, 1996). Many times, the mere chance to get to know an activity in advance actually increases interest and enthusiasm to participate and ends up turning the new activity into a favorite choice. For more information, see the example at the end of this chapter about using priming during extracurricular activities.

Make Play Dates Short and Sweet A final key aspect of preparation is planning how to conclude the play date. Suggest to parents that they consider arranging drop-off and pick-up times beforehand with the other parent(s) as another helpful step in planning. Having the child or peer be picked up right after finishing the activity helps to avoid down-time and prevents the children from becoming bored. The play date should end on a positive note with both children wanting to play again. Having some tears or frustration because the children want the activity to last longer is a much better problem than their not wanting another play date!

Even with all of these ideas, it can be hard to predict what will work for a particular child. Remind the family that play dates do not have to be perfect. The more they try, the more they will learn what works. The goal is to keep trying ideas and building or expanding the child's interests so that planning play dates becomes easier and it becomes more likely that children will have interests in common.

Step 3: Keep It Cooperative

Once parents have chosen a great activity (or a few) and the children have arrived, the parents' job is to keep the interaction going throughout the play date by setting up repeated opportunities for cooperation. Almost any activity can be modified to enhance cooperation between children. Remember, even though parents may have to prompt interaction at first, if they establish cooperative arrangements, the children will eventually interact with each other without prompting because their enjoyment of the activity will depend on it. The sections that follow describe how to set up cooperative arrangements initially and ensure they are ongoing throughout the play date.

Initial Cooperative Arrangements Consider the following contrasting examples that illustrate how a parent can choose to use cooperative arrangements to enhance interactions naturally.

Scenario 1: Typical snacktime. Suppose the parent plans to give the children a snack because they look hungry after playing so hard outside. The parent could tell the children it's snack time, bring them into the kitchen, and set an individual snack down in front of each child. To keep interaction going, he or she could ask the children about what they were doing outside or (for older children) ask about their weekend plans. The children would likely enjoy the snack and answer the adult's questions.

Scenario 2: "Make your friend's nachos." Now let's imagine that same situation with cooperative arrangements. When the children come in from outside, the parent announces that the snack for the day is "make-your-friend's nachos." (Remember, activities—even snacks—with multiple pieces will make cooperative arrangements easier.) The adult puts one child in charge of the chips, salsa, and olives and the other child in charge of the cheese, guacamole, and beans. Next, the adult explains that the children will each make a plate of nachos for their friend by asking what the friend wants on his or her plate and following the friend's instructions. The parent can help the children decide who will go first to make the snack, considering which child is most motivated by the food or will have the hardest time waiting. If necessary, the parent can prompt the child with ASD to ask, "How many chips do you want?" "How much cheese?" "Do you want olives or guacamole?" "Does this look good?" and to respond to the peer's instructions. Next, when it is the child's turn to direct the making of his or her nachos, parents can help the child not just respond to the peer's questions but also initiate requests by saying things such as, "That's enough chips," "Could you put some more cheese?" "I don't want any salsa," "Can I have three more olives?" and so on. The child might even be motivated enough to say, "Thank you" right before receiving the yummy snack. Keep in mind that if the children each have access to only some of the ingredients, when they want seconds it will seem obvious to ask the peer for the other ingredients. Parents can prompt if necessary, making their prompts increasingly subtle as the children show initiative to interact on their own.

The previous example illustrates how setting up an activity with shared control of the materials can encourage cooperation. The chapter authors use this quite a lot on play dates. Parents can even tell children to bring favorite items from home to a play date. For instance, they might consider asking the children to each bring their favorite costumes, action figures, ice cream toppings, or sand toys. If they do, the children will have an immediate excuse for interaction upon arrival, especially if the children have brought enough to share with friends.

Another way to set up initial cooperative arrangements is to embed cooperation within the structure or rules of the game or activity. For instance, in our practice we sometimes play games like Buddy Freeze Tag, in which the children need a buddy to "un-freeze" them—creating an immediate reason for interaction and communication. Similarly, in Buddy Red Light/Green Light, the children hold hands or interlock elbows and have to move together to win the game. Adults can modify the rules of existing games as much as the children will tolerate to make cooperation part of the way the game is played. It is important to think about whether the children will have more reasons to interact and cooperate if they are actually playing on the same team. For instance, once when the authors were playing Pictionary with children on a play date, we decided to put the two children on the same team playing against an adult. This arrangement actually helped them have more reasons to interact (deciding what to draw and how to give clues). Working together to "beat" the adult added an extra boost to their developing friendship.

Parents or other adults can also design activities around a child's special interest. One child we worked with loved mazes, so we set up an activity that involved creating a giant maze. Another loved sharks, so we tried to incorporate sea-creature themes across activities (a bingo game, treasure hunt, baking projects). An early study of this technique showed the benefit of structuring social games to involve the expertise of children with ASD (Baker, Koegel, & Koegel, 1998). In this study, the researchers saw that one child knew all the states and capitals in the United States and designed a tag game played on a giant outline of a U.S. map painted on the school's blacktop. (Incorporating a child's restricted interests in designing group activities for peers is discussed in detail in Chapter 12; interest clubs can be a great way to engage older children, teens, and adults around topics of high interest.)

Ongoing Cooperative Arrangements Ongoing cooperative arrangements are also a great way to enhance cooperation once the play date is already in full swing. The trick to success is to get good at predicting what each child is likely to want next. Here are a few examples to illustrate the point.

Facilitate Requesting and Offering Play Materials Suppose a family of a child with ASD invites a few children over who love to play with play dough. The parents have already set up a great initial activity, making play dough. They had success with cooperation by putting one of the peers who can read well in charge of the instructions and the other children in charge of the ingredients (flour, salt, oil, etc.). With some prompting, they got the children to ask questions like "How much flour do I put in?" "Can you measure 1 cup of salt for me?" "Can I take a turn stirring?" "Should we make it red or blue?" The child with ASD even said "I want more play dough" spontaneously to his peer when requesting the finished product. Now the children are happily playing with the play dough, but the parents have noticed that without an excuse for cooperation, the interaction has died down. They need a new strategy for promoting cooperation.

Scenario 1: Facilitate making requests. First, parents can watch what the children are doing with the play dough and try to predict what their child will do next. If they can figure out what the child will do next, they can make sure he or she needs something that a peer has. This will motivate the child to interact. For instance, let's say the parents see their child using a rolling pin to flatten the play dough. They could predict that next, he or she might want to use a cookie cutter or play dough knife to cut out a shape. They can then make sure the peers have the desired item(s)—if necessary, discreetly moving the items over next to the peer—and then prompt their child to look around and ask for what he or she wants. Another helpful strategy is for children with ASD to request desired items from peers (e.g., asking for the scissors, more play dough, a specific cookie cutter). Not only do the opportunities strengthen children's communication with peers, they also motivate children to want to attend to peers and stay involved in the activities.

Scenario 2: Facilitate making offers. When children are doing well making requests of peers, they may be ready to initiate in a slightly more complicated way by asking the peer if he or she wants something the child has. The natural reinforcer for this behavior is not as direct (which makes it harder and less motivating for some children). If parents think their child is motivated enough by the interaction and the overall activity to respond to a few prompts for this more advanced skill, they can go ahead and try it. For example, they could give the cookie cutters to the child with ASD and prompt him or her to offer them at the moment the peer finishes rolling play dough: "Which cutter do you want?" Parents could also watch what the peer is doing and try to predict what he or she may need next. For instance, suppose parents notice a peer rolling out letters to spell his name. They know the last letter of his name, so they could encourage their child to make an E (for instance) and offer it to the peer just as he is finishing the name: "Do you want an E?"

Facilitate Expanding Comments and Conversations We have found that the best way to enhance comments and conversations is to create a motivating context with plenty of cooperation. Following are some ways that adults can help spark conversations. Remember, though, just prompting children to talk will not have the same beneficial long-term effect as creating a context in which they are motivated and initiate these acts on their own and receive natural reinforcement for doing so. Self-management is also a strategy that can be helpful for enhancing conversation skills (Koegel, Park, & Koegel, 2014). This strategy is discussed in Chapter 10.

The following example illustrates how parents (or other adults) can expand social conversation by first getting the children to join in a common play theme (making faces with their snack materials) and then using subtle prompts to suggest ways the topic could be expanded.

Scenario: Facilitate expanding a conversation topic. After their fun afternoon working with play dough, the children are now eating a snack. One of the parents suggests (by whispering to one of the peers) that the children make faces out of their snack materials. The peer then suggests, "Hey, let's make faces with our snacks." The children look like they like the idea but still don't seem to be talking much. The parent prompts the children to talk about their plans by saying, "I wonder what you guys are going to do for making mouths." One peer offers, "I'm going to make my mouth with raisins." If the child with ASD doesn't make a similar comment, the parent could suggest that the peer that ask the child about his or her plans: "What are you going to use?" Some children may even be able to have conversations about past or future events, for example, "One time I made a face out of sticks and leaves in my yard," or, "Next time we get together, let's make pizza faces." Parents can hint at these topics by saying things like, "I wonder if any of you have ever made silly faces like this before?" or "Would it be fun to do another kind of face next time?" If the adult can manage to say these things in subtle way—that is, in a quiet tone, while seeming to walk off to get more ingredients—the children may take the hint but direct their comments to each other (which is ideal) rather than to the adult. If parents have tried this but their child still seems to need heavy prompting or clear reinforcement to practice comments, they can always take advantage of the final moments before the child eats the snack he or she created (the tangible natural reinforcer for participating in the conversation) and prompt him to show his snack creation to the peers before eating ("Look how silly my rice-cake face looks"). Parents can also introduce the idea to the children by taking a turn to do this with their own snack items, should more support be necessary in the beginning.

Step 4: Review and Recycle

Once the play date is over (and parents have had a chance to catch their breath), they can reflect on how it went for both (or all) children, as well as for the parent(s). Some questions for parents to consider are as follows:

- Was the peer I selected a good match for my child (considering age, social functioning, flexibility, interests)?
- Did the play date end at the right time, while both children were still interacting and having fun with each other?

- Did the choice of activity encourage enough opportunities for interaction and communication to occur between the children?
- Did the child with ASD know how to participate and help the peer (if opportunity developed) in the activity?
- Was the parent (as the adult facilitator) able to direct children's interaction and communication toward one another and not just through the parent?
- Did the parent (facilitator) have back-up activities planned?
- Was the parent (facilitator) sensitive and aware of both (or all) children's moods?
- Was the play date a positive, enjoyable experience for the children?
- Was the play date a positive, enjoyable experience for the parent?

If the parent(s) answered "No" to any of these questions, then the next step is to determine which component(s) of the play date to add, take away, or adapt before the next one. Sometimes it is tempting to make spontaneous choices in the middle of a play date, such as continuing it beyond the planned activity or trying an activity unfamiliar to the child with ASD. Keep in mind, however, the importance of sticking to the plan for both children's benefit. It takes time for children to get to know and feel comfortable with each other and to build friendships. Parents should let the children first develop the rapport, relationship, and positive experiences from which friendship grows and then consider extending play dates or making activities more spontaneous or complex. Remind parents that at the end of the day, they should try not to feel discouraged or disappointed by anything that happened. These are opportunities for all children to improve their social, communication, and play skills; to learn important lessons of sharing, conflict resolution, and emotional regulation; and to facilitate friendships. Parents may wish to talk with the child with ASD (and perhaps the parents of the peer) about what they learned from the children and the play date, if possible. Then parents can plan ahead for what to keep the same and what to do differently next time.

BEYOND PLAY DATES: EXPANDING FRIENDSHIP OPPORTUNITIES ACROSS SETTINGS

Similar to play dates at home, the strategies discussed in this chapter can also promote social interaction and friendships in other social settings. The authors have had the privilege of being involved in a number of inclusive group programs. Following are some examples from our work at Stanford and Early Emory (formerly known as the Walden Early Childhood Center) to further illustrate how these strategies can be used across a variety of contexts.

Toddler Group Play in Educational Settings

With toddlers in a playgroup program, the key is to keep the activities simple and fun to encourage social-communicative exchanges and interaction. When preparing each activity, the teacher will want to take time to organize and adapt materials and think through a lesson plan for turn-taking, sharing, co-construction, showing, imitating, or other cooperative arrangements to occur between the children.

The arrangement of the classroom space is also important to children's learning. Other materials or toys unrelated to the designated learning activities are put away or out of access to avoid distractions and to support children's attention to the choice of activities available to them. Each learning activity is set up in a specific spot in the room, using child-sized furniture to help demarcate its space and boundaries. For example, play dough is at the table in one corner of the room, musical instruments and songs on the colorful carpet in the opposite corner, and a sleeve of books with beanbags in another corner. Paying attention is the first step to becoming motivated to do something, and it starts with the way in which materials and the activities unfold. Once children choose their preferred activity, the teacher involves the children to set up the activity, thereby facilitating social-communication opportunities right at the start. Children tell, or point to, which color paint they want in the clear plastic container in the middle of the table, or they say or point to which musical instrument they want in the bag in the middle of the group circle. More learning opportunities can be embedded in the set-up based upon children's familiarity with the activity and motivation to participate. Examples include choosing other paint colors or tools to use to make a picture, choosing the song to sing from pictures on a poster board, or choosing which book to read first and who is going to read the page.

Next, children can engage in the activity as a large group or in pairs, depending on the play theme and materials. Children can collectively make one large collage, adding their own color to the masterpiece, or materials can be shared in pairs as children work on individual projects (e.g., a paint brush, roller, glitter, cars to roll through the paint, animals to make footprints on it). For large group activities, such as singing songs or reading books, children can still have individual moments to participate. A child can fill in the word, verse, or action to a song or have a musical solo to shake or play his or her musical instrument. Alternatively, a child can touch, point, or name a picture on a page. Pictures of a character, object, or action can be photocopied and laminated for the child to match to where it goes on the page. Children can also act out actions or scenes on the page, individually or with partners or props (e.g., puppets, toys, clothes). Children who already know, or especially like, a particular song or story can help the teacher lead the group activity.

Once it is time to end the activity, the teacher can just as easily work opportunities for engagement and learning into cleaning up the materials. Children can choose their role and/or partner to clean up with, or the act itself can be turned into a game (e.g., "Put away something blue," "Find something with bells and put it in the bag," "If your partner is Sammy, put away your toys").

Generally speaking, the more motivated the child is to engage in the activity, the more he or she will want to participate in the steps leading up to it. Don't forget, though, that the reward still has to match the effort! If the child is still learning how to use a particular behavior, then the child at first exerts more attention, thinking, and effort to carry out the skill before it becomes automatic through practice. Teachers should make sure the child enjoys the fruit of his or her labor before going on to the next learning moment and should be mindful of whether the child is motivated and ready to tackle another new behavior or one or two already developed skills in his or her repertoire. Letting a child practice behaviors he or she can already do is not taking a step backward in the child's ability to learn.

If anything, the practice continues to strengthen the behavior and maintain it in the child's skill set, and it promotes confidence.

Group Activities in School Classrooms and Social Skills Groups

In school settings, teachers can design group activities to incorporate the interests of a child with ASD. This will help promote cooperative interactions. These same techniques can easily be used in social skills groups. Depending on the complexity of the child's interest and cognitive skill, teachers can develop simple or elaborate schemes for incorporating the child's interests. We remember one child who came to class every day and immediately went over to the play cupboard and grabbed as many plastic fish from one of the board games as he could. The teachers realized that they could motivate that child to complete class lessons and interact with peers if the children at his small group table were holding plastic fish. Another classroom included a child who loved elevators. Luckily, quite a few of the other children were interested in related topics such as building, how machines work, and travel/transportation. The teacher could incorporate the topic of elevators into quite a few lessons that provided opportunities for the child with ASD to make valuable contributions to the classroom activities.

Sometimes children with ASD have advanced knowledge about a particular topic, such as the solar system. Games and classroom activities can be designed around these special areas of interest to capitalize on the child's expertise and create cooperation. We did this in one classroom by designing a bingo-like game in which children drew names of different planets and had to match them with the pictures of planets on their bingo cards. All of the children learned about the solar system, and the child with ASD stayed engaged much longer than he typically did. Teachers can think about how the lessons they want to teach may relate to the interests of any child in their class with ASD. If possible, teachers can set up the lesson so the child with ASD can serve as an expert on the topic. This creates a natural cooperative arrangement in which the child with ASD will get practice interacting socially, while the peers are learning new information.

Cooperation in Extracurricular Activities and Summer Camps

Program directors for children's activities can also have a strong role in creating environments that promote cooperation. Parents of a child with ASD can ask for cooperation to be built into extracurricular programs their child attends. Many benefits can result when the people planning group activities take the child's interests and needs into account. For instance, suppose a craft activity is planned for the day. If the program leaders decide to deliberately limit the number of scissors on the tables, the children will have a reason to interact when they need scissors that another child is using. Teachers or program directors can also arrange cooperative activities. For instance, instead of making individual collages, children can be instructed to work with a buddy to decide together what pictures to cut out and paste on their paper. A teacher can encourage socialization during a small group task by putting one peer in charge of the magazines, one in charge of the cutting, one in charge of the glue, and one in charge of deciding where to place the pictures on a large poster board. In this way, the children have practice with each of the following skills:

- Initiating actions (e.g., "Can you cut out the puppy picture?" "We're gonna need more glue for this one," "Should I put the tree in the top corner or bottom corner?")
- Responding to peers' suggestions (e.g., "First I'm going to cut out this big fish," "Here's more glue," "No, let's just put one tree")
- Working together toward a common goal

Another great strategy that can be easily applied in summer camps, extracurricular settings, and schools is priming. Priming is the practice of exposing a child to an upcoming activity in advance, in way that is a high-reinforcement (fun) and low-demand (easy). The authors of this chapter studied this strategy with four children with ASD with mild support needs who were struggling with peer interactions (Gengoux, 2015). We found that when children with ASD participated in games and activities for brief (10-minute) priming sessions the previous day, they used more initiations and statements reflecting competence when that same activity was introduced in their summer camp setting the next day, without the need for an interventionist during the actual activity. In contrast, when the children had not had priming, they generally spent their unstructured times alone. In addition, the children with ASD also showed improvements in happiness, interest, and comfort when they were primed. Perhaps most important, their peers engaged significantly more frequently, asked more questions, and made more positive statements about that child's competence in the activity when the child with ASD had familiarity with the game. It's a little surprising that just 10 minutes of practice the day before could help a child with ASD initiate an activity, without prompting, the very next day, but this strategy is definitely worth a try. Children (and adults, for that matter) are more motivated to do things they are good at. In our experience, the confidence boost can be quite dramatic when a child sees a familiar activity and thinks, "I know how to play that game!"

Key Insights ||| Expanding Friendship Opportunities

Creating social opportunities for children with ASD across settings is critical. The more children have an opportunity to practice social skills with peers, the stronger these skills will get. Parents, teachers, services providers, and practitioners should keep the following points in mind:

- **Use intervention strategies when teaching social skills:** Although access to peers is important, it is really not enough if not accompanied by systematic, evidence-based interventions.
- **Understand that adults play an important role:** Parents and providers can do a lot to help improve a child's chances of having interactions with peers that are truly enjoyable and making friends. In this chapter, we discuss ways in which adults can support a child's social relationships, with a special focus on setting up successful play dates.
- **Adults should prepare thoroughly for play date activities to ensure they are fun, high-interest, cooperative, and familiar:** For instance, any time you

are aiming to enhance peer interactions, having a fun activity that is of high interest to the child with ASD will be of utmost importance. Also, figuring out a way to engineer cooperation into any peer activity and practicing or preparing the child with ASD ahead of the activity will help support positive social behaviors and reciprocity.

SUMMARY

Researchers have referred to friendship as a relationship providing companionship, mutual support, and affection (cf., Freeman & Kasari, 1998). Friendships require understanding and perception of what another person is feeling. Interpersonal skills are necessary to be a good listener; to be open, honest, and willing to share information; to have fun; to help each other when there is a need; and to express and exchange ideas, feelings, and thoughts. These skills can be challenging but are certainly not impossible to teach children with ASD (Kasari, Chamberlain, & Bauminger, 2001; Kasari & Sigman, 1996). Although research in the area of socialization is still sorely needed, we routinely hear parents' frustrations and concerns that their child has no social program and no or few social goals on their IEPs. Socialization is a challenge for all children with ASD, and active, multi-component interventions should be a part of every child's program.

Active efforts of parents, family members, teachers, service providers, and other autism advocates can make dramatic improvements in the social abilities and networking skills of children with ASD. Also important to keep in mind is the wide range of levels of social involvement. Not every child with or without a developmental disability needs or wants to be the life of the party. Some children may be satisfied by the reciprocal support they receive from a limited number of friendships. We may need to rethink or expand our concept of friendship to consider what will be beneficial for each child as an individual (Chamberlain, Kasari, & Rotheram-Fuller, 2007). Wherever the child falls on the sociability scale, the goal of acceptance and integration with peers will help protect children from social isolation. By identifying and lending support, parents, educators, and clinicians can help create a context for children with ASD to understand themselves in relation to their peers and encourage their active participation in making friends.

STUDY QUESTIONS

1. Describe the challenges that can interfere with friendship development for children with ASD.
2. What might be an appropriate first step for a child who has few peer interactions at school?
3. Describe the play date intervention package for promoting positive social experiences between children with ASD and their typically developing peers.
4. What can the adult do as the facilitator in the play date to encourage but not overly prompt social interaction between children with ASD and typically developing peers?

5. How could the play date intervention package apply to other social/natural settings and with other adult partners to promote existing and new friendships?
6. How is motivation addressed for both children with ASD and their peers when planning a play date?
7. What are important red flags to be aware of during a play date?
8. Describe a potential play date activity and socialization techniques used with two children (one with ASD and one with typical development) who both like science.
9. Discuss the impact that play dates can have on other aspects of social interaction and development for children with ASD.
10. What do you think is the most important next step for research on expanding the social networks for children with disabilities?

REFERENCES

Anderson, A., Moore, D. W., Godfrey, R., & Fletcher-Flinn, C. M. (2004). Social skills assessment of children with autism in freeplay situations. *Autism, 8,* 369–385.

Baker, M. J., Koegel, R. L., & Koegel, L. K. (1998). Increasing the social behavior of young children with autism using their obsessive behaviors. *Journal of the Association of Persons with Severe Handicaps, 23,* 300–308.

Buhrmester, D. (1990). Intimacy of friendship, interpersonal competence, and adjustment during preadolescence and adolescence. *Child Development, 61,* 1101–1111.

Burgess, K. B., Wojslawowicz, J. C., Rubin, K. H., Rose-Krasnor, L., Booth-LaForce, C. (2006). Social information processing and coping strategies of shy/withdrawn and aggressive children: Does friendship matter? *Child Development, 77,* 371–383.

Chamberlain, B., Kasari, C., & Rotheram-Fuller, E. (2007). Involvement or isolation? The social networks of children with autism in regular classrooms. *Journal of Autism and Developmental Disorders, 37,* 230–242.

Chang, Y., Shih, W., & Kasari, C. (2016). Friendships in preschool children with autism spectrum disorder: What holds them back, child characteristics or teacher behavior? *Autism, 20,* 65–74.

Frankel, F. (2010). *Friends forever: How parents can help their kids make and keep good friends.* San Francisco: John Wiley & Sons.

Frankel, F. D., Gorospe, C. M., Chang, Y., & Sugar, C. A. (2011). Mothers' reports of play dates and observation of school playground behavior of children having high-functioning autism spectrum disorders. *Journal of Child Psychology and Psychiatry, 52,* 571–579.

Frankel, F., & Myatt, R. (2003). *Children's friendship training.* New York: Brunner-Routledge.

Fredeen, R. M. (2005). *Increasing initiations toward peers in children with autism using Pivotal Response Training and collateral gains in quality of initiations.* Unpublished doctoral dissertation, University of California, Santa Barbara.

Freeman, S. F. N., & Kasari, C. (1998). Friendships in children with developmental disabilities. *Early Education and Development, 9,* 341–355.

Gengoux, G.W. (2015). Priming for social activities: Effects on interactions between children with autism and typically developing peers. *Journal of Positive Behavior Interventions, 17,* 181–192.

Gottman, J. M. (1983). How children become friends. *Monographs of the Society for Research in Child Development, 48*(3), 1–85.

Gresham, F. M. (1981). Social skills training with handicapped children: A review. *Review of Educational Research, 51,* 139–176.

Grindle, C. F., Hastings, R. P., Saville, M., Hughes, J. C., Huxley, K., Kovshoff, H. . . . & Remington, B. (2012). Outcomes of a behavioral education model for children with autism in a mainstream school setting. *Behavior Modification, 36,* 298–319.

Hartup, W. W., & Stevens, N. (1997). Friendships and adaptations in the life course. *Psychological Bulletin, 121*(3), 355–370.
Kasari, C., Chamberlain, B., & Bauminger, N. (2001). Social emotions and social relationships: Can children with autism compensate? In J. Burack & T. Charman (Eds.), *The development of autism: Perspectives from theory and research* (pp. 309–323). Mahwah, NJ: Lawrence Erlbaum Associates.
Kasari, C., Locke, J., Gulsrud, A., & Rotheram-Fuller, E. (2011). Social networks and friendships at school: Comparing children with and without ASD. *Journal of Autism and Developmental Disorders, 41,* 533–544.
Kasari, C., Rotheram-Fuller, E., Locke, J., & Gulsrud, A. (2012). Making the connection: randomized controlled trial of social skills at school for children with autism spectrum disorders. *Journal of Child Psychology and Psychiatry, 53,* 431–439.
Kasari, C., & Sigman, M. (1996). Expression and understanding of emotion in atypical development: Autism and Down syndrome. In M. Lewis & M.W. Sullivan (Eds.), *Emotional development in atypical children* (pp. 109–130). Mahwah, NJ: Lawrence Erlbaum Associates.
Kim, S., Koegel, R. L., & Koegel, L. K. (2017). Training paraprofessionals to target socialization in students with ASD: Fidelity of implementation and social validity. *Journal of Positive Behavior Interventions 2017, 19,* 102–114.
Koegel, L. K., Koegel, R. L., Frea, W. D., & Fredeen, R. M. (2001). Identifying early intervention targets for children with autism in inclusive school settings. *Behavior Modification, 25,* 745–761.
Koegel, L. K., Kuriakose, S., Singh, A. K., & Koegel, R. L. (2012). Improving generalization of peer socialization gains in inclusive school settings using initiations training. *Behavior Modification, 36,* 361–377.
Koegel, L. K., Park, M. N., & Koegel, R. L. (2014). Using self-management to improve the reciprocal social conversation of children with autism spectrum disorder. *Journal of Autism and Developmental Disorders, 44,* 1055–1063.
Koegel, L. K., Vernon, T. W., Koegel, R. L., Koegel, B. L., & Paullin, A. W. (2012). Improving social engagement and initiations between children with autism spectrum disorder and their peers in inclusive settings. *Journal of Positive Behavior Interventions, 14,* 220–227.
Koegel, R. L., Bradshaw, J. L., Ashbaugh, K., & Koegel, L. K. (2014). Improving question-asking initiations in young children with autism using Pivotal Response Treatment. *Journal of Autism and Developmental Disorders, 44,* 816–827.
Koegel, R.L., Kim, S., & Koegel, L.K. (2014). Training paraprofessionals to improve socialization in students with ASD. *Journal of Autism and Developmental Disorders, 44,* 2197–2208.
Koegel, R.L., Werner, G.A., Vismara, L., & Koegel, L.K. (2005). The effectiveness of contextually supported play date interactions between children with autism and typically developing peers. *Research and Practice for Persons with Severe Disabilities, 30,* 93–102.
Kretzmann, M., Shih, W., & Kasari, C. (2015). Improving peer engagement of children with autism on the school playground: A randomized controlled trial. *Behavior Therapy, 46,* 20–28.
Ladd, G. W., Hart, C. H., Wadsworth, E. M., & Golter, B. S. (1988). Preschoolers' peer networks in nonschool settings: Relationship to family characteristics and school adjustment. In S. Salzinger, J. S. Antrobus, & M. Hammer (Eds.), *Social networks of children, adolescents, and college students* (pp. 61–92). Mahwah, NJ: Lawrence Erlbaum Associates.
Locke, J., Williams, J., Shih, W., & Kasari, C. (2017). Characteristics of socially successful elementary school-aged children with autism. *Journal of Child Psychology and Psychiatry, 58,* 94–102.
McConnell, S. R. (2002). Interventions to facilitate social interaction for young children with autism: Review of available research and recommendations for educational intervention and future research. *Journal of Autism and Developmental Disorders, 32,* 351–372.
McGee, G. G., Feldman, R. S., & Morrier, M. J. (1997). Benchmarks of social treatment for children with autism. *Journal of Autism and Developmental Disorders, 27,* 353–364.
Minjarez, M. B., Williams, S. E., Mercier, E. M., & Hardan, A. Y. (2011). Pivotal response group treatment program for parents of children with autism. *Journal of Autism and Developmental Disorders, 41*(1), 92–101.
Nelson, J., & Aboud, F.E. (1985). The resolution of social conflict between friends. *Child Development, 56,* 1009–1017.

Rafferty, Y., Piscitelli, V., & Boettcher, C. (2003). The impact of inclusion on language development and social competence among preschoolers with disabilities. *Exceptional Children, 69,* 467–479.
Sigman, M., & Ruskin, E. (1999). Continuity and change in the social competence of children with autism, Down syndrome, and developmental delays. *Monographs of the Society for Research in Child Development, 64,* v–114.
Strain, P. S., & Bovey, E. H. (2011). Randomized, controlled trial of the LEAP model of early intervention for young children with autism spectrum disorders. *Topics in Early Childhood Special Education, 31,* 133–154
Werner, G. A., Vismara, L. A., Koegel, R. L., & Koegel, L. K. (2006). Play dates, social interactions, and friendships. In R. L. Koegel & L. K. Koegel (Eds.), *Pivotal Response Treatments for autism: Communication, social and academic development* (pp. 199–213). Baltimore, MD: Paul H. Brookes Publishing Co.
Wolfberg, P., DeWitt, M., Young, G. S., & Nguyen, T. (2015). Integrated play groups: Promoting symbolic play and social engagement with typical peers in children with ASD across settings. *Journal of Autism and Developmental Disorders, 45,* 830–845.
Zanolli, K., Daggett, J., & Adams, T. (1996). Teaching preschool age autistic children to make spontaneous initiations to peers using priming. *Journal of Autism and Developmental Disorders, 26,* 407–422.

III

Childhood

Treatment Options at Home and at School

7

Parent Education in Pivotal Response Treatment

Lynn Kern Koegel, Kelsey Oliver, and Robert L. Koegel

CHAPTER GOALS

Goal 1. The reader will understand effective, evidence-based delivery models of Pivotal Response Treatment (PRT) for parent education programs.

Goal 2. The reader will become familiar with specific strategies used to teach parents how to implement PRT.

Goal 3. The reader will learn positive outcomes associated with providing parents with education in PRT.

Goal 4. The reader will understand how Fidelity of Implementation (FoI) for PRT is assessed.

Goal 5. The reader will be able to recognize examples of effective parent education strategies.

This chapter discusses the importance of parent education and differential outcomes related to a seamless implementation of goals across all environments in contrast to challenges of generalization and maintenance if parents are not involved in the intervention. Next, we discuss important considerations when providing feedback to parents. Relatedly, we describe how to measure FoI to ensure the interventions are being correctly and systematically implemented. Finally, we discuss various PRT parent education programs, including working with an individual family, group parent education, and working with families who are geographically distant from a PRT intervention center.

THE IMPORTANCE OF PARENT EDUCATION

Parent education is recognized as a critical part of the habilitation process if successful outcomes for children with autism are to be achieved. Parent involvement and participation in treatment programming, including the implementation of evidence-based interventions, are highly desirable and recommended by the National Research Council (Brookman-Frazee, Vismara, Drahota, Stahmer, & Openden, 2009; Koegel & Schreibman, 1996; National Research Council, 2001). In fact, a systematic review of the literature showed that when parents of children with autism spectrum disorder (ASD) participate in parent education programs, they gain knowledge, skills, and performance. Further, they have reductions in stress and their children improve in language and behavior. Parents report that skills learned in parent education programs are also helpful with their other children (McConachie & Diggle, 2007). The importance of parent education was demonstrated in an early study that compared a clinical model of treatment, in which only clinicians worked one-to-one with children with ASD, with a parent education model, in which a clinician trained the parent to work one-to-one with his or her child (Koegel, Schreibman, Britten, Burke, & O'Neill, 1982). While all children participating in the study demonstrated improved levels of appropriate behavior postintervention, only the children whose parents had received parent education continued to maintain the improvements in their skills 3 months after the program ended. Children whose parents did not participate in parent education demonstrated a decrease in appropriate behaviors over time once the clinician stopped doing intervention. This clearly shows the necessity of having parents actively involved in their children's intervention programs. Following, we discuss foundational topics related to parent education: current understandings in the field, areas in need of further research, the relationship between parent education and parent stress, general how-to's, specific strategies, and criteria to use when assessing parents' fidelity of implementation of PRT.

Our Understanding of Parent Education

The importance of parent education and parent involvement has been recognized in many areas. However, several issues need to be considered when developing programs for parent education. For example, although best practices for parent education are considered essential, they have not been well studied. We do know that parent support, in which the parent is provided with encouragement and social support, is not sufficient for ensuring that goals are implemented correctly. Parents need to be provided with specific feedback, whether it be through individualized coaching from a specialist during interactions or having a specialist observe videotapes of parent-child interactions and discuss intervention procedures (Mahoney et al., 1999). In addition, when developing parent education programs, practitioners should give particular attention to cultural variables, parent needs and learning styles, parent stress levels, and families' limited time and resources (Mahoney et al., 1999). Very few existing publications relate to parent education curriculums and FoI, the relative effectiveness of group versus individual parent education, and best practices in relation to the number of hours provided in parent education programs (Schultz, Schmidt, & Stichter, 2011).

Areas That Need Further Research

Given the relatively limited research on parent education, the following topics are in particular need of further research:

- Curriculum: What works best as it relates to the ease and accuracy of implementing PRT?
- Size of instruction group: Are group sessions as effective as individual sessions?
- Hours: How many weekly hours of parent education result in the best outcomes?
- Measurement: How are parent and child gains most effectively measured?
- Duration: How long should parent education programs last?
- Settings: What is the best setting for parent education? A clinic? In home? In community settings? A combination of settings?

Parent Education and Parent Stress

Parent stress can be especially high among parents whose child has very challenging or problem behaviors or high support needs and among parents who may have more difficulty accessing services (Krakovich, McGrew, Yu, & Ruble, 2016). However, given that all parents of children with ASD experience particularly high levels of stress, parent education needs to be designed in a way that helps alleviate stress. For example, research has shown that programs that require busy parents to set aside time from their daily activities to work with their children in a drill-type format actually increase their stress. In contrast, programs that incorporate teaching into naturally occurring activities throughout the day can decrease parent stress (Koegel, Bimbela, & Schreibman, 1996).

Because PRT is a naturalistic approach, it requires less "extra" time outside of a family's everyday routine to be implemented (Steiner, Koegel, Koegel, & Ence, 2011), providing children with the opportunity to receive round-the-clock intervention during everyday naturally occurring activities (Koegel, Koegel, Frea, & Smith, 1995; Koegel, Koegel, Kellegrew, & Mullen, 1996). For example, when parents are taught how to incorporate PRT strategies into families' daily routines, such as mealtime—as compared with a more structured parent education model—there are observed increases in their happiness as well as improvements in their positive communication with their child (Koegel, Bimbela, & Schreibman, 1996). Furthermore, parent education contributes to generalization of a child's skills, as parents can implement PRT in a wide variety of contexts both in the home and the community. Thus, in terms of spread of effect, more rapid learning, and maintenance of gains, parent education in PRT is a cost-effective method of disseminating evidence-based intervention and a highly efficacious approach for improving child and family outcomes.

General *How To* Issues Regarding Parent Education in PRT

A body of literature has focused on the positive collateral benefits that parent education programs can provide for parents and families, including reduced stress levels, increased self-efficacy, increased positive affect, improved quality of parent–child interactions, and improved quality of sibling interactions (Bandura, 1997; Brookman-Frazee & Koegel, 2004; Koegel, Bimbela, & Schreibman, 1996; Koegel, Steibel, & Koegel, 1998; Moes, 1995; Schreibman, Kaneko, & Koegel, 1991; Stahmer & Gist, 2001; Steiner, 2011). However, research is still lacking regarding best practices for parent education programs. Nevertheless, we do have some studies that provide helpful guiding strategies during PRT parent education sessions. One strategy that has been shown to be effective at empowering parents and decreasing their stress is utilizing a collaborative partnership approach during PRT parent training. For example, Brookman-Frazee and Koegel (2004) compared a clinician-directed model of parent training in PRT (i.e., the clinician determined the child's target skills, activities, and language opportunities) to a parent–clinician partnership approach (i.e., the clinician and parent collaboratively determined the activities, input was frequently elicited from the parent, and choices were provided to the parent). It was found that using a parent–clinician partnership approach to parent education resulted in very low levels of observed parent stress and increased levels of parent confidence during parent–child interactions. Furthermore, using the parent–clinician partnership model, children demonstrated significantly higher levels of positive affect and engagement with their parents, in addition to greater verbal responsiveness to language opportunities. These findings suggest that parent education programs emphasizing collaboration and partnership between parents and clinicians can be effective at improving both child and family well-being.

Similarly, research compared a strength-based approach to a deficit-based approach to parent education in PRT (Steiner, 2011). While providing feedback to parents regarding their implementation of PRT with their child, therapists made statements that either highlighted strengths of the child (e.g., "He seems to be interested in many toys today") or emphasized certain deficits (e.g., "He's having trouble staying engaged with one toy at a time"). Dependent measures included parent affect following therapist statements, parent affect while playing with their child, physical affection between the parent and child, and the child's verbal responsiveness to the parent. It was found that during the strength-based condition, parents exhibited improved overall affect. Results also indicated that in this condition, compared to a deficit-based approach to parent education, parents made more positive statements about their child and exhibited more physical affection toward their child. Child responsiveness was also higher. This study emphasizes the importance of focusing on a child's strengths and capabilities during the implementation of parent education sessions, as it results in improvements in the quality of social interactions between the parent and child as well as increases in child verbal communication.

Strategies for Parent Education Programs

Given these findings, we recommend the following strategies for parent education programs:

- ***Goals – Have parents co-create goals.*** This way the goals will be practical and will increase parents' motivation to teach them.
- ***Treatment – Don't "tell" parents what to do.*** Work in partnerships with parents to develop methods to solve problems. As such, the intervention will better fit into the family's values and personal style.

- ***Strengths – Focus on strengths.*** Point out the child's positive behaviors and how the parent can take advantage of those, rather than focusing on the child's deficits.
- ***Rewards – Reward the parents.*** Always discuss areas where the parent is having success. If a parent makes a mistake, suggest they adjust on the next trial but highlight what the parent is doing correctly.

FIDELITY OF IMPLEMENTATION OF PRT

Now that we have discussed some general issues related to parent education, it is important to discuss specifics. Parents need to be provided with explicit and clear strategies that will help their child. Often parents observe sessions and are unable to replicate the procedures at home. The FoI of PRT provides parents with specific feedback, beginning with the motivational strategies discussed in Chapter 1. Generally, parents are asked to interact with their child for 10 minutes, and each minute is scored for the following: 1) child attention, 2) clear opportunity, 3) choice, 4) contingent reinforcement, 5) task variation, 6) interspersal of maintenance and acquisition tasks, 7) use of natural reinforcers, and 8) reinforcement of attempts. These scoring categories are discussed in the following section.

1. ***Child attention:*** This includes ensuring that the parent secured the child's attention before beginning a teaching opportunity. For example, if the child is staring out the window when the parent presents an instruction, this category is not recorded as correct.
2. ***Clear opportunity:*** In addition to securing the child's attention, the parent needs to provide a clear opportunity that is not confusing for the child and is appropriate to the child's target behavior. For example, if the child is learning first words and the parent says, "This is such a cute toy and I know you like to play with it. Can you say *toy*?" the instruction is too complex for a child learning first words. In contrast, if the parent holds up the toy and models the word "toy," the instruction is clear and appropriate to the child's developmental level.
3. ***Choice:*** The next area scored is child choice. If the child is interested in a smartphone and the parent says, "Look over here, there's a stuffed doggie and it barks, ruff ruff," the parent, while well intentioned, isn't providing child choice and would not be scored as correct for that category. Alternatively, if the parent has the smartphone (or pauses the ongoing activity briefly) and asks the child what animal is on the screen or has the child ask to use the phone, the parent is correctly using child choice.
4. ***Contingent reinforcement:*** Next, the parent needs to provide immediate and contingent reinforcement to the child. For instance, if a child learning to use first words requests "swing" to be pushed on the swing, and the parent says, "Just a minute, I need to tie your shoe first," the consequence will be delayed. However, if the parent immediately pushes the child on the swing after the child spontaneously requests, the parent would be scored as correct.

5. ***Task variation:*** Also important is varying the task. That is, if the parent drills the child repeatedly on a target behavior, this category is not recorded as correct. If the parent varies the activities to decrease boredom and monotony, the category is recorded as correct.

6. ***Interspersal of maintenance and acquisition tasks:*** Closely related to task variation is interspersing acquisition and maintenance tasks. For example, if the target behavior is learning subtraction and the child already knows addition, the parent would not be scored as correct if he or she presented only subtraction problems. In contrast, if the parent mixes subtraction with addition problems, the parent would be scored as correct in this category.

7. ***Use of natural reinforcers:*** The parent needs to provide a natural reward after correct responses. For example, if a child is learning to count and the parent has the child count dots on a page, then rewards the child with a token or cookie, the parent would not be scored as correct in that category. Alternatively, if the parent has the child count small pieces of cookies, then gives the child the cookie pieces, it would be considered correct implementation of the procedure.

8. ***Reinforcement of attempts:*** Finally, the parent is scored for reinforcing attempts. If the parent uses a strict shaping paradigm without rewarding the child for trying, the parent is not scored as correct. In contrast, if the child's clear attempts are rewarded, even if they aren't completely correct, the parent is recorded as correct in this category.

Because it is rare that a parent (or anyone for that matter) implements all of the procedures correctly 100% of the time, a criterion of 80% in each category is required to meet FoI. Because each minute is scored, parents must provide at least one learning opportunity per minute (and we prefer two trials a minute). If a parent provides more than one opportunity per minute, each trial is scored, and the parent needs to be correct on all trials to receive a correct score for that minute. Parents can be scored via videotape samples or in vivo. No feedback is provided during the 10-minute sample. With the specific information provided by the scoring, parents can be provided with very detailed and unambiguous feedback regarding their implementation of the procedures.

MODELS OF PARENT EDUCATION

Now that we've discussed scoring for FoI and other issues that are foundational to parent education, we discuss various PRT delivery models for parent education.

Individual Models

A variety of service models exist for parent education in PRT, models that are effective for improving both child and parent outcomes. Variations of PRT parent education models continue to emerge in the literature to help address the increasing need for treatment. That is, while most of the early models focused on one child and his or her parent working with a clinician, later models have focused on teaching groups of parents to meet increasing demands, as the incidence of ASD has increased.

There is an extensive amount of research demonstrating the efficacy of delivering PRT parent-education programs individually to one family at a time (Schreibman & Koegel, 2005; Stahmer & Gist, 2001; Steiner, Gengoux, Klin, & Chawarska, 2013; Steiner et al., 2012; Symon, 2005; Vernon, 2014; Vernon, Koegel, Dauterman, & Stolen, 2012). This approach can be advantageous because it allows each child's intervention to be highly individualized and provides parents with opportunities to practice techniques while receiving direct feedback (Kaiser & Hancock, 2003; Steiner et al., 2012). For some families, a different PRT point is targeted each week, and feedback is provided on each weekly point until all of the points are worked through. Other times, the points are discussed simultaneously, and feedback is provided for all the points together. During individual sessions, the clinician models the PRT, then provides the parent with an opportunity to deliver PRT and receive feedback. The exact percentage of time that the parents implement the procedures varies, but the parent is *always* required to work with his or her child and feedback is always provided.

For example, in a large-scale community-based PRT education program, clinicians provided individual parent education sessions to parents of 158 children ranging from 2 to 10 years of age (Baker-Ericzen, Stahmer, & Burns, 2007). The largest percentage of families in this sample identified as Hispanic (35%), while 27.4% identified as white. The clinician and the family met individually in a clinical setting for 1 hour every week for 12 weeks. The primary outcome measure used in this study was the *Vineland Adaptive Behavior Scales-II* (Vineland-II; Sparrow et al., 2005), with a series of statistical analyses to determine relationships among domains. Parents were provided with a copy of a PRT training manual (available from Koegel Autism Consultants), either in Spanish or English, during initial sessions. Clinicians taught the parents the outlined motivational techniques while they worked with their children. In addition, parents were provided with homework assignments every week to practice various techniques within their home and community. Following the 12-week parent education intervention, statistical analyses showed significant improvements on multiple child measures, regardless of the child's age, gender, or race/ethnicity. On average, the children demonstrated significant increases on measures of the *VABS-II*, including the areas of communication, daily living skills, socialization, motor skills, and adaptive behavior. Children who were 3 years of age or younger exhibited the greatest improvement from baseline to postintervention, although all children improved.

Additional research has demonstrated the efficacy of PRT parent education delivered individually (Coolican, Smith, & Bryson, 2010). This study used a nonconcurrent multiple baseline design across participants to examine the effects of PRT parent education on parents' and preschool children's outcomes. Specific child outcome measures included disruptive behavior and the children's frequency and type of child utterance (e.g., appropriate/inappropriate, prompted/independent). Parent outcome measures included FoI, perceived self-efficacy, and satisfaction with the program. Intervention consisted of three 2-hour individual parent-education sessions, with the first two sessions in a clinical setting and the third in the families' homes. Prior to the start of the parent education, parents were provided with training materials on how to teach PRT and how to teach first words (available from Koegel Autism Consultants). Sessions included an overview of PRT techniques. Clinicians modeled the skills in addition to providing direct coaching and in-vivo feedback on the parent's implementation of PRT. After intervention, increases in functional language were observed for all eight children, with significant gains for six of these children. In addition, the responsiveness for all children significantly increased and maintained at follow-up.

Intensive Short-Term Individual Intervention PRT Services

Intensive short-term intervention programs, involving practice with feedback for a week with individual families, have been shown to be a feasible and effective way to provide introductory education in PRT and other behavioral techniques to families who are awaiting services or who are geographically distant from a treatment center (Koegel, Symon, & Koegel, 2002). For example, parents were taught to implement the motivational procedures of PRT during a five-day, 25-hour education program (5 hours per day). In this program, parents submitted baseline video clips of themselves working with their child at home. After completion of the week-long program, the parents submitted additional video clips. The videotapes were scored on parents' use of PRT procedures and the children's expressive communication. As well, the level of enjoyment the parent experienced while interacting with his or her child was rated on a Likert scale. Results indicated that following intervention, the parents successfully mastered the PRT motivational techniques, and these gains maintained for 3 months to 1 year following completion of the week-long intensive parent education program. Subsequent improvements in social-communication occurred for all children participating in the study. In addition, upon completion of the program parents were scored as happier and less stressed during interactions with their child. These encouraging findings suggest that in a relatively brief period of time, parents can effectively learn basic PRT techniques while reducing their stress and increasing their child's social communication skills.

Group Models

Many parent education programs have focused on the clinician delivering instruction to one parent–child dyad at a time (e.g., Baker-Ericzen et al., 2007; Koegel et al., 2002; Symon, 2005). However, in an effort to address the growing discrepancy between accessible evidence-based treatment options and the large number of children in need of intervention, research has also examined the effectiveness of delivering PRT parent education using a group model. For example, one study evaluated PRT implementation by parents after they participated in a brief, 10-week PRT education program presented primarily in a group format (Minjarez, Williams, Mercier, & Harden, 2011). This research assessed whether parents were able to learn PRT in a group context well enough to reach the 80% criterion for FoI and whether parent fidelity would be related to child communication gains. Seventeen children, sixteen with a diagnosis of ASD and one with a diagnosis of pervasive developmental disability, not otherwise specified (PDD-NOS), and their parents were included in this study. Children ranged in age from 2 years to 6 years, 11 months. Parent education content was based on published manuals of PRT techniques (Koegel et. al., 1989). Concepts covered included: 1) ensuring that the parents were securing their child's attention and presenting clear language opportunities; 2) varying the task presented by including both maintenance and acquisition tasks; 3) including child choice and shared control; 4) providing immediate, contingent, and natural reinforcement; and 5) reinforcing the child's verbal attempts. These concepts were taught to parents by providing examples during group discussions and presentations, reviewing videos that parents brought in from home, setting treatment goals, and assigning homework for the parents to complete. Parent education sessions were conducted for 10 weeks and included weekly group meetings for 90 minutes. In addition, each parent–child dyad had one individual in-vivo education session for 50 minutes at the end of the 10 weeks. Following the group parent education intervention, there was a significant increase in parent FoI of PRT. In addition, the participants' children demonstrated statistically significant increases in functional utterances after their parents participated in the program. These results show that a brief group education intervention can be effective for improving parents' teaching of PRT and illustrate the collateral gains demonstrated by the children of participating parents once specialized procedures are being implemented correctly.

As a follow-up to this study, Minjarez, Mercier, Williams, and Harden (2012) explored how this brief clinic-based group parent education program influenced families' levels of stress and feelings of empowerment. To supplement the data from their previous study, these researchers collected baseline and follow-up ratings of parent stress, as measured by the *Parenting Stress Index/Short Form* (Abidin, 1995), and parent empowerment, as measured by the *Family Empowerment Scale (FES)* (Koren et al., 1992). After the 10-week parent education program, significant improvements were observed in both the *Parenting Stress Index* and the *Family Empowerment Scale.* Specifically, parents reported increased levels of empowerment and significantly lower levels of stress after participating in the parent education program. This suggests that group PRT education not only produces positive outcomes for children with ASD but also contributes to positive collateral benefits in quality of life for the parents.

Other researchers have examined large-scale delivery of a group parent education programs (Harden et al., 2015). These authors used a randomized controlled trial (RCT) and large sample size to further establish the efficacy of delivering PRT parent education in a group format. Participating in this study were 53 children between ages 2 and 6 years and their parents. Families were randomly assigned to the PRT parent education group (similar to that outlined by Minjarez et al., 2011) or a psychoeducational group, in which parents learned general information regarding autism but not specifics related to PRT. Intervention lasted for 12 weeks. The PRT group parent education condition consisted of one 90-minute group session per week for 8 weeks, followed by one visit per week for 4 weeks, during which a clinician met individually with each parent-child dyad. During the program, groups of four to six parents were led by one or two clinicians through PRT teaching materials, including presentations and video examples (available from Koegel Autism Consultants). The researchers found that children whose parents participated in the PRT condition exhibited significantly greater improvements in their frequency and intelligibility of verbal utterances, compared with children randomly assigned to the psychoeducation condition. Children in the PRT condition also had greater scores on the Vineland-II for adaptive communication skills (Sparrow et al., 2005). In addition, a high percentage of the parents assigned to the PRT condition (84%) were able to meet the criterion for FoI of PRT by the end of the 12-week intervention, with many parents achieving fidelity sooner. This RCT demonstrated on a large scale that group-delivered PRT programs can effectively teach parents PRT techniques, which subsequently improves their child's functional communication.

As a follow up to this large-scale RCT assessing PRT parent education in a group format, an additional study assessed whether treatment effects were maintained for 23 families 3 months after completing the program (Gengoux et al., 2015). Specifically, data were collected from 10-minute videos of parent-child interactions on the frequency of the child's functional utterances and the the parents' FoI of PRT. The results showed that while the criterion for parent FoI of PRT was met by about half of the families 12 weeks after completion of the parent education, all of the children had significantly improved in the frequency of their functional utterances at follow-up. This indicates maintenance of treatment gains from the parent education intervention for all of the children and most of the parents. Further, the children showed significant generalized gains on standardized tests, including the Mullen Scales of Early Learning Composite (MSEL; Mullen, 1995) and the Vineland communication domain score (Vineland-II; Sparrow et al., 2005). The findings of this study suggest that the improvements in a child's communication and maintenance of language, following a brief PRT parent education program delivered primarily in a group format, can be maintained for up to 12 weeks posttreatment.

Parent Education for Geographically Distant Families

To address the service-need discrepancy and the lack of "state of the art" services in some geographical areas, some research has sought to establish effective strategies for providing interim and short-term parent education programs to families. Using a randomized clinical trial and a wait-list control group, research by Nefdt, Koegel, Singer, and Gerber (2010) examined the delivery of an introductory PRT parent education program through a self-directed learning program to parents of children who were not currently receiving, or were waiting for, treatment. Specifically, parents randomly assigned to the treatment condition were provided with an interactive, self-guided DVD containing lessons, quizzes, and video clips regarding PRT strategies in addition to physical copies of PRT manuals (Koegel et al., 1989). The procedure consisted of the following steps:

1. Parents were given a DVD consisting of 14 chapters with accompanying quizzes covering basic behavior principles and the motivational PRT procedures.
2. Parents were asked to complete each quiz before moving to the next chapter.
3. At the end of the chapter, a review of the material was presented.
4. The parents were provided with an interactive task wherein parents could score other parents implementing the intervention procedures.
5. A completed scoring sheet with explanation was provided to each parent so that he or she could compare answers with a professional.

Results of the study showed that the majority of the parents demonstrated acquisition of the PRT procedures, reported high satisfaction with the program, and exhibited high levels of confidence when interacting with their child following the intervention program. Furthermore, the children of the parents who received intervention showed significantly higher levels of verbal utterances following their parents' completion of the program. In contrast, the control group showed a small decrease in verbal utterances. This study demonstrated that a self-directed learning program in PRT is effective for providing parents with introductory knowledge and skills to implement evidence-based practice while awaiting more intensive services.

CASE HISTORY
Improving Amil's Communication and Social Skills Through PRT and Parent Education

Amil was 3 years and 2 months old when he came to the authors' center for a week-long individual program. He lived with both his parents in a remote area that had very few services to offer for ASD. Amil had been diagnosed with autism at the age of 2 1/2, at which time the diagnosing psychologist told the parents that it was unlikely he would ever talk, that he probably wouldn't have friends, and that they should plan for care needs for the rest of his life. Amil was bussed to school, which required him to sit on the bus for 45 minutes per day—each direction—to a larger city where he attended a special education preschool with about nine other preschool children.

Prior to attending the week-long program, Amil's parents sent in video clips from a variety of settings. Amil was not using verbalizations or words to communicate in any setting. At home, he led his parents to desired items that were out of reach. He was still in diapers and had regular meltdowns when he was frustrated or when his parents couldn't understand what he wanted. In addition to the teacher, the school provided three aides in the classroom who sat behind the children at circle time and desk activities, gently physically leading the children back to their chairs if the children attempted to leave the area. Observations of many clips over many different school activities revealed that the adults never prompted expressive communication from the children, nor any social interactions with peers. Further, the bulk of Amil's preschool peers—most of whom also had autism—had significant communication delays and appeared uninterested in engaging with their classmates.

During the week-long parent education program, we focused on verbal expressive communication. Using the PRT procedures, we spent the majority of the day prompting expressive communication while extinguishing disruptive and crying behaviors. All target behaviors were discussed with the family, and goals were developed as a group. During the first day, Amil made a few word attempts, which his parents immediately rewarded. When providing the family with feedback, we stressed his strengths, how many great sounds he could say, and how many toys captured his interest. Each subsequent day, he made a few additional word attempts. Although his words were highly unintelligible, each and every attempt was rewarded. By the fifth and final day, Amil was making verbal word attempts following a model around 60% of the time. His tantrums borne out of frustration had greatly decreased, and his social communication improved once he realized that trying communication got him a lot further than a lengthy meltdown. Throughout the week, Amil's parents improved on their FoI of the PRT procedures. Initially, they tended to try and draw his attention to a variety of items, rather than using the activity in which he was engaged as a stimulus for word attempts. However, with feedback from their clinician, they quickly improved in their ability to use child choice. Another area that needed improvement was their ability to provide immediate and contingent rewards. Initially, they were so excited by Amil's newly learned word attempts that they often tried to have him say several words before providing him with the natural reinforcer. Again, with feedback, they learned not to delay the reward for Amil's great attempts, but to provide a natural reward for each and every one, no matter how far it was from the adult word.

At the end of the week Amil's parents returned home and continued to work with him and maintained their high level of FoI with their use of the PRT procedures. Within a month, Amil was attempting to imitate almost 100% of the words his parents modeled and was—on rare occasions—saying a spontaneous word. Within 2 months, Amil had quite a large vocabulary consisting of close to 80 words. At that point, his parents began to have him put together two of his known words to create the beginning of sentences. So, instead of prompting him to say "ball," they prompted "throw ball," and instead of prompting "cookie," they prompted him to say, "more cookie," making sure to vary the combinations of words so he didn't simply memorize the two-word combination.

By the end of summer, almost 3 months after he had completed our week-long program, Amil began to show a great interest in books and letters in addition to his growth in expressive communication. He could label each letter and loved going through the alphabet. And, while most children despise flash cards, Amil regularly sought out a stack of letter flash cards, enthusiastically brought them to his parents, and enjoyed pulling out and labeling random letters. He also showed an interest in numbers and would seek out number books, which he brought to his parents and spontaneously labeled each number. Because of his interest in numbers, his parents helped him learn how to count his favorite things. Cheetos were a much-desired treat, and after just a few weeks, he easily counted up to 100 Cheetos. In fact, his parents learned to break the Cheetos into very tiny pieces as his counting skills improved, so he wouldn't satiate during the enjoyable activity.

Although he was improving verbally and academically and he enjoyed interacting with his parents, Amil expressed very little interest in other children. Given his lack of interest, along with his apparent intelligence in academic areas, we recommended that the family consider a regular education setting. This would provide him with typical and competent peers with whom he could practice his social-verbal interactions as well as engage in a regular preschool curriculum. His parents also requested that he receive one-to-one support. The school reluctantly agreed because they had no inclusive classroom in that area, he had made little to no progress in their special education program, and he had made rapid and significant progress following their parent education program.

Amil's parents found a nice preschool in their neighborhood and talked with the preschool staff about including him with support. The school welcomed him, along with his aide, with open arms and expressed a true interest in helping him succeed. Initially, he chose to run in circles and ignore his friends, but with constant prompting from his aide, he began to improve. All goals were coordinated with the family, and Amil's parents began to have short play dates with pre-planned activities around Amil's interests. After several months of intervention, he began spontaneously interacting with peers, taking turns, playing simple games with peers, and engaging in some reciprocal conversation. With his parents' efforts and dedication, Amil continues to make steady gains and shows greatly decreasing symptoms of autism. He knows far more than most adults about the human body, planets, science, and many other topics. His social skills are improving, particularly when lunch groups include his interests. His mother has been able to demonstrate procedures to the school staff and assist with training teachers and paraprofessionals. Although her bachelor's degree was in the sciences, she has become an expert on intervention for autism, especially as it pertains to her child. |||

Key Insights ||| Helping Parents Effectively Teach Their Children With ASD

The following guidelines are helpful for practitioners who work with parents (or other adult family members) of children with ASD, so that they may effectively teach their children.

- **Include parents:** A seamless intervention must be implemented across all daily environments for the individual with autism. Therapists, teachers, aides, and other educators may change, but the parents remain constant. They play a critical role in ensuring consistent and evidence-based quality services.
- **Parents need "practice-with-feedback":** There are a variety of parent education methods, but generally it appears to be most helpful if parents can be provided with feedback while actually working with their child. That way, practitioners can provide parents with specific and individualized pointers. This can be accomplished in vivo or by observing recorded clips of the parent(s) working with their children.
- **Keep it positive:** Focusing on the individual with ASD's weaknesses just adds to parent stress. In contrast, focusing on the strengths of the child reduces parent stress and provides a good starting point for intervention. For each goal being targeted, frame the intervention in a positive way to accentuate the positive behaviors of the individual with ASD.
- **Teamwork:** All goals should be coordinated with the family and developed as a team. As well, intervention procedures should be developed in coordination with the family. If goals or intervention procedures don't match the family's needs and desires, the family probably won't work on them. In contrast, if goals are important to the family and procedures fit into their cultural values and parenting style, they'll make the effort to work with their child.
- **Use routines and natural activities:** Requiring parents to sit down and drill their child increases parent stress. Goals need to be worked on regularly throughout the day during ongoing activities. This will decrease family stress.
- **Consider cultural variables:** Most of the literature on parent education has been conducted with European American families. Many variables, such as family support, how a disability is regarded, involvement of extended family, priority of target behaviors, selection of target behaviors, and so on, may vary across cultures. Sensitivity to these issues is important, so is providing

clinicians with the same cultural background whenever possible. (See Chapter 3 for more information on working effectively with families from diverse cultures.)

SUMMARY

In summary, parent involvement in the intervention process is not a luxury but a necessity if goals are to be achieved rapidly. Without a coordinated program, there is likely to be "behavioral contrast." This means the child with ASD will perform differently across settings, oftentimes showing challenging behaviors in other settings if the intervention programs are not coordinated and contingencies aren't consistent in all settings. In contrast, with parent education, we see more rapid gains on targeted behaviors, widespread generalization, long-term maintenance, and a myriad of other more positive outcomes. However, parent education programs must be carefully designed so that they improve the family's functioning. High levels of stress are observed among parents of children with ASD; therefore, programs need to support parents and siblings and ensure that parent stress is reduced. Working hand and hand with families can be very rewarding when rapid child gains are realized, and very carefully planned parent education programs may achieve that goal.

STUDY QUESTIONS

1. Why is parent involvement in the intervention process critical for child outcomes?
2. In what ways does PRT education decrease parent stress?
3. What are the positive benefits that parent education programs can provide for parents, siblings, and children with ASD?
4. What are some collateral benefits experienced by children whose parents participate in PRT education programs?
5. Why is it important to focus on a child's strengths rather than his or her weaknesses during parent education programs?
6. What is the minimum criterion level for fidelity of PRT implementation? What is the rationale for this criteria level?
7. How is fidelity of PRT implementation scored?
8. How are parent education programs in PRT delivered to parents and families?
9. What are some evidence-based treatment options for families who want to receive education in PRT but are geographically distant from a treatment center or are waiting to receive treatment?

REFERENCES

Abiden, R. R. (1995). Parenting Stress Index (PSI) Manual. Charlottesville, VA: Pediatric Psychology Press.

Baker-Ericzen, M. J., Stahmer, A. C., & Burns, A. (2007). Child demographics associated with outcomes in a community-based pivotal response training program. *Journal of Positive Behavior Interventions, 9*(1), 52–60. doi:10.1177/10983007070090010601

Bandura, A. (1997). *Self-efficacy*. New York: Freeman.
Brookman-Frazee, L., & Koegel, R. L. (2004). Using parent/clinician partnerships in parent education programs for children with autism. *Journal of Positive Behavior Interventions, 6*(4), 195–213. doi:10.1177/10983007040060040201
Brookman-Frazee, L., Vismara, L., Drahota, A., Stahmer, A., & Openden, D. (2009). Parent training interventions for children with autism spectrum disorders. In J. L. Matson (Ed.), *Applied behavior analysis for children with autism spectrum disorders*. New York City, NY: Springer.
Coolican, J., Smith, I. M., & Bryson, S. E. (2010). Brief parent training in pivotal response treatment for preschoolers with autism. *Journal of Child Psychology and Psychiatry, 51*(12), 1321–1330. doi:10.1111/j.1469-7610.2010.02326.x
Gengoux, G. W., Berquist, K. L., Salzman, E., Schapp, S., Phillips, J. M., Frazier, T. W., Minjarez, M. B., & Hardan, A. Y. (2015). Pivotal response treatment parent training for autism: Findings from a 3-month follow-up evaluation. *Journal of Autism and Developmental Disorders, 45*, 2889–2898. doi:10.1007/s10803-015-2452-3
Harden, A. Y., Gengoux, G.W., Berquist, K. L., Libove, R. A., Ardel, C. M., Phillips, J., Frazier, T. W., & Minjarez, M. B. (2015). A randomized controlled trial of pivotal response treatment group for parents of children with autism. *Journal of Child Psychology and Psychiatry, 56*(8), 884–892.
Kaiser, A., & Hancock, T. (2003). Teaching parents new skills to support their young children's development. *Infants and Young Children, 16*, 9–21.
Koegel, R. L., Bimbela, A., & Schreibman, L. (1996). Collateral effects of parent training on family interactions. *Journal of Autism and Developmental Disorders, 26*(3), 347–359.
Koegel, L. K., Koegel, R. L., Kellegrew, D., & Mullen, K. (1996). Parent education for prevention and reduction of severe problem behaviors. In L. K. Koegel, R. L. Koegel, & G. Dunlap (Eds.), *Positive behavioral support: Including people with difficult behavior in the community* (pp. 3–30). Baltimore, MD: Paul H. Brookes Publishing Co.
Koegel, L. K., Steibel, D., & Koegel, R. L. (1998). Reducing aggression in children with autism toward infant or toddler siblings. *Journal of the Association for Persons with Severe Handicaps, 23*, 111–118.
Koegel, R. L., Koegel, L. K., Frea, W. D., & Smith, A. E. (1995). Emerging intervention for children with autism: Longitundinal and lifestyle applications. In R. L. Koegel & L. K. Koegel (Eds.), *Teaching children with autism: strategies for initiating positive interactions and improving learning opportunities* (pp. 1–15). Baltimore, MD: Paul H. Brookes Publishing Co.
Koegel, R. L., O'Dell, M. C., & Koegel, L. K. (1987). A natural language teaching paradigm for nonverbal autistic children. *Journal of Autism and Developmental Disorders, 17*(2), 187–200.
Koegel, R. L., & Schreibman, L. (1996). Fostering self-management: Parent-directed pivotal response training for children with autistic disorder. In E. D. Hibbs & P. S. Jenson (Eds.), *Psychosocial treatments for child and adolescent disorders* (pp. 525–552). Washington, DC: American Psychological Association.
Koegel, R. L., Schreibman, L., Britten, K. R., Burke, J. C., & O'Neill, R. E. (1982). A comparison of parent training to direct child treatment. In R.L. Koegel, A. Rincover, & A.L. Egel (Eds.), *Educating and understanding autistic children* (pp. 260–279). San Diego, CA: College-Hill Press.
Koegel, R. L., Schreibman, L., Good, A., Cerniglia, L., Murphy, C., & Koegel, L. K. (1989). How to teach pivotal behaviors to children with autism: A training manual. Santa Barbara: University of California.
Koegel, R. L., Symon, J. B., & Koegel, L. K. (2002). Parent education for families of children with autism living in geographically distant areas. *Journal of Positive Behavior Interventions, 4*(2), 88–103.
Koren, P. E., DeChillo, N., & Friesen, B. J. (1992). Measuring empowerment in families whose children have emotional disabilities: a brief questionnaire. *Rehabilitation Psychology, 37*(4), 305.
Krakovich, T. M., McGrew, J. H., Yu, Y., & Ruble, L. A. (2016). Stress in parents of children with autism spectrum disorder: An exploration of demands and resources. *Journal of Autism and Developmental Disorders, 46*(6), 2042–2053.
Mahoney, G., Kaiser, A., Girolametto, L., MacDonald, J., Robinson, C., Safford, P., & Spiker, D. (1999). Parent education in early intervention: A call for a renewed focus. *Topics in Early Childhood Special Education, 19*(3), 131–140.

McConachie, H., & Diggle, T. (2007). Parent implemented early intervention for young children with autism spectrum disorder: A systematic review. *Journal of Evaluation in Clinical Practice, 13*(1), 120–129.

Minjarez, M. B., Mercier, E. M., Williams, S. E., & Harden, A. Y. (2012). Impact of pivotal response training group therapy on stress and empowerment in parents of children with autism. *Journal of Positive Behavior Interventions, 15*(2), 71–78. doi:10.1177/1098300712449055

Minjarez, M. B., Williams, S. E., Mercier, E. M., & Harden, A. Y. (2011). Pivotal response group treatment programs for parents of children with autism. *Journal of Autism and Developmental Disorders, 41,* 92–101. doi:10.1007/s10803-010-1027-6

Mullen, E. M. (1995). *Mullen scales of early learning* (pp. 58-64). Circle Pines, MN: AGS.

National Research Council. (2001). *Educating children with autism.* Washington, DC: National Academy Press.

Nefdt, N., Koegel, R., Singer, G., & Gerber, M. (2010). The use of a self-directed learning program to provide introductory training in pivotal response treatment to parents of children with autism. *Journal of Positive Behavior Interventions, 12,* 23–32. doi:10.1177/1098300709334796

Moes, D. (1995). Parent education and parenting stress. In R. L. Koegel & L. K. Koegel (Eds.), *Teaching children with autism: Strategies for initiating positive interactions and improving learning opportunities* (pp. 79–93). Baltimore, MD: Paul H. Brookes Publishing Co.

Schreibman, L., Kaneko, W. M., & Koegel, R. L. (1991). Positive affect of parents of autistic children: A comparison across two teaching techniques. *Behavior Therapy, 22,* 479–490.

Schreibman, L., & Koegel, R. L. (2005). Training for parents of children with autism: Pivotal responses, generalization, and individualization of interventions. In E. D. Hibbs & P. S. Jensen (Eds.), *Psychosocial treatments for child and adolescent disorders: Empirically based strategies for clinical practice* (2nd ed., pp. 605–631). Washington, DC: American Psychological Association.

Schultz, T. R., Schmidt, C. T., Stichter, J. P. (2011). A review of parent education programs for parents of children with autism spectrum disorders. *Focus on Autism and Other Developmental Disabilities, 26*(2), 96–104.

Sparrow, S. S., Cicchetti, D. V., Balla, D. A., & Doll, E. A. (2005). *Vineland adaptive behavior-scales: Survey forms manual.* American Guidance Service.

Stahmer, A. C., & Gist, K. (2001). The effects of an accelerated parent education program on technique mastery and child outcome. *Journal of Positive Behavior Interventions, 3*(2), 75–82.

Steiner, A. M. (2011). A strength-based approach to parent education for children with autism. *Journal of Positive Behavior Interventions, 13*(3), 178–190.

Steiner, A. M., Gengoux, G. W., Klin, A., & Chawarska, K. (2013). Pivotal response treatment for infants at-risk for autism spectrum disorders: A pilot study. *Journal of Autism and Developmental Disorders, 43,* 91–102.

Steiner, A. M., Koegel, L. K., Koegel, R. L., & Ence, W. A. (2012). Issues and theoretical constructs regarding parent education for autism spectrum disorders. *Journal of Autism and Developmental Disorders, 42*(1), 1218–1227.

Symon, J. B. (2005). Expanding interventions for children with autism: Parents as trainers. *Journal of Positive Behavior Interventions, 7*(3), 159–173.

Vernon, T. W. (2014). Fostering a social child with autism: A moment-by-moment sequential analysis of an early social engagement intervention. *Journal of Autism and Developmental Disorders, 44,* 3072–3082.

Vernon, T. W., Koegel, R. L., Dauterman, H., & Stolen, K. (2012). An early social engagement intervention for young children with autism and their parents. *Journal of Autism and Developmental Disorders, 42,* 2702–2717.

8

Inclusive Education

Robert L. Koegel and Kelsey Oliver

CHAPTER GOALS

Goal 1. The reader will describe early education models for autism spectrum disorders (ASD).

Goal 2. The reader will learn the differences between integration and full inclusion programs.

Goal 3. The reader will discuss issues relating to the arguments for and against inclusion.

Goal 4. The reader will describe various effective interventions for inclusion.

Goal 5. The reader will list advantages of inclusion for typically developing students and students with ASD.

This chapter describes challenges and solutions for educating children with ASD alongside their typically developing peers in general education (GE) classrooms. Teachers, and other school personnel working in conjunction with parents, will be able to learn about implementing powerful educational strategies based upon Pivotal Response Treatment (PRT). While it may seem straightforward that children with ASD need to be educated so that they may achieve their maximum potential, they haven't always been considered "educable" and were at one time systematically excluded from public school. Consequently, without an education, they did not progress and their outcomes were poor. In addition, the majority of children with autism were institutionalized by adolescence, and many even earlier. Dr. Bob Koegel, co-author of this chapter and the co-developer of PRT, first encountered some of these issues related to these children's lack of a happy future, and the resulting significant family stress, in the 1970s when some very dramatic and tragic events occurred in Santa Barbara.

CASE HISTORY
The Horrifying Problem

When the father of a child with autism in our community was diagnosed with terminal cancer, he made it his top priority to try and find a satisfactory placement for his child, where the child would be cared for after his father passed away. Although in some ways the 1970s do not seem all that long ago (compared with the thousands of years of teaching history) in the grand scheme of things, with respect to the treatment and education of children with autism it was practically the Dark Ages. These children were not allowed to go to school in the community because they were considered uneducable. To the extreme stress of families, by the time the children reached adolescence, almost all were placed in mental hospitals, where they ended up spending the majority of their lives. When this father discovered that institutionalization would be a likely outcome for his child, he went to observe a mental hospital and was horrified to find that the environment was not the cheerful place he had hoped and prayed it would be. Some children were sitting on the floor in pools of urine; others were tied to their beds to prevent them from severely injuring themselves; and there was loud screaming almost all of the time.

The father was horrified to the point that he could not think clearly. He knew he was going to die from cancer, and he now felt that his child would likely end up with a horrible future. In a state of blind terror, he went home and killed his son—an act he considered a "mercy killing." Society and the courts reacted swiftly, and the father was convicted of murder and sentenced to life in prison.

Although it seemed as if this father's situation could not get any worse, it did when his terminal cancer reversed and he entered an extended period of remission. In this case, being cured of cancer was not a relief. The guilt he experienced was a far greater punishment than any prison sentence could ever impose. A network television documentary was produced about this story, and eventually the Governor of California commuted the prison sentence, freeing the father. Yet, he was not freed from his own mental prison. He lived the rest of his life in a state of mental torture. It didn't matter to him if he was in prison or not; his life was completely ruined.

MAKING EDUCATION A TOP PRIORITY FOR CHILDREN WITH ASD

Although this entire story seems about as bad as anyone could ever imagine, eventually there came a silver lining that affected the entire country and continues to have an impact throughout the world. This family's tragic outcome became widely known. Several prime-time television documentaries appeared on major networks to show how society had failed this father. Subsequently, educators, citizens, families of children with autism, and others expressed sympathy for the painful situation and burden placed upon him. The development of an educational system that could meet the needs of families with a child with autism became a top priority. The California legislature then began to take action! They wanted to solve this problem, and legislators in other states were beginning to feel the same way. However, when they read the literature on autism, they had trouble finding research studies showing that children with this disability could learn. (At that time, research and clinical practice focused on autism only; it was not until later that the field developed more understanding of the cluster of related disabilities now called ASD.)

At that time, I (Bob) was just graduating from the University of California at Los Angeles and planning to move to the University of California at Santa Barbara. Given the widely publicized situation there, the Santa Barbara County Schools were at the forefront of the movement to try to find solutions for educating children with autism. Officials within the school system applied for a federal grant to help with this endeavor. They reached out to the university seeking someone who might be able to help them develop a program for these children who were regarded as "seemingly impossible." I had previously been a doctoral student of Ivar Lovaas, so the university told them that I was trained in the behavioral interventions that Lovaas and his students had shown might be very effective in teaching children with autism. When the Santa Barbara County Schools contacted me, I was beginning to get involved in developing behavioral interventions that might be useable in a school context, and I agreed to help develop a classroom model for teaching children with autism. However, the research coming out of Lovaas's lab was demonstrating an effective teaching intervention carried out in a one-to-one clinic setting, not in a group or classroom setting. Naïvely, I thought this was a minor difference.

Meanwhile, although autism had rarely received media attention prior to the mercy killing in Santa Barbara, this attention occurred more frequently afterward. When I was contacted by the print and television media, I told them it should be a simple process to adapt the clinic procedures to a school setting. Reporters told me that people working in the schools thought it was not a simple process. Unfortunately, I somewhat arrogantly told members of the news media that the schools might be having trouble because school personnel were not trained well. This was a big blunder on my part. Not only did it (temporarily) alienate the school personnel, but it turned out that they were correct! The process was far more complicated than I had anticipated. It took years of systematic research for our team to develop a program that was effective with groups of children and that teachers could be trained to replicate. Details concerning this research are presented in the sections that follow.

Phase 1: Developing the School-Based Treatment Model

Along with the personnel in the Santa Barbara Schools, I was awarded a federal grant to try to develop a model based on the successful one-to-one procedures Lovaas's researchers had developed, but one that could be carried out in a school setting. The problems were difficult but not insurmountable when attacked through systematic research. Initially, we worked in a classroom of eight children with ASD, one teacher, and two aides. I thought this ratio would be fine; however, once the children arrived, we had great difficulty getting the children from the bus to the classroom, and once inside, it was impossible to get them to sit in their seats all at the same time. However, we knew Lovaas's procedures worked with individual children, so we began to work with each child one at a time. Under those conditions, just as the initial studies conducted in Lovaas's lab showed, there were no unexpected problems. The children all responded well to the teaching in a one-to-one situation.

Next, I tried to work with two children at a time. Everything fell apart. No matter how hard I tried, I was unable to make progress when more than one child at a time was present. This difficulty led to a research project that ultimately was extremely successful in creating an effective classroom model for teaching children with autism (Koegel & Koegel, 1995; Russo & Koegel, 1977).

We began the lesson by having a teacher at the head of the classroom giving instruction to the "students," even though there was only one student who was being prompted to respond and then reinforced by an aide who sat behind the child giving prompts and reinforcers related to the teacher's instructions.

Once this was working successfully, we incorporated a second child, now using the one-to-one instructional format for both children, but with the teacher still at the head of the classroom and an aide behind each child providing prompts and reinforcers.

Next, we thinned the schedule of reinforcement so that we could fade out the presence of one of the aides. This resulted in a format where the teacher was at the head of the class and the two students were prompted and reinforced by one aide.

After this procedure was working successfully, we duplicated it with a second group of two children. At the end of that stage, the instructional format was to have one teacher at the head of the class, teaching two groups of two children, with each group being prompted and reinforced by an aide (i.e., one teacher, four children, and two aides).

Again, we then thinned the schedule of reinforcement and faded out the presence of one of the aides. At this point we had one teacher, four children, and one aide.

We then duplicated this entire procedure with another group of children, until we eventually ended up with one teacher, two groups of four children, and two aides (one for each group).

At this point, we had planned to thin the schedule of reinforcement further so we could fade the presence of one of the aides. However, the state of California was then moving toward regulations suggesting a classroom with two aides would be fine. Therefore, from the practical perspective of suggesting a model that could be implemented statewide, and eventually nationwide, we finalized the model with the ratio of one teacher, eight children, and two aides.

Phase 2: Developing a New Model to Address Children's Heterogeneity

With the first (group) phase of the model working quite well, many people assumed the problem of trying to educate children with autism in a school context was solved. We began disseminating the findings of the classroom model, and many school districts began implementing special day classes using this model, or a very similar one. However, our clinical observations indicated a problem that might require further research and refinement of the model. For example, we rapidly realized that some children could barely hold onto a pencil even with help, while other children were not only capable of holding the pencil but also able to print words or even sentences with it. That is, the heterogeneity among the children was vast, and we felt that more research was needed in order for the model to account for this great variability. This required individualization of instruction for each child within the group.

Specifically, in order to work with children with vastly different ability levels and interests, we needed to individualize their instruction within the context of existing classrooms. We approached this in two ways:

1. *We focused on teaching tasks that left a record of the children's responding* (e.g., writing letters or words, using arithmetic worksheets, spelling worksheets).
2. *We gradually taught the children to respond for extended periods of time without direct supervision or prompting.*

For example, we worked on writing assignments by teaching a child to first draw letters, then short words, then short phrases, and ultimately sentences. As the instruction progressed to the higher levels (e.g., writing sentences), the children were responding for longer and longer periods of time. Because the writing assignment took some time, the teacher had opportunities to move around the classroom to check on other children. Similarly, with math, we taught the children to complete a problem, then added several more. We continued this approach until the children were producing fairly lengthy responses, sometimes working for 15 minutes or more, before the teacher provided additional direct supervision and reinforcement.

Implications for Including Children With ASD in General Education Classrooms

While we were doing this, we realized that not only were we treating each child as an individual, we also were able to capitalize on their strengths to maximize their learning. This seemed like something that would benefit *all children*, not just children with autism. At that point we realized that we should be focusing on teaching *children* of all different levels and abilities, not just *children with autism*. If we used the approach within any GE classroom—teaching all of the children in ways that focused on their individual strengths—then there was no reason to exclude children with autism from the GE classrooms.

INCLUSION OF CHILDREN WITH ASD

We liked the idea of inclusion. It seemed like it provided an opportunity for children with ASD to be with their typical peer role models, and it also respected all of the children's human rights. As such, it seemed like

1. Inclusion would be beneficial for all of the children, both typically developing children and children with ASD.
2. It was the right thing to do.

What could go wrong?

Well, like many great ideas that seem simple at first, it turned out to be much more complex than we had imagined; even though the procedures worked, a great many issues needed to be dealt with in order for an inclusive model to be accepted. Many members of society thought that a full inclusion approach would never work (cf. Mesibov & Shea, 1996), and they vehemently resisted it for fear that it would ruin the educational system. And, they were right that this would be the case if one approached full inclusion by just placing the children together and hoping for the best. Such an approach was (and still is) guaranteed to lead to disaster. Inclusion needed to be done systematically in order for it to work. When it was done properly, however, it produced tremendous benefits for all children, not just for the children with disabilities. Consider the following issues that needed to be addressed in order for the model to work: the meaning of inclusion; perceptions and attitudes regarding inclusion and students with ASD; and parents' anxieties and desires concerning inclusion. These issues are discussed in the following sections.

The Meaning of Inclusion

The term *inclusion* presents a multiplicity of definitions and interpretations to parents, teachers, and school administrators (Lindsay, 2007; Murphy, 1996; Odom et al., 2004). Many misconceptions exist regarding inclusion and how it differs from earlier movements such as integration and mainstreaming (Lindsay, 2007). Frequently, the terms *mainstreaming, inclusion,* and *least restrictive environment* are mistakenly used interchangeably (Yell, 2012). Many who do not know otherwise assume that mainstreaming, or the "consistent part-time placement in general education" (Kasari, Freeman, Bauminger, & Alkin, 1999), is synonymous with inclusion. Some still observe this once-prevalent attitude even now. However, advocates for inclusion posit that there should be no such thing as part-time inclusion. They feel that if it is part-time inclusion, then it is *not* inclusion (Lynch & Irvine, 2009). Thus, the term *full inclusion* is now used.

A key difference between a philosophy favoring full inclusion and philosophies such as mainstreaming is that full inclusion assumes the GE classroom to be a child's home base the entirety of the day (Mesibov & Shea, 1996; Murphy, 1996). While there appears to be variation in how full inclusion is defined, "the fundamental concept is that students with special needs can and should be educated in the same setting as their normally developing peers, with appropriate support services, rather than being placed in special education classrooms or schools" (Mesibov & Shea, 1996, p. 337). Further, full inclusion has been defined as complete integration in general, age-appropriate classrooms regardless of the extent of a student's needs, with support services provided within the context of the GE classroom (Murphy, 1996). Related concepts/movements have emerged: 1) multi-tiered systems of support that provide increasingly intensive levels of support for students with mild/moderate and moderate/complex support needs, and 2) universal design for learning. (Although a detailed discussion of these topics is beyond the scope of this book, we mention them here for readers who may wish to seek out further reading on related topics.)

Perceptions and Attitudes

From early on in the movement toward inclusive education, it has been shown that a key factor in determining the success of inclusion is the attitudes and perceptions of GE teachers, special education teachers, administrators, and school districts (Hannah & Pliner, 1983; Kavale, 2002; Kavale & Forness, 2000; Lindsay, 2007; Simpson, de Boer-Ott, & Smith-Myles, 2003). Students with ASD have been considered difficult to teach and are often perceived by those who are not thoroughly familiar with disabilities to have lower capacity to perform well academically. In addition, these children often have more behavior regulation difficulties and impaired social-emotional functioning (Cassady, 2011; Emam & Farrell, 2009; Sansoti & Sansoti, 2012). Research also suggests that, historically, GE teachers have been more likely to report less positive attitudes about inclusion than special education teachers or school psychologists (McHatton & McCray, 2007; Pearman, Barnhart, Huang, & Mellblom, 1992; Segall & Campbell, 2012; Shippen, Crites, Houchins, Ramsey, & Simon, 2005), with concerns that students with ASD might require more specialized support (Carter et al., 2014; Majoko, 2016; Sansoti & Sansoti, 2012), which may be difficult to provide while simultaneously teaching the rest of the class (Cassady, 2011). Thus, GE teachers thought inclusion might compromise the education of the typical learners in their classrooms (Murphy, 1996). Similarly, GE teachers appeared to be less inclined to support full inclusion when a student demonstrated difficult behavior or complex needs (Avramidis & Norwich, 2002; Lindsay, 2007; Murphy, 1996). Some teachers even expressed resentment related to being required to make modifications or accommodations (Emam & Farrell, 2009).

Pre-service GE teachers have also reported mixed attitudes on inclusion of students with ASD in their classroom, though they often tend to report being more concerned about disruptive behavior than academic skills (Barned, Flanagan Knapp, & Neuharth-Pritchett, 2011; Lindsay, Proulx, Thomson, & Scott, 2013; McCray & McHatton, 2011; McHatton & Parker, 2013). While they generally have positive attitudes on inclusion, they report less positive attitudes toward inclusion with students who are more severely impacted (Barned et al., 2011). Consistent with previous research, this suggests that while preservice GE teachers may express positive attitudes regarding inclusion, they may not consider it to be an appropriate placement for all students with ASD (Grider, 1995).

These findings are especially concerning when considering a study by Robertson, Chamberlain, and Kasari (2003) that found when GE teachers had more positive perceptions and attitudes regarding their relationship with their student with ASD, the student was more likely to be socially included in the class. This suggests that educators' perceptions of students with ASD can have an effect on their classroom practices, which, in turn, can affect the students' success. In Robertson et al.'s study, teacher perceptions became a self-fulfilling prophecy!

Attitudes and perceptions of principals and school administrators regarding inclusion of students with disabilities have also consistently been shown to have an effect on the success of inclusive schools (Cook, Semmel, & Gerber, 1999; DeMatthews & Mawhinney, 2014). Horrocks, White, and Roberts (2008) noted, "The most significant factor in predicting both a positive attitude toward inclusion, and higher recommendations of placements for children with autism, was the principal's belief that children with autism could be included in a regular education classroom (p. 1462)." Research has found that principals who experienced positive interactions with students with disabilities and had exposure to concepts related to special education were more likely to have a positive attitude regarding inclusion (Praisner, 2003). Further, principals with positive attitudes towards inclusion were more likely to place students with disabilities in settings that were less restrictive (i.e., GE classrooms) (Praisner, 2003). This implies that a positive cycle could be produced. If principals and administrators can be provided with successful experiences and information on disabilities, their attitudes and perceptions towards inclusion will tend to improve, thus increasing the likelihood of successful inclusion.

Despite these findings, administrators report having less knowledge of ASD and less awareness and use of effective practices than special education teachers and school psychologists (Segall & Campbell, 2012). GE teachers and administrators also report beliefs about ASD that are inaccurate, such as the etiology of the disorder. Themes occur in what principals focus on for successful inclusion, including "school culture building, resource allocation, and ongoing professional development," suggesting that these are important topics to address during professional development trainings (DeMatthews & Mawhinney, 2014; Guzman, 1997; Salisbury & McGregor, 2002).

Parents' Anxieties and Desires

Several factors influence the likelihood that parents of children with ASD will choose an inclusive setting for their child's education. These factors include 1) teacher training and preparedness, 2) parents' overall perceptions about, and involvement in, their child's school, and 3) the size of the GE classroom and the degree of structure within that classroom. These factors are further discussed.

Teacher training and preparedness have been found to influence parents' perceptions and placement decisions. Parents are less likely to pursue placing their child in an inclusive setting if they perceive the GE teacher to be ill-prepared or lack training necessary to support the student with ASD's success (Connor & Ferri, 2007; Kasari et al., 1999). Thus, a child's placement might be influenced by the perceived level of appropriate support for that student, rather than reflecting what is truly that student's level of ability and least restrictive environment. Similarly, GE teachers' attitudes and knowledge of characteristics associated with ASD and with inclusive school practice are predictive of parents' satisfaction with their child's schooling experience (Falkmer, Anderson, Joosten, & Falkmer, 2015).

In addition to the perceptions of teachers and administrators, parent perceptions and involvement can have a large effect on the school placement of students with ASD (Falkmer et al., 2015; Iovannone, Dunlap, Huber, & Kincaid, 2003; Odom et al., 2004). Many parents of children with disabilities express positive attitudes toward full inclusion, though they often have some anxiety and hesitancy (Bitterman, Daley, Misra, Carlson, & Markowitz, 2008; Connor & Ferri, 2007; de Boer, Pijl, & Minnaert, 2010; Kavale & Forness, 2000). Relatedly, some parents posit that public schools do not employ staff who are qualified to meet the needs of students with ASD in an inclusive context and that school personnel lack a thorough understanding of ASD, while others worry that placing a student with ASD in full inclusion could lead to mistreatment and ridicule from typically developing students (Abu-Hamour & Muhaidat,

2014b; Connor & Ferri, 2007; Falkmer et al., 2015; Leyser & Kirk, 2004; Murphy, 1997; Turnbull & Ruef, 1997; Yssel, Engelbrecht, Oswald, Eloff, & Swart, 2007).

Finally, parents of children with ASD may also be concerned with GE classrooms that are much larger and less structured than specialized classrooms (Mesibov & Shea, 1996; Odom et al., 2004). Research has also suggested that many parents view full inclusion as an inappropriate placement for students with ASD who are severely impacted by their symptoms, and that these parents have concerns that the GE classroom won't be accommodating enough for their child's level of functioning (Abu-Hamour & Muhaidat, 2014b; de Boer et al., 2010; Kasari et al., 1999; Leyser & Kirk, 2004).

Unfortunately, parents of children with and without disabilities have reported less positive attitudes about including a child with ASD compared to a child with a physical or sensory disability, especially if the child with ASD has behavioral difficulties (Barned et al., 2011; Lindsay, Proulx, Thomson, & Scott, 2013; McCray & McHatton, 2011; McHatton & Parker, 2013; Rafferty, Boettcher, & Griffin, 2001). Behavioral difficulties seem to be a common theme when considering barriers to full inclusion for ASD. As a whole, more efforts are necessary in a variety of areas. For example, research consistently recommends that teachers of inclusive classrooms communicate and collaborate with parents so that families are kept informed about their child's progress and any difficulties or problems that may arise (Iovannone et al., 2003; Stoner & Angell, 2006; Stoner, Angell, House, & Bock, 2007; Stoner et al., 2005; Turnbull & Ruef, 1997; Turnbull, Turnbull, & Blue-Banning, 1994). This is particularly important considering that parents' satisfaction with a child's inclusive school experience is strongly correlated with their trust and communication with GE teachers (Stoner et al., 2005). Thus, for inclusion for students with ASD to work, there must be ongoing positive communication and collaboration with parents. More support and training are needed.

Teacher Training, Support, and Resources

A longstanding issue relating to inclusion is the fundamental lack of adequate training and resources for GE teachers to support learners with disabilities (Abu-Hamour & Muhaidat, 2014a; Allen, 2008; Burack, Root, & Zigler, 1997; Kauffman, 1995; Kavale, 2002; Kavale & Forness, 2000; Mather & Roberts, 1994; McGregor & Campbell, 2001; McHatton & McCray, 2007). It has been argued that with the right support and preparation, inclusion can result in successful outcomes for students with ASD. However, there still exist too few models and procedures to facilitate the successful placement and maintenance of learners with ASD in GE classrooms (Simpson et al., 2003). Regardless of the stance on inclusion, GE teachers continuously emphasize the need for extensive and ongoing professional development opportunities regarding how to best meet the wide-ranging needs of students with ASD (Able, Sreckovic, Schultz, Garwood, & Sherman, 2015; Corkum et al., 2014). Even though school personnel may express positive attitudes regarding inclusion, this does not guarantee that they have sufficient understanding of characteristics of ASD or effective intervention strategies. Educators' attitudes (i.e., attitudes of GE teachers, special education teachers, administrators, and school psychologists) are not always a significant predictor of awareness or their use of empirically supported interventions (Segall & Campbell, 2012), which highlights the importance of providing specific training and knowledge regarding evidence-based practices to educators regardless of whether they are in favor of the notion of inclusion. In fact, GE teachers consistently report concerns related to their skills and the resources necessary to make inclusion successful (Able et al., 2015; Allen, 2008; Corkum et al., 2014; Lindsay, Proulx, Scott, & Thomson, 2013; Lindsay, Proulx, Thomson, & Scott, 2013; McGregor & Campbell, 2001; Odom et al., 2004; Sansoti & Sansoti, 2012; Scruggs & Mastropieri, 1996). Most notably, educators report concerns with how to respond effectively to disruptive behavior (Lindsay, Proulx, Thomson, & Scott, 2013), how to structure cooperative learning groups, and how and when to intervene with behaviors that interfere with the student's academic and social success (Able et al., 2015).

It is cause for optimism that GE teachers who have had more experience with ASD have demonstrated and reported greater confidence in responding to students with autism (Engstrand & Roll-Pettersson, 2012; McGregor & Campbell, 2001; Odom et al., 2004), suggesting that providing GE teachers training and experience with supporting learners with ASD could have a positive impact on teachers' skills in successfully applying strategies in the classroom. Teachers note that their initial teacher training program could have been more effective if they had been given the opportunity to interact directly with students with disabilities (Able et al., 2015). In fact, the more special education units that GE teachers acquire during their teacher training programs, the more positive their attitudes toward inclusion and ASD (Engstrand & Roll-Pettersson, 2012).

As a whole, hands-on training is critical. The efficacy of even brief training programs can also increase teachers' confidence and understanding of evidence-based practices. Pre-service teacher training programs that center upon cross-departmental collaboration between special education and general education can improve attitudes and perceptions toward inclusive education (McHatton & Parker, 2013).

Support From Paraprofessionals: One-to-One Aides In regard to resources, many GE teachers posit that students with ASD need specialized support in GE classrooms, such as an educational aide (Carter et al., 2014; Glashan, MacKay, & Grieve, 2004; Lindsay, 2007; Odom et al., 2004; Odom, Buysse, & Soukakou, 2011). However, many educators adopt the mentality that if a student is reliant on a full-time, one-to-one aide for support, he or she cannot be truly considered as fully included in the GE classroom (Sansoti & Sansoti, 2012). Relatedly, it has also been reported that unless the use of an aide is handled correctly, having a full-time aide could inhibit a student from becoming fully integrated into the GE environment or make the student overly dependent on the paraprofessional (Mesibov & Shea, 1996; Sansoti & Sansoti, 2012).

Despite these concerns, however, there is extensive research regarding training paraprofessionals to support the GE teacher in including students with ASD (e.g., Carter et al., 2014; Crosland & Dunlap, 2012; Harrower & Dunlap, 2001; Koegel, Kim, & Koegel, 2014; Robinson, 2011), suggesting that these concerns regarding paraprofessional support could be moot if professionals are truly up to date on the research literature. This includes training paraprofessionals to implement specific, individualized interventions while maintaining an appropriate proximity to the student—that is, not too close, but also not too far away (Koegel et al., 2014; Simpson et al., 2003). Research has also suggested that if children with ASD receive intensive behavioral intervention early, the likelihood that they will later need support from an aide in a GE classroom is reduced (Jacobson & Mulick, 2000). This alludes to the importance of providing intensive, evidence-based intervention with paraprofessional support as early as possible in order to reduce a student's reliance on an aide in the future.

Support From Paraprofessionals: Co-Teaching Co-teaching has been one of the most widely used inclusion models (Lipsky & Gartner, 1997), and paraprofessionals are frequently the primary adults directly supporting students with ASD in inclusive settings (Robinson, 2011; Young, Simpson, Smith-Myles, & Kamps, 1997). Research has acknowledged the benefits of teaching assistants for GE teachers (Lindsay, 2007). There are many different types of co-teaching models in which an aide or other paraprofessional assists the teacher in instructing students with ASD, and there are even co-teaching models in which two teachers work together. The important point here is that whoever is doing the teaching needs to be trained in specific teaching techniques that work. As is the case for GE teachers, simply placing an educational aide in a classroom without proper training is not an effective strategy for inclusion. Rather, educational aides, co-teachers, and other paraprofessionals in the classroom should also be provided with thorough and ongoing training regarding how to support students with ASD in full inclusion contexts (Jacobson & Mulick, 2000). As previously mentioned, this concern is being addressed by current research on evidence-based programs specifically designed to teach paraprofessionals to support individuals with ASD in inclusive settings (Koegel et al., 2014; Robinson, 2011).

Support From the School Culture and Leadership Support, structure, and attitudes towards inclusion have been reported in the literature as being very important for success (McCray & McHatton, 2011). Authors such as DeMatthews and Mawhinney (2014) go so far as to suggest that such attitudes are vital to success. Thus, effective inclusion of students with ASD may require not just training individual personnel but rather a shift in the school culture toward inclusion. Researchers agree that a full inclusion approach will necessitate restructuring general and special education at many different levels, including desirable changes in the organization of the classroom curricula in addition to a beneficial comprehensive shift in the attitudes and perceptions of those working in administration (DeMatthews & Mawhinney, 2014; Murphy, 1996). Such shifts can be helpful not only for those with disabilities but indeed for everyone in the school.

In an in-depth analysis, McLesky and Waldron (2015) suggested important factors for developing and sustaining effective inclusive school environments and emphasized principal leadership, collecting progress data, and a system for professional development. It seems that researchers and school personnel alike recognize the importance of building a collaborative inclusive school community for inclusion to be most effective. The extent and quality of communication and/or collaboration among school personnel might be factors worth examining when comparing successful and unsuccessful cases of full inclusion.

Improving Socialization in Inclusive Schools

When full inclusion is done correctly, it is successful in many ways, bringing out the best in all children. However, when it is done incorrectly, there can be reason for serious concern. Without proper implementation, social rejection, isolation, and bullying are common themes in inclusion research across the world (Majoko, 2016; Sreckovic, Brunsting, & Able, 2014). Research has suggested that typical peers' lack of informed understanding about a peer's ASD could contribute to rejection and/or isolation of the peer with ASD. For example, when peers were unaware of a student's ASD diagnosis and associated symptoms, researchers noted an observed increase in isolation and neglect of the student (Ochs, Kremer-Sadlik, Solomon, & Sirota, 2011). This is consistent with additional literature that found that students with ASD who were less impaired by their symptoms experienced higher levels of bullying or rejection (Kasari, Locke, Gulsrud, & Rotheram-Fuller, 2011; Rowley et al., 2012). More detailed research has shown that boys tend to be actively rejected, while girls tend to be overlooked, rather than rejected, by same-gender peers (Chamberlain, Kasari, & Rotheram-Fuller, 2007).

Generally speaking, without some appropriate information about disabilities, a fair number of typically developing students seem ill-prepared to understand, support, interact with, and communicate with their classmates with disabilities (Cooper, Griffith, & Filer, 1999), which seems especially true when students have mitigated ASD symptoms that are less apparent to their typically developing peers (Kasari et al., 2011; Ochs et al., 2001). By contrast, students who readily stand out from peers tend to experience greater acceptance, perhaps because the typically developing peers form different expectations of that student and assume more of a protective role (Kasari et al., 2011). Overall, students with ASD are likely to need intensive support with social skills for inclusion to be successful (Able et al., 2015; Carter et al., 2014; Locke, Ishijima, Kasari, & London 2010; Rotheram-Fuller, Kasari, Chamberlain, & Locke, 2010).

There is a large body of research supporting the efficacy of disability awareness programs for improving peers' knowledge and attitudes regarding disabilities (Lindsay & Edwards, 2013). For example, providing typical peers with information on autism characteristics leads to increased positive inclusion initiations toward their classmates with ASD, such as inviting the student with ASD to join an activity (Ochs et al., 2001). It appears that when typical classroom peers are informed, and especially if the typical children have some appropriate peer training, children with ASD "are more included in the social structure of their typical classrooms." Related to this point, acceptance of children with disabilities is more common in younger grades than in older grades (Rotheram-Fuller, 2005). Relatedly, even when peers are not trained, children with ASD seem better accepted in elementary school compared with middle and high school (Able et al., 2015). Possibly this is the case because of a smaller developmental difference between younger children with and without disabilities, compared with the more noticeable differences that may emerge with older children in middle and upper grades when academic and social demands increase (Simpson et al., 2003). These findings allude to the importance of early intervention and providing typically developing children and children with ASD the opportunity to learn side-by-side in the same classroom as early as possible.

Although some research on social inclusion of students with ASD may seem quite negative, many articles describe positive effects of inclusion on peers and peer relationships (Odom et al., 2011). Typically developing children who have had consistent contact in the GE classroom with peers with ASD indicated more positive attitudes and intentions toward those peers when compared with typical children who did not experience contact with peers on the autism spectrum (Mavropoulou & Sideridis, 2014). In addition, the in-class proximity of the student with ASD to typical peers did not seem to have an effect on peers' positive attitudes, meaning that the student with ASD did not have to be in close proximity to typical peers in order to have a positive impact on them (Mavropoulou & Sideridis, 2014). This suggests that the student with ASD's presence in the classroom in and of itself was sufficient to have a positive influence on typical peers. This is consistent with past research claiming that general contact with students with disabilities in inclusive settings has a positive effect on typically developing peers' understanding of and attitudes toward disabilities (Odom et al., 2004).

GE teachers have reported that including students with ASD in their classrooms increased typically developing students' acceptance of ASD, and diversity in general, and contributed to their leadership skills through acting as a role model to their peers (Finke, McNaughton, & Drager, 2009). Thus, carefully planned inclusion programs maximize the growth of both typical students and those with autism (Simpson & Sasso, 1992).

Potential Negative Effects of Segregation The points raised in the preceding section suggest some major negative implications for what might happen to a typically developing child who never has an opportunity to interact with peers with disabilities and learn about disabilities. Statistically speaking, it is a certainty that many of these typically developing children will themselves one day have a child who has a disability. If they have had the opportunity during childhood to experience being with children with disabilities in full inclusion classrooms and to appreciate these children's positive qualities, it is likely that as adults, parents of children with disabilities will experience a higher quality of life than if their understanding of disabilities is based largely on frightening innuendo and rumors.

Benefits of Peer-Mediated Intervention In addition to informing typically developing peers about disabilities, peer-mediated interventions in inclusive settings have extensive empirical support and are effective for promoting academic and social skills for students with ASD (Harrower & Dunlap, 2001; Odom & Strain, 1984; Watkins et al., 2015). Teaching target behaviors, such as verbal initiations to peers and turn-taking (Harper, Symon, & Frea, 2008) for students with ASD in preschool through high school (Watkins et al., 2015), has been greatly effective using peer-mediated strategies. As such, students can be given the opportunity to take on an active, meaningful role in facilitating skills and developing relationships with their peers with ASD. Peer support also has the potential to reduce the strain on the GE teacher and students by facilitating optimal development for all of the children in the class. In this way, it is clear that typically developing peers could be considered an enormous benefit to inclusion, both for themselves and for children with ASD.

REVISITING THE DEBATE OVER FULL INCLUSION

The debate over full inclusion is often obscured by issues pertaining to ethics and morality. Ethical arguments pertaining to inclusion and ASD are generally categorized into two schools of thought: the "rights-based" perspective and the "needs-based" perspective (Ravet, 2011). It is a fallacy that these two perspectives are mutually exclusive, and we argue throughout this book that both empirical evidence and values need to be considered in developing any intervention approach. The "rights-based" perspective is in large part a values-based perspective that seeks to end educational segregation in any form. Individuals with this philosophy emphasize a student's being completely included in all aspects of GE at school, both socially and academically. This perspective prioritizes the importance of modifying schools to make necessary accommodations. Conversely, the "needs-based" perspective tends to emphasize the relative lack of large bodies of empirical evidence and the potential negative effects of inclusion if it is carried out without appropriate supports. Individuals supporting the needs-based perspective tend to value preserving a variety of placement options and services to best meet a wide variety of needs. They posit that empirical evidence takes precedence over doing the "right thing." Again, throughout this book we argue that the "right thing" should include *both empirical evidence and values.*

Some educational researchers tend to argue from a needs-based perspective (Ravet, 2011); empirical evidence outweighs values and ideologies. However, we suggest that empirical evidence is merely one factor in the formation of public policy and that politics are also shaped by the ideologies and aspirations of society (Lindsay, 2007). Thus, some researchers suggest adopting a more integrative perspective that incorporates core values of both the rights- and needs-based perspectives (Ravet, 2011).

Early Arguments Against Inclusion

Early critics of inclusion felt that sometimes inclusion is just used as a buzzword without actual actions to promote inclusion (Murphy, 1996). Those in favor of the needs-based perspective also contend that proponents for full inclusion ignore or compromise empirically validated interventions in order to "do the right or proper thing" by fully including a child (Simpson & Sasso, 1992), which they think might jeopardize the individualized nature of educational programming (Borthwick-Duffy, Palmer, & Lane, 1996; Fuchs & Fuchs, 1994).

It has been argued (we believe incorrectly) that the full inclusion movement differs from prior integration efforts, such as mainstreaming, in that full inclusion places a greater emphasis on maximum exposure to typically developing peers, more so than on the individual needs of each student (Simpson, 1995; Simpson & Sasso, 1992). Some early opponents posited that the emphasis on social integration and academic skills in full inclusion models surpassed emphasis on teaching important independent functional living skills, such as counting money or identifying signs and traffic signals (Borthwick-Duffy et al., 1996; Grider, 1995). Others argued that students with disabilities would receive far less individual instruction from the GE teacher than typically developing students (Jenkins & Pious, 1991). Consequently, some scholars of the needs-based perspective at one time felt (we believe incorrectly) that full inclusion was an inappropriate placement for some students compared with smaller, more highly structured contexts (i.e., a special day class) and that being able to offer a wide variety of placement options would be beneficial (Kauffman, 1995; Mesibov & Shea, 1996; Simpson & Sasso, 1992).

Advances in Research Supporting Full Inclusion

There have been extensive advances that counter these early arguments against inclusion and tend to render them invalid. With individualized training, teachers, educational assistants, and paraprofessionals can successfully learn how to appropriately respond to students with disabilities within a GE context and how to individualize each student's goals and interventions to their developmental level (Allday, Neilsen-Gatti, & Hudson, 2013; de Boer, 2009; Jacobson & Mulick, 2000; Koegel et al, 2014; Koegel, Koegel, Frea, & Fredeen, 2001; Koegel, Vernon, Koegel, Koegel, & Paullin, 2012; Leach & Duffy, 2009; Leblanc, Richardson, & Burns, 2009; McHatton & Parker, 2013; Robinson, 2011; Stahmer, Suhrheinrich, Reed, Bolduc, & Schreibman, 2010). The great advantage of research is that it does not lock one into unsolvable dilemmas, but rather provides an avenue for solving problems. At present, research is solving the potential problems brought to our attention in the early literature, making it possible to provide the most effective education in the more natural environment of full inclusion. This exposure to normal stimuli, in a GE classroom with typically developing peers, is also consistent with all developmental models from early on (e.g., Hebb, 1958) that argue the nervous system requires normal stimulation in order to develop normally.

In addition to ethical and moral debates, a number of legal debates have been advanced. The first law enacted to guarantee the right of students with disabilities to be educated with their typically developing peers was PL 94-142 (National Education Association of the United States (1978). It was rapidly followed by the Individuals with Disabilities Education Act (IDEA) (2004), mandating that students with disabilities be educated with their typically developing peers in the least restrictive environment (LRE) to the maximum extent appropriate. However, the extent to which individuals with disabilities should be educated alongside their peers and how that is defined for each student have historically been topics of debate (Kavale & Forness, 2000). In fact, LRE is one of the most frequently litigated components of IDEA (Yell, 2012; Yell, Katsiyannis, Drasgow, & Herbst, 2003).

Many opponents of full inclusion believe it is violating PL 94-142 (1975), the law stating that all students with disabilities are entitled "to a free public education in the least restrictive environment," because they believe that some students are unable to feasibly receive education within a GE classroom (Huefner, 1994; Mather & Roberts, 1994). These opponents view supporters of full inclusion as ignoring the severity of certain conditions and the need for individualized and specialized services (Grider, 1995; Mather & Roberts, 1994). They argue that it is both illegal and inadvisable for school administration to require a blanket approach to educating students with disabilities (Huefner, 1994). Put another way, they argue that full inclusion has been presented as a "one-size-fits-all" approach rather than one option on a continuum of available educational placement options (Borthwick-Duffy et al., 1996; Fuchs & Fuchs, 1994). We believe, and the research cited in this chapter and elsewhere in this book supports the argument, that full inclusion is appropriate and that it is appropriate to have a one-size-fits-all approach for a right to an appropriate education in a full inclusion classroom along with one's typically developing peers, just as it is okay to have a right to life, liberty, and the pursuit of happiness. In such cases, we believe one size fits all.

The proponents of full inclusion feel that the right to freedom and dignity are rights that should be available to all, and if that is one size fits all, then it is okay. Such an important right should be available to all if it is at all possible to provide a quality education in such an environment. Related to this point, a considerable amount of empirical evidence shows that, when done properly, educational programming can be effectively individualized within the context of full inclusion to meet the diverse and unique needs of students with ASD. However, such research suggests that inclusive education may not be effective unless appropriate supports are used and proper staff training has taken place (cf. Koegel et al., 2014). The data show that children educated in full inclusion environments learn at least as well, if not better than, children in more restricted environments (see following section on data on full inclusion versus segregated educational settings), while at the same time preserving their freedom and dignity.

Cost of Full Inclusion Versus Segregation Finally, some critics of full inclusion have suggested (incorrectly) that its costs may be too high (Odom et al., 2011; Odom et al., 2001; Yell, 2012). They have speculated that planning and implementing behavioral interventions might possibly be too time- and labor-intensive, and some consider the possibility that state-of-the-art services for ASD might be more expensive than services for other disabilities (Jacobson & Mulick, 2000). However, inclusion, especially at the preschool level, tends to be no more expensive than segregated programs (Barton & Smith, 2015; Odom et al., 2001). Thus, there are strong arguments that full inclusion is not more expensive than special day classes. Furthermore, one needs to consider the benefit of the intervention and needs to be aware that according to the law, cost cannot take precedence over what is legally deemed the child's LRE (IDEA, 2004; Yell, 2012).

Efficacy of Full Inclusion Versus Segregation The efficacy of inclusive programs compared with more segregated special education settings has historically been a topic of debate, as mixed results are reported in the literature (Barton & Smith, 2015; Carlberg & Kavale, 1980; Lindsay, 2007; Mesibov & Shea, 1996; Odom et al., 2004; Sainato, Morrison, Jung, Axe, & Nixon, 2015). Some researchers have contended that mainstream or full inclusion classroom settings are unable to provide the same quality learning experiences as special classes (Murphy, 1996); however, many studies demonstrate the potential benefits of full inclusion (Barton & Smith, 2015; Odom et al., 2004; Sainato et al., 2015; Strain & Bovey, 2011). For example, when compared with a control group, an inclusive kindergarten classroom was found to have significant positive effects on children with ASD's verbal communication, in addition to positive effects on adaptive behavior

(Sainato et al., 2015). Research has also found that children with severe disabilities in inclusive classrooms score better on standardized language assessments than children in more segregated settings (Rafferty, Piscitelli, & Boettcher, 2003). Despite continual evidence of positive outcomes for both children with ASD and their peers as a result of inclusion, students with ASD have been found to spend significantly more time in special education classrooms compared with students with other disabilities (Bitterman et al., 2008). We believe this discrepancy in placement is due to a lack of training and education on full inclusion procedures (cf. Koegel et al., 2014).

There is no doubt that a student with ASD cannot simply be placed in a standard GE classroom without any sort of accommodations or modifications (Mesibov & Shea, 1996; Odom, Buysse, & Soukakou, 2011; Odom et al., 2001; Simpson et al., 2003; Simpson & Sasso, 1992). High-quality inclusive classrooms generally have high ratios of competent peers as models, specialized instruction and intervention, adaptations of materials and/or space, facilitation of social interactions with peers by adults, and individualization of goals (Simpson et al., 2003; Soukakou, 2012; Strain & Bovey, 2011).

High-quality inclusive programming has collaboration as its core and may include modification of the environment and curriculum, classroom support and training, attitudinal support, coordinated team efforts and commitment, regular data collection and program evaluation, and home-school collaboration (Simpson et al., 2003). Not surprising, these components directly address the reported barriers to inclusion. The indicators of high-quality programs are critical to address and implement if inclusive programs are truly to provide more beneficial environments and outcomes than segregated settings.

Key Insights ||| Providing Inclusive Education for Children With ASD

The following insights concerning inclusive education are important to keep in mind when working with students with ASD:

- An extensive line of research has shown not only that educating children with autism and related disorders is possible, but also that it may be best achieved in full inclusion classrooms.
- A vast body of literature exists to demonstrate that educational interventions, especially those in inclusive contexts, improve social, academic, and behavioral functioning for students with ASD (e.g., Crosland & Dunlap, 2012; Harrower & Dunlap, 2001; Koegel, Kim, & Koegel, 2014; Koegel, Koegel, Frea, & Fredeen, 2001; Koegel, Vernon, Koegel, Koegel, & Paullin, 2012; Stahmer, Carter, Baker, & Miwa, 2010).
- Training programs and manuals have been developed by ourselves and others specifically to support educators and school administrators in developing appropriate inclusive programs (e.g., de Boer, 2009).
- As more people have been educated in the procedures and results related to high-quality inclusive educational models, advocacy and acceptance have increased.

- General education teachers need access to training and support in methods that facilitate inclusion, along with hands-on practice with feedback, during their pre-service education.
- When a school promotes a positive attitude, provides support and resources, and encourages team collaboration, this results in effective inclusive programs.
- Children with and without disabilities benefit from inclusion.

SUMMARY

Since the 1970s when the educational system first began to formally consider children with autism to be educable, beliefs and practices related to the education of children with ASD have changed dramatically. These students were once considered uneducable; however, perspectives among educators, researchers and clinicians, and the general public have shifted over time. Now, it is far more widely recognized that children with ASD have a right to a free and appropriate public education in the least restrictive environment possible—and that, not only are they capable of learning, they can learn alongside their typically developing peers in general education classrooms. The lead author's early work in this area developed school-based models in which 1) one-to-one support from aides could be gradually faded, and 2) educational methods and supports could be individualized to address students' heterogeneity.

To ensure inclusive education of children with ASD is effective, several factors must be considered: perceptions and attitudes toward inclusion (e.g., educators', parents'); parental anxieties and desires for their child; teacher training, support, and resources; and socialization with peers, which is just as important as academic success. When these factors are taken into account and addressed, the benefits of inclusion—not only for students with ASD, but for their peers as well—ultimately outweigh the costs.

STUDY QUESTIONS

1. How were the early classroom models for children with autism arranged?
2. How was heterogeneity addressed in the early classroom models?
3. Describe the different definitions of inclusion.
4. Discuss perceptions and attitudes toward inclusion from various perspectives (e.g., administrators, teachers, parents).
5. List reasons why inclusion sometimes fails.
6. What are some strategies to promote inclusion?
7. Discuss peer attitudes toward students with disabilities.
8. Discuss the interpretation of the least restrictive environment laws regarding inclusion.

9. List ways in which peers can become involved and improve their attitudes toward students with disabilities.

10. What are some characteristics of high-quality inclusive programs?

REFERENCES

Abu-Hamour, B., & Muhaidat, M. (2014a). Special education teachers' attitudes towards inclusion of students with autism in Jordan. *Journal of the International Association of Special Education, 14,* 34–40.

Abu-Hamour, B., & Muhaidat, M. (2014b). Parents' attitudes towards inclusion of students with autism in Jordan. *International Journal of Inclusive Education, 18*(6), 567–579.

Able, H., Sreckovic, M. A., Schultz, T. R., Garwood, J. D., & Sherman, J. (2015). Views from the trenches: Teacher and student supports needed for full inclusion of students with ASD. *Teacher Education and Special Education, 38,* 44–57.

Allday, A., Neilsen-Gatti, S., & Hudson, T. M. (2013). Preparation for inclusion in teacher education pre-service curricula. *Teacher Education Division of the Council for Exceptional Children, 36*(4), 298–311.

Allen, J. (2008). *Rethinking inclusive education: The philosophers of difference in practice.* London: Springer.

Avramidis, E., & Norwich, B. (2002). Teachers' attitudes towards integration/inclusion: A review of the literature. *European Journal of Special Needs Education, 17,* 129–147.

Barned, N. E., Flanagan Knapp, N., & Neuharth-Pritchett, S. (2011). Knowledge and attitudes of early childhood preservice teachers regarding the inclusion of children with autism spectrum disorder. *Journal of Early Childhood Teacher Education, 32*(4), 302–321.

Barton, E. E., & Smith, B. J. (2015). Advancing high-quality preschool inclusion: A discussion and recommendations for the field. *Topics in Early Childhood Special Education, 35*(2), 69–78.

Bitterman, A., Daley, T. C., Misra, S., Carlson, E., & Markowitz, J. (2008). A national sample of preschoolers with autism spectrum disorders: Special education services and parent satisfaction. *Journal of Autism and Developmental Disorders, 38,* 1509–1517.

Borthwick-Duffy, S. A., Palmer, D. S., & Lane, K. L. (1996). One size doesn't fit all: Full inclusion and individual differences. *Journal of Behavioral Education, 6*(3), 311–329.

Burack, J., Root, R., & Zigler, E. (1997). Inclusive education for students with autism: Reviewing ideological, empirical and community considerations. In D. Cohen & F. Volkmor (Eds.), *Handbook of autism and developmental disorders* (2nd ed.). Chichester, England: Wiley.

Carlberg, C., & Kavale, K. (1980). The efficacy of special versus regular class placement for exceptional children: A meta-analysis. *The Journal of Special Education, 14*(3), 295–309.

Carter, E. W., Common, E. A., Sreckovic, M. A., Huber, H. B., Botteman-Beutel, K., Gustafson, J., Dykstra, J., & Hume, K. (2014). Promoting social competence and peer relationships for adolescents with autism spectrum disorders. *Remedial and Special Education, 35*(2), 91–101.

Cassady, J. M. (2011). Teachers' attitudes toward the inclusion of students with autism and Emotional Behavioral Disorder. *Electronic Journal for Inclusive Education, 2*(7).

Chamberlain, B., Kasari, C., & Rotheram-Fuller, E. (2007). Involvement or isolation? The social networks of children with autism in regular classrooms. *Journal of Autism and Developmental Disorders, 37*(2), 230–242.

Connor, D. J., & Ferri, B. A. (2007). The conflict within: Resistance to inclusion and other paradoxes in special education. *Disability and Society, 22,* 63–77.

Cook, B. G., Semmel, M. I., & Gerber, M. M. (1999). Attitudes of principals and special education teachers toward the inclusion of students with mild disabilities: Critical differences of opinion. *Remedial and Special Education, 20*(4), 199–207.

Cooper, M. J., Griffith, K. G., & Filer, J. (1999). School intervention for inclusion of students with and without disabilities. *Focus on Autism and Other Developmental Disabilities, 14*(2), 110–115.

Corkum, P., Bryson, S. E., Smith, I. M., Giffen, C., Hume, K., et al. (2014). Professional development needs for educators working with children with autism spectrum disorders in inclusive school environments. *Exceptionality Education International, 24,* 33–47.

Crosland, K., & Dunlap, G. (2012). Effective strategies for the inclusion of children with autism in general education classrooms. *Behavior Modification, 36*(3), 251–269.

de Boer, S. R. (2009). *Successful inclusion for students with autism: Creating a complete, effective ASD inclusion program.* San Francisco, CA: Jossey-Bass.

de Boer, A., Pijl, S. J., & Minnaert, A. (2010). Attitudes of parents towards inclusive education: A review of the literature. *European Journal of Special Needs Education, 25*(2), 165–181.

DeMatthews, D., & Mawhinney, H. (2014). Social justice leadership and inclusion: Exploring challenges in an urban district struggling to address inequities. *Educational Administration Quarterly, 50*(5), 844–881.

Emam, M. M., & Farrell, P. (2009). Tensions experienced by teachers and their views of support for pupils with autism spectrum disorders in mainstream schools. *European Journal of Special Needs Education, 24*(4), 407–422.

Engstrand, R. Z., & Roll-Pettersson, L. (2012). Inclusion of preschool children with autism in Sweden: attitudes and perceived efficacy of preschool teachers. *Journal of Research in Special Education Needs, 14*(3), 170–179.

Falkmer, M., Anderson, K., Joosten, A., & Falkmer, T. (2015). Parents' perspectives on inclusive schools for children with autism spectrum conditions. *International Journal of Disability, Development, and Education, 62,* 1–23.

Finke, E. H., McNaughton, D. B., & Drager, K. D. R. (2009). All children can and should have the opportunity to learn: General education teachers' perspectives on including children with autism spectrum disorder who require AAC. *Augmentative and Alternative Communication, 25*(2), 110–122.

Fuchs, D., & Fuchs, L. S. (1994). Inclusive schools movement and the radicalization of special education reform. *Exceptional Children, 60,* 294–309.

Glashan, L., MacKay, G., & Grieve, A. (2004). Teachers' experience of support in the mainstream education of pupils with autism. *Improving Schools, 7,* 49–60.

Grider, J. R. (1995). Full inclusion: A practitioner's perspective. *Focus on Autistic Behavior, 10*(4), 1–11.

Guzman, N. (1997). Leadership for successful inclusive schools: A study of principal behaviours. *Journal of Educational Administration, 35*(5), 439–450.

Hannah, M. E., & Pliner, S. (1983). Teacher attitudes toward handicapped children: A review and synthesis. *School Psychology Review, 12,* 12–25.

Harper, C. B., Symon, J. B. G., & Frea, W. D. (2008). Recess is time-in: Using peers to improve social skills of children with autism. *Journal of Autism and Developmental Disorders, 38,* 815–826.

Harrower, J. K., & Dunlap, G. (2001). Including children with autism in general education classrooms: A review of effective strategies. *Behavior Modification, 25*(5), 762–784.

Hebb, D. O. (1958). The motivating effects of exteroceptive stimulation. *American Psychologist, 13*(3), 109–113.

Horrocks, J. L., White, G., & Roberts, L. (2008). Principals' attitudes regarding inclusion of children with autism in Pennsylvania public schools. *Journal of Autism and Developmental Disorders, 38,* 1462–1473.

Huefner, D. S. (1994). The mainstreaming cases: Tensions and trends for school administrators. *Educational Administration Quarterly, 30,* 27–55.

Iovannone, R., Dunlap, G., Huber, H., & Kincaid, D. (2003). Effective educational practices for students with autism spectrum disorders. *Focus on Autism and Other Developmental Disabilities, 18,* 150–165.

Individuals with Disabilities Education Act (IDEA) of 2004, PL 108-446, 20 U.S.C. §§ 1400 *et seq.*

Jacobson, J. W., & Mulick, J. A. (2000). System and cost research issues in treatments for people with autistic disorders. *Journal of Autism and Developmental Disorders, 30*(6), 585–593.

Jenkins, J. R., & Pious, C. G. (1991). Full inclusion and the REI: A reply to Thousand and Villa. *Exceptional Children, 57*(6), 562–64.

Kasari, C., Freeman, S. F. N., Bauminger, N., & Alkin, M. C. (1999). Parental perspectives on inclusion: Effects of autism and Down syndrome. *Journal of Autism and Developmental Disorders, 29,* 297–305.

Kasari, C., Locke, J., Gulsrud, A., & Rotheram-Fuller (2011). Social networks and friendships at school: Comparing children with and without ASD. *Journal of Autism and Developmental Disorders, 41,* 533–544.

Kauffman, J. M. (1995). Why we must celebrate a diversity of restrictive environments. *Learning Disabilities Research & Practice, 10*(4), 225–232.

Kavale, K. A. (2002). Mainstreaming to full inclusion: From orthogenesis to pathogenesis of an idea. *International Journal of Disability, Development, and Education, 49*(2), 201–214.

Kavale, K. A., & Forness, S. R. (2000). History, rhetoric, and reality: Analysis of the inclusion debate. *Remedial and Special Education, 21*(5), 279–296.

Koegel, R. L., & Koegel, L. K. (1995). *Teaching children with autism: Strategies forinitiating positive interactions and improving learning opportunities*. Baltimore: MD: Paul H. Brookes Publishing, Co.

Koegel, L. K., Koegel, R. L., Frea, W. D., & Fredeen, R. M. (2001). Identifying early intervention targets for children with autism in inclusive school settings. *Behavior Modification, 25,* 745–762.

Koegel, L. K., Vernon, T. W., Koegel, R. L., Koegel, B. L., & Paullin, A. W. (2012). Improving social engagement and initiations between children with autism spectrum disorder and their peers in inclusive settings. *Journal of Positive Behavior Interventions,* 1–8.

Koegel, R. L., Kim, S., & Koegel, L. K. (2014). Training paraprofessionals to improve socialization in students with ASD. *Journal of Autism and Developmental Disorders, 44*(9), 2197–2208.

Leach, D., & Duffy, M. L. (2009). Supporting students with autism spectrum disorders in inclusive settings. *Intervention in School and Clinic, 45,* 31–37.

Leblanc, L., Richardson, W., & Burns, K. A. (2009). Autism spectrum disorder and the inclusive classroom: Effective training to enhance knowledge of ASD and evidence-based practices. *Teacher Education and Special Education, 32*(2), 166–179.

Leyser, Y., & Kirk, R. (2004). Evaluating inclusion: An examination of parent views and factors influencing their perspectives. *International Journal of Disability Development and Education, 51,* 271–285.

Lindsay, G. (2007). Educational psychology and the effectiveness of inclusive education/mainstreaming. *British Journal of Educational Psychology, 77,* 1–24.

Lindsay, S., & Edwards, A. (2013). A systematic review of disability awareness interventions for children and youth. *Disability and Rehabilitation, 35,* 623–646.

Lindsay, S., Proulx, M., Scott, H., & Thomson, N. (2013). Exploring teachers' strategies for including children with autism spectrum disorder in mainstream classrooms. *International Journal of Inclusive Education, 18*(2), 101–122.

Lindsay, S., Proulx, M., Thomson, N., & Scott, H. (2013). Educators' challenges of including children with autism spectrum disorder in mainstream classrooms. *Journal of Disability, Development, and Education, 60*(4), 347–362.

Lipsky, D. K., & Gartner, A. (1997). *Inclusion and school reform: Transforming America's classroom.* Baltimore, MD: Paul H. Brookes Publishing Co.

Locke, J., Ishijima, E. H., Kasari, C., & London, N. (2010). Loneliness, friendship quality and the social networks of adolescents with high-functioning autism in an inclusive school setting. *Journal of Research in Special Educational Needs, 10*(2), 74–81.

Lynch, S. L., & Irvine, A. N. (2009). Inclusive education and best practice for children with autism spectrum disorder: an integrated approach. *International Journal of Inclusive Education, 13*(8), 845–859.

Majoko, T. (2016). Inclusion of children with autism spectrum disorders: Listening and hearing to voices from the grassroots. *Journal of Autism and Developmental Disorders, 46*(4),

Mather, N., & Roberts, R. (1994). Learning disabilities: A field in danger of extinction? *Learning Disabilities Research and Practice* 9(1), 49–58.

Mavropoulou, S., & Sideridis, G. D. (2014). Knowledge of autism and attitudes of children toward partially integrated peers with autism spectrum disorders. *Journal of Autism and Developmental Disorders, 44,* 1867–1885.

McCray, E. D., & McHatton, P. A. (2011). "Less afraid to have *them* in my classroom": Understanding pre-service general educators' perceptions about inclusion. *Teacher Education Quarterly, 38*(4) 135–155.
McGregor, E., & Campbell, E. (2001). The attitudes of teachers in Scotland to the integration of children with autism into mainstream schools. *Autism, 5*(2), 189–207.
McHatton, P., & McCray, E. D. (2007). Inclination toward inclusion: Perceptions of elementary and secondary education teacher candidates. *Action in Teacher Education, 29*(3), 25–32.
McHatton, P. A. & Parker, A. (2013). Purposeful preparation: Longitudinally exploring inclusion attitudes of general and special education pre-service teachers. *Education and Educational Research, 36*(3), 186–203.
McLeskey, J., & Waldron, N. L. (2015). Effective leadership makes schools truly inclusive. *Phi Delta Kappan, 96*(5), 68–73.
Mesibov, G. B., & Shea, V. (1996). Full inclusion and students with autism. *Journal of Autism and Developmental Disorders, 26*(3), 337–346.
Murphy, D. M. (1996). Implications of inclusion for general and special education. *The Elementary School Journal, 96*(5), 469–493.
National Education Association of the United States. (1978). *PL 94-142: Related federal legislation for handicapped children and implications for coordination*. Washington: The Association.
Ochs, E., Kremer-Sadlik, T., Solomon, O., & Sirota, K. G. (2001). Inclusion as social practice: views of children with autism. *Social Development, 10*(3), 399–419.
Odom, S. L., Buysse, V., & Soukakou, E. (2011). Inclusion for young children with disabilities: A quarter century of research perpsectives. *Journal of Early Intervention, 33*(4), 344–356.
Odom, S. L., Hanson, M. J., Lieber, J., Marquart, K., Sandall, S., Wolery, R., & Chambers, J. (2001). The costs of preschool inclusion. *Topics in Early Childhood Special Education, 21,* 46–55.
Odom, S. L., & Strain, P. S. (1984). Peer-mediated approaches to promoting children's social interaction: A review. *American Journal of Orthopsychiatry, 54*(4), 544–557.
Odom, S. L., Vitztum, J., Wolery, R., Lieber, J., Sandall, S., Hanson, M. J., Beckman, P., Schwartz, I., & Horn, E. (2004). Preschool inclusion in the United States: A review of research from an ecological systems perspective. *Research in Special Educational Needs, 4,* 17–49.
Pearman, E. L., Barnhart, M. W., Huang, A. M., & Mellblom, C. (1992). Educating all students in school: Attitudes and beliefs about inclusion. *Education and Training in Mental Retardation, 27,* 177–182
Praisner, C. L. (2003). Attitudes of elementary school principals toward the inclusion of students with disabilities. *Exceptional Children, 69*(2), 135–145.
Rafferty, Y., Boettcher, C., & Griffin, K. W. (2001). Benefits and risks of reverse inclusion for preschoolers with and without disabilities: Parents' perspectives. *Journal of Early Intervention, 24,* 266–286.
Rafferty, Y., Piscitelli, V., & Boettcher, C. (2003). The impact of inclusion on language development and social competence among preschoolers with disabilities, *Exceptional Children, 69*(4), 467–479.
Ravet, J. (2011). Inclusive/exclusive? Contradictory perspectives on autism and inclusion: The case for an integrative position. *International Journal of Inclusive Education, 15*(6), 667–682.
Robertson, K., Chamberlain, B., & Kasari, C. (2003). General education teachers' relationships with included students with autism. *Journal of Autism and Developmental Disorders, 33,* 123–130.
Robinson, S. E. (2011). Teaching paraprofessionals of students with autism to implement Pivotal Response Treatment in inclusive school settings using a brief video feedback training package. *Focus on Autism and Other Developmental Disabilities, 26*(2), 105–118.
Rotheram-Fuller, E. (2005). Age-related changes in the social inclusion of children with autism in general education classrooms (Doctoral dissertation). Retrieved from ProQuest Dissertations Publishing (3181739).
Rotheram-Fuller, E., Kasari, C., Chamberlain, B., & Locke, J. (2010). Social involvement of children with autism spectrum disorders in elementary school classrooms. *Journal of Child Psychology and Psychiatry, 51*(11), 1227–1234.

Rowley, E., Chandler, S., Baird, G., Simonoff, E., Pickles, A., Loucas, T., & Charman, T. (2012). The experience of friendship, victimization and bullying in children with an autism spectrum disorder: Associations with child characteristics and school placement. *Research in Autism Spectrum Disorders, 6*(3), 1126–1134.

Russo, D. C., & Koegel, R. L. (1977). A method for integrating an autistic child into a normal Public-school classroom. *Journal of Applied Behavior Analysis, 10*(4), 579–590.

Sainato, D. M., Morrison, R. S., Jung, S., Axe, J., & Nixon, P. A. (2015). A comprehensive inclusion program for kindergarten children with autism spectrum disorder. *Journal of Early Intervention, 37*(3), 208–225.

Salisbury, C. L., & McGregor, G. (2002). The administrative climate and context of inclusive elementary schools. *Exceptional Children, 68,* 259–274.

Sansoti, J. M., & Sansoti, F. J. (2012). Inclusion for students with high-functioning autism spectrum disorders: Definitions and decision making. *Psychology in the Schools, 49*(10), 917–931.

Scruggs, T. E., & Mastropieri, M. A. (1996). Teacher perceptions of mainstreaming/inclusion, 1958–1995: A research synthesis. *Exceptional Children, 63,* 59–74.

Segall, M. J., & Campbell, J. M. (2012). Factors relating to education professionals' classroom practices for the inclusion of students with autism spectrum disorders. *Research in Autism Spectrum Disorders, 6,* 1156–1167.

Shippen, M. E., Crites, S. A., Houchins, D. E., Ramsey, M. L., & Simon, M. (2005). Preservice teachers' perceptions of including students with disabilities. *Teacher Education and Special Education, 28*(2), 92–99.

Simpson, R. L. (1995). Children and youth with autism in an age of reform: A perspective on current issues. *Behavioral Disorders,* 21, 7–20.

Simpson, R. L., de Boer-Ott, S. R., & Smith-Myles, B. (2003). Inclusion of learners with autism spectrum disorders in general education settings. *Topics in Language Disorders, 23(*2), 116–133.

Simpson, R. L., & Sasso, G. M. (1992). Full inclusion of students with autism in general education settings: Values versus science. *Focus on Autistic Behavior, 7*(3), 1–13.

Soukakou, E. P. (2012). Measuring quality in inclusive preschool classroom: Development and validation of the Inclusive Classroom Profile. *Early Childhood Research Quarterly, 27*(3), 478–488.

Sreckovic, M. A., Brunsting, N. C., & Able, H. (2014). Victimization of students with autism spectrum disorder: a review of prevalence and risk factors. *Research in Autism Spectrum Disorders, 8,* 1155–1172.

Stahmer, A., Carter, C., Baker, M., & Miwa, K. (2010). Parent perspectives on their toddlers' development: comparison of regular and inclusion childcare. *Early Child Development and Care, 173*(5), 477–488.

Stahmer, A. C., Suhrheinrich, J., Reed, S., Bolduc, C., & Schreibman, L. (2010). Pivotal response teaching in the classroom setting. *Preventing School Failure: Alternative Education for Children and Youth, 54*(4), 265–274.

Stoner, J., & Angell, M. E. (2006). Parent perspectives on role engagement: An investigation of parents of children with ASD and their self-reported roles with education professionals (autism spectrum disorder). *Focus on Autism and Other Developmental Disabilities, 21,* 177–189.

Stoner, J., Angell, M. E., House, J. J., & Bock, S. J. (2007). Transitions: Perspectives from parents of young children with autism spectrum disorder (ASD). *Journal of Developmental and Physical Disabilities, 19,* 23–39.

Stoner, J., Bock, S. J., Thompson, J. R., Angell, M. E., Heyl, B. S., & Crowley, E. P. (2005). Welcome to our world: Parent perceptions of interactions between parents of young children with ASD and education professionals. *Focus on Autism and Other Developmental Disabilities, 20,* 39–51.

Strain, P. S., & Bovey, E. H. (2011). Randomized, controlled trial of the LEAP model of early intervention for young children with autism spectrum disorders. *Early Childhood Special Education, 31,* 133–154.

Turnbull, A. P., & Ruef, M. (1997). Family perspectives on inclusive lifestyle issues for people with problem behavior. *Exceptional Children, 63,* 211–227.

Turnbull, A. P., Turnbull, H. R., & Blue-Banning, M. (1994). Enhancing inclusion of infants and toddlers with disabilities and their families: A theoretical and programmatic analysis. *Infants and Young Children, 7*(2).

Watkins, L., O'Reilly, M., Kuhn, M., Gevarter, C., Lancioni, G. E., Sigafoos, J., & Lang, R. (2015). A review of peer-mediated social interaction interactions for students with autism in inclusive settings. *Journal of Autism and Developmental Disorders, 45*(4), 1070–1083.

Wilde, L. D., Koegel, L. K., & Koegel, R. L. (1992). *Increasing success in school through priming: A training manual.* Santa Barbara: University of California.

Yell, M. L. (2012). *The law and special education* (3rd ed.). Upper Saddle River, NJ: Pearson.

Yell, M. L., Katsiyannis, A., Drasgow, E., & Herbst, M. (2003). Developing legally correct and educationally appropriate programs for students with autism spectrum disorders. *Focus on Autism and Other Developmental Disabilities, 18*(3), 182–191.

Young, B., Simpson, R. L., Smith-Myles, B., & Kamps, D. M. (1997). An examination of paraprofessional involvement in supporting inclusion of students with autism. *Focus on Autism and Other Developmental Disabilities, 12,* 31–38.

Yssel, N., Engelbrecht, P., Oswald, M. M., Eloff, I., & Swart, E. (2007). Views of inclusion: A comparative study of parents' perceptions in South Africa and the United States. *Remedial and Special Education, 28*(6), 356–365.

9

Motivational Academics

Lynn Kern Koegel and Samantha K. Poyser

CHAPTER GOALS

Goal 1. The reader will understand why it is important for children with autism spectrum disorders (ASD) to be included with their typically developing peers.

Goal 2. The reader will understand why disruptive behaviors are often present both in school and at home during academic tasks.

Goal 3. The reader will learn how to incorporate motivational components into schoolwork to improve motivation to engage in academic activities.

Goal 4. The reader will understand how creating motivation for engaging in academic work will simultaneously reduce or eliminate disruptive behavior.

Goal 5. The reader will understand why parental involvement in their child's education is important.

This chapter discusses challenging behaviors that are commonly seen when academic activities are presented at school and home. We also discuss inclusion in general education (GE) settings and the use of partial participation, so that children with ASD can engage to the maximum extent possible with their typically developing peers. Next, we describe specific motivational procedures that can be included in the curriculum, as an antecedent intervention, to decrease the likelihood of disruptive behavior. Finally, we discuss parent collaboration and procedures that can be implemented in the home to improve academic engagement and decrease disruptive behaviors across settings.

BACKGROUND: THE RELATIONSHIP BETWEEN BEHAVIOR AND ACADEMICS

Many students with ASD engage in challenging behavior during academic activities, which presents a problem for the student, their parents, and the involved professionals (Koegel, Koegel, Harrower, & Carter, 1999; Koegel, Singh, & Koegel, 2010). That is, getting students with ASD who demonstrate disruptive behaviors to participate in classroom activities and complete their homework assignments can be a daily difficulty that wears on the child, parents, and teachers. Children with ASD will often display disruptive or avoidance behaviors when academic tasks are too difficult or unrelated to their preferred interests. However, research has shown that incorporating motivational variables into the academic assignments decreases disruptive behaviors and increases the student with ASD's interest and performance (Koegel et al., 2010; Mancil & Pearl, 2008). To do this, academic programs must be individualized using core Pivotal Response Treatment (PRT) motivational components with regular data collection to be sure that the student is responding positively to the intervention (Koegel, Dunlap, & Koegel, 1996).

Disruptive Behaviors

Before beginning to discuss intervention procedures for improving academics, it is important to more thoroughly understand the relationship between academic activities and disruptive behaviors. Disruptive behaviors are often displayed in both the school and home environment when students with ASD are presented with academic assignments. Research has suggested that these students most frequently engage in disruptive behavior to escape or avoid the task at hand (Gunter, Denny, Jack, Shores, & Nelson, 1994; Ochs, Kremer-Sadlik, Solomon, & Sirota, 2001). The function of this disruptive behavior may be to escape the academic task because it is too difficult or uninteresting. That is, when a task is presented with overly complicated instructions or difficult problems, when it is repetitive and boring, and/or when it seems meaningless, the student with ASD may display disruptive behavior to get out of, or escape, the task. Undoubtedly, this can stand in the way of students with ASD reaching their full academic potential (Gunter et al., 1994 Koegel, O'Dell, & Koegel, 1987). Once the student with ASD's communication skills improve or replacement behaviors are taught, such as asking for help or asking to take a break, disruptive behavior should decrease (Koegel, Koegel, & Surratt, 1992); however, incorporating motivational strategies and making the activities meaningful will further encourage the student to complete work without avoidance- or escape-motivated behaviors. Incorporating the PRT motivational variables, and other techniques designed to help the child with ASD succeed, should result in decreases in disruptive behavior. Implementing such antecedent intervention procedures reduces the need to target the problem behaviors directly, thereby creating conditions conducive to active learning and engagement (Koegel et al., 2010).

Inclusive Classrooms and Partial Participation

In addition to receiving academic assignments that are modified to be motivational, in recent decades many more children with ASD are being included with their typically developing peers in the least restrictive environment (LRE) (IDEA,

2004). The LRE is often the GE classroom, and the primary adult responsible for the child with ASD's academic program is often the classroom teacher (Fisher & Meyer, 2002) with support from special education staff. Indeed, there are several benefits to educating students with disabilities in the same classroom as their typically developing peers (Fryxell & Kennedy, 1995; Helmstetter, Curry, Brennan, & Sampson-Saul, 1998; Hunt, Farron-Davis, Beckstead, Curtis, & Goetz, 1994). For example, in inclusive classrooms, typically developing peers can serve both as supports and positive role models, while facilitating an environment for friendships. Longitudinal group studies demonstrate that students with ASD have greater success in inclusive settings, compared with those placed in special education classrooms (Fisher & Meyer, 2002).

For inclusion of children with ASD to be successful, it is important that they are able to engage in academic assignments along with their classmates without disruptive behaviors interfering. Even if the child is not academically at the same level as typically developing peers in the classroom, it is important that the children be exposed to the same curriculum. This can be accomplished through *partial participation*, wherein the student with ASD is engaging in the same assignment as his or her typical peers, but the assignment is modified to require the maximum participation possible within the student's ability level. Note that partial participation allows the students to be included full time and learn alongside their typically developing peers. The partial participation model firmly rejects a developmental order or logic for curriculum decision making in which the child with ASD is placed in a lower academic level and, instead, focuses on the child's active participation in real, age-appropriate activities (Ferguson & Baumgart, 1991). This involves teachers' selection of areas to target that will have the greatest impact on helping their students become independent and competent in their natural settings (Ferguson & Baumgart, 1991). Such strategies, if implemented correctly, result in a dramatically more meaningful and effective educational program for the student with ASD. Some examples of assignment modifications are shown in Figures 9.1 and 9.2.

Partial Participation Example–Math In this example, the child with ASD is able to add numbers in the ones column but has not yet learned to carry. Note that the child is still participating in the same assignment as the peers, but it has been modified for his level.

Typical student	Student with ASD
403	3
+ 39	+ 9

Figure 9.1. Example of how a math problem might be modified to allow for partial participation.

Partial Participation Example–Spelling In this example, the child with ASD is able to identify words by the first letter. Thus, the child has to recognize the correct spelling based on the remaining letters.

Partial participation is a method of exposing the child to the same activities in which the typical peers engage. As a result, the children are learning the same skill or academic areas as their peers, but at their own level. It is analogous to a family

Typical student	Student with ASD	
Write the words that the teacher reads.	*Circle the correct word that the teacher reads.*	
blue	blue	brown
table	toy	table
glass	glass	game
and	and	another
money	money	many
friend	friend	funny

Figure 9.2. Example of how a spelling activity might be modified to allow for partial participation.

cleaning the dishes after dinner. The younger children in the family may help clear the spoons and forks from the table and load them in the dishwasher, while the older children and adults are clearing and loading the breakable items, such as glassware and plates. By partially participating, the younger children are learning how to clear the table and load the dishwasher, but at their own level. Without having them partially participate, they wouldn't learn the skill at all. The principle underlying this simple example is the same for academics. Exposing the children to the same activity ensures they will be able to participate in the academic activities expected of their typical peers, even if it is just a part of the assignment. This is a vast difference from the days when children with ASD who were included in GE classrooms sat in the back corner with their aides working on completely different assignments. And, because the academics are not beyond the student's capabilities, the disruptive behavior that comes from frustration with overly difficult assignments is reduced.

INCORPORATING MOTIVATIONAL VARIABLES TO IMPROVE ACADEMIC ENGAGEMENT AND BEHAVIOR

Incorporating specific PRT motivational components, such as child choice, interspersal of maintenance tasks, preferred interests, and natural reinforcers, has been shown to improve motivation in academics (Koegel et al., 2010; Mancil & Pearl, 2008; Moes, 1998), thereby improving academic performance, engagement, and enthusiasm for learning. Key motivational strategies identified in the research literature are discussed in the following sections, along with suggestions for how educators and families might implement these strategies during in-class academic activities and homework.

Key Strategies: Child Choice, Task Interspersal, and Natural Rewards

In a systematic review of the implementation of child choice in the school environment, researchers found that providing the student with choice within academic assignments can produce increases in work completion, task duration, positive affect, and interest, while decreasing disruptive behaviors and latency in the time it takes the child to begin academic tasks (Reutebuch, El Zein, & Roberts, 2015). Choice can be provided in a variety of different ways, depending on how flexible the teacher is. That is, some teachers will agree to a considerable amount of modification, such as having the student use different stimulus materials while working on the same task. Others insist that the assignment that the other students are given should not be modified. Keep this in mind when assisting parents in developing a plan for their child. For example, we know that child choice is important. However, if the assignment cannot be modified, choice can also be implemented by providing an opportunity for the student to select the order in which each activity is completed during the school day. While the student may choose non-academic activities at the start of the day, research shows that eventually the student will engage in all of the classroom activities (Kern, Childs, Dunlap, Clarke, & Falk, 1994). Other research has shown that permitting a student to select the writing utensil and the color of paper can be helpful. Similarly, the student may decide where he or she would like to sit while completing a homework assignment (Moes, 1998). If the teacher is flexible, the student may be given a choice of materials, such as choosing which book to read or which math activity to complete. For example, if the child with ASD doesn't like the tiny colored blocks the class uses for learning patterns but enjoys working with Legos at home, Legos can be used for patterning. Similarly, if the child isn't interested in the phonic drills the teacher presents, phonics can be taught using the letters that spell the names of the child's favorite foods or toys after which the child can be naturally rewarded with an opportunity to eat the favorite food or play with the favorite toy. Again, reviews have found that providing choice, regardless of the type of choice, is a promising intervention for improving academic outcomes (Reutebuch et al., 2015).

Similarly, research has demonstrated that choice, along with other motivational variables, improves student performance and interest during homework assignments (Koegel et al., 2010). Specifically, academic tasks (writing and math) were targeted for four students with ASD, ranging in age from 4 to 7 years, who demonstrated significant disruptive behaviors (e.g., aggression, property destruction, tantrums, leaving the work area, refusal to come to the work area and engage in the task). The children were included in GE classrooms, and intervention was implemented with teacher-assigned classroom activities. However, the assignments were modified for each child using motivational components. That is, during the baseline condition, the students participated in typical instructional activities and were provided with individualized rewards; although the rewards were chosen by the students, they were not related to the task. Further, one task was presented at a time until it was completed. Finally, no consideration was given to varying the difficulty level. The students were required to engage in the academic task assigned by the teacher.

In the intervention condition, the same academic activity was targeted (i.e., math or writing), but it was modified to incorporate motivational variables. For example, easy activities that the students had previously mastered were interspersed with more difficult ones. During writing tasks, single words were interspersed with the assigned full sentences. In addition, the task was directly related to the reward, and child-specific interests were incorporated into the task. For example, if the teacher assigned the students to write a story about what they did over the weekend, the student with ASD could choose the topic of the story. Generally, they chose to write about their perseverative interest or favorite items or activities, after which they could play with the item or engage in that activity. Finally, the activities were varied so that the task was less drill-like and tedious. In addition, the child was provided with other choices, such as what materials they wanted to use and where they wanted to complete the assignment.

For all four students, the amount of time it took to begin the activity, or *latency*, as well as disruptive behavior, decreased and remained low throughout intervention. In addition, postintervention measures were collected at least 2 weeks after the intervention had been faded. In the postintervention measure, an adult unfamiliar to the child and unfamiliar with the study was asked to engage the child in a math or writing task. The children's rate of completion for writing and math problems, along with their measured interest, increased during the postintervention sessions and remained high even after the motivational components were no longer incorporated. This research suggests that part of the students' initial problem may have been that they engaged in generalized avoidance and escape behaviors. However, once the students were exposed to the curriculum using motivational strategies, generalization in appropriate behavior also occurred, meaning students demonstrated appropriate behavior and engagement during assignments that weren't part of the treatment condition. These types of improvements suggest that the motivational components helped the students with ASD develop a genuine love of learning, so that learning itself most likely became reinforcing.

Motivational components can also be included within the classroom curriculum with minimal modifications for students with ASD who are fully included. That is, the authors have incorporated motivational variables into the standard classroom worksheets for assignments such as reading and writing. Intervention procedures included the use of natural reinforcement, child choice, and interspersed maintenance and acquisitions tasks. As an example of a natural reinforcer, if the student enjoyed taking walks and wrote sentences using the word "walk," he could then go on a walk. The results from these modifications were consistent with the homework study results. During the baseline measures, the students were largely unengaged and uninterested. In contrast, when motivational variables were incorporated into the worksheets and other assignments, ratings of interest and happiness were higher. The students also increased the number of academic tasks they completed independently and needed less prompting to complete the tasks.

A similar study also demonstrated that using the child's preferred interests as motivators can also be effective in improving academic engagement (Mancil & Pearl, 2008). That is, embedding preferred interests into the curriculum motivated students with ASD to stay engaged during otherwise difficult or uninteresting tasks. For example, one student's preferred interest was a popular cartoon train character, so for math tasks a picture of this character was placed next to the numbers she had to add together. Instead of adding "13 + 7," the student was now finding out how many of her favorite trains there were. Again, this study showed that when preferred interests were incorporated into the math assignments, disruptive behaviors decreased.

In summary, key motivational strategies for academics include

- Child choice
- Interspersal of easy and difficulty tasks
- Natural rewards

It is critical to look for ways to link academic tasks to a motivating outcome for students with ASD. This also results in making the assignment meaningful for the student. For example, instead of requiring the student to add random numbers on a worksheet, he or she can add the prices of favorite toys they would like to purchase. Similarly, instead of learning to read with books that are chosen by the teacher, having the students read clues in a scavenger hunt leading to a desired treasure can improve the student's willingness to engage in the task. Likewise, writing letters to family members can be a fun and meaningful activity and is likely to result in collateral acquisition of knowledge such as the location on the envelope of the recipient's address, the return address, and stamp. In addition, a scavenger hunt around the classroom that requires the child to read each clue to move to the next step can help the teacher assess for reading comprehension. Most important, adding in these specific and researched motivational components can greatly increase the student's desire to learn.

Priming

Another helpful motivational procedure for students with ASD is priming, or previewing classroom materials in a nondemanding manner before they are presented in class. This simple and fun-to-implement procedure can be effective in both decreasing disruptive behaviors and improving the child's interest (Koegel, Koegel, Frea & Green-Hopkins, 2003; Wilde, Koegel, & Koegel, 1992). Priming can occur at home the night before school. Parents are asked to preview the materials in a relaxing, fun manner, such as reading an upcoming story to the child in a relaxing context—as a bedtime story—the night before it will be read at school. The point of the priming is not to teach materials in their entirety, but to expose the child to the academic activity in an enjoyable and relaxed way so that avoidance or escape behaviors are reduced when the actual activity occurs. If parents are unable or unwilling to prime the child, a teacher or special educator may also do this in a nondemanding manner after school, the day before the information is presented in class. Conceptually, when presented outside of the classroom, the material becomes low-demand with many opportunities for reinforcement. Thus, when the students are later exposed to the academic activity in class, the material is no longer a stimulus for escape or avoidance and the children no longer engage in disruptive behaviors to escape the task.

In another study, the authors used priming to increase appropriate behavior and academic responding for students in inclusive classrooms (Koegel et al., 2003). Priming sessions, which lasted for approximately 1 hour each day, were conducted in the evening with the student's parents or during "pull-out" services with a special educator. The study used an alternating treatment design, whereby children alternated between being primed on classroom material or going into the day as usual with no preview. Again, between the two conditions, students showed dramatic differences in both rates of disruptive behavior and academic responding. That is, when students participated in priming sessions, there were always increases in academic responding and reductions in problem behavior. Appropriate behavior was significantly higher in the priming conditions as well. This effect reversed immediately when the assignments were not primed. In addition to yielding academic and behavioral gains, home–school coordination with upcoming curriculum can be an enjoyable way to work collaboratively to greatly improve the student's behavior and academic motivation.

CASE EXAMPLE
Using Priming to Improve Ricky's Engagement in Class

Ricky was 5 years old and was fully included in a GE kindergarten class. He had slight delays academically, socially, and communicatively. He knew his letters and could count but was unwilling to sit for most academic activities. Socially, he was interested in the other children, but most frequently isolated himself and needed regular prompting to join in his classmates' activities and socially interact with them. Communicatively, he had a large vocabulary and could create grammatically correct sentences, but social conversation and receptive communication were challenges. When sentences and instructions were lengthy, he was lost.

One of the biggest challenges for Ricky was circle time. Because it was a highly verbal activity, he paid no attention. Story time was even more challenging. Although he probably could have picked up a word here and there, whenever the teacher grabbed a book and began to read it to the class, he erupted in severely disruptive screaming at the top of his lungs. He screamed single words, out of context, after which he'd laugh, roll on the floor, and flop around, disrupting the whole class.

Anyone who has worked with a school-based team knows how tough it is scheduling a date for an IEP meeting that will work for all of the people involved; however, this was not the case for Ricky's IEP meeting. Because of his disruptive behavior, the school pulled one together in a matter of days. School personnel wanted him out of the GE classroom. They didn't feel it was fair that he was disrupting the education for the other 20+ students in his class. However, before the IEP meeting, we started priming Ricky daily on the story the class would hear at story time the following day. His teacher gave his mother a copy of the books she was going to read, and his mother read them to him while he relaxed in bed each evening before dozing off. Ricky found the stories relaxing and fun when his mother sat beside his bed reading the books. Fortuitously, the priming had a dramatic effect on his behavior. Soon, instead of engaging in his usual disruption, screaming out one of his favorite words like, "refrigerator," "Uranus," or "Chucky-cheese," Ricky scurried up to the front of the classroom, sitting attentively and absorbing every word when the story—which now was familiar and had a positive history—was read. There was no more disruptive behavior. The intervention made such a difference that we began priming him on other activities—use of academic classroom centers, independent work, and even playtime activities. Ricky was able to remain in the GE classroom and began to engage appropriately in the activities with his classmates, particularly when they were primed. He actively listened, was engaged throughout the day, and was thoroughly interested in the activities. He no longer engaged in escape and avoidance behaviors at school.

PARENT INVOLVEMENT

As mentioned in other chapters, having a consistent educational plan that is coordinated between the home and school environment can be very important and helpful for improving the motivation of students with ASD. The literature shows that parent involvement is important for improving the child's academic achievement and helps the child develop a positive attitude toward work (Cooper & Nye,

1994; Hampshire, Butera, & Bellini, 2016; Walker, Hoover-Dempsey, Whetsel, & Green, 2004). Implementing intervention in a consistent manner across settings will increase the likelihood that students will make rapid progress, and this consistency has been shown to result in positive behavior change maintaining over time (Koegel & Koegel, 2006; Koegel et al., 2003). The research suggests that if parents are taught to incorporate PRT motivational techniques into homework, disruptive behavior decreases, child affect improves, positive comments improve, and homework performance improves (Koegel & Koegel, 2006). Further, parents can prime their children on academic activities to reduce disruptive behaviors at school. Collaborative implementation of goals, interventions, and behavior plans across the children's day can greatly reduce or eliminate disruptive behaviors.

Key Insights ||| Improving Academics and Behavior Through Motivational Strategies

The motivational strategies discussed in this chapter can significantly improve children's engagement in academic work at school and at home, resulting in reductions in disruptive behavior and improvements in socialization. The following key insights are important for practitioners to keep in mind when they work with school-age children with ASD, their families, their teachers, and other school-based professionals.

- **Academic inclusion is important:** When students with disabilities are included in the general education classroom, they are provided with more opportunities for friendship, academic growth, and positive models of appropriate behaviors. The earlier students with ASD are able to participate with their typically developing peers, the more positive their academic trajectory can be.
- **Parental involvement is key:** Coordinating educational plans between the classroom and the home is important to ensure consistency and improve motivation in the child's academic environment. Coordination is especially important if an intervention is done systematically, as in the case of priming, in which close home–school collaboration on assignments improves students' engagement and behavior.
- **Include natural reinforcers:** Look for ways to embed natural reinforcers into the task so that the student is able to directly relate his or her hard work to a desired natural reinforcing outcome.
- **Incorporate preferred interests:** Use the child's preferred interests to make tasks more interesting for the child, and use them as a reward for once the assignment is completed. Including the child's interests will help him to continue working even when the task is unfamiliar or difficult.
- **Give the student choices:** Allow the children to have as many choices as possible when it comes to academic assignments. When the activity cannot be individualized, they can choose which stimulus materials to use, where to complete the assignment, in what order to complete homework pages, and so on.

- **Preview classroom activities:** "Priming," or previewing, upcoming classroom activities can help improve students' interest and motivation to engage. When activities have been presented previously in a positive and low-demand manner, students will be more inclined to engage in a given activity when they see it again. Previewing material makes it easier for the child to understand in the classroom. And previewing in a nondemanding and rewarding manner will make the child less likely to try and escape or avoid the academic material when it is presented in class.
- **Add in maintenance tasks:** Intersperse maintenance tasks along with acquisition tasks so that students can gain momentum through the maintenance tasks and do not become overwhelmed with the portions of the tasks being difficult.

SUMMARY

So often, children with disabilities are underestimated in terms of what they can accomplish. They are especially susceptible to low expectations in the school environment, where the teacher–student ratio is low and paraprofessionals may not have the skills to work effectively with a child with ASD who exhibits disruptive behaviors. As mentioned in Chapter 2 on assessment, many students with ASD are given a curriculum far below their ability levels because their disruptive behaviors have interfered with task engagement during testing. In fact, research shows that teachers frequently revise and decrease the demands of the curriculum based on a student's disruptive behaviors (Carr, Taylor, & Robinson, 1991). However, with the addition of motivational components and appropriate modifications made to class curriculum, the children can thrive. Often students with ASD are not as naturally motivated as other students, and they need explicit and clear links between their hard work and a desired outcome. Once they are motivated, through systematic revision of the curriculum and priming they often start to develop a generalized desire to learn without special curricular manipulations, and their disruptive behavior decrease to very low levels. As well, appropriate behaviors, free of disruption, make it easier for students with ASD to develop social relationships with their peers.

STUDY QUESTIONS

1. Why is it important for children with ASD to be included in classrooms with their typically developing peers?
2. Why is it important to coordinate educational plans between home and school?
3. How can parents help make homework time a more positive experience?
4. List reasons why children with ASD might display disruptive behaviors during school and during homework time.
5. Describe ways to adapt the student's assignment to their academic level.
6. How does priming the child with upcoming classroom material help them to participate in classroom activities?

7. What type of choices can be offered to the child to increase their motivation?
8. How can a child's preferred interests be used to improve their academic performance?
9. How can natural reinforcers be embedded into assignments?
10. Why is it important to provide natural reinforcers within academic tasks?

REFERENCES

Carr, E. G., Taylor, J. C., & Robinson, S. (1991). The effects of severe behavior problems in children on the teaching behavior of adults. *Journal of Applied Behavior Analysis, 24*(3), 523–535.

Cooper, H., & Nye, B. (1994). Homework for students with learning disabilities: The implications of research for policy and practice. *Journal of Learning Disabilities, 27*(8), 470–479.

Ferguson, D. L., & Baumgart, D. (1991). Partial participation revisited. *Journal of the Association for Persons with Severe Handicaps, 16*(4), 218–227.

Fisher, M., & Meyer, L. H. (2002). Development and social competence after two years for students enrolled in inclusive and self-contained educational programs. *Research and Practice for Persons with Severe Disabilities, 27*, 165–174.

Fryxell, D., & Kennedy, C. H. (1995). Placement along the continuum of services and its impact on students' social relationships. *Journal of the Association for Persons With Severe Handicaps, 20*, 259–269.

Gunter, P. L., Denny, R. K., Jack, S. L., Shores, R. E., & Nelson, C. M. (1994). Aversive stimuli in academic interactions between students with serious emotional disturbance and their teachers. *Behavioral Disorders, 18*, 265–274.

Hampshire, P. K., Butera, G. D., & Bellini, S. (2016). Self-management and parents as interventionists to improve homework independence in students with autism spectrum disorders. *Preventing School Failure, 60*(1), 22–34.

Helmstetter, E., Curry, C., Brennan, M., & Sampson-Saul, M. (1998). Comparison of general and special education classrooms of students with severe disabilities. *Education and Training in Mental Retardation and Developmental Disabilities, 33*(3), 216–227.

Hunt, P., Farron-Davis, F., Beckstead, S., Curtis, D., & Goetz, L. (1994). Evaluating the effects of placement of students with severe disabilities in general education versus special classes. *Journal of the Association for Persons With Severe Handicaps, 19*, 200–214.

Individuals with Disabilities Education Act (IDEA) of 2004, PL 108-446, 20 U.S.C. §§ 1400 *et seq.*

Kern, L., Childs, K. E., Dunlap, G., Clarke, S., & Falk, G. D. (1994). Using assessment-based curricular intervention to improve the classroom behavior of a student with emotional and behavioral challenges. *Journal of Applied Behavior Analysis, 27*(1), 7–19.

Koegel, L. K., Dunlap, G., & Koegel, R. L. (1996). *Positive behavioral support: Including people with difficult behavior in the community.* Baltimore, MD: Paul H. Brookes Publishing Co.

Koegel, L. K., Koegel, R. L., Frea, W., & Green-Hopkins, I. (2003). Priming as a method of coordinating educational services for students with autism. *Language, Speech, and Hearing Services in Schools, 34*(3), 228–235.

Koegel, L. K., Koegel, R. L., Harrower, J. K., & Carter, C. M. (1999). Pivotal response intervention I: Overview of approach. *Journal of the Association for Persons with Severe Handicaps, 24*(3), 174–185.

Koegel, R. L., & Koegel, L. K. (2006). *Pivotal response treatments for autism: Communication, social, and academic development.* Baltimore, MD: Paul H. Brookes Publishing Co.

Koegel, R. L., Koegel, L. K., & Surratt, A. (1992). Language intervention and disruptive behavior in preschool children with autism. *Journal of Autism and Developmental Disorders, 22*(2), 141–153.

Koegel, R. L., O'Dell, M., & Koegel, L. K. (1987). A natural language paradigm for nonverbal autistic children. *Journal of Autism and Developmental Disorders, 17*(2), 187–200.

Koegel, L. K., Singh, A. K., & Koegel, R. L. (2010). Improving motivation for academics in children with autism. *Journal of Autism and Developmental Disorders, 40*(9), 1057–1066.

Mancil, R. G., & Pearl, C. E. (2008). Restricted interests as motivators: Improving academic engagement and outcomes of children on the autism spectrum. *TEACHING Exceptional Children Plus, 4*(6), 15.

Moes, D. R. (1998). Integrating choice-making opportunities within teacher-assigned academic tasks to facilitate the performance of children with autism. *Journal of the Association for Persons with Severe Handicaps, 23,* 319–328.

Ochs, E., Kremer-Sadlik, T., Solomon, O., & Sirota, K. (2001). Inclusion as social practice: Views of children with autism. *Social Development, 10*(3), 399–419.

Reutebuch, C. K., El Zein, F., & Roberts, G. J. (2015). A systematic review of the effects of choice on academic outcomes for students with autism spectrum disorder. *Research in Autism Spectrum Disorders, 20,* 1–16.

Walker, J. M., Hoover-Dempsey, K., Whetsel, D. R., & Green, C. L. (2004). *Parental involvement in homework: A review of current research and its implications for teachers, after school program staff, and parent leaders.* Harvard Family Research Project, Harvard Graduate School of Education, 3 Garden Street, Cambridge, MA 02138.

Wilde, L. D., Koegel, L. K., & Koegel, R. L. (1992). *Increasing success in school through priming: A training manual.* Santa Barbara: University of California.

IV

Adolescence and Young Adulthood

Moving Toward Independence

10

Functional Behavior Assessment and Self-Management

Brittany Lynn Koegel and Lynn Kern Koegel

CHAPTER GOALS

Goal 1. The reader will understand procedures for implementing a functional assessment for individuals with autism spectrum disorders (ASD).

Goal 2. The reader will become familiar with empirically based articles relating to functional assessment with individuals with ASD.

Goal 3. The reader will understand procedures for developing a self-management program.

Goal 4. The reader will understand how to develop a self-management program that is appropriate for the target behavior.

Goal 5. The reader will be able to develop positive goals at appropriate time levels for maximizing the likelihood of positive reinforcement in a self-management program.

Goal 6. The reader will become familiar with various successful evidence-based self-management programs for individuals with ASD.

Before we begin discussing methods for dealing with challenging behaviors, it's important to consider the importance of making sure antecedent procedures are in place to reduce the likelihood of behavior problems occurring in the first place. Because Pivotal Response Treatment (PRT) motivates children to want to participate in their therapy, they exhibit very little disruptive behavior. In fact, in an early study using an alternating treatment design where the authors of this book included the PRT motivational procedures, then reversed to using no motivational procedures, and so on, we found that disruptive and challenging behaviors were lower during every single session that included motivational procedures (Koegel,

Koegel, & Surratt, 1992). Thus, PRT operates as an antecedent to prevent the occurrence of disruptive behavior, and therefore one does not usually need to focus much time or energy on developing responsive procedures to eliminating these behaviors (Koegel et al., 1992). For these reasons, this chapter and subsequent chapters place greater emphasis upon using the PRT motivational procedures than upon functional behavior assessment (FBA) and self-management.

However, some children spend time in environments that aren't particularly motivating. Some teachers do not incorporate motivational procedures, and some children still exhibit disruptive behaviors even when a large part of their day includes engaging activities. Further, sometimes children learn that it's easier to aggress toward another child so that child does not take a toy or when they don't want to share. In these instances, a behavior plan will be necessary. This chapter describes how to conduct a functional assessment and develop appropriate replacement behaviors that serve the same communicative function as the targeted disruptive behavior. It also describes how to teach self-management procedures for improving appropriate behaviors and reducing challenging behaviors.

THE HISTORY OF BEHAVIORAL INTERVENTIONS

Prior to the 1980s, most challenging behaviors that individuals with autism exhibited beyond the first few years of life were viewed as aberrant and were dealt with through punitive consequences. That is, in order to eliminate behaviors such as tantrums, aggression, property destruction, and self-injury, punishment principles of operant conditioning were being used (cf. Lovaas, 1977). For example, punishing disruptive behavior using a myriad of aversive and often painful procedures was common. In fact, the research literature was suggesting that the most effective method of dealing with disruptive behavior was the use of aversive stimulation. These methods included water mists in the face (Bailey, Pokrzywinski, & Bryant, 1983), electric shock (Lovaas, Schaeffer, & Simmons, 1965; Risley, 1968), aromatic ammonia (Tanner & Zeiler, 1975), and other painful or uncomfortable procedures. While these procedures were effective in reducing the behaviors in the presence of the clinician, there were issues with generalization and maintenance of the gains. In addition, many people did not want to use punishment, stating that such methods do not respect the dignity of the individual with autism (c.f., Horner, Carr, Strain, Todd, & Reed, 2002). As a direct consequence of this sentiment, the field of positive behavior support (PBS) was created.

The Development of Positive Behavior Support

Researchers in this area sought to develop scientifically sound methods to minimize or eliminate challenging behavior while enhancing the quality of life for individuals with disabilities. Most of this research began when the United States government, wanting to avoid the use of aversive interventions, announced that it would award a very large federal grant for the purpose of developing non-aversive interventions. Many researchers, parents, and practitioners participated in this effort (Koegel, Koegel, & Dunlap, 1996). The field of PBS focuses on prevention of problem behavior but also uses intervention strategies in natural community settings that include lifestyle and systems change in addition to using positive strategies rather than punishment (Horner et al., 2002).

From the start, the field of PBS focused considerably on re-evaluating assessment procedures, so that instead of simply recording instances of challenging behavior, the field emphasized understanding the function of these behaviors. To do this, researchers and practitioners focused on analyzing both antecedents and consequences that might be maintaining the behavior, with antecedents including setting variables (e.g., hunger, fatigue), the presence of certain individuals (e.g., those who placed heavy demands on the child), time of day, possible physical issues, and so on. In particular, this focus on examining antecedents and consequences led to understanding the communicative intent of a challenging behavior. That is, in addition to recording the occurrence of a challenging behavior, the "why" is also assessed. That is, why did the individual engage in the behavior and what was he or she trying to communicate? Based on this type of assessment, replacement behaviors that serve the same communicative functions can be developed and taught. Researchers found that once individuals learned that they could obtain their reinforcer (e.g., attention, escape from a difficult task) through communication using appropriate means, they tended to rapidly stop being disruptive. It makes sense. Why would individuals scream, injure themselves, or destroy their belongings if they could be taught to say they needed a break or that they needed help? Verbal or augmentative communication to replace challenging behavior is not only desirable for others in the environment, it is also desirable for the individual with ASD.

In general, while challenging behaviors can have many possible functions, they can frequently be attributed to a few common functions: 1) gaining access to preferred items or activities; 2) escaping or avoiding nonpreferred items or activities; or 3) feeling momentary anxiety or discomfort as a result of changes in routine or environment (cf. Reese, Richman, Belmont, & Morse, 2005).

If disruptive behaviors are to be eliminated, is important to identify the function of the behavior through FBA in order to better inform the appropriate intervention for the child. That is, if the child does not learn to use a functionally equivalent replacement behavior (FERB), the challenging behaviors are likely to return as they are often efficient and effective in obtaining the desired function and, therefore, maintained. This is the case even if the challenging behaviors are punished and eliminated; they are likely to return if the individual does not have an appropriate way to communicate. However, if intervention addresses each function and the individual practices the replacement behavior often during non-crisis situations, the replacement behavior can become a strong part of the individual's repertoire. Consequently, the disruptive behavior becomes inefficient and unnecessary and can be reduced or eliminated, particularly if the disruptive behaviors are ignored so they are ineffective. For example, if we see through a functional assessment that a child is exhibiting tantrums in order to obtain attention, then we could teach the child a replacement behavior such as saying, "Look!" or "Look at my book!" in order to obtain attention, rather than tantrumming.

Analyzing a Behavior's Function and Teaching Replacement Behaviors

So, how do we do a functional assessment? A variety of procedures, including indirect, descriptive, and experimental assessment methods, have been used to identify the factors maintaining an individual's problematic behavior. At times, to completely understand the problem behavior a functional analysis needs to be conducted, which consists of manipulating the situation, alternating between situations that may or may not produce behavior problems. However, oftentimes very informal and simple procedures—such as observation and a parent, teacher, or care provider's report—can be helpful in determining the cause (function) of a behavior. By simply conducting a functional assessment of the current situation, one doesn't necessarily need to place the individual under circumstances in which challenging behavior may occur, so often this is preferable. Some researchers have even found that verbal children with disabilities can sometimes accurately report why they are exhibiting the disruptive behavior (Kern, Dunlap, Clarke, & Childs, 1994).

The main point here is, *regardless of method, it is important to understand why the behavior is occurring* and then, based on this information, to develop an intervention plan that makes the challenging behavior unnecessary and teaches an acceptable and appropriate replacement behavior. This type of assessment and intervention can be used to address a variety of behavioral challenges at home, at school, or in other settings. The examples that follow describe how FBA may be used with younger children. Subsequent sections of the chapter explain how to teach self-management procedures to older children, adolescents, and adults to help them monitor and manage their own behavior.

Example: Functional Assessment and Intervention in the Home Koegel, Stiebel, and Koegel (1998) used functional analysis within the context of a multiple baseline design for three children with autism between 4 and 5 years of age who demonstrated significant aggression toward their 6- to 8-month-old infant siblings. Aggression included yelling, pinching, hitting, shoving, rolling and sitting on top of the infant, head-butting, poking, grabbing objects away from the infant, and kicking the infant. In order to fully understand when and why the aggression occurred, the children were observed, and clinicians met with the parents. The times of day and the activities involved during at the time of the aggression were recorded.

For example, one child with ASD engaged in aggression most frequently during dinner time, and four specific antecedent stimuli were associated with the aggression. These included times when her infant sister kicked or banged her spoon on the metal tray of the high chair, when her infant sister made vocal noises, when her sister cried, and when the children were sitting alone at the table while their mother finished preparing the dinner. To address each function of the aggression, environmental and behavioral manipulations were made. First, it was hypothesized that the infant's banging on the metal tray caused escape-motivated aggression, as the sound was aversive. Thus, the metal tray was replaced with a plastic tray to decrease the noise. Second, to decrease the aggression when the infant made noises, the parents prompted their older child to respond to the baby by saying phrases such as, "She's talking," "What do you think she's saying?" and "Maybe she needs help." The mother then taught the child how to "help" her sibling (e.g., handing the infant a pacifier that was just out of reach). Such behaviors were easy for the child to do, and this approach quickly eliminated the aversive noises the baby was making. Finally, it was hypothesized that the aggression during the "down time" before dinner might also have an attention-seeking function. The mother then decided to fully prepare the meal before seating the children at the table so she could give them attention when they were together. This child's severe aggression levels reduced from about 6% of the time during baseline to no aggression at all during seven of the twelve sessions and no aggression at all at follow up.

For the second child-infant dyad, three situations were identified that reliably produced aggressive behavior. The first was when the mother went to a different room to talk on the telephone. The second was when the infant touched, interfered with, or took his sibling's toys. The third was probably somewhat related to interfering with the toys but occurred when the infant was approaching his brother's toys while he was playing. We hypothesized that the aggression that occurred while the mother was on the telephone served the function of gaining attention. In relation to the infant approaching or touching the toys, we hypothesized that the aggression occurred because the older boy with autism wanted to maintain possession of the toys. Thus, there were two hypothesized functions for the aggression (obtaining attention and stopping interference with his toys). Therefore, for the attention-motivated disruptive behavior, we changed the contingency so that the child was provided with contingent attention from his mother when he exhibited progressively longer intervals of independent play. To respond to the behavior's other hypothesized function of maintaining possession of the toys, we placed a basket full of infant toys in the play area and taught the boy to give his baby brother a toy from the basket when he approached or interfered with the older sibling's toys. During times when the infant still continued to try to take the older boy's toys, we also taught him to say, "Take [sibling's name]" to his mother, after which she immediately picked up the infant and removed him from the area near his brother's toys. During baseline, aggression occurred about 18% of the time. However, following intervention, there was no aggression for seven of the eleven sessions and no aggression at all during follow up.

For the third infant-child dyad, aggression was observed in association with the infant sibling touching his brother's toys, touching his body, and crying and making other noises that the child with autism perceived as aversive. Again, desire to maintain possession of the toys was hypothesized to be causing the aggression, along with some escape-motivated aggression to terminate the aversive touching and noise. Similar to the previous child, we made infant toys available for the older child to trade with his infant brother whenever his baby brother took his toys. In regard to the touching and noise, we taught him to verbally communicate to his mother, "Take [infant's name]" to minimize the aversive noises and crying as well as to reduce the infant sibling's interference with his toys. During baseline, this child with ASD exhibited aggression toward his sibling about 69% of the time. During intervention, a steady decline in aggression was noted, with none at all occurring during the last session. As you can probably imagine, the reduction in aggression was accompanied by greatly improved happiness scores on a Likert scale, with "unhappy/uncomfortable scores" at baseline improving to "happy and comfortable" following the intervention. These scores improved for parents, for the children with ASD, and for neutral individuals observing the sessions. In short, everyone was happy when the aggression was eliminated.

Because of the seriousness of these behaviors (infants were in danger of being seriously injured), we taught the parents how to do the intervention so that they could implement the procedures throughout their children's waking hours. Thus, with the parent education component practice could be frequent, avoiding a potentially disastrous situation.

Example: Functional Assessment and Intervention at School Interventions that involve conducting a FBA and teaching a functionally equivalent, socially appropriate replacement behavior can also be used to reduce challenging behaviors that occur at school, as was done for Jack in his inclusive classroom.

CASE HISTORY
Teaching Jack Appropriate Classroom Behaviors

Jack was an 8-year-old boy diagnosed with ASD who participated in a full-inclusion first-grade classroom. He struggled to follow verbal multi-step directions (e.g., "Finish your math worksheet and place it in the basket, then take out your reading book and begin reading Chapter Two"). When Jack became confused, he resorted to poking and disturbing the student next to him. This commonly resulted in punishment by the teacher, followed by an explosive tantrum from Jack. Generally, a tantrum resulted in him being removed from the classroom for a period of time until he calmed down. Unfortunately, the removal functioned as a reward for Jack, as he then did not have to comply with the difficult instructions. That is, Jack's initial off-task behavior of poking and disturbing his classmate led to punishment followed by Jack's more severe tantrum behavior, which had a routine consequence: removal from the classroom. This consequence served a desired function for Jack: escape from a nonpreferred task.

Because Jack's behavior was worsening, the staff decided to use an FBA strategy to identify the antecedents to Jack's behavior. The school staff recognized that a majority of Jack's off-task and disruptive behavior occurred when the teacher verbally provided multi-step directions. The teacher therefore began to implement a simple intervention of writing multi-step directions on the board. This seemed to benefit all of the children in the class, as the oral presentation of multi-step instructions was sometimes difficult for all of the students. At first Jack needed a few verbal prompts to look to the visual aid; soon afterward, Jack was able to stay on task and complete multi-step directions independently, and his disruptive behaviors decreased dramatically.

As you can see, Jack's teachers successfully identified the antecedents to his disruptive behavior (verbal multi-step directions) and provided an appropriate and effective replacement behavior (visual cues with minimal verbal prompts). When we understand why a child struggles, we can set up opportunities to reduce triggers, provide adaptive skills, and increase success. When treating disruptive behaviors, it is important to be proactive, rather than reactive. FBA procedures should be used as a prevention strategy to reduce or eliminate challenging behavior early on, rather than allow it to escalate into more serious issues (Kamps, Wendland, & Culpepper, 2006). Research has demonstrated that it is critical to use a function-based approach in order to improve behavior outcomes within school settings (Durand & Carr, 1991; McIntosh, Horner, Chard, Dickey, & Braun, 2008) and in home and community settings across the age span (Carr, 1994).

Figure 10.1 provides a guide for functional assessment. As can be seen, the procedure involves first writing the behavior and the time and place it occurred. Next, the most common antecedents are noted—for example, the individual was told to do something, there was a change in activity, and so on. Then, the consequence is noted, and again common ones are indicated, for example, the individual was given attention, punished, or ignored. Finally, and often most important, the "why" or function is recorded. For example, did the individual want to get out of some activity (escape-motivated behavior)? Did the disruptive behavior occur during a transition? Was it to obtain an item or activity? Or did the individual want attention? Was the disruptive behavior exhibited to avoid a person, place, or activity? Once this information is collected, a well-informed intervention plan can be developed that addresses the function of the disruptive behavior. This type of intervention, rather than punishment, will lead to a higher likelihood of elimination of the unwanted behaviors, as the individual learns appropriate ways to communicate the same function the disruptive behavior was serving.

The Role of Reinforcement in Maintaining Replacement Behaviors

One last note: When an individual is taught the replacement behaviors, he or she will need to learn that the disruptive behaviors are no longer functional. This means making sure the disruptive behaviors are not reinforced, by ignoring them. As with any behavior, this lack of reinforcement may cause an extinction burst (i.e., a brief escalation in the behavior), so anyone working with the child will need to be warned. Also, if the individual is receiving reinforcement on a thin schedule, such as getting rewarded every once in a while, disruptive behaviors may persist for a while before they extinguish. That is, intermittent rewards make behaviors more resistant to extinction. We see this in the classroom when a teacher answers a child occasionally when they call out instead of raising their hands. Because the child is used to the teacher answering on occasion, it makes that behavior more resistant to change and so it continues to occur even when it's being ignored. Similarly, if a disruptive behavior is being rewarded in some environments, it is likely to take longer before it completely extinguishes. That's why using a team approach, with consistency across all people and environments, is critical if disruptive behavior is to be eliminated rapidly and permanently.

It's also important to note that some replacement behaviors are complex and take a while to teach. For example, teaching a child to carry on a conversation with another child instead of getting the peer's attention through inappropriate behaviors may take some time. Until the skills are learned, some system needs to be in place that can make reinforcement available in the early stages as the child begins learning the skill. Self-management can meet this need, because it teaches the child to evaluate his or her own behavior, after which reinforcement is provided in the early steps, while acquiring the skill. This self-reflection and reinforcement occurs before the child has acquired the replacement behavior at a level complex enough to yield natural reinforcement from the environment. Self-management can be used alone or in combination with other techniques. For example, often treatment

Name ______________________________ Date ______________

	BEHAVIORS								
TIME									
PLACE									
BEFORE (ANTECEDENT)									
Told to do something									
Change in activity									
Moved to different area									
Was alone									
Was interrupted									
Was told "no"									
AFTER (CONSEQUENCE)									
Was given attention									
Was given desired item									
Lost desired item									
Was removed from area									
Was ignored									
Was punished									
Had an adult's request withdrawn									
WHY (FUNCTION)									
To escape or get out of ... [specify]									
Transition									
To obtain ... [specify]									
To get attention									
To avoid ... [specify person/place]									
Other [specify]									

Figure 10.1. This is an example functional assessment form for understanding the antecedents, consequences, and functions of an individual's challenging behaviors.

programs have the individual self-manage occurrences of components of the replacement behavior until the replacement behavior becomes strong enough and/or complex enough to result in natural reinforcement. These procedures can result in a more independent use of the replacement behaviors. Read on for details of how to implement self-management.

SELF-MANAGEMENT AS A BEHAVIORAL INTERVENTION

Self-management is a technique used to teach an individual to become aware of his or her own behaviors and to either increase or decrease the occurrence of certain behaviors (Chia, Anderson, & McLean, 2018; Watkins, Kuhn, Ledbetter-Cho, Gevarter, & O'Reilly, 2017). This procedure has a great deal of success when consequences of behaviors are either too far delayed or too small to influence the frequency of a behavior (Malott, 1984). There are a series of steps involved in the process of self-management. First, it requires teaching the individual to discriminate between instances when a specific behavior has occurred versus instances when it has not occurred. Second, for the process to become totally independent on the child's part, implementing self-management involves teaching the child to obtain a reward for exhibiting the behavior. Consider the following example. If a child is not paying attention in class, it may be difficult to teach the child exactly what "paying attention" means. Therefore, at the beginning of the self-management program, the team implementing the intervention would provide examples of the correct versus the incorrect behavior. They might have the child slouch in his seat while looking away from the teacher, and then teach the child to label those behaviors as not paying attention. Conversely, to teach the correct behavior, the team would have the child sit up straight in his chair and look at the teacher and teach the child to label that as paying attention to the teacher.

Once the child can perform and label both of the behaviors (not paying attention versus paying attention), then the team can move on to the next phase: teaching the child to record instances of the correct behavior (e.g., paying attention). Then, the team would teach the child to obtain a reward for successful engagement in a target behavior and recording that success (Baer, 1984). For example, the child may be given a sheet and taught to give himself a check after a time interval of performing the target behavior (in this case, paying attention). The intervention would begin by focusing on small intervals of time, with the amount of time gradually expanded. The team would provide a timer for the child to use (e.g., a chiming watch). In the beginning, the child might be rewarded for giving himself a check mark for paying attention for 5 seconds. Then the team would gradually and systematically increase the time period, so the child gives himself a check mark for paying attention for 10 seconds, then 15, and so on. Eventually, the child is sitting at his desk, paying attention for several minutes, before giving himself a check mark. The intervention team can then tell him that he can obtain rewards (which could be larger and more desirable) if he can earns a lot of check marks. At that point, the child may be sitting at his desk, giving himself check marks for a whole academic period, before he cashes in his check marks for a reward.

Benefits and Versatility

Self-management programs have been effectively applied to a myriad of behaviors, even though the specific techniques for self-monitoring and self-reinforcement vary considerably. For example, individuals can self-monitor by making hash marks on a sheet of paper, using a counting device, using a smartphone, or collecting marbles or other tokens then exchanging the tokens for a rewarding item or activity (Rosine & Martin, 1983; Sowers, Verdi, Bourbeau, & Sheehan, 1985). (Subsequent chapters of this book describe how to use self-management procedures in conjunction with other high- and low-tech interventions, such as video modeling, to improve communicative, social, and daily living skills and manage responsibilities at school and at work.)

Self-management is a flexible system that can be used as an intervention for a variety of different behaviors, can be used with individuals of many intellectual functioning levels, and can be implemented in a variety of different settings (e.g., home, school, camp, work). Further, once the skill is acquired, it can be programmed to occur in the absence of an interventionist, thereby making the intervention less stigmatizing, more time and cost effective, and creating a potentially accelerated program because the individual takes an active role in the intervention process (Whitman, 1990).

Self-management has been discussed as an extremely important tool for individuals to use in order to increase autonomy and decrease the necessity of constant attention or treatment. This is important not only because society values independence (O'Leary & Dubey, 1979), but also because people prefer to engage in activities in which they are in control (Bannerman, Sheldon, Sherman, & Harchik, 1990). For example, a person may need to monitor her diet and exercise in order to stay healthy. He or she may need to exercise every day, make healthy eating choices, and so on, in order to live the best quality of life (Bodenheimer, Lorig, Holman, & Grumbach, 2002). In the absence of constant vigilance by a doctor, nutritionist, or support person, he or she will need to learn effective self-management skills to make these desired choices in everyday life.

Another important benefit of self-management is that individuals can learn behaviors in the following circumstances: 1) where natural contingencies or reinforcers are not available, 2) where the contingencies are too delayed to control a behavior, or 3) where the natural rewards are too small to maintain the behaviors. For example, a teacher may insist that a child complete a worksheet in class that does not provide any natural reinforcer. Ideally, we would want to teach the teacher how to use natural reinforcers. However, if that is not a possibility, self-management can serve as a temporary tool to get the child through the activity while at the same time teaching the child self-regulatory skills.

Consider the following examples where self-management might serve to be quite useful:

- A child may make humming noises throughout the day that interfere with teaching and learning in a general education setting. Self-management can be used as a tool to get the child through the activity without humming while also teaching the child pivotal self-regulatory skills.

- An adult may forget to engage in appropriate hygiene, interfering with social relationships and employment. Self-management can be used as a tool to teach hygiene while simultaneously teaching self-regulation and improving the adult's social life.
- A behavior may be taught in one setting without generalizing to another setting. Self-management can be used as a tool to get the behavior to occur across a variety of settings.

For decades, self-management has been shown to be effective with generalization and maintenance of learned behaviors (Fowler, 1984; Malott, 1984) by functionally giving control over the behavior to the child or other person receiving intervention, so that external treatment providers do not need to be present.

Using Self-Management With Individuals With ASD

Although self-management has been a successful technique for many years, it was not until the late 1980s that it became a pivotal area in the treatment of individuals with ASD. In 2012, The National Standards Project determined that self-management was an empirically validated intervention for children with ASD. Self-management has been successfully used to reduce challenging behaviors (Koegel, Harrower, & Koegel, 1999). Self-stimulatory behaviors (Koegel & Koegel, 1990), increase responsiveness (Koegel, Koegel, Hurley, & Frea, 1992), and improve classroom behaviors and social skills (Koegel, Harrower, & Koegel, 1999). One advantage of self-management for children with ASD is that children can learn to monitor and engage in appropriate behaviors on their own and can often learn to administer their own rewards, resulting in less time needed with an interventionist and more independence.

One extremely important issue when generating a self-management plan is making sure the goals are realistic and something an individual can accomplish (see Table 10.1). If people are successful in their self-developed plans, they are much more likely to reach desired goals (Corbin & Strauss, 1988). This is similar for any type of self-management plan created. An example of this is creating a daily living skills chart for an individual with ASD and severe food inflexibility. The interventionist may not want to ask the child to try three new foods at every meal, but rather ask the child to try one new food every day. In other words, making the goal appropriate and obtainable will result in a greater likelihood of success.

One major advantage of self-management is that it is broadly effective and can impact the individual for many behaviors and in many settings, such as in school (Baer, Fowler, & Carden-Smith, 1984) and in community settings (Koegel & Koegel, 1990). It has been effective for teaching a variety of skills, such as social skills (Wheeler, Bates, Marshall, & Miller, 1988) and job skills (Hughes & Peterson, 1989) to individuals with ASD, both with and without intellectual disability (ID). This is important to note in regard to the widespread applicability of the procedures. For many years it was thought that only individuals with verbal expressive communication and higher intelligence could manage their own procedures,

Table 10.1. Appropriate self-management plans to increase likelihood of reaching goals

Problem	Goal	Bad Plan	Good Plan
An adolescent with ASD does not engage in physical activities and is overweight.	Increase daily exercise.	• Run 5 miles per day (too hard). • Run 5 miles per week (not specific enough).	• Walk 20 minutes a day after lunch Monday-Friday. • Increase pace over a 2-month period. • Begin 30-second intervals of running when adolescent can walk briskly for 20 minutes.
An adult with ASD needs to ask questions during conversation. Baseline measures shows that no questions are asked.	Improve question-asking during social conversation.	Ask questions throughout the conversation.	Begin with asking two questions with prompting during a 5-minute conversation.
A child with ASD needs to increase the number of hours spent with friends outside of school.	A typical child spends 20 hours per week in social activities outside of school.	Spend 20 hours outside of school with friends.	Plan at least one short (30-minute) desired social activity per week with a friend. Use self-management for engagement.

but research has shown that the intervention can be adapted for individuals with greater support needs.

Using Self-Management for Individuals With Greater Support Needs

One way to teach self-management to individuals with ASD and ID, who will likely have greater support needs, is to use assistive technology. For example, prompting tools such as pictorial prompts (cue cards) or computer-aided systems may be important for teaching individuals with disabilities who are nonverbal. One benefit of using assistive technology, such as picture prompts, is that the individual does not have to wait for an adult to prompt him or her to engage in a certain behavior (Riffel et al., 2005). Another benefit is that the individual does not have to memorize an entire set of instructions. Yet, even though the technology is simple to use, when an individual learns to self-manage with assistive technology, the process is very similar to the antecedent procedures used to teach self-management using verbal prompts. First, an individual is taught to discriminate between appropriate and inappropriate behaviors using a picture, or multiple pictures, to prompt the individual through the appropriate behaviors in a task. Then, he or she is taught to self-reward for engaging in the appropriate behaviors. An example of this is a study in which Singh, Oswald, Ellis, and Singh (1995) taught individuals to self-prepare a meal using a picture-based cookbook. In this study, individuals with significant intellectual disabilities were shown images of desserts they could learn to make. After learning each step (paired with a picture), individuals were able to self-reward based on their completion of individual steps until they finished the final step and were able to eat the dessert.

Another tool researchers have used is teaching participants to make directive statements to themselves about a task. For example, the individual can be taught to self-instruct, as a type of reminder, at predetermined intervals. These statements can be either general statements ("Go fast") or more specific ("First, take the bread out of the package").

In one example, Dettmer, Simpson, Myles, and Ganz (2000) used a picture-cued activity schedule to teach children with autism to self-manage transitions between activities both at home and in the classroom. Participants were shown picture schedules of what to do and how to behave during transitions. Pictures showed students moving quickly from each activity to the next and from car to classroom. Participants used the pictures before each activity as a reminder to independently engage in the appropriate behaviors. Following successful transitions, the children could exchange points for rewards. As a result of this self-management program, the children were able to independently transition faster and decrease the number of prompts needed during transitions.

Tactile prompts, such as a vibrating pager, have also shown some success with individuals with ASD. For example, Finn, Ramasamy, Dukes, and Scott (2015) used a vibrating prompt watch and self-graphing to improve the on-task behavior of elementary school students. Targeted behaviors included engaging in academic tasks (reading/writing), raising one's hand for help, putting work away, and so on. Off-task behaviors included looking around the room, playing with items, making noises, staring at one's paper unengaged, and other nonproductive behaviors. The watch vibrated every 2 minutes, and students were taught to mark a "yes" on a checklist for intervals in which their behavior was on task. Intervals were later lengthened. High levels of on-task behavior occurred following the intervention for all children and maintained even after the watch and graphing sheets were completely removed. Of importance is that the children were able to complete this program with minimal involvement from an interventionist, making the procedure very useful in applied settings and creating an important skill of autonomous appropriate functioning for the children.

Personal computers have also been successful for teaching self-management. This method is often similar to methods involving picture prompts, but the pictures are stored on personal computers. The benefit of this method is that the system may be easier to organize, change, and adapt on a computer. Also, often rewards can be programmed to be provided at various intervals in the absence of an interventionist. For example, Lancioni and Oliva (1988) taught two teenagers with significant developmental delays to use personal computers to learn to engage in simple daily living tasks (e.g., putting a food item on a plate). In this study, when participants stepped on a mat, a sensor triggered a picture to appear on their screen; this image prompted the participants to collect the food item and cued the next picture on the computer. This process was repeated until the activity was completed. Reward cards can also be placed randomly within the picture prompts, such as cards prompting the participants where and when to obtain a reinforcer.

As can be noted, a variety of methods to alert the individual when to self-manage, including alarming or vibrating watches, computers, or picture cards. Various recording systems can also be used including a simple piece of paper, a wrist counter, or an electronic device. Matching the materials with the capabilities and needs of the individual as well as the appropriate method for recording is important. More details are provided below.

HOW TO DEVELOP A SELF-MANAGEMENT PROGRAM

Now that we have discussed various applications of self-management, let's go over the 10 specific steps in developing a self-management program (each is explained in further detail in the sections that follow):

Preliminary Steps (1–5)

1. Define the target behavior.
2. Measure the target behavior.
3. Choose a reward.
4. Set an initial goal.
5. Gather materials.

Teaching Steps (6–7)

6. Teach discrimination between behaviors.
7. Record (monitor) the behavior.

Final Steps to Create Independence (8–10)

8. Fade reliance on prompts.
9. Increase time intervals or tallies required for rewards.
10. Fade the presence of the treatment provider.

Step 1: Define the Target Behavior

First of all, you need to write a very clear definition of the target behavior. For example, describing a desired appropriate behavior as "good behavior" is too vague. In contrast, you as the interventionist must be specific in defining both the appropriate and inappropriate behaviors, such as "talking out when the teacher asks the class a question instead of raising hand," that is clear to everyone. Similarly, the phrase "doesn't respond" is not as clear as "gives a verbal answer consisting of at least one word, when a conversational partner asks a question."

Step 2: Measure the Target Behavior

Measuring the behavior you want to target is important for several reasons. First, you will want to have a baseline of the individual's pre-intervention levels of the behavior you are targeting for increasing or decreasing. That way you can assess whether your self-management program is effective. Second, baselines will help you decide on a beginning point for intervention. For example, if the target behavior is to have the child stay in his seat for an hour at school, but right now he can only stay in his seat for one minute, you'll want to start with less than a minute during your first self-management intervals so that he'll experience success. Also remember, when you start to collect data, you'll want to decide on a specific time period for measuring the behavior that will stay constant throughout the intervention. For example, suppose you are measuring the number of social verbal initiations an adolescent makes during conversation; one interval has 10 initiations and another has 5 initiations, but the time periods differ. In this instance, the data are meaningless because the length of the intervals is inconsistent. In contrast, if both time periods were equal (e.g., 5 minutes), then it is clear that the difference in the child's number of verbal initiations during each interval means something.

Sometimes it is impossible to avoid measuring a behavior in circumstances in which the time intervals differ; there are some solutions a treatment provider can use to ensure the measurement is meaningful. For example, if you were measuring initiations during play periods that vary from day to day, you could divide the number of responses by the number of minutes to get a rate per minute. Or you could measure just part of the play period (e.g., the first 10 minutes), keeping the length of the interval measured constant from day to day.

Another important issue relates to the interval you use for recording behaviors that may go on for a while, such as disruption, tantrums, and self-stimulation. For these type of behaviors, you can choose a time interval, such as 10 seconds, 20 seconds, or 30 seconds, and record whether the behavior occurred in each smaller interval for a designated time period. Be sure to select a time interval that will be sensitive to occurrences of the behavior. If the behavior occurs frequently, you may need to select a shorter time interval. If the behavior occurs less frequently, you might simply want to count the number of seconds it occurs within a specific time period, such as an hour. These methods will help you determine percentages of how often a behavior is occurring within a given time period.

Step 3: Choose a Reward

This is the fun part! Give whoever you're working with a chance to choose rewards that will be motivating. Make sure to select several small rewards that can be given more frequently when the intervals are close together, along with some larger ones for later successes when the intervals are longer. For example, in our clinic, we worked with an 11-year-old who wouldn't let her parents leave the room without engaging in disruptive behaviors. We started by rewarding her for letting her parents leave the room for 10-second intervals, and after every five successes, we increased the time by 5 seconds. For her successes during the shorter intervals, we rewarded her with stickers, small toys, and small candies she chose. However, she really wanted to earn a video game, so we let her know that when she was able to let her parents leave the room for 20 minutes for 5 consecutive days, she could earn the video game. That way, she had little rewards for successes along the way, and a big reward for achieving our end goal.

Step 4: Set an Initial Goal

This is the time for you to take a look at your baseline data. It's important to start with an initial goal that is easily achievable so the individual experiences immediate success during the beginning steps of the self-management program. You can scale up this goal gradually and systematically—for example, by increasing the length of intervals or the number of responses required to receive a reward—but make it easy at first. If question asking is your goal and the person you're working with never asks a question, you would probably want to start by setting a goal of asking one question and checking off one box for the self-management then give an initial reward. Similarly, if a child exhibits one disruptive behavior every 10 minutes, you could start by setting a goal that the child will not engage in this behavior for a time interval 8 or 9 minutes. In sum, when setting initial behavioral goals, use baseline data to determine goals that are modest enough to ensure that the individual can achieve them fairly easily and thus experience success right away.

Step 5: Gather Materials

Now that you have your preliminary planning and baseline completed, make sure you have your rewards handy and a self-management device for the individual to record his or her responses. This can be a simple piece of paper with checkboxes for discrete behaviors or time intervals. Using a countdown alarm on a smartphone works well for recording time intervals with good behavior; in fact, the individual can use any type of program that can be set to alert him or her when the interval finishes. If discrete behaviors are being counted, a wrist or hand-held counter (e.g., a golf counter) will work. If the intervention program is being developed for an individual who is nonverbal or minimally verbal and will use picture prompts, the interventionist can get pictures organized either on the computer or using picture cards held together on a ring.

Once these preliminary steps have been completed, the following intermediate steps can help you prepare the individual to engage in, and keep track of, appropriate behaviors, so that he or she can ultimately practice self-management independently.

Step 6: Teach Discrimination Between Behaviors

Now it's time for teaching. An important step is making sure the person you're working with understands what to manage. In our own practice, we've seen plenty of programs in which the behavioral goal is so vague that the person really has no idea what the target behaviors are or how he or she is supposed to behave. First of all, you'll want to demonstrate both appropriate and inappropriate behaviors to make sure that the person really understands both. Once he or she is able to discriminate between behaviors and identify what behavior is expected, as shown by responding whether your examples are appropriate or inappropriate, have the individual demonstrate the behaviors. Just a few times is fine. For example, ask the person to show you a quiet student who raising his hand and sitting nicely, or whatever the target behavior is. Once he gets it, you can start the monitoring process.

Step 7: Record (Monitor) the Behavior

Now that the individual you're working with has a clear understanding of the target behavior, you can explain how the monitoring will be accomplished. Maybe it's a timer that sounds when it's time to monitor, maybe it's recognizing that she answered a question and gets a point on her wrist counter, or maybe you are using a vibrating watch that cues her in to when she should mark the small piece of paper taped on her desk. Even iPads can be used for monitoring (Xin, Sheppard, & Brown, 2017). The individual will need to practice both engaging in the appropriate behavior and monitoring occurrences of the desired behavior. One thing to be careful of at this point is that the person truly is evaluating and monitoring the behavior *independently*. If you say, "Great, that was wonderful, give yourself a point," then she isn't really *self*-managing. In contrast, if you say, "How do you think you did?" you're giving the individual an opportunity to think about his or her own behavior, and that's what we really want.

After completing these teaching steps, it's time to increase the independence of the individual with whom you are working. This needs to be accomplished carefully and systematically in order to be effective. The remaining steps will help you fade your own presence so the self-management program is being independently implemented.

Step 8: Fade Reliance on Prompts

During the first seven steps of self-management, you will be pretty active teaching and prompting. You will be reminding the individual to monitor, rewarding him or her for good behavior and accurate monitoring, and helping him or her to access rewards. In Step 8, it's time to gradually fade out the individual's reliance on these prompts. As in any other teaching program, you can reduce the number of prompts, gradually and systematically make them less salient (e.g., gestures instead of verbal prompts), and encourage the individual to complete the steps independently.

Step 9: Increase Time Intervals or Tallies Required for Rewards

When we develop first steps of self-management, we use baseline measurements to create a time interval that will result in success. Sometimes that interval is short. For individuals who are tallying behaviors, we have them monitor a small number of responses initially. Once the person can accurately and independently monitor his or her own behavior and responses, it is time to start gradually increasing the length of time intervals or number of responses before he or she can turn in the recorded tally for a reward.

For example, suppose you started a self-management program by having a child monitor sitting nicely and quietly for 15-second intervals, and the child has checked off five boxes, indicating that she successfully completed this behavioral goal for five intervals. At this point, you may want to increase the time interval by 10 seconds, so that the child now practices sitting quietly for 25-second intervals. After another five boxes are checked off, you could add an additional 10 seconds, so that the child's goal is now to sit quietly for 35 seconds at a time. If the child continues to do well, you could increase the increments by 20 or 30 seconds or even a minute at a time. Similarly, if the child is getting a reward after tallying each successful response he makes to a peer, you may want to increase the number of responses needed to obtain a reward, to two, then four, then six, then ten, and so on. However, if you find you've increased the goal too much or too quickly and the child isn't having success, back down a bit. Remember, we want to create goals that are small enough to ensure the child, adolescent, or adult is successful but large enough to make progress. At this point in the intervention process, the individual with whom you work should be monitoring increasingly longer intervals that are repeated for the desired periods of time.

Step 10: Fade the Presence of the Treatment Provider

Now you are going to gradually fade out your own presence so that the individual is self-managing in your absence. Again, you will want to do this gradually and systematically. At first, we like to fade out for very brief periods of time and then check in with someone who can validate that the person receiving intervention engaged in the desired behavior and self-recorded accurately. Depending on where the self-management is taking place, this can be a teacher, aide, employer, and so on. For example, if a child is monitoring his or her behavior in the classroom, you can step out briefly, then ask the teacher how the student behaved in your absence. If the student is successful when you are gone, you can increase your absence to longer and longer intervals. By now, the self-management should be going smoothly and independently.

An important part of creating independence is that the interventionist must introduce behaviors in steps that the individuals are capable of completing on their own. That is, individuals can alter their lifestyles in small, manageable steps. Self-management for individuals with ASD needs to be completed in steps that result in success. If a step seems unmanageable or too difficult, the individual may never reach the end goal (Corbin & Strauss, 1988).

Making Sure Self-Management Will Occur in Additional Settings

The nice thing about self-management is it's a portable strategy and can be implemented without the vigilance of a treatment provider. We all self-manage behaviors (e.g., shopping lists, to-do lists, calendars of events), and we all learn to become independent by self-managing our behaviors. Sometimes we have specialized programs we create for ourselves, such as programs for weight management, eating healthy, giving compliments, and any other area we wish to improve. Individuals can use self-management systems in any setting where engaging in the target behavior is desirable—for example, in other classes, on field trips, at home or at school, and so on. Also, sometimes you can teach the self-administration of a reward. For example, we had one student who learned to self-manage being quiet in class. He was able to carry his self-management sheets to many different settings. He chose to listen to jazz tapes when he received a certain number of points from tallying up his quiet intervals; and whenever he earned the designated number of points, he was able to independently go to the back of the classroom and listen to a song. Not only was he able to self-manage in a variety of settings, he also could give himself his reward, which made him completely independent.

The Widespread Applicability of Self-Management

In addition to individually designed programs, self-management has also seen success in teacher training. Teachers who were trained to self-manage certain behaviors made better instructional decisions (Browder, Liberty, Heller, & D'Huyvetters,

1986). For example, teachers who self-managed changing instructional practices based on student's academic performances showed more individualized teaching in classrooms. And furthermore, teachers who self-managed their own behaviors had better student performances than teachers who did not self-manage (Allinder, Bolling, Oats, & Gagnon, 2000). Thus, it isn't just individuals with ASD who can directly benefit from self-management. Indirect benefits to students can also ensue when teachers track their own behaviors.

Self-management plans have been effective for a variety of different areas for older individuals with ASD, including social skills (Koegel & Frea, 1993) and increasing the amount of activities in which teens with ASD engage (Newman et al., 1995). It has also been effective for children with low (or no) expressive verbal skills for completing daily living skills and chores.

Stahmer and Schreibman (1992) also showed that children with autism could learn appropriate play skills in community settings. In this multiple-baseline design, three children were taught to manage their own appropriate play skills in play areas (clinic settings or bedroom). This study also found that two of three children were able to generalize their newly learned play skills to unsupervised environments. Further, as appropriate play increased, inappropriate restricted and repetitive behaviors (RRBs) decreased.

Cautions When Using Self-Management

There are a few cautionary issues related to self-management. First, self-management should not be considered an alternative for teaching FERBs in situations where an individual frequently engages in disruptive or challenging behavior. Although the challenging behavior may be reduced immediately using self-management, if an individual does not have appropriate ways of communication, the behavior is likely to return. Next, be aware that an interventionist may not be able to fade the self-management entirely (meaning the desired behavior becomes so automatic the individual no longer needs a self-management system), especially in situations where the motivating factors for inappropriate behaviors remain too strong. For example, self-management for weight loss may be difficult to fade if desirable food is present, or the urge to engage in RRBs may be too great when self-management is removed. Finally, some behaviors respond best to a multi-component program. Self-management is one strategy—an important skill—but some individuals and/or especially resistant behaviors may require a combination of programs implemented simultaneously for the desired end result.

Key Insights ||| Using Positive Behavioral Interventions and Fostering Independence

The following principles are important to keep in mind when implementing positive behavioral interventions.

- **Aversive consequences do not lead to long-lasting behavioral improvement:** Nor do they respect the dignity and autonomy of people with disabilities. Although the use of punishment may work temporarily, the individual is not learning how to respond appropriately in the given situation. Understanding why challenging behaviors occur and addressing their function by teaching appropriate responses leads to improved behavior over time.

- **Teach functionally equivalent replacement behaviors:** Once the function of the challenging behavior is apparent, a replacement behavior can be developed and taught. The replacement behavior needs to be practiced frequently during non-crisis times so that it becomes automatic and readily used when it is needed.
- **Coordinate intervention across settings:** The most rapid reductions in challenging behaviors occur when intervention procedures are consistent across all settings. Replacement behaviors should be coordinated with the individual's family and caregivers to be sure they fit their lifestyles and values.
- **Combine programs:** Most interventions do not result in complete elimination of all undesired behaviors. Therefore, a combination of programs is often recommended.
- **Self-management can increase independence:** By teaching an individual to be aware of, and monitor, his or her own behaviors, greater independence can be achieved. This lessens the need for constant vigilance from a treatment provider.

SUMMARY

Self-management can be effective people across the spectrum, ranging from those who are unable to speak to highly verbal individuals. Having individuals track their own demonstration of a desired behavior or skill increases self-awareness and decreases the need for prompting by an adult or therapist. In addition, self-management commonly results in the individual's increased self-efficacy, independence, and motivation for change. In combination with FBA, self-management has shown to be an effective treatment for increasing appropriate behaviors (Kern & Clemons, 2007). Again, this is cost-efficient and also may reduce any stigmatization that may occur when an interventionist is present.

STUDY QUESTIONS

1. Discuss changes relating to the way in which challenging behaviors have been addressed for individuals with ASD over time.
2. What are examples of precursors that may cause challenging behavior?
3. What are examples of consequences that may maintain challenging behaviors?
4. List some examples of common functions of challenging behaviors.
5. What are functionally equivalent replacement behaviors?
6. What are some advantages of using self-management?
7. List the steps of a self-management program.
8. How can self-management be combined with teaching functionally equivalent replacement behaviors?

9. List ways self-management can be faded.
10. Discuss the benefits of self-management.

REFERENCES

Allinder, R. M., Bolling, R. M., Oats, R. G., & Gagnon, W. A. (2000). Effects of teacher self-monitoring on implementation of curriculum-based measurement and mathematics computation achievement of students with disabilities. *Remedial and Special Education, 21*(4), 219–226.

Baer, D. M. (1984). Does research on self-control need more control? *Analysis & Intervention in Developmental Disabilities. 4,* no. 2 (1984): 211–218

Baer, M., Fowler, S. A., & Carden-Smith, L. (1984). Using reinforcement and independent grading to promote and maintain task accuracy in a mainstreamed class. *Analysis and Intervention in Developmental Disabilities, 4*(2), 157–169.

Bailey, S. L., Pokrzywinski, J., & Bryant, L. E. (1983). Using water mist to reduce self injurious and stereotypic behavior. *Applied Research in Mental Retardation, 4*(3), 229–241.

Bannerman, D. J., Sheldon, J. B., Sherman, J. A., & Harchik, A. E. (1990). Balancing the right to habilitation with the right to personal liberties: The rights of people with developmental disabilities to eat too many doughnuts and take a nap. *Journal of Applied Behavior Analysis, 23*(1), 79–89.

Bodenheimer, T., Lorig, K., Holman, H., & Grumbach, K. (2002). Patient self-management of chronic disease in primary care. *JAMA, 288*(19), 2469–2475.

Browder, D. M., Liberty, K., Heller, M., & D'huyvetters, K. K. (1986). Self-management by teachers: Improving instructional decision making. *Professional School Psychology, 1*(3), 165.

Carr, E. G. (1994). Emerging themes in the functional analysis of problem behavior. *Journal of Applied Behavior Analysis, 27*(2), 393–399.

Carr, E. G., & Durand, V. M. (1985). Reducing behavior problems through functional communication training. *Journal of Applied Behavior Analysis, 18*(2), 111–126.

Chia, G. L. C., Anderson, A., & McLean, L. A. (2018). Use of technology to support self m management in individuals with autism: Systematic review. *Review Journal of Autism and Developmental Disorders,* 1–14.

Corbin, J., & Strauss, A. (1988) *Unending work and care: Managing chronic illness at home.* San Francisco, Ca: Jossey-Bass Publishers.

Dettmer, S., Simpson, R. L., Myles, B. S., & Ganz, J. B. (2000). The use of visual supports to facilitate transitions of students with autism. *Focus on Autism and Other Developmental Disabilities, 15*(3), 163–169.

Durand, V. M., & Carr, E. G. (1991). Functional communication training to reduce challenging behavior: Maintenance and application in new settings. *Journal of Applied Behavior Analysis, 24*(2), 251–264.

Finn, L., Ramasamy, R., Dukes, C., & Scott, J. (2015). Using WatchMinder to increase the on task behavior of students with autism spectrum disorder. *Journal of Autism and Developmental Disorders, 45*(5), 1408–1418.

Fowler, S. A. (1984). Introductory comments: The pragmatics of self-management for the developmentally disabled. *Analysis and Intervention in Developmental Disabilities, 4*(2), 85–89.

Horner, R. H., Carr, E. G., Strain, P. S., Todd, A. W., & Reed, H. K. (2002). Problem behavior interventions for young children with autism: A research synthesis. *Journal of Autism and Developmental Disorders, 32*(5), 423–446.

Hughes, C., & Petersen, D. L. (1989). Utilizing a self-instructional training package to increase on-task behavior and work performance. *Education and Training in Mental Retardation,* 114–120.

Kamps, D., Wendland, M., & Culpepper, M. (2006). Active teacher participation in functional behavior assessment for students with emotional and behavioral disorders risks in general education classrooms. *Behavioral Disorders, 31*(2), 128–146.

Kern, L., & Clemens, N. H. (2007). Antecedent strategies to promote appropriate classroom behavior. *Psychology in the Schools, 44*(1), 65–75.

Kern, L., Dunlap, G., Clarke, S., & Childs, K. E. (1994). Student-assisted functional assessment interview. *Assessment for Effective Intervention, 19*(2–3), 29–39.

Koegel, L. K., Harrower, J. K., & Koegel, R. L. (1999). Support for children with developmental disabilities in full inclusion classrooms through self-management. *Journal of Positive Behavior Interventions, 1*(1), 26-34.

Koegel, L. K. F., Koegel, R. L., & Dunlap, G. E. (1996). *Positive behavioral support: Including people with difficult behavior in the community*. Baltimore, MD: Paul H Brookes Publishing Co.

Koegel, L. K., Koegel, R. L., Hurley, C., & Frea, W. D. (1992). Improving social skills and disruptive behavior in children with autism through self-management. *Journal of Applied Behavior Analysis, 25*(2), 341-353.

Koegel, L. K., Stiebel, D., & Koegel, R. L. (1998). Reducing aggression in children with autism toward infant or toddler siblings. *Research and Practice for Persons with Severe Disabilities, 23*(2), 111–118.

Koegel, R. L., & Frea, W. D. (1993). Treatment of social behavior in autism through the modification of pivotal social skills. *Journal of Applied Behavior Analysis, 26*(3), 369–377.

Koegel, R. L., & Koegel, L. K. (1990). Extended reductions in stereotypic behavior of students with autism through a self-management treatment package. *Journal of Applied Behavior Analysis, 23*(1), 119–127.

Koegel, R. L., Koegel, L. K., & Surratt, A. (1992). Language intervention and disruptive behavior in preschool children with autism. *Journal of Autism and Developmental Disorders, 22*(2), 141–153.

Lancioni, G. E., & Oliva, D. (1988). A computer-aided programme for promoting unsupervised activities for multihandicapped adolescents. *Journal of Intellectual Disability Research, 32*(2), 125–136.

Lovaas, O. I. (1977). *The autistic child: Language development through behavior modification.* Oxford: England: Irvington.

Lovaas, O. I., Schaeffer, B., & Simmons, J. Q. (1965). Building social behavior in autistic children by use of electric shock. *Journal of Experimental Research in Personality*. 1(2), 99–109.

Malott, R. W. (1984). Rule-governed behavior, self-management, and the developmentally disabled: A theoretical analysis. *Analysis and Intervention in Developmental Disabilities, 4*(2), 199–209.

McIntosh, K., Horner, R. H., Chard, D. J., Dickey, C. R., & Braun, D. H. (2008). Reading skills and function of problem behavior in typical school settings. *The Journal of Special Education, 42*(3), 131–147.

Newman, B., Buffington, D. M., O'Grady, M. A., McDonald, M. E., Poulson, C. L., & Hemmes, N. S. (1995). Self-management of schedule following in three teenagers with autism. *Behavioral Disorders, 20*(3), 190–196.

O'Leary, S. G., & Dubey, D. R. (1979). Applications of self-control procedures by children: A review. *Journal of Applied Behavior Analysis, 12*(3), 449–465.

Reese, R. M., Richman, D. M., Belmont, J. M., & Morse, P. (2005). Functional characteristics of disruptive behavior in developmentally disabled children with and without autism. *Journal of Autism and Developmental Disorders, 35*(4), 419–428.

Riffel, L. A., Wehmeyer, M. L., Turnbull, A. P., Lattimore, J., Davies, D., Stock, S., & Fisher, S. (2005). Promoting independent performance of transition-related tasks using a palmtop PC-based self-directed visual and auditory prompting system. *Journal of Special Education Technology, 20*(2), 5–14.

Risley, T. R. (1968). The effects and side effects of punishing the autistic behaviors of a deviant child. *Journal of Applied Behavior Analysis 1*(1): 21–34.

Rosine, L. P., & Martin, G. L. (1983). Self-management training to decrease undesirable behavior of mentally handicapped adults. *Rehabilitation Psychology, 28*(4), 195.

Singh, N. N., Oswald, D. P., Ellis, C. R., & Singh, S. D. (1995). Community-based instruction for independent meal preparation by adults with profound mental retardation. *Journal of Behavioral Education, 5*(1), 77–91.

Sowers, J. A., Verdi, M., Bourbeau, P., & Sheehan, M. (1985). Teaching job independence and flexibility to mentally retarded students through the use of a self-control package. *Journal of Applied Behavior Analysis, 18*(1), 81–85.

Stahmer, A. C., & Schreibman, L. (1992). Teaching children with autism appropriate play in unsupervised environments using a self-management treatment package. *Journal of Applied Behavior Analysis, 25*(2), 447–459.

Tanner, B. A., & Zeiler, M. (1975). Punishment of self-injurious behavior using aromatic ammonia as the aversive stimulus. *Journal of Applied Behavior Analysis*, *8*(1), 53–57.

Watkins, L., Kuhn, M., Ledbetter-Cho, K., Gevarter, C., & O'Reilly, M. (2017). Evidence-based social communication interventions for children with autism spectrum disorder. *The Indian Journal of Pediatrics*, *84*(1), 68–75.

Wheeler, J. J., Bates, P., Marshall, K. J., & Miller, S. R. (1988). Teaching appropriate social behaviors to a young man with moderate mental retardation in a supported competitive employment setting. *Education and Training in Mental Retardation*, 105–116.

Whitman, T. L. (1990). Self-regulation and mental retardation. *American Journal on Mental Retardation*.

Xin, J. F., Sheppard, M. E., & Brown, M. (2017). Brief report: Using iPads for self-monitoring of students with autism. *Journal of Autism and Developmental Disorders*, *47*(5), 1559–1567.

11

Improving Communication Skills in Adolescents and Adults With ASD

Lynn Kern Koegel and Shereen J. Cohen

CHAPTER GOALS

Goal 1. The reader will identify the ways in which improving communication skills can improve long-term social, educational, and employment outcomes for individuals with autism spectrum disorders (ASD).

Goal 2. The reader will understand how video feedback can be used to improve social conversation.

Goal 3. The reader will learn the steps to create a self-management program to improve social conversation.

Goal 4. The reader will understand the use of visual frameworks to improve social conversation.

Goal 5. The reader will become familiar with question banks to improve social conversation.

Goal 6. The reader will be able to select appropriate interventions for various conversational target behaviors, such as empathy, positive commenting, appropriate detail, and prosody.

Transitioning to adulthood can be particularly difficult for individuals on the autism spectrum, as most confront significant obstacles in many areas while attempting to navigate college, work, community participation, leisure activities, socialization, and independent living (Hendricks & Wehman, 2009). In fact, while it is difficult to compare studies because of the heterogeneity of the population of individuals diagnosed with ASD, all studies report very low levels of paid employment, with the most optimistic outcome suggesting that only about a third of individuals with ASD will secure paid employment, with intellectual functioning being highly correlated with employment (Howlin, Goode, Hutton, & Rutter, 2004). Other studies suggest much lower levels of employment among this population. What is also concerning is that individuals with ASD who work are likely to earn low wages, work in restrictive settings, and experience challenges relating to adjusting to the work setting (Howlin, 2000). In addition to struggles regarding employment, independent living is also a concern, as most adults with ASD remain highly dependent on their parents throughout the lifespan.

One contributing factor that often affects these adults' ability to obtain and keep rewarding employment, live independently, and have meaningful social relationships is their challenge with social communication. Individuals with ASD may struggle with various aspects of everyday communication such as initiating and sustaining conversations, showing appropriate interest in others, expressing empathy, asking questions, using an appropriate level of detail in conversation, and responding positively to others. While many of these areas can improve with intervention, deficits in these skills affect social interactions across many different contexts—at school, at work, in the community, and in personal relationships. Typically developing young adults learn these skills as a matter of course, or at least learn them well enough to manage in the contexts listed previously. Their interactions with peers and getting feedback from peers helps them refine social conversation and social interactions. Unfortunately, many individuals with ASD don't have the opportunity to interact with typical peers and/or receive feedback and social support. Therefore, young adults with ASD may need explicit instruction and deliberate practice to become fluent with everyday communication skills. Targeted interventions increase the likelihood that these individuals will get and keep jobs, form meaningful relationships, and navigate their social world successfully.

These challenges may seem daunting. However, some research has evoked optimism in these areas. The following sections describe programs that have been effective for improving behaviors that may interfere with gaining employment, socialization, and independent living for adolescents and adults with ASD, with the ultimate goal of gaining meaningful and enjoyable employment with satisfying interpersonal and social relationships. Specific interventions discussed in this chapter include 1) using visual frameworks; 2) video modeling of social skills, including video self-modeling; 3) instruction in empathy; 4) teaching appropriate use of questioning; and 5) self-management.

VISUAL FRAMEWORKS

Individuals with ASD often have visual strengths; thus, visually cued instruction can facilitate learning and can be used to decrease more salient prompts. A visual framework is a schematic or other visual representation used to teach skills needed in a particular situation. Generally, visual frameworks have few printed words but use symbols to prompt an individual with ASD. In general, visual cues can accompany oral instruction and can be helpful with language and social conversation (Quill, 1997). Most recently, we have used visual frameworks to prompt appropriate conversations during social interactions.

For example, this method can be used for individuals who provide too few or too many details during conversation. Specifically, the schematic shown in Figure 11.1 has three circles. The first two circles indicate that the individual with

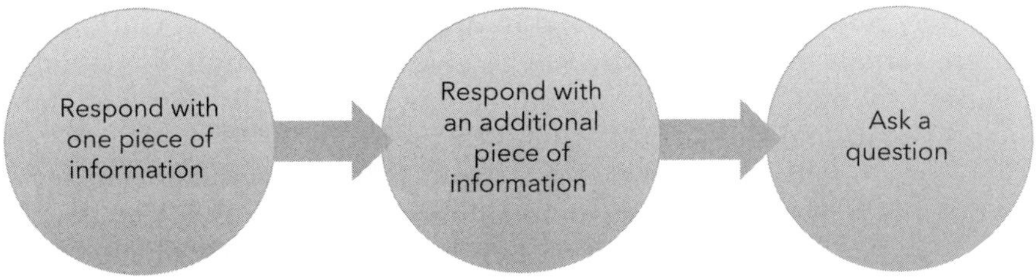

Figure 11.1. A visual framework for improving social conversation for individuals who tend to add too little or too much information.

ASD should respond to a question with two pieces of information, and the third prompts the individual to ask a question. To practice this, the clinician begins with asking a question. Next, the clinician helps the individual practice with either a lengthier response, if the client tends to answer in single words or give minimal responses, or a shorter response, if the individual tends to provide too many details. The value of the visual framework is that after practice, the clinician needs to provide only visual prompts for the individual with ASD by pointing to the circle. This reduces the interference that verbal prompting might create during social conversation.

Visual frameworks can accompany any type of social program and can be used alone or in combination with other programs such as self-management, as described in this chapter's section on self-management. The section that follows describes how video modeling may be used to teach individuals with ASD how to express appropriate empathetic responses during social conversation.

VIDEO MODELING IN PRT

Another technique used for teaching individuals with ASD is video modeling. This is based on theories of social learning, whereby people learn through observation of behaviors and consequences (Bandura, 1977). Video modeling has been successfully used with learners of all ages, from early childhood through adulthood, to teach a variety of skills, including social, communication, and vocational skills. Video modeling has been shown to be effective as a solitary intervention for teaching a specific skill or in combination with other helpful techniques, such as self-management or visual frameworks.

Video modeling has been empirically supported as an effective method to teach play skills (Akmanoglu, Yanardag, & Batu, 2014; Hine & Wolery, 2006; Ozen, Batu, & Birkan, 2012), social/communication skills (Plavnick, MacFarland, & Ferreri, 2014), and self-care/daily living skills (Acar & Diken, 2012). For example, Plavnick and colleagues (2014) used video modeling to teach initiations to children ages 5–6, specifically, how to join another child's game. For adolescents, this technique has been used to teach social skills (O'Handley, Radley, & Whipple, 2015), independent living skills (Allen, Vatland, Bowen, & Burke, 2015; Smith, Ayres, Mechling, & Smith, 2013), academic skills (Burton, Anderson, Prater, & Dyches, 2013; Hart & Whalon, 2012) and vocational skills (Alexander, Ayres, Smith, Shepley, & Mataras, 2013; Allen et al., 2010; Kellems & Morningstar, 2012; Van Laarhoven, Winiarski, Blood, & Chan, 2012). For adults, video modeling has been used to improve social conversation (Koegel, Ashbaugh, Navab, & Koegel, 2016; Koegel, Navab, Ashbaugh, & Koegel, 2016), independent living skills (Canella-Malone, Sigafoos, Reilly, Cruz, & Lancioni, 2006), and vocational skills (Kellems & Morningstar, 2012).

There are a number of different ways to conduct video modeling. One method to consider when designing a video modeling intervention is the model. That is, it can be "self," meaning the person receiving the intervention is recorded engaging in desired behaviors, or "other", meaning another peer or adult engages in the behavior). Generally, when using the latter two options, it is recommended that the model be as similar as possible to the person receiving the intervention in terms of age, gender, ethnicity, and so forth. Another method to consider is point of view (i.e., performer or observer). In this type of video modeling, someone usually completes the steps while videotaping, so that the person receiving the intervention can be presented with the situation that will occur from his or her own perspective. Additional considerations in video modeling include the length of the video (i.e., full sequence versus short clips), as well as the presence or absence of narration. These various methodologies and their applications are explained in the following sections.

Video Modeling Featuring Oneself, Peer, or an Adult

One method for video modeling that has been helpful in the treatment of individuals with ASD is video self-modeling (VSM) (Hart & Whalon, 2012; Koegel, Ashbaugh, et al., 2015). With VSM, the individual diagnosed with ASD is videotaped engaging in an activity and, later, watches clips of his or her own performance. Some clips later shown to the individual include a correct response, and others show instances in which the individual "needs improvement." During these feedback sessions, the clinician provides suggestions and engages in discussion regarding ways in which the individual could improve the behavior. Subsequent videos are collected and the intervention is repeated until the individual is able to successfully engage in the target behaviors.

For example, Koegel, Ashbaugh, et al. (2015) used this intervention strategy with adults who engaged in excessive negative comments and/or self-deprecation during social conversation. After an initial session discussing the intervention, the individual is shown specific clips in which improvement is needed. Generally, these are sandwiched in between clips of successful social interactions, for which the individual does not need intervention. The clinician and the individual with ASD then collaborate to develop a positive spin on situations, wherein the individual could replace a statement such as "I had a horrible weekend, I didn't do anything" with "I had a relaxing weekend reading books." This positive reframing has been shown to decrease negative comments among the individuals with ASD and simultaneously garner them as more favorable communicative partners during generalized conversations with peers. Textbox 11.1 describes a few simple examples of reframed response statements that an individual could be taught to use to replace overly negative comments.

Video self-modeling can also be used for other areas in which individuals with ASD struggle, such as asking questions to initiate, maintain, and show interest in another during social conversation. The procedure for using VSM to teach

TEXTBOX 11.1. Reframed Responses: Examples

Example 1. Communicative partner asks, "How was your weekend?".

Negative response: "I hate weekends. I never have anything to do."

Reframed: "I didn't do much. Just a low-key relaxing weekend."

Example 2. Communicative partner asks, "How's school going?".

Negative response: "Terrible, I have two midterms this week."

Reframed: "I'm studying hard because I have two midterms this week, but I like all my classes."

Example 3. Communicative partner asks, "What are you doing for the holidays?".

Negative response: "They aren't going to be fun at all since my brother is studying overseas."

Reframed: "I will miss my brother, who is overseas, but it's always fun seeing the rest of my family."

question-asking is similar to that described for reducing negative comments and self-deprecation (Koegel, Ashbaugh, et al., 2015). First, a learner is recorded engaging in a conversation with a peer. The interventionist and the individual with ASD then watch the video together. After hearing the learner ask his or her conversational partner a question, the interventionist pauses the video to say, "Great question!" Subsequently, during an awkward pause in the conversation or times when a question would be appropriate, the interventionist would pause the video and say, "What might be a good question you could have asked here?" Then the interventionist and learner collaboratively generate a few options for what could have been asked at that point in the conversation so that the learner gets a better sense of what type of response would be appropriate and also learns how to generate a good response in that moment. Video self-modeling creates the opportunity to provide feedback after a real-life conversation, and the collaborative effort helps the individual with ASD develop questions that are comfortable and individualized. Next, the learner practices another conversation with a peer, which is again recorded for later viewing and feedback. This can be repeated until the learner responds appropriately and expresses comfort during the social conversation. The same methodology can also be used with individuals who tend to perseverate about one topic during social conversation.

Other studies have used videos featuring others as a model, such as similarly aged peers (Akmanoglu et al., 2014; Plavnick et al., 2014) or adults (O'Handley et al., 2015; Van Laarhoven et al., 2012). In these situations, a peer or adult is videotaped engaging in the desired targeted behavior for the individual with ASD, who is then provided with opportunities to view these clips. For example, when training adolescents and young adults with ASD to perform job duties as a mascot in a store, Allen and colleagues (2010) showed the participants videos of an adult engaging in the targeted behaviors, such as walking around the store, waving, and manipulating the facial expression of the costume through levers inside the costume. In both of these studies, the investigators demonstrated that all participants increased the frequency and diversity of modeled behaviors.

Point of View

Another method to consider when implementing video modeling is point of view. This involves the choice to record the clips showing the behavior from the perspective of the *observer* or the *performer* of the behavior. For example, one study taught play skills by filming over the shoulder of the person demonstrating the skills, such that when watching the video, one could see hands playing with toys, as if one were watching oneself performing the action (Hine & Wolery, 2006). In most cases the video is filmed from the viewpoint of the observer so the individual watching the clips gets an idea of what to do in that situation (Burke et al., 2013).

Additional Variables

Additional variables to consider when implementing video modeling relate to the editorial process. Video modeling may be conducted by having the participant view the full sequence of events and then perform the task, or the video may be broken down into smaller steps, such that the participant can use the video to prompt discrete behaviors. This variation of video modeling may also be known as video prompting (Canella-Malone et al., 2006). In addition, the video may contain narration or other auditory stimuli to create a multisensory learning experience (Smith et al., 2013). For example, the video model may resemble an instructional video, in which a model is performing a task with narration: "First you open the bag, then you take out the milk. Then you carry the milk to the fridge, open the fridge, and put the milk inside the fridge." Narration may also be used to reinforce behavior, with commentary such as, "Billy is making great eye contact. Way to go, Billy!" (O'Handley et al., 2015). Alternately, if the video model aims to teach or improve social interactions (conversation or play), the individual receiving the intervention may simply watch a conversation or activity, as if watching a movie (Ozen et al., 2012). This type of video modeling may or may not be effective for individuals with ASD if they do not receive direct feedback, as performing a skill modeled by another is sometimes challenging.

As a whole, video modeling is a relatively new intervention procedure that has potential for individuals with ASD. To date, most interventions have focused on individuals with expressive verbal communication, because the intervention usually involves discussing the clips. Some literature has suggested that individuals with ASD who enjoy watching videotapes may be more positively affected by the intervention than those who prefer direct feedback, which involves the social interaction with another person (Charlop-Christy, Le, & Freeman, 2000). Also, self- and peer-video modeling may be more effective for individuals with ASD than teacher video modeling, and imitation skills may be necessary for acquiring skills, but additional research is needed in this area (McCoy & Hermansen, 2007). Further, as mentioned, some type of active teaching often needs to accompany the video segments as observational learning generally doesn't seem to occur when adolescents and adults simply watch video segments. As the field progresses, researchers and clinicians will most likely explore methods for using video modeling with a wider range of target behaviors and with individuals with greater support needs.

INSTRUCTION IN EMPATHY

As previously stated, individuals diagnosed with ASD have difficulties with social communication. These can include challenges with expressions of emotional and conversational reciprocity during conversation, as well as deficits in one's ability to read facial and other nonverbal cues (Bons et al., 2013; Deschamps, Been, & Matthys, 2014) and perspective taking (Schwenck et al., 2012). In consonance with this perspective, some have conceptualized ASD as a disorder of empathy. However, empathy is a multi-faceted concept with both cognitive and emotional components. The notion that individuals with ASD lack empathy should not be misunderstood as implying that ASD is a form of sociopathy or the inability to care for the well-being of others (Krahn & Fenton, 2009).

Challenges with empathy and social interaction may also be compounded by the fact that so many individuals with ASD have very little access to typically developing peers while growing up. Historically children with ASD have often been educated in self-contained classrooms with other children who exhibit significant communication challenges and generally have not participated in after-school and extracurricular activities or sports. During naturally occurring peer interactions, children become better at socializing, receive social support from friends, and get feedback from peers on their social communication and behaviors. Children who are isolated from these interactions will not reap their benefits. Thus, their isolation means that to some extent they may not learn many important behaviors, which is likely to have a negative impact. However, our research suggests that some interventions may be helpful with empathy. So, what is empathy, and in what ways do individuals with ASD struggle with it?

What Is Empathy?

The general consensus in the literature suggests that empathy comprises two main components: *cognitive empathy (CE)* and *emotional empathy (EE)* (Krahn & Fenton, 2009; Oxley, 2011; Smith, 2009a). CE refers to the ability to identify the emotion that another person is feeling, while EE refers to one's ability to emotionally respond in kind to the other person's feelings or, by some definitions, to actually feel what the other person is feeling. As demonstrated by Winczewski, Bowen, and Collins (2016), accurately identifying another person's emotional state is insufficient for a satisfactory empathic interaction. One must also communicate concern for the other person's emotional state. The ability to infer another person's emotions from their behavior, feel the other person's emotion, care how they feel, and communicate understanding and caring, are all components of the overall construct of empathy. For example, when seeing a friend crying, a typical individual might perceive their friend as feeling sad, feel slightly sad themselves, and say something supportive to their friend, such as "What's wrong?" or "I'm sorry you are feeling this way."

Research suggests that individuals with ASD tend to lack the expression of *cognitive* empathy but not emotional empathy (Bellebaum, Brodmann, & Thoma, 2014; Dziobek et al., 2008; Jones, Happé, Gilbert, Burnett, & Viding, 2010). Some studies have even suggested that individuals with ASD may have higher emotional empathy than typical (Gu et al., 2015; Smith, 2009a). In other words, individuals with ASD care very much how others feel, but may have difficulty deducing what emotion someone is feeling. Finally, due to social communication difficulties, they also may have difficulty communicating their empathy, although they experience a physiological and emotional empathic reaction (Charman et al., 1997; Koegel, Ashbaugh et al., 2015). These cognitive and communicative components of empathy have been targeted in treatment research.

An important first question is how we measure empathy. Measures of empathy include standardized pencil-and-paper measures (The Interpersonal Reactivity Index (IRI), Davis [1983]; The Questionnaire Measure of Emotional Empathy (QMEE), Mehrabian & Epstein [1972]; The Empathy Quotient (EQ), Baron-Cohen & Wheelwright [2004]), as well as physiological measures such as heart rate and skin conductance and neurological (e.g., fMRI studies, mirror neuron system, fusiform gyrus, medial prefrontal cortex). However, as clinicians and researchers, we tend to look at behavioral symptoms. That is, we set up situations in which people typically exhibit empathy, such as social conversation, and assess the individual with ASD's response. For example, we may have the individual engage in a social conversation with a similarly aged peer. The peer can make statements that should evoke empathy, such as "I'm not feeling well today" or "I had a really fun weekend." If the individual with ASD responds with "Oh" or "I went to a physics lecture last night" or just doesn't respond at all, we consider this area in need of intervention.

Can Empathy Be Taught?: A Summary of Research

The next relevant question is whether we can teach empathy. Rameson, Morelli, and Lieberman (2012) found that empathy may not be entirely automatic, suggesting that it may be subject to change. A number of researchers have sought to teach skills associated with cognitive empathy and empathic communication to both neurotypical individuals and individuals affected by ASD. A variety of interventions have been developed, utilizing such interventions as in vivo prompting, video modeling, visual frameworks, and reinforcement schedules (both naturalistic and token economy). Studies aiming to teach empathic skills to children and adults with ASD are discussed in the following sections.

Teaching Empathic Skills Through Software Training Golan and Baron-Cohen (2006) tested the efficacy of Mind Reading software training program in adults with Asperger syndrome or high-functioning autism. Their DVDs include emotional expressions in the voices and faces of actors to help learn about emotions. Participants were randomly assigned to the computer training program or a no-treatment control group. In the second part of the study, another group of adults with ASD were randomly assigned to participate in the computer training program, plus weekly counseling, or a treatment-as-usual social skills training group. The program required entailed 2 hours per week for 10 weeks. In both variations of this experiment, participants who used the software training program improved significantly on a variety of measures of cognitive empathy and showed greater improvement than control groups. Unfortunately, results did not generalize to novel stimuli or settings. Thus, additional intervention following computerized interventions appears to be necessary.

Teaching Empathic Skills Through Vignettes Schrandt, Townsend, and Poulson (2009) tested an intervention to train children with ASD to respond empathically to vignettes, such as a story of a doll bumping its leg and saying "Ow." This study utilized a multiple baseline across response category for four children with ASD. During baseline, all participants were responding to zero opportunities for empathic responding. During intervention, an adult prompted a correct response from the child which was rewarded with a token. All participants learned to respond empathically to pain and sadness, and some participants learned to respond across all emotional categories (sadness, pain, happiness, excitement, and frustration). All participants also generalized the skills, responding correctly when presented with novel stimuli or in a novel setting.

Teaching Empathic Skills Through Video Modeling Axe and Evans (2012) used video modeling to teach three children to respond to facial expressions. Using a multiple baseline across response design, the authors tested the efficacy of a video modeling intervention to teach verbal responses to a variety of facial expressions. Participants watched clips that showed a facial expression, followed by a person modeling an appropriate response. The participant echoed the response and then practiced responding to just the expression. Verbal praise was delivered for correct responses. All participants learned to respond appropriately to the facial expressions, and all participants generalized to novel settings and stimuli.

Combining Video Modeling With Visual Frameworks In another study Koegel, Ashbaugh, et al. (2015) used video modeling, in addition to a visual framework, to teach adults with ASD to respond using empathic statements and empathic questions during social conversations. The authors tested the efficacy of this intervention using a multiple baseline across participant design with adults between 19 and 26 years of age. Intervention sessions were conducted once weekly, with each session lasting about 40 minutes. Prior to intervention, baseline conversation probes were collected while each participant engaged in conversation with a similarly aged peer. To assess whether empathy occurred during the social conversation, participants were presented with opportunities to respond empathically. For example, the clinician might say something like, "I did something really fun yesterday," "I had a really hard week," or "I have a hard test coming up and I'm really stressed out." The baseline revealed that the adult participants responded with an empathetic statement (e.g., "Oh, sorry to hear you're stressed" or "That's rough") 0%–37% of the time, on average, and asked an empathetic question an average of 12%–33% of the time. For intervention, we used a visual framework as a schematic guide. This framework, shown in Figure 11.2, contained three boxes with examples. The first box listed several types of emotional statements, with examples of each type.

- *Sick*—"I'm not feeling that well today."
- *Stressed*—"I'm nervous about my finals."
- *Excited*—"My friend is coming to visit me this week."

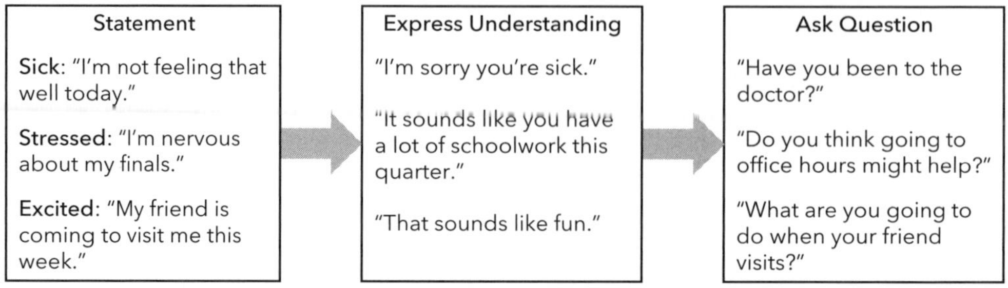

Figure 11.2. A visual framework to help individuals learn to give empathic responses during social conversation.

The second box was labeled "Express Understanding" and listed examples that would show understanding of this emotional state, such as "I'm sorry you're sick" or "It sounds like you have a lot of schoolwork this quarter" or "That sounds like fun." Expressing understanding was important for two reasons. First, of course, people having a conversation want to acknowledge that they understand how the communicative partner is feeling. Second, as clinicians, we wanted to make sure that the individuals with ASD were responding to the emotional state rather than to another aspect of the conversation. For example, if the communicative partner said, "My computer crashed today, and I lost all the work I had been doing, and I think I may lose my job now" an appropriate response to express understanding might be, "That would be horrible if you lost your job" or "You might be able to retrieve some of the information on the hard drive" In contrast, an inappropriate response would be "Where do you work?" "Oh, well I always back up my files so that never happens to me" or "What kind of computer do you have?" Similarly, if someone says, "My sister and I got in a disagreement last night, and I think she's mad at me," an appropriate response might be "That's too bad," or "I can see why you feel terrible." An inappropriate response would be "How old is your sister?" or "I don't like to get involved in people's family problems."

The third box of the visual framework was labeled, "Ask Question" and contained examples, such as "Have you been to the doctor?" if the communicative partner indicates that he or she is not feeling well, or "Do you think going to office hours might help?" when the communicative partner indicates that she didn't do well on a test, or "What are going to do when your friend visits?" after a communicative partner says a friend from out of town is visiting. This visual framework was provided to the individual with ASD to practice, using the examples. For instance, the clinician might say "I had a great weekend," after which the individual with ASD would be prompted to produce an empathic statement, followed by an empathic response, for example: "That's great! What did you do?" Or if the clinician said, "Last week was so stressful," the individual with ASD would be prompted to express empathetic understanding and ask an empathetic question, such as "I'm sorry you had a hard week. What happened?"

In addition to the prompting, a conversation probe was recorded similar to the one used during baseline in which similarly aged peers engaged in social conversation and inserted various statements of both positive and negative emotion each week. During the weekly intervention sessions conversational clips were shown to the individual with ASD. If the individual generated an appropriate empathetic response, the clinician discussed how great the response was. This also provided a positive model for the empathetic responses. Next, conversational examples that "needed improvement" were shown, and the clinician and individual with ASD discussed potential responses that could have been used in that situation.

Following the intervention, all participants significantly improved in both their empathetic responses and questions. Specifically, in regard to empathetic statements, participants improved from an average of 0%–37% at baseline, to 71%–87% following intervention and averaged 50%–100% at follow-up. Use of empathetic questions improved from average baseline levels of 12%–33% to average postintervention levels of 82%–97%, with empathetic questions asked 90%–100% of the time at follow-up. Thus, the combination of practice with a visual framework along with video modeling in real life conversations dramatically improved the participants' verbal use of empathy during social conversation. What's more, following intervention, all participants improved on standardized tests of empathy and reported improvements in self-confidence during social conversation. This self-report of improved confidence is important, as many adults with ASD report anxiety regarding socialization as well as depression regarding their lack of friendships and social interactions.

QUESTION ASKING AND QUESTION BANKS

As discussed throughout this chapter, difficulty with social conversation can negatively affect the building of relationships, gaining and maintaining employment, and fully participating in the community for recreational and other activities. Although there are relatively few evidence-based procedures for improving social skills in adolescents and adults with ASD, the literature suggests that careful and systematic interventions can help them make improvements. One potential area for improvement is question asking (Koegel, Koegel, Green-Hopkins, & Barnes, 2010; Palmen, Didden, & Arts, 2008). The analysis of language samples of individuals who are highly verbal and those who are verbal with significant language delays suggest that their functions of language are often limited to requests, protests, and some comments, while question asking is low or absent (cf., Koegel, Koegel, Harrower, & Carter, 1999). Questions are important for initiating conversation and social interactions, for maintaining social conversation, and for self-initiated learning; they are a necessary language function for communicative competence. As well, long-term outcomes are improved when a young child's communication includes initiations, including questions (Koegel, Koegel, Shoshan, & McNerney, 1999).

For adolescents and adults, question-asking can be taught in several ways. One method is through priming. For example, practitioners can develop question banks with a variety of questions pre-printed on index cards. These serve as conversation starters, such as "How was your weekend?" "What kinds of food do you enjoy?" "Have you seen any good movies lately?" and so on. Individuals receiving interventions can practice asking these questions with a clinician or parent using appropriate eye contact, intonation, and body language. In our own clinical experience, after about four sessions of practice, we notice generalization of the question asking with adolescents and adults who are able to form sentences and engage in conversation but who lack appropriate question asking during social conversation.

Questions can also be taught using leading statements. These serve as a prompt for the individual with ASD to learn strategies to keep the conversation going and avoid long awkward pauses. To practice, the conversational partner makes statements such as "I'm going to see my best friend this weekend." The individual with ASD is then prompted to come up with three different possible appropriate responses to the statement. For example, he may ask, "Where does your friend live?" or "What are you going to do?" or "How often do you see her?" This is practiced until the individual can create questions without prompting. Over time, the individual with ASD learns appropriate responses that keep the conversation active and show interest in the conversational partner during everyday conversations.

SELF-MANAGEMENT

Finally, self-management, as discussed in the previous chapter, is another intervention that can be used to improve social conversation in adults. We will not review the procedures in detail here; however, self-management, using the general steps described in Chapter 10, can be used alone or in combination with many interventions to improve communication skills. For example, we have had adults self-manage minutes during conversation that they stayed on topic. Time periods of on-topic engagement can be monitored. The schematic shown in Figure 11.1 shows a program that has been used to prompt an individual to provide the correct amount of detail during conversation. Simply add boxes below the schematic so the individual with ASD can monitor each time the correct amount of detail is added. We have also had adolescents and adults self-manage the use of empathetic statements. Question-asking can also be self-managed. For example, if an adolescent or adult is not asking questions, the interventionist can prepare a checklist for the individual with ASD to use to monitor questions he or she asked during a conversation. Again, self-management is a pivotal area. Once an individual is able to self-control his or her own behaviors, improvements in many areas occur. The case history of Jacob, below, illustrates how the intervention strategies described in this chapter can be used to improve communication skills in young adults with ASD.

CASE HISTORY
Improving Jacob's Social Communication Skills

Jacob was 22 years old with a diagnosis of Asperger syndrome. He was brilliant and attended an Ivy League school until depression got the best of him. Although he had a few friends in high school, moving to college was difficult. At college, he couldn't muster the courage to ask a friend out to a social event. Consequently, he began to play video games late into the night and found it increasingly difficult to get up in the morning. He began missing classes. Despite his history of straight A's, his grades plunged to–at best– C's, with a few D's and F's. As time went on, he fell deeper into the darkness of depression and even had thoughts of suicide.

When Jacob started failing all of his courses, his parents took action. They collected him and all of his belongings and enrolled him at the university where we worked, which could provide support for the social challenges that face college students with ASD. Some universities only provide a standard package of procedures that address academic challenges—extra time on tests, tests in a quiet room, a note taker, and so on. Fewer programs tackle the social challenges faced by individuals with ASD. When Jacob began our program, we collected a language sample of him conversing with a similarly aged peer. During supervision, we chatted about his strengths and weaknesses. He was smart and could answer each question intelligently and interestingly. He was well-groomed, clean-shaven, and appeared to have good hygiene. His prosody was fine; he spoke at an appropriate rate using great intonation patterns and the right volume level.

Now the issues: His biggest communication issue was that he never asked a question. This resulted in long, painful, awkward pauses throughout the conversations if the partner didn't pick up the slack. Generally, his conversational partner did the majority of the talking, but only because of his lack of initiating and questions. Jacob confided that he had dated a few times but never got a second date. This wasn't hard to imagine, given his long, silent pauses. A few other less important issues also stood out. His posture was stiff, and his hand movements were awkward. In addition, he on occasion gave a hug that was meant to be warm and sweet but practically broke the nose of the person being hugged. And finally, he wore the same shorts, flip flops, and short-sleeved t-shirt every day, no matter what the weather—rain or shine, and according to his mother, snow too.

First impressions are important, so we started out by taking Jacob on a shopping trip for clothes. His mother reported that she had been bugging him for years about his clothing without success. But as a young adult with Asperger syndrome, Jacob was now highly motivated to make friends and have a girlfriend. With an enthusiastic graduate student to take him shopping, the clothing suggestions were likely to become a reality. After one shopping trip, this good-looking young man began dressing like a fashion model (on a student's budget, of course).

Next, we addressed the hugs. We suggested practicing some gentle hugs—the kind with one arm just lightly placed around the other person. That was a quick fix.

Finally, we began to delve into the social conversation. We used video modeling to show Jacob examples of his long pauses during the social conversation. Each time there was a long pause, we stopped the clip and helped him come up with three questions he could ask to keep the conversation going. Shortly thereafter the clinician faded her assistance, and Jacob was able to come up with the questions on his own. After 4 weeks with 1 hour of practice per week on the questions, he was able to carry on a conversation that flowed well and showed his conversational partner that he was interested in him or her. The graduate student working with Jacob also took him on a few outings to practice the newly learned question asking with new people. We also practiced having him sit in a relaxed manner during social conversation without making awkward hand and body movements.

After the intervention, Jacob began dating a woman within a few months and moved out of his parents' home and into a house with many other students. He eventually completed college with excellent grades and was admitted to graduate school. Interestingly, he reported that he had seen a psychotherapist for many years. During each visit they chatted about why he couldn't make friends. He said he didn't have a clue that the question asking was missing from his social conversation and that was what was inhibiting his ability to socialize. As mentioned in Chapter 2, behavioral observations are critical to understanding important behaviors that may be interfering with success. ▮▮▮

Key Insights ||| Improving Young Adults' Communication Skills

Keep the following points in mind when working to help young adults with ASD improve their communication skills.

- **Transitioning to adulthood can be challenging:** Some individuals with ASD have difficulty with social conversation in college, the work setting, and during social events. Intervention for social conversation can result in improvements and should be targeted in adulthood.
- **Video modeling can be a helpful intervention strategy:** Video modeling can be implemented in a variety of ways. For social conversation, it is often helpful to use clips from recent social conversation to discuss specific strategies that can be used in future conversations. This provides the individual with ASD an opportunity to view his or her own behaviors and get feedback on ways to improve.
- **Visual frameworks can be helpful intervention tools:** Many individuals with ASD respond well to visual cues. For social conversation, visual frameworks can be used to prompt the right amount of social conversation for those who give too little or too much detail or to prompt other skills. Oftentimes, visual frameworks reduce the need for oral feedback during social conversation.
- **Empathy can be taught:** Many individuals with ASD have challenges verbally communicating emotions. Studies now show that it is possible to teach adults with ASD to respond empathetically during social conversation.
- **Question asking can be taught:** Questions are important for starting conversations and keeping them going. Question asking is often low in individuals with ASD. Question asking can be improved in individuals with ASD in several ways, which, in turn, improves social interaction.
- **Self-management can improve social conversation:** As with other behaviors, there is a point when the individual who wants to improve social conversation skills needs to take control of his or her own intervention. Self-management is a great tool for social conversation, because conversations will happen throughout the day in the absence of an interventionist. Having the right tool available in natural settings can be a helpful reminder to ask a question, respond to others, or work on any other area that may need intervention.

SUMMARY

In summary, communication is important throughout life, and intervention programs are showing that social conversation can be improved. As with any other behavior, a careful analysis of areas that may be interfering with making friends, getting along at the work site, or engaging in social leisure activities is important. Once those areas are determined, whether they be question asking, responsiveness, empathy, positive statements, or any other behavior, an appropriate intervention will need to be developed. This may involve video modeling, self-management, visual frameworks, or other procedures. The important point is that it is never too late to provide intervention. Social conversation skills can be improved, and often this makes a huge difference for an individual with ASD who wants to make friends, have a job, engage in leisure social activities, and feel more attached socially.

STUDY QUESTIONS

1. Describe some common concerns for individuals with ASD in adulthood.
2. How can video modeling be used to improve social conversation?
3. What is empathy?
4. Discuss how empathy can be improved in individuals with ASD who lack these verbal responses.
5. What are some advantages of visual frameworks?
6. How can visual frameworks be used to improve social conversation in individuals with ASD?
7. Discuss some advantages of self-management.
8. Describe a self-management program for an individual with ASD.
9. Discuss ways self-management can be combined with other interventions.
10. What are some common communicative challenges in adults with ASD?
11. Describe visual frameworks and how they can assist with social conversation.

REFERENCES

Acar, C., & Diken, I. H. (2012). Reviewing instructional studies conducted using video modeling to children with autism. *Kuram Ve Uygulamada Egitim Bilimleri, 12*(4), 2731–2735.

Akmanoglu, N., Yanardag, M., & Batu, S. E. (2014). Comparing video modeling and graduated guidance together and video modeling alone for teaching role playing skills to children with autism. *Education and Training in Autism and Developmental Disabilities, 49*(1), 17–31.

Alexander, J. L., Ayres, K. M., Smith, K. A., Shepley, S. B., & Mataras, T. K. (2013). Using video modeling on an iPad to teach generalized matching on a sorting mail task to adolescents with autism. *Research in Autism Spectrum Disorders, 7*(11), 1346–1357.

Allen, K. D., Vatland, C., Bowen, S. L., & Burke, R. V. (2015). An evaluation of parent-produced video self-modeling to improve independence in an adolescent with intellectual developmental disorder and an autism spectrum disorder: A controlled case study. *Behavior Modification, 39*(4), 542–556.

Allen, K. D., Wallace, D. P., Greene, D. J., Bowen, S. L., & Burke, R. V. (2010). Community-based vocational instruction using videotaped modeling for young adults with autism spectrum disorders performing in air-inflated mascots. *Focus on Autism and Other Developmental Disabilities, 25*(3), 186–192.

Allen, K. D., Wallace, D. P., Renes, D., Bowen, S. L., & Burke, R. V. (2010). Use of video modeling to teach vocational skills to adolescents and young adults with autism spectrum disorders. *Education & Treatment of Children, 33*(3), 339–349.

Axe, J. B., & Evans, C. J. (2012). Using video modeling to teach children with PDD-NOS to respond to facial expressions. *Research in Autism Spectrum Disorders, 6*(3), 1176–1185.

Bandura, A. (1977). Social learning theory. Englewood Cliffs, NJ: Prentice-Hall.

Baron-Cohen, S., & Wheelwright, S. (2004). The empathy quotient: An investigation of adults with Asperger syndrome or high-functioning autism, and normal sex differences. *Journal of Autism and Developmental Disorders, 34*(2), 163–175.

Bellebaum, C., Brodmann, K., & Thoma, P. (2014). Active and observational reward learning in adults with autism spectrum disorder: relationship with empathy in an atypical sample. *Cognitive Neuropsychiatry, 19*(3), 205–225.

Bons, D., Van Den Broek, E., Scheepers, F., Herpers, P., Rommelse, N., & Buitelaaar, J. K. (2013). Motor, emotional, and cognitive empathy in children and adolescents with autism spectrum disorder and conduct disorder. *Journal of Abnormal Child Psychology, 41*(3), 425–443.

Burke, R. V., Allen, K. D., Howard, M. R., Downey, D., Matz, M. G., & Bowen, S. L. (2013). Tablet-based video modeling and prompting in the workplace for individuals with autism. *Journal of Vocational Rehabilitation, 38*(1), 1–14.

Burton, C. E., Anderson, D. H., Prater, M. A., & Dyches, T. T. (2013). Video self-modeling on an iPad to teach functional math skills to adolescents with autism and intellectual disability. *Focus on Autism and Other Developmental Disabilities, 28*(2), 67–77.

Cannella-Malone, H., Sigafoos, J., Reilly, M. O., Cruz, B. D., & Lancioni, G. E. (2006). Comparing video prompting to video modeling for teaching daily living skills to six adults with developmental disabilities. *Education and Training, 41*(December), 344–356.

Charlop-Christy, M. H., Le, L., & Freeman, K. A. (2000). A comparison of video modeling with in vivo modeling for teaching children with autism. *Journal of Autism and Developmental Disorders, 30*(6), 537–552.

Charman, T., Swettenham, J., Baron-Cohen, S., Cox, A., Baird, G., & Drew, A. (1997). Infants with autism: An investigation of empathy, pretend play, joint attention, and imitation. *Developmental Psychology, 33*(5), 781–789.

Davis, M. H. (1983). Measuring individual differences in empathy: Evidence for a multidimensional approach. *Journal of personality and social psychology, 44*(1), 113.

Deschamps, P. K. H., Been, M., & Matthys, W. (2014). Empathy and empathy induced prosocial behavior in 6- and 7-year-olds with autism spectrum disorder. *Journal of Autism and Developmental Disorders, 44*(7), 1749–1758.

Dziobek, I., Rogers, K., Fleck, S., Bahnemann, M., Heekeren, H. R., Wolf, O. T., & Convit, A. (2008). Dissociation of cognitive and emotional empathy in adults with Asperger syndrome using the Multifaceted Empathy Test (MET). *Journal of Autism and Developmental Disorders, 38*(3), 464–473.

Golan, O., & Baron-Cohen, S. (2006). Systemizing empathy: Teaching adults with Asperger syndrome or high-functioning autism to recognize complex emotions using interactive multimedia. *Development and Psychopathology, 18*, 591–617.

Gu, X., Eilam-Stock, T., Zhou, T., Anagnostou, E., Kolevzon, A., Soorya, L., & Fan, J. (2015). Autonomic and brain responses associated with empathy deficits in autism spectrum disorder. *Human Brain Mapping, 36*(9), 3323–3338.

Hart, J. E., & Whalon, K. J. (2012). Using video self-modeling via iPads to increase academic responding of an adolescent with autism spectrum disorder and intellectual disability. *Education and Training in Autism and Developmental Disabilities, 47*(4), 438–446.

Hendricks, D. R., & Wehman, P. (2009). Transition from school to adulthood for youth with autism spectrum disorders: Review and recommendations. *Focus on Autism and Other Developmental Disabilities, 24*(2), 77-88.

Howlin, P. (2000). Outcome in adult life for more able individuals with autism or Asperger syndrome. *Autism, 4*(1), 63-83.

Howlin, P., Goode, S., Hutton, J., & Rutter, M. (2004). Adult outcome for children with autism. *Journal of Child Psychology and Psychiatry, 45*(2), 212–229.

Hine, J. F., & Wolery, M. (2006). Using point-of-view video modeling to teach play to preschoolers with autism. *Topics in Early Childhood Special Education, 26*(2), 83–93.

Jones, A. P., Happé, F. G. E., Gilbert, F., Burnett, S., & Viding, E. (2010). Feeling, caring, knowing: different types of empathy deficit in boys with psychopathic tendencies and autism spectrum disorder. *Journal of Child Psychology and Psychiatry, and Allied Disciplines, 51*(11), 1188–1197.

Kellems, R., & Morningstar, M. E. (2012). Using video modeling delivered through iPads to teach vocational tasks to young adults with autism spectrum disorders (ASD). *Career Development and Transition for Exceptional Individuals, 35*(3), 155–167.

Koegel, L. K., Ashbaugh, K., Navab, A., & Koegel, R. L. (2015). Improving empathic communication skills in adults with autism spectrum disorder. *Journal of Autism and Developmental Disorders.*

Koegel, L. K., Koegel, R. L., Green-Hopkins, I., & Barnes, C. C. (2010). Brief report: Question asking and collateral language acquisition in children with autism. *Journal of Autism and Developmental Disorders, 40*(4), 509–515.
Koegel, L. K., Koegel, R. L., Harrower, J. K., & Carter, C. M. (1999). Pivotal response intervention I: Overview of approach. *The Journal of the Association for Persons with Severe Handicaps. 24*(3), 174–186.
Koegel, L. K., Koegel, R. L., Shoshan, Y., & McNerney, E. (1999). Pivotal response intervention II: Preliminary long-term outcome data. *Research and Practice for Persons with Severe Disabilities, 24*(3), 186–198.
Koegel, L. K., Navab, A., Ashbaugh, K., & Koegel, R. L. (2016). Using reframing to reduce negative statements in social conversation for adults with autism spectrum disorder. *Journal of Positive Behavior Interventions, 18*(3), 133–144.
Krahn, T., & Fenton, A. (2009). Autism, empathy and questions of moral agency. *Journal for the Theory of Social Behaviour, 39*(2), 145–166.
McCoy, K., & Hermansen, E. (2007). Video modeling for individuals with autism: A review of model types and effects. *Education and Treatment of Children,* 183–213.
Mehrabian, A., & Epstein, N. (1972). A measure of emotional empathy. *Journal of Personality, 40*(4), 525–543.
O'Handley, R. D., Radley, K. C., & Whipple, H. M. (2015). The relative effects of social stories and video modeling toward increasing eye contact of adolescents with autism spectrum disorder. *Research in Autism Spectrum Disorders, 11,* 101–111.
Oxley, J. C. (2011). What is empathy? In *The Moral Dimensions of Empathy*. Palgrave Macmillan, Macmillan Publishers Limited, London, England.
Ozen, A., Batu, S., & Birkan, B. (2012). Teaching play skills to children with autism through video modeling: Small group arrangement and observational learning. *Education and Training in Autism and Developmental Disabilities, 47*(1), 84–96.
Palmen, A., Didden, R., & Arts, M. (2008). Improving question asking in high-functioning adolescents with autism spectrum disorders: Effectiveness of small-group training. *Autism, 12*(1), 83–98.
Plavnick, J. B., MacFarland, M. C., & Ferreri, S. J. (2014). Variability in the effectiveness of a video modeling intervention package for children with autism. *Journal of Positive Behavior Interventions, 17*(2), 105–155.
Quill, K. A. (1997). Instructional considerations for young children with autism: The rationale for visually cued instruction. *Journal of Autism and Developmental Disorders, 27*(6), 697–714.
Rameson, L. T., Morelli, S. A., & Lieberman, M. D. (2012). The neural correlates of empathy: Experience, automaticity, and prosocial behavior. *Journal of Cognitive Neuroscience, 24*(1), 235–245.
Schrandt, J. A., Townsend, D. B., & Poulson, C. L. (2009). Teaching empathy skills to children with autism. *Journal of Applied Behavior Analysis, 42*(1), 17–32.
Schwenck, C., Mergenthaler, J., Keller, K., Zech, J., Salehi, S., Taurines, R., & Freitag, C. M. (2012). Empathy in children with autism and conduct disorder: Group-specific profiles and developmental aspects. *Journal of Child Psychology and Psychiatry and Allied Disciplines, 53*(6), 651–659.
Smith, A. (2009a). Emotional empathy in autism spectrum conditions: Weak, intact, or heightened? *Journal of Autism and Developmental Disorders, 39*(12), 1747–1748.
Smith, A. (2009b). The empathy imbalance hypothesis of autism: A theoretical approach to cognitive and emotional empathy in autistic development. *Psychological Record, 59*(3), 489–510.
Smith, M., Ayres, K., Mechling, L., & Smith, K. (2013). Comparison of the effects of video modeling with narration vs. video modeling on the functional skill acquisition of adolescents with autism. *Education and Training in Autism and Developmental Disabilities, 48*(2), 164–178.
Van Laarhoven, T., Winiarski, L., Blood, E., & Chan, J. M. (2012). Maintaining vocational skills of individuals with autism and developmental disabilities through video modeling. *Education and Training in Autism and Developmental Disabilities, 47*(4), 447–461.
Winczewski, L. A., Bowen, J. D., & Collins, N. L. (2016). Is empathic accuracy enough to facilitate responsive behavior in dyadic interaction? Distinguishing ability from motivation. *Psychological Science, 27*(3), 394–404.

12

Improving Socialization in Adolescents and Adults With ASD

Lynn Kern Koegel, Kristen Ashbaugh, and Daina Tagavi

CHAPTER GOALS

Goal 1. The reader will understand socialization issues in individuals with autism spectrum disorders (ASD).

Goal 2. The reader will discuss the importance of implementing social interventions for ASD.

Goal 3. The reader will describe procedures to develop social groups for adolescents with ASD involving their restricted interests.

Goal 4. The reader will describe comprehensive programs for improving socialization and social communication for individuals with ASD.

Goal 5. The reader will discuss research related to long-term social outcomes for individuals with ASD.

This chapter discusses common social challenges in individuals with ASD and consequential co-morbidities that may develop. In addition, we discuss the disadvantages social challenges often present in regard to psychological well-being, limitations in friendship development, engagement in leisure activities, and educational opportunities. We then describe intervention techniques to create increased opportunities for peer socialization in school, college, and the workplace. We emphasize the importance of interventions focusing on the individual with ASD's strengths to create social motivation and quality of life. Throughout the chapter, we emphasize a need for comprehensive social intervention programs, implemented throughout the lifespan, aimed toward improving friendships, employment opportunities, and overall quality of life.

THE IMPACT OF SOCIAL DIFFICULTIES

Socialization is a core difficulty that impacts individuals with ASD of all ages and development levels (American Psychiatric Association, 2013; Seltzer, Shattuck, Abbeduto, & Greenberg, 2004). The literature has shown that young adults with ASD report that they would like to form social relationships and contribute to their community, but they often experience loneliness due to a lack of involvement and social skill deficits (Adreon & Durocher, 2007; Hendricks & Wehman, 2009; Howlin, Mawhood, & Rutter, 2000; Muller, Schuler, & Yates, 2008). Fortunately, there are many evidence-based and clinical intervention strategies to help improve social engagement for adolescents and adults with ASD. Thus, it is important that individuals with ASD wanting to improve in this area receive support and treatment to help them improve their socialization with peers and co-workers.

Although signs of ASD emerge early in life and diagnoses are usually made in early childhood, symptoms tend to persist throughout the lifespan, particularly in socialization, and can greatly impact the quality of life of individuals with ASD and their caregivers. Adults with ASD often face a plethora of challenges on a daily basis. Research has found that individuals with ASD have significant hardship finding and securing postsecondary employment, particularly due to their unique impairments in communication and socialization (Hendricks, 2010; Müller, Schuler, Burton, & Yates, 2003). According to Seltzer and colleagues (2004), it is challenging for many adults with ASD to live independently, get married, obtain higher education, secure competitive employment, or develop meaningful and long-term relationships or social networks. In fact, a large majority of individuals with ASD continue to remain highly dependent on family members and professional service providers throughout their lives (Seltzer et al., 2004). In a review of the literature by Levy and Perry, it was determined that approximately 50%–60% of adults with ASD fail to meet academic milestones and/or are not provided with adequate vocational preparation in school, and more than 75% are unable to find work, stemming primarily with their difficulties with socialization (Levy & Perry, 2011).

Research has also demonstrated that very few adults with ASD (as low as 8%) report having friendships with same-age peers that are reciprocal in nature and occur outside of prearranged settings such as work and school (Howlin et al., 2000; Orsmond, Krauss, & Seltzer, 2004). People with ASD often lack the social skills and social communication skills to appropriately pursue and maintain a romantic relationship, despite reporting a desire for these types of relationships as frequently as their typically developing peers (Mehzabin & Stokes, 2011). These individuals also endorse feelings of loneliness and report wanting meaningful social relationships, but often lack the social skills to initiate and sustain successful social interactions (Howlin et al., 2000). These socialization deficits in young adults with ASD have been linked to lower rates of success in higher education opportunities, which, in turn, are associated with lower employment rates, quality of life, self-confidence, and skill development (Vanbergeijk, Klin, & Volkmar, 2008). Although studies vary on their level of optimism in regard to outcomes in this area and can relate to the type of support individuals with ASD receive, clearly there is a need for additional research and attention to these issues.

Adults with ASD display high rates of co-morbid disorders, which further affect their daily functioning and outcome. Adults with ASD and a higher IQ, who have the greatest likelihood of achieving optimal functioning and outcomes according to the literature, also tend to experience more social isolation, withdrawal, and peer victimization (Shtayermman, 2007; Sterling, Dawson, Estes, & Greenson, 2008). Klin and Volkmar (1996) found anxiety and depression to be the most common co-occurring disorders in young adults with higher functioning ASD, or Asperger syndrome. Symptoms of depression are hypothesized to result from repeated failures in several domains throughout life (e.g., education, socialization, language development), while symptoms of anxiety are thought to be caused by challenges in trying to interact in a society that places a high value on appropriate social interactions (Klin, McPartland, & Volkmar, 2005). Depression and anxiety may also stem from high levels of learned helplessness that individuals with ASD tend to develop over the course of their upbringing.

This phenomenon, which has been shown to be present in large numbers of individuals with ASD, and the resulting anxious and depressive symptomology are believed to develop in response to consistent failures to succeed (Seligman, 1975). Targeting these specific areas that may contribute to co-morbid symptomology, such as deficits in socialization or the resulting feelings of learned helplessness, is correlated with decreases in co-morbid symptoms and even overall ASD symptomology. For example, Koegel, Ashbaugh, Koegel, Detar, and Regester (2013) demonstrated that a structured social planning intervention led to increased socialization for college students with ASD, which resulted in higher satisfaction with their peer interactions, overall college experience, and quality of life. Hillier, Fish, Siegel, and Beversdorf (2011) found that a discussion-based intervention focused on improving social and vocational skills for young adults with ASD greatly reduced symptoms of anxiety and depression.

INTERVENTIONS FOR IMPROVING SOCIALIZATION

If untreated, social challenges can persist throughout the lifespan in individuals with ASD. Compared with typically developing individuals, individuals with ASD are reported to have less access than their peers in regard to learning social and romantic skills (Stokes, Newton, & Kaur, 2007), which can lead to challenges in understanding appropriate ways in which to interact to develop friendships and romantic relationships. This unfortunate lack of access may result from many factors, including (but not limited to)

- The individual with ASD's self-isolation
- Society's lack of inclusion of individuals with ASD
- Placement in special education programs with other individuals who have communication and social delays
- The lack of social intervention programs
- Untrained school staff
- The lack of implementation of available social programs

An unwanted cycle is created in which the core deficits of ASD and exclusion from effective programs and typical peers interferes with those with ASD's abilities to engage in peer relationships (Stokes et al., 2007).

However, there is some research relating to the types of social activities in which individuals with ASD engage when they do socialize. Specifically, research suggests that about 40% of the adolescents and adults who live at home attend weekly social activities relating to a hobby, and almost all adults and adolescents with ASD engage in hobby-related activities to a lesser extent during the year (Orsmond et al., 2004). This suggests that if an individual with ASD attends social activities, these activities are likely to be based on the individual's interests.

To that end, our research suggests that it may be particularly important to consider reinforcement hierarchies when developing a social program for someone with ASD. That is, when practitioners rank potential reinforcers from most to least desirable, restricted interests are often on the top of the hierarchy. Oftentimes an individual with ASD who is participating in a restricted interest is unlikely to satiate and can find it extremely disturbing or difficult to transition away from the activity. Thus, from a theoretical point of view, if restricted interests were used as a natural reinforcer for engagement in social interaction, the individual with ASD would be highly motivated to socialize. This hypothesis has proven true in several studies.

FOUNDATIONAL STUDIES USING RESTRICTED AND PREFERRED INTERESTS TO IMPROVE SOCIALIZATION

The authors' earliest work in this area began with exploring using the restricted interests of children with ASD who ranged in age from 5 years, 4 months to 8 years, 9 months and engaged in very low levels of social interaction with their classmates during the school lunch period (Baker, Koegel, & Koegel, 1998). In this study, we found that if we identified each child's individual restricted interest (through parent and teacher interviews and observations) and incorporated those interests into a group activity, we could greatly improve peer socialization and affect. For example, a fourth grader spent all of her lunch and recess periods swinging on the kindergarten swing. In fact, she had been doing this since kindergarten, and whenever one of the other children requested that she share the swing, she began screaming, crying, and throwing tantrums. At first, it appeared that this was her only interest. However, when interviewed, her mother reported that her daughter spent all of her free time watching movies. Consequently, she had learned every current movie's title and characters and had memorized most of the movie scripts. Social activities that incorporated this child's restricted interest could potentially be more motivating to her than social activities that did not. Therefore, as a lunchtime activity we incorporated movie themes into a tag game using photographs of movie stars that were placed around the field. During the game a "caller" quoted a line from the movie, the name of a character, or a scene in the movie, at which point the children needed to run to the laminated picture corresponding to the movie described in order to be "safe." If the child was tagged before reaching the laminated picture, he or she became the "caller." As you might have guessed, because movies were one of the child's repetitive and restricted interests, she immediately hopped off the swing to engage in the tag game with her peers.

In this initial study, when the restricted interests were incorporated into the group activities, the children all greatly increased their social engagement with peers during the games, and this increased engagement generalized to other activities. That is, after intervention began, they also increased their levels of socialization during other playground activities that were not associated with their perseverative and restricted interests. What's more, all of the children with ASD, as well as their typically developing classmates, improved in their affect ratings of interest and happiness on Likert scales following the intervention. This initial research suggested that using a restricted interest as the theme of a group activity may be highly motivating to the individual with ASD and a simple way to promote prosocial behaviors. Before participating in these social activities that had been specially developed around their perseverative and restricted interests, the children with ASD had rarely interacted with peers despite being prompted to engage. In contrast, the children rapidly and enthusiastically engaged in the group activities related to their restricted interests.

DEVELOPING INTEREST-BASED SOCIAL OPPORTUNITIES FOR ADOLESCENTS AND YOUNG ADULTS

Based on these initial findings (Baker et al., 1998), we expanded the intervention to use with adolescents and young adults. For example, in another study, adolescents with ASD who attended middle school and spent their lunch periods completely alone were selected to participate. In this study, social clubs—advertised via flyers and announcements, and with light refreshments provided—were formed around each student's interest (Koegel, Fredeen, Kim, Danial, Rubinstein, & Koegel, 2012). For example, one student had a perseverative interest in movies, so we developed a movie trivia club in which an adult asked the students questions, in a format similar to a game show, and groups of two to four students were given 10 seconds to discuss the answer they would provide. The first team to get seven correct answers was given a small prize, such as a candy bar. A second student's perseverative interest involved comic books, cartooning, and card games. For him, a comic book and gaming club was created. The students were taught to draw cartoons and could create group pictures that they discussed after completion. A card game club was developed for a third student whose perseverative interest was card games. Age-appropriate card games were played at the club meeting during his lunch period. The results of this study showed that the socially isolated students increased their interactions with peers immediately after the start of the clubs and remained engaged close to 100% of the time throughout the activity (see Figure 12.1). The results also showed concomitant gains in untreated social-verbal initiations, with all of the middle school students improving in their social initiations with peers. Thus, incorporating perseverative and restricted interests into group activities greatly improved the social engagement of adolescents with ASD. However, this study did suggest that social gains might not generalize and maintain if the students moved to a new school where a club related to their restricted interest was not available. Thus, it may be important to include this support into the student's individualized education program (IEP) to assure maintenance of social improvements.

Following this study, we conducted a similar study in high schools (Koegel, Kim, Koegel, & Schwartzman, 2013). In this study, clubs were developed for seven high school students who were referred because of social isolation during lunch period. Clubs developed for the high schoolers around their restricted interests included a movie trivia club, a Frisbee club, a video game club, an intramural

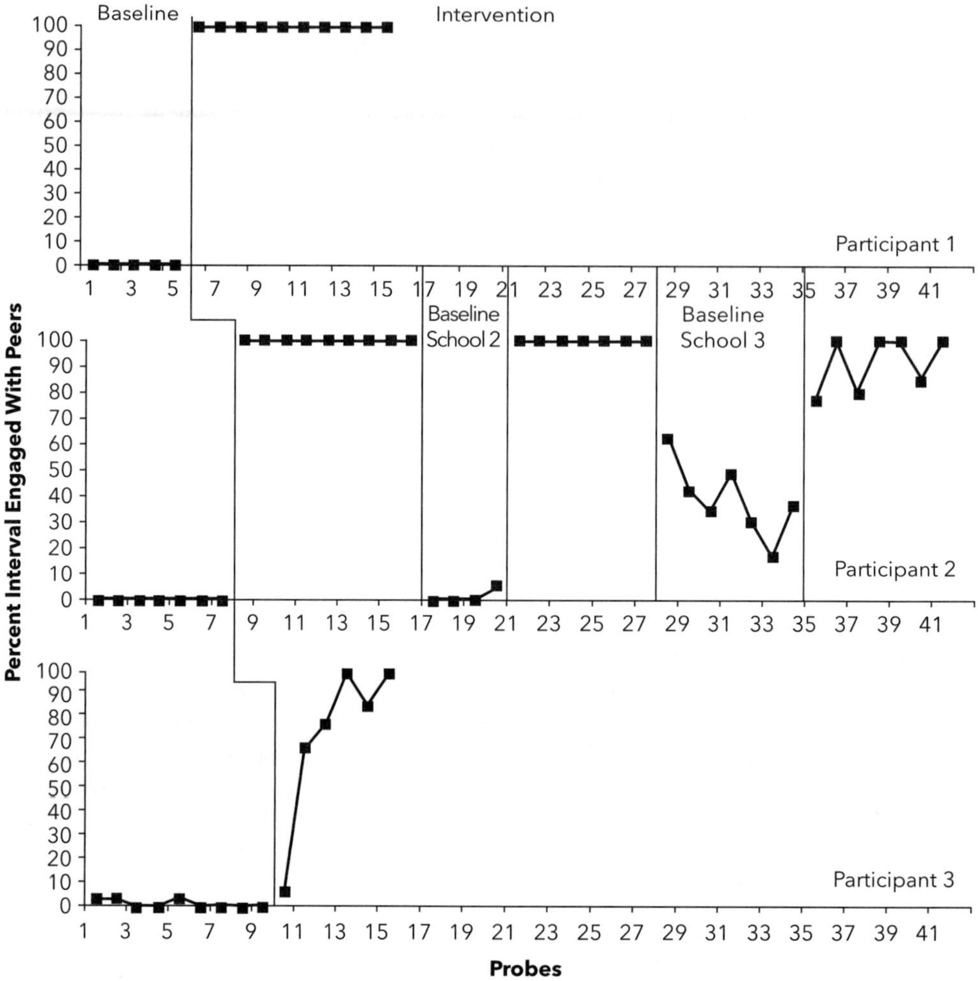

Figure 12.1. Target participants' percentage of intervals engaged with typically developing peers. (From Koegel, R. L., Fredeen, R., Kim, S., Danial, J., Rubinstein, D., & Koegel, L. [2012]. Using perseverative interests to improve interactions between adolescents with autism and their typical peers in school settings. *Journal of Positive Behavior Interventions*, *14*[3], p. 137. Reprinted by permission.)

basketball club, a computer graphics club, and a cooking club. Similar to the elementary and middle school students, the participants spent most of their time alone during baseline. In contrast, once clubs were created around their restricted interests, they demonstrated immediate improvements in socialization with their typically developing peers. In addition to engagement, all of the participants also showed large improvements in their number of social initiations toward their peers—an unexpected collateral gain of the clubs. Interestingly, on a social validation questionnaire administered just after the intervention, the students with ASD as well as their typically developing peers reported enjoying the clubs and making new friends, and they noted that the clubs made them feel "happy." Some even requested more frequent club meetings. Anecdotally, we observed that many of the students with ASD were nominated to be the club president, due to their vast accumulation of knowledge relating to the club theme. Thus, not only did the club provide an opportunity for socialization around a topic they found enjoyable and motivating, but they were also frequently considered to be the most valued member of the club due to their high level of knowledge and competence for that topic.

While the clubs were a huge success, this study also showed that if the school discontinued the club the students were likely to revert back to social isolation. However, if the club was continued or the student could join a very similarly themed club, the gains maintained after the completion of interventions.

TRAINING PARAPROFESSIONALS TO IMPLEMENT SOCIAL PROGRAMS

In these foundational studies, skilled individuals with clinical experience implemented the interventions; however, several studies suggest that paraprofessionals can easily be trained to implement social interventions. For instance, Robinson (2011) conducted a study showing that a brief video feedback training package can be an efficient and effective method of training paraprofessionals to provide improved socialization in their students with ASD. In this package, the trainer modeled the implementation of Pivotal Response Treatment (PRT) for approximately 15 minutes with each student while the paraprofessional observed. The PRT intervention strategies consisted of finding a child-chosen activity, providing clear opportunities for each child's target behavior, using shared control, and providing natural and contingent reinforcement to the student. After viewing the trainer's modeling session and hearing a brief description of PRT, the paraprofessionals implemented the PRT while being videotaped. The trainers then reviewed approximately 15 minutes of videotape (fast-forwarding if necessary) and discussed the session with the paraprofessionals, pausing for corrective feedback and praising correct implementation of the social programs. Each session concluded with praise and encouragement. Study results indicated that during baseline, the paraprofessionals rarely, if ever, prompted socialization with their students, but instead either hovered or remained uninvolved with their students. However, after two to four training sessions, the paraprofessionals achieved fidelity of implementation (FoI) on the PRT procedures and were able to implement and monitor effective interventions. As well, the paraprofessionals maintained their skills 1–2 months later. The children with ASD also demonstrated great improvements following the paraprofessional training. In addition, all of the students' affect improved after the paraprofessionals were trained to implement the PRT social interventions.

A similar study conducted a 1.5-hour PRT training, then provided paraprofessionals with in-vivo feedback relating to their implementation of the PRT social skills (Feldman & Matos, 2013). Again, paraprofessionals were measured for their use of child choice, clear and specific instructions, prompting, and the delivery of natural rewards. The results of this study suggested that following a 3-day training period, with feedback approximately every 2 minutes during a 15- to 20-minute period, all of the paraprofessionals improved in their FoI on one activity. Further, after being trained, some paraprofessionals showed generalization of skills to other activities for which they were not trained; with an additional training period, those who initially did not show generalization did reach FoI on activities for which they were not trained. As with the Robinson (2011) study, all paraprofessionals reduced their hovering and/or lack of involvement and improved in their social facilitation and monitoring following training. In addition, all indicated high satisfaction with the training, said they would recommend the training to others, and reported that they would continue using the procedures (as also indicated by their high levels of fidelity at follow-up).

Taken together, these studies suggest two important principles:

- Educators and practitioners can be optimistic about greatly improving the socialization of individuals with ASD.
- It is relatively easy to train school staff to implement social interventions with high fidelity.

STRUCTURED SOCIAL PLANNING: IMPROVING OPPORTUNITIES FOR ADULTS

The interventions described thus far assessed individuals with ASD's interests, so as to develop interest-based social activities and thereby increase their motivation to socialize with peers. A similar idea was captured in our work with adults with an intervention called *structured social planning*. Structured social planning incorporates the underlying motivational strategies of PRT to help increase social activities for adolescents and adults with ASD (Ashbaugh, Koegel, & Koegel, 2017; Koegel, Ashbaugh et al., 2013). This intervention incorporates principles of PRT and consists of the following components:

1. Identify motivational interests for social activities
2. Create a menu of social activities
3. Give training in executive functioning skills
4. Provide peer mentorship
5. Implement individualized social skills intervention

Table 12.1 briefly describes these five components and their connection to core PRT strategies. Each component is further described in Steps 1–5 below. The textboxes accompanying each step illustrate how the intervention could be put into practice with a young woman named Nina.

Table 12.1. Structured social planning and underlying PRT strategies

Structured Social Planning	Description	PRT Strategy
1. Identify motivational interests for social activities	Individual's preferred and motivational interests are identified and incorporated into social activities.	Increase motivation
2. Create a menu of social activities	Individual is given a menu of at least three possible social activities to attend that match their motivational interests, and they choose one activity from the menu.	Choice
3. Give training in executive functioning skills	Individual is trained in executive functioning skills related to the social activity.	Direct and natural reinforcement
4. Provide peer mentorship	Individual is matched with a similar-age peer mentor for support at the social activity.	Naturalistic support
5. Implement individualized social skills training	Individual is trained in social skills related to the peer social activity.	Interspersal Natural reinforcement

Step 1: Identify Motivational Interests for Social Activities

The first step to increasing social activities for adolescents and adults with ASD is to identify preferred interests, likes, and hobbies that can be incorporated into socialization with peers. Just as PRT incorporates the individual's motivational interests into treatment, structured social planning uses these preferred interests when determining which social activities may be a good match. As discussed, the literature suggests that adults with ASD are most successful with, and prefer participating in, shared-interest social activities, meaning activities that incorporate their preferred interests (Koegel, Dyer, & Bell, 1987; Muller et al., 2008; Wenzel & Rowley, 2010). To assess for preferred interests, the treatment provider discusses the individual's interests, likes, dislikes, and preferences. It is also helpful to probe for information regarding the adolescent or adult's personal hobbies, social activities of interest, previous extracurricular activities, career path, and goals for the future, as in the example in Textbox 12.1. When possible, parents can also provide helpful information regarding the individual's interests and preferred activities.

Step 2: Create a Menu of Social Activities

The next step is for the treatment provider to research social activities based on the preferred interests. Individuals with ASD generally want to interact with peers but often they have not learned the skills to find available social activities in the community (Muller et al., 2008). To help relieve this difficulty, the treatment provider creates a list of at least three possible activities. See Table 12.2 for a comprehensive menu of social activities for adults.

The individual then selects activities he or she would like to attend. Just as PRT focuses on child choice, structured social planning involves the adolescent or adult using the menu of social activities to choose an activity to attend. This is thought to increase the individual's sense of personal control and independence. Helpful places to look when researching social activities include school clubs, recreational or leisure classes, community-based classes and events, camps, meetup groups, community service groups, church programs, libraries, social media pages, volunteer opportunities (e.g., the animal shelter), or neighborhood groups.

Textbox 12.2 describes how Nina's treatment provider conducted research to create a menu of choices for her. Nina was given the list of options, and she chose to try the recreational dance class.

TEXTBOX 12.1. Structured Social Planning: Step 1 Example

Nina is an 18-year-old female who discussed wanting to make more friends and join more activities. She spent most of her time alone at home or going out in the community with her parents. The treatment provider worked with Nina to identify her interests and hobbies so that the provider could later find social activities based on these interests. After talking with Nina, the treatment provider identified that Nina loved to paint at home, watch anime shows, sew costumes, and practice meditation and that she had previously taken dance classes as a child.

Table 12.2. Examples of social activities for individuals with ASD

Academics	Arts	Culture/Language	Community
Science Club	Anime Club	Any cultural interest group	Community festivals
Debate Club	Art Club	Foreign language classes	Habitat for Humanity
Writing Club	Art classes	International club	Key Club
History Club	Ceramics		Newspaper
Honor's Society	Fashion design		Radio
Robotics Club	Graphic design		Magazine
Study Groups	Photography		
Writing Club	Sewing		
Music	**Performance Art**	**Religious**	**Roleplay/Fantasy**
Music interest clubs	Comedy shows	Church groups	Cosplay
Choir	Film clubs	Youth groups	Dungeons and Dragons
Band	Film Productivity	Bible studies	Gaming clubs
Music classes	Dance		Live-action roleplaying (LARPing)
Orchestra	Drama		
Concerts	School/Community theater		
Special Interest	**Sports/Recreation**	**Technology**	**Volunteering**
Board Game groups	Any sport team	Computer clubs	Local charities
Book Club	Any sporting event	Web Design Club	Local soup kitchen
Chess Club	Martial arts	Videogame Club	Pet shelters
Cooking groups	Recreation classes		Best Buddy International
Equestrian Club	Intramurals		Hospital volunteer
Movies	Tennis classes		American Red Cross
Political groups	Yoga		
Quilt-making	Fencing		
	Cycling		
	Bowling leagues		
	Hiking clubs		
	Walking groups		

Step 3: Give Training in Executive Functioning Skills

After the adolescent or adult with ASD chooses a social activity to attend, the next step is to provide training in related executive functioning skills. Research shows that adolescents and adults with ASD have difficulty with executive functioning

TEXTBOX 12.2. Structured Social Planning: Step 2 Example

After Nina's motivational interests were identified, the treatment provider researched social activities based on Nina's preferred interests and created a menu of three activities for her to choose from. The menu included a painting class at the community center, a local anime club, and a recreational dance class. Nina was given the list of options, and she chose to try the recreational dance class.

skills, including planning, managing time, task initiation, memory, and organization (O'Hearn, Asato, Ordaz, & Luna, 2008). These challenges with executive functioning can create another barrier to socialization. To successfully participate in social activities, an individual must be able to plan for the activity, manage their time to attend it, and organize the necessary materials and details. Many social activities require signing up for the activity or submitting an RSVP, arranging transportation, bringing materials or being prepared, planning ahead, and time management.

With structured social planning, weekly training is provided on how to register for social activities, look up directions, coordinate bus or parking information, and find out what is required for the activity. In addition, many individuals with ASD need psycho-educational training on how to use a calendar or planner and how to set an alarm or reminder to remind them of the social activity. It is helpful for the adolescent or adult to show the treatment provider how they input the activity into their calendar or planner to assess for accuracy. Providing training in executive functioning skills aligns with the underlying PRT strategy of direct and natural reinforcement, in that the individual plans for the social activity and is then reinforced by going to the social activity. Textbox 12.3 describes how Nina's treatment provider helped her use the executive functioning skills needed to participate in the dance class she had selected.

Step 4: Provide Peer Mentorship

To help individuals with ASD feel more confident and supported at the actual social activity, it is extremely helpful for the individual to be paired with a typically developing peer mentor (Chan et al., 2009; Dillon, 2007; Koegel, Ashbaugh, et. al., 2013). As a treatment provider, it is valuable to identify and select peers who are motivated and enthusiastic about helping individuals with ASD. These peers can be trained to become peer mentors—that is, they receive brief training about autism and basic support strategies to help individuals with ASD (Hart, Grigal, & Weir, 2010). Peer mentors can offer individualized support that is unique to the particular student's needs and that involves flexibility regarding the activity, time, and location, which has been shown to be beneficial for working with students

TEXTBOX 12.3. Structured Social Planning: Step 3 Example

Nina chose the recreational dance class for her social activity, but she indicated that she did not know how to attend the class. The treatment provider taught her how to sign up for the class online, helped her locate the building and room, and assisted her in reading the class description to see if she needed to bring any materials to the first class. Additionally, the treatment provider prompted her to look up the bus route she would take to the class and asked Nina to input the class time in her telephone and set an alarm reminder for an hour beforehand. Lastly, the treatment provider prompted Nina to save the phone number of the recreation center in case she got lost or had questions and needed to get in touch with a staff member.

with ASD (Adreon & Durocher, 2007; Dillon, 2007). Furthermore, the peer mentor component of structured social planning aims to provide social assistance in the natural environment in a non-stigmatizing manner. To achieve this aim, the peer mentor is instructed to engage like a typical friend of the individual with ASD during social activities (Ashbaugh et al., 2017; Koegel et al., 2013). Similar to PRT's emphasis on providing treatment in the natural environment, peer mentorship involves proving support at the actual social activity. Peer mentors can help model appropriate social behavior, discreetly prompt individuals with ASD to engage with peers, and provide feedback on the individual's social behavior following the activity (Hart et al., 2010; Koegel, Ashbaugh et al., 2013). Feedback can be given in vivo or at a later time with the treatment provider. This strategy can be very helpful for adolescents and young adults with ASD. In fact, all of the adolescents and adults with whom we work have requested to be connected with a peer mentor rather than attend the social event alone. Textbox 12.4 describes how peer mentorship was incorporated into structured social planning for Nina.

Step 5: Implement Individualized Social Skills Training

To help individuals with ASD successfully engage with others at social activities, we provide training in social skills related to their upcoming social event. Research shows that instruction and rehearsal of social skills related to participation in social activities can help improve social behavior for young adults with ASD (Gantman, Kapp, Orenski, & Laugeson, 2012). For example, instruction and priming on the following areas have been shown to benefit individuals with ASD: conversation skills (e.g., how to introduce oneself, ask questions of peers, discuss appropriate topics of conversation), electronic communication (e.g. using social media such as Facebook, e-mailing, text messaging), and appearance (e.g. hygiene, appropriate clothes)

TEXTBOX 12.4. Structured Social Planning: Step 4 Example

Nina signed up for the dance class and set a reminder to attend the class in her phone. She was nervous about attending the class and indicated that she was unsure if she still wanted to go. The treatment provider matched Nina with a peer mentor, Allison, and facilitated a meeting with Nina and Allison to help build rapport. Allison told Nina that she would call her the morning of the class, and they would plan on meeting outside of the class 15 minutes before the class began. During the dance class, Allison introduced herself and Nina to others and helped sustain conversations with group members. After the class, Allison and Nina spent 15 minutes talking about Nina's experience at the class, and Allison provided verbal praise for social behavior that Nina did well (e.g., smiling at others, saying hello, arriving on time) as well as constructive feedback (e.g., next time it would be helpful to ask questions to express interest about other members and say goodbye to others at the end of class). Nina reported that she felt much more comfortable having a peer mentor at the activity, and the treatment provider was able to work with Nina on asking more questions and saying goodbye.

TEXTBOX 12.5. Structured Social Planning: Step 5 Example

Nina was starting to attend the dance class on a weekly basis. She told her treatment provider that she enjoyed going to the class, but she requested help with social skills to increase her engagement and interactions with others at the class. Using visual frameworks, video feedback, and self-management (see Chapters 10 and 11), Nina improved her ability to appropriately greet others, ask questions to express interest in other people, end conversations, and connect with others on social media. Her peer mentor reported that after receiving social skills intervention, Nina started to have more interactions with others at the dance class and was beginning to form friendships with peers.

(Laugeson, Frankel, Gantman, Dillon, & Mogil, 2011). In addition, parents have reported that instruction in, and rehearsal of, social skills can improve young adults' overall social skills, social responsiveness, and frequency of get-togethers (Gantman et al., 2012). Social skills training should be continuously implemented for individuals with ASD as they begin to attend more social activities with peers. Coordinating with the peer mentor regarding areas of need is valuable, as illustrated in Textbox 12.5. See Chapter 11 for more information about improving communication skills.

Benefits of Structured Social Planning

Structured social planning has been shown to improve socialization for individuals with ASD (Ashbaugh et al., 2017; Koegel, Ashbaugh, et. al., 2013). The underlying motivational strategies of PRT can be incorporated into a packaged intervention to help adolescents and adults with ASD successfully engage in more social activities. Research has found that structured social planning can increase social integration for people with ASD, helping them to attend more community-based social activities, increase their involvement in extracurricular activities, and increase the number of peers they interact with during social activities. Furthermore, studies suggest that using motivational strategies of PRT to help increase socialization has collateral benefits, including improved academic performance for students, increased quality of life, and increased satisfaction and happiness of individuals with ASD (Ashbaugh et al., 2017; Koegel et al., 2013).

Key Insights ||| Targeting Socialization

To improve socialization in adolescents and adults with ASD, the following issues are important to consider:

- Although signs of ASD emerge early in life, symptoms tend to persist throughout the lifespan and greatly impact quality of life and, therefore, need to be targeted consistently and comprehensively.
- Individuals with ASD frequently endorse feelings of loneliness, but often lack the social skills necessary to initiate and maintain social interactions. Thus, this area needs to be targeted.

- In addition to social challenges, adults with ASD often display high rates of co-morbid disorders, which further affect their daily functioning.
- Research has shown that targeting deficits in socialization can lead to decreases in co-morbid symptoms and even overall ASD symptomology.
- Using restricted and highly preferred interests as natural reinforcers or as a theme of activities during engagement in social interaction helps motivate individuals with ASD.
- Structured social planning has been highly successful in motivating adults with ASD to engage in social activities. This intervention consists of the following steps: 1) identify motivational interests for social activities, 2) create a menu of social activities, 3) train the individual in needed executive functioning skills, 4) provide peer mentorship, and 5) implement individualized social skills training.
- Using these techniques to increase socialization can help individuals with ASD succeed in higher education, obtain competitive employment, live independently, and improve their overall quality of life.

SUMMARY

Socialization is a major deficit area for individuals with ASD that impacts overall functioning in multiple domains throughout the lifespan. Although adults with ASD report desiring close friendships and romantic relationships, they often experience loneliness and anxiety and depression because they have not developed the necessary social and communicative skills to initiate and sustain these types of relationships. Social challenges and resulting co-morbidities often result in difficulties succeeding in higher education, starting successful careers, and being satisfied with life overall. Clinicians working with people with ASD can target these areas and improve overall functioning by incorporating these individuals' restricted interests, which have been shown to be highly motivating and effective. Using peer mentors, executive functioning training, and menus of acceptable social activities have been shown to be successful interventions with this population. With appropriate training and intervention, adults with ASD can show improvements in socialization, leading to advancements in other domains of life and a better chance of successful daily functioning and full inclusion in society. These benefits of intervention are summarized in Figure 12.2.

STUDY QUESTIONS

1. Discuss the importance of socialization in individuals with ASD.
2. Describe co-morbidities that may develop in individuals with ASD who have difficulties with socialization.
3. Discuss the importance of the use of restricted interests in social programs for individuals with ASD.

4. Describe an intervention that uses restricted interests for improving socialization in an individual with ASD.
5. What are some collateral benefits experienced by children, adolescents, and adults who engage PRT social programs?
6. Describe methods for training paraprofessionals to implement PRT programs for socialization.
7. What is structured social planning?
8. List the steps to creating a structured social program for an adult or adolescent with ASD.
9. How is motivation incorporated into designing social programs?
10. Discuss the positive collateral gains when individuals with ASD begin socializing.

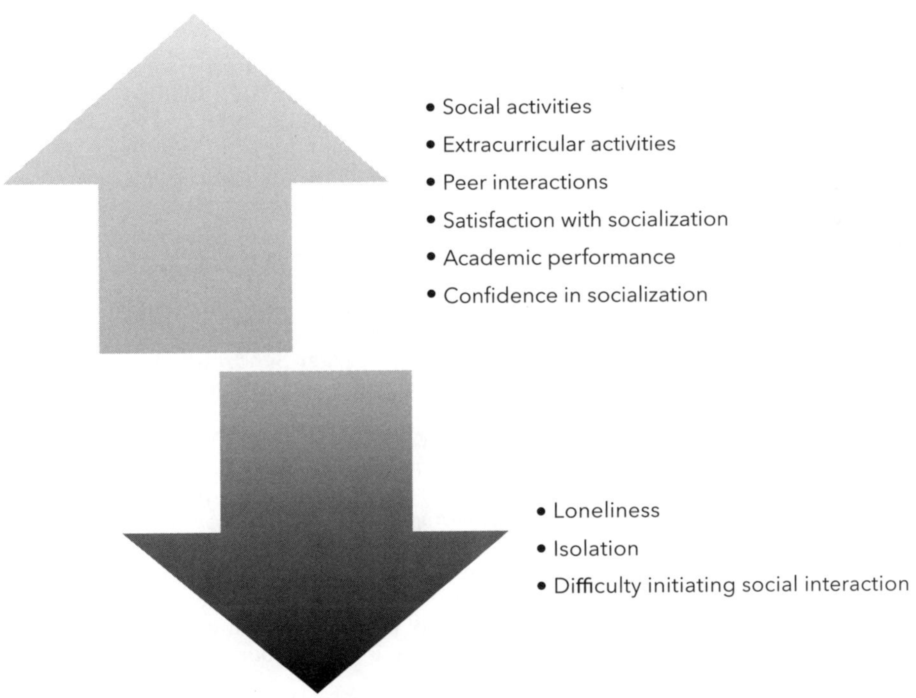

Figure 12.2. How structured social planning increases positive outcomes and decreases negative outcomes.

REFERENCES

Adreon, D., & Durocher, J. (2007). Evaluating the college transition needs of individuals with high-functioning autism spectrum disorders. *Intervention in School and Clinic, 42*(5), 271–279.

American Psychiatric Association. (2013). *Diagnostic and statistical manual of mental disorders (5th edition; DSM-5)*. Washington, DC: Author.

Ashbaugh, K., Koegel, L., & Koegel, R. (2017). Increasing social integration for college students with autism spectrum disorder. *Behavioral Development Bulletin, 22*(1), 183–196.

Baker, M. J., Koegel, R. L., & Koegel, L. K. (1998). Increasing the social behavior of young children with autism using their obsessive behaviors. *Journal of the Association for Persons with Severe Handicaps, 23*(4), 300–308.

Chan, J. M., Lang, R., Rispoli, M., O'Reilly, M., Sigafoos, J., & Cole, H. (2009). Use of peer-mediated interventions in the treatment of autism spectrum disorders: A systematic review. *Research in Autism Spectrum Disorders, 3*(4), 876–889.

Dillon, M. (2007). Creating supports for college students with Asperger syndrome through collaboration. *College Student Journal, 41*(2), 499–504.

Feldman, E. K., & Matos, R. (2013). Training paraprofessionals to facilitate social interactions between children with autism and their typically developing peers. *Journal of Positive Behavior Interventions, 15*(3), 169–179.

Gantman, A., Kapp, S. K., Orenski, K., & Laugeson, E. A. (2012). Social skills training for young adults with high-functioning autism spectrum disorders: A randomized controlled pilot study. *Journal of Autism and Developmental Disorders, 42*(6), 1094–1103.

Hart, D., Grigal, M., & Weir, C. (2010). Expanding the paradigm: Postsecondary education options for individuals with autism spectrum disorder and intellectual disabilities. *Focus on Autism and Other Developmental Disabilities, 25*(3), 134–150.

Hendricks, D. R., & Wehman, P. (2009). Transition from school to adulthood for youth with autism spectrum disorders: Review and recommendations. *Focus on Autism and Other Developmental Disabilities, 24*(2), 77–88.

Hendricks, D. (2010). Employment and adults with autism spectrum disorders: Challenges and strategies for success. *Journal of Vocational Rehabilitation, 32*(2), 125–134.

Hillier, A. J., Fish, T., Siegel, J. H., & Beversdorf, D. Q. (2011). Social and vocational skills training reduces self-reported anxiety and depression among young adults on the autism spectrum. *Journal of Developmental and Physical Disabilities, 23*(3), 267–276.

Howlin, P., Mawhood, L., & Rutter, M. (2000). Autism and developmental receptive language disorder—A follow-up comparison in early adult life. II: Social behavioural, and psychiatric outcomes. *Journal of Child Psychology and Psychiatry and Allied Disciplines*, 41, 561–578.

Klin, A., & Volkmar, F. R. (1996). *Asperger syndrome: Treatment and Intervention: Some Guidelines for Parents*. Learning Disabilities Association of America.

Klin, A., McPartland, J., & Volkmar, F. R. (2005). Asperger Syndrome. In F. R. Volkmar, R. Paul, A. Klin, & D. Cohen (Eds.), *Handbook of autism and pervasive, developmental disorders* (3rd ed., pp. 88–125). Hoboken, NJ: Wiley.

Koegel, L., Ashbaugh, K., Koegel, R., Detar, W., & Regester, A. (2013). Increasing socialization in adults with Asperger's Syndrome. *Psychology in the Schools, 50*(9).

Koegel, R. L., Dyer, K., & Bell, L. K. (1987). The influence of child-preferred activities on autistic children's social behavior. *Journal of Applied Behavior Analysis, 20*, 243–252.

Koegel, R. L., Fredeen, R., Kim, S., Danial, J., Rubinstein, D., & Koegel, L. (2012). Using perseverative interests to improve interactions between adolescents with autism and their typical peers in school settings. *Journal of Positive Behavior Interventions, 14*(3), 133–141.

Koegel, R., Kim, S., Koegel, L., & Schwartzman, B. (2013). Improving socialization for high school students with ASD by using their preferred interests. *Journal of Autism and Developmental Disorders, 43*(9), 2121–2134.

Levy, A., & Perry, A. (2011). Outcomes in adolescents and adults with autism: A review of the literature. *Research in Autism Spectrum Disorders, 5*(4), 1271–1282.

Laugeson, E. A., Frankel, F., Gantman, A., Dillon, A. R., & Mogil, C. (2012). Evidence based social skills training for adolescents with autism spectrum disorders: The UCLA PEERS program. *Journal of Autism and Developmental Disorders,42*(6), 1025–1036.

Mehzabin, P., & Stokes, M. A. (2011). Self-assessed sexuality in young adults with high-functioning autism. *Research in Autism Spectrum Disorders, 5*(1), 614–621.

Müller, E., Schuler, A., Burton, B. A., & Yates, G. B. (2003). Meeting the vocational support needs of individuals with Asperger syndrome and other autism spectrum disabilities. *Journal of Vocational Rehabilitation, 18*(3), 163–175.

Müller, E., Schuler, A., & Yates, G. (2008). Social challenges and supports from the perspective of individuals with Asperger syndrome and other autism spectrum disabilities. *Autism, 12*(2), 173–190.

O'Hearn, K., Asato, M., Ordaz, S., & Luna, B. (2008). Neurodevelopment and executive function in autism. *Development and Psychopathology, 20*(4), 1103–1132.

Orsmond, G. I., Krauss, M. W., & Seltzer, M. M. (2004). Peer relationships and social and recreational activities among adolescents and adults with autism. *Journal of Autism and Developmental Disorders, 34*(3), 245–256.

Robinson, S. E. (2011). Teaching paraprofessionals of students with autism to implement pivotal response treatment in inclusive school settings using a brief video feedback training package. *Focus on Autism and Other Developmental Disabilities, 26*(2), 105–118.

Seligman, M. E. (1975). *Helplessness: On depression, development, and death.* New York, NY: WH Freeman/Times Books/Henry Holt & Co.

Seltzer, M. M., Shattuck, P., Abbeduto, L., & Greenberg, J. S. (2004). Trajectory of development in adolescents and adults with autism. *Mental Retardation and Developmental Disabilities Research Reviews, 10*(4), 234–247.

Shtayermman, O. (2007). Peer victimization in adolescents and young adults diagnosed with Asperger's Syndrome: a link to depressive symptomatology, anxiety symptomatology and suicidal ideation. *Issues in Comprehensive Pediatric Nursing, 30*(3), 87–107.

Sterling, L., Dawson, G., Estes, A., & Greenson, J. (2008). Characteristics associated with presence of depressive symptoms in adults with autism spectrum disorder. *Journal of Autism and Developmental Disorders, 38*(6), 1011–1018.

Stokes, M., Newton, N., & Kaur, A. (2007). Stalking, and social and romantic functioning among adolescents and adults with autism spectrum disorder. *Journal of Autism and Developmental Disorders, 37*(10), 1969–1986.

VanBergeijk, E., Klin, A., & Volkmar, F. (2008). Supporting more able students on the autism spectrum: College and beyond. *Journal of Autism and Developmental Disorders, 38*(7), 1359–1370.

Wenzel, C. & Rowley, L. (2010). Teaching social skills and academic strategies to college students with Asperger's syndrome. *TEACHING Exceptional Children, 42*(5), 44–50.

V

Adulthood

Higher Education and Employment

13

Improving Outcomes in Higher Education for Adults With ASD

Kristen Ashbaugh, Erin Engstrom, Lynn Kern Koegel, and Katarina Ford

CHAPTER GOALS

Goal 1. The reader will describe common challenges that adults with autism spectrum disorders (ASD) face in higher education settings.

Goal 2. The reader will discuss factors to consider when choosing a college for a student with ASD.

Goal 3. The reader will describe strategies to promote success in academics, social integration, executive functioning, and daily living skills for students with ASD in higher education settings.

Goal 4. The reader will discuss campus and community resources that may be helpful for college students with disabilities.

Goal 5. The reader will describe ways in which the strengths of individuals with ASD can be used to improve outcomes in higher education.

ASD is one of the fastest growing disability categories (Cimera & Cowan, 2009). It is estimated that rates of autism increased 373% between 1980 and 1994 (Dales, Hammer, & Smith, 2001), leading to skyrocketing incidence rates of individuals with ASD now entering adulthood. The challenges of integrating this population into community settings are becoming evident, as is the importance of addressing the specific needs of adults with ASD. This chapter describes some of the unique strengths and challenges that adults with ASD face as they enter higher education settings and provides information regarding specific interventions and supports that will help reduce the gap in positive outcomes between these adults and their peers who do not have ASD.

SUPPORTING INDIVIDUALS WITH ASD IN HIGHER EDUCATION

Research and the literature indicate that individuals benefit from a college education and the college experience (Dowrick, Anderson, Heyer, & Acosta, 2005; Grigal, Neubart, & Moon, 2001; Hart, Grigal, & Weir, 2010; Zafft, Hart, & Zimbrich, 2004). College is an environment designed to promote academic and personal skill building, future employment, increased self-confidence, and integration into a community (Webb, Patterson, Syverud, & Seabrooks-Blackmore, 2008; Zafft et al., 2004). For students with disabilities, college should be a natural and inclusive environment in which they can integrate with students without disabilities and build self-confidence as they navigate the campus environment and acquire independent living skills (Hart et al., 2010). Figure 13.1 summarizes the ways higher education can benefit these students.

Postsecondary education is also a predictor of successful employment outcomes (Dowrick et al., 2005; Zafft et al., 2004). Data show that students with disabilities who participate in postsecondary education have higher rates of competitive employment, utilize fewer work-related supports (e.g. job coaches), and earn higher wages when compared with individuals with disabilities who did not participate in postsecondary education (Zafft et al., 2004). Despite these benefits, many individuals with ASD do not enter or complete college due to a variety of difficulties in areas such as social integration, organization and time management, and daily living skills that are not addressed in most intervention programs (Van Bergeijk, Klin, & Volkmar, 2008). This makes clear the importance of identifying the challenges that students with ASD face in higher education settings and developing intervention strategies to support students with ASD to succeed in postsecondary education.

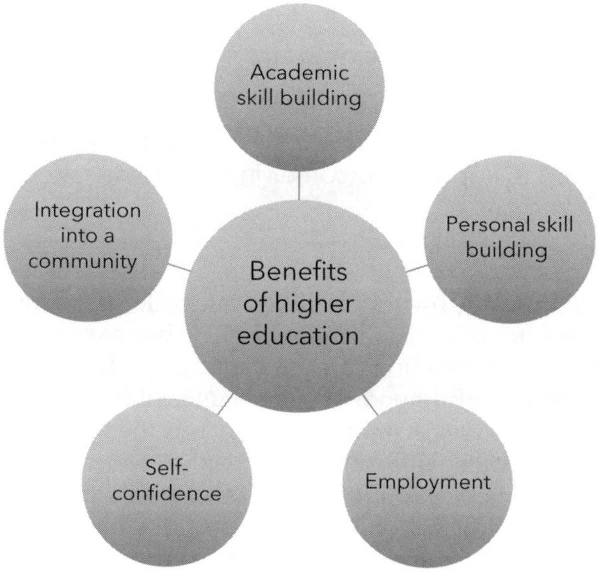

Figure 13.1. Benefits of higher education.

COMMON CHALLENGES

Students with ASD who pursue higher education may encounter a number of different challenges, including fewer individualized supports than they had available in high school, difficulty with social integration into campus life, and struggles with the executive functioning and daily living skills needed for independence and academic success.

Decrease in Individualized Supports

When students with ASD graduate from high school, they are no longer protected under IDEA (Individuals with Disabilities Education Improvement Act, 2004), a piece of legislation designed to provide students with individualized intervention programs, accommodations, and modifications (Adreon & Durocher, 2007). Although IDEA requires that a student's individualized education program (IEP) include transition planning based on the student's preferences, strengths and interests, higher education settings do not always provide individualized services, such as an IEP did in elementary, middle, and high school (Van Bergeijk et al., 2008). At the postsecondary level, the Americans with Disabilities Act (ADA) and the Rehabilitation Act are mandates for provision of services (Americans with Disabilities Act, 1990; Graetz & Spampinato, 2008). The ADA prohibits any public institution from discriminating against individuals with a disability (ADA, 1990). Under this mandate, universities typically offer a general menu of accommodations, but support services are not necessarily individually tailored to the needs of a specific student (Graetz & Spampinato, 2008). Historically, most universities have offered "one-size-fits-all" services for all students with a range of disabilities that focus on academic performance, such as extended time on exams and notetakers. However, these services often do not address the unique areas of need for the student with ASD, particularly in the areas of communication and socialization (Graetz & Spampinato, 2008). There is often a lack of funding and training to provide the level of services that adults with ASD may need to succeed in the higher education setting (Graetz & Spampinato, 2008), although more postsecondary education options and programs for students with ASD (e.g., summer transition programs) have begun to emerge (Barnhill, 2014; Hart et al., 2010).

In addition to services at the college level typically being more limited and general, students with ASD generally must self-advocate to receive assistance (Adreon & Durocher, 2007; Stodden & Mruzek, 2010). In contrast to the years spanning from preschool through high school, during which teachers and staff are legally required to provide services to address targeted goals, students in higher education must take the initiative themselves to disclose their disability and self-advocate for accommodations (Dowrick et al., 2005). ADA shifts the responsibility for making decisions about services from parents and school personnel to the student with ASD (Stodden & Mruzek, 2010). Unfortunately, it is common for students with ASD to have difficulty knowing which services they need to succeed at the college level and how to access the appropriate resources (Adreon & Durocher, 2007). Thus, special arrangements need to be made during the college years. The literature clearly indicates the need for self-advocacy skill training for college students with disabilities (Webb et al., 2008). For example, individuals must know how to initiate contact with the school's disability office, approach professors to communicate the accommodations that they need to be successful, and follow through on utilizing the resources, as well as navigate their new and complex social surroundings. Students with disabilities at postsecondary education settings have reported that they are not always aware of what services they need, which accommodations are available to them, and how to access services (Dowrick et al., 2005).

Difficulty With Social Integration

Current services offered by colleges and universities do not always include supports in social areas. However, socialization is one of the most important areas to address for students with ASD and often creates a substantial barrier to success at the college level (Nevill & White, 2011). Adjusting to the social pressures of postsecondary education and independent living is extremely challenging for college students with disabilities. The literature suggests that success at the undergraduate and graduate levels requires an individual to demonstrate advanced social skills (Nevill & White, 2011; Webb et al., 2008). Students with ASD typically struggle with the transition to college, not because they lack the cognitive abilities to complete the work but because they experience challenges with new social interactions in an unfamiliar place (Wenzel & Rowley, 2010).

Research shows that many higher education students with ASD report feeling isolated, resign themselves to their lack of relationships, and do not attempt to improve their feelings of loneliness (Muller, Schuler, & Yates, 2008). For students with ASD, leisure time can frequently involve solitary activities, such as playing video games, using the Internet, or watching television (Hendricks & Wehman, 2009). Despite difficulties with initiating social interactions, most adults with ASD have a desire to contribute to their community and integrate into it (Adreon & Durocher; 2007; Muller et al., 2008). The discrepancy between experiencing social challenges and longing for integration indicates that effective social interventions for college students with ASD are needed.

Social challenges may be one of the primary reasons that as many as half of individuals with ASD, whose symptoms continue into adulthood, develop comorbid disorders such as depression and anxiety (Kring, Greenberg, & Seltzer, 2008). Data indicate that compared with a typical community sample, individuals with ASD have a higher rate of depression (Hendricks & Wheman, 2009; Stewart, Barnard, Pearson, Hasan, & O'Brien, 2006). Research shows that students with ASD have difficulty engaging in positive social relationships with peers, which can result in rejection, isolation, and academic failure (Webb et al., 2008). College students with ASD often report having few friends and feeling lonely, which can interfere with their intellectual skills to excel in academics (Dillon, 2007). Individuals with ASD too often receive poor grades or fail out of college due to feeling isolated and depressed because they are not able to establish and maintain relationships (Dillon, 2007).

In short, socialization—a key area for success in postsecondary education—is one of the most difficult areas for college students with ASD (Ashbaugh,

Koegel, & Koegel, 2017). Thus, it is critical to consider social integration with peers and the campus community when designing support strategies for students with ASD.

Executive Functioning and Daily Living Skills

Many individuals with ASD have challenges in their daily living skills relative to their cognitive functioning (Bal, Kim, Cheong, & Lord, 2015). This includes skills such as personal hygiene, meal preparation, health and medication management, budgeting, and managing transportation within the community. The gap between cognitive and adaptive functioning skills appears to continue into adulthood and increase with age (Matthews et al., 2015). Challenges with adaptive functioning skills can create a barrier to success in higher education given the increased demands for independent functioning in these areas. Postsecondary students with ASD often move away from home and are independently managing their activities of daily living for the first time. These skills are important areas to target when providing supports for higher education students with ASD.

Executive functioning skills can also be challenging for students with ASD, creating difficulties in the higher education setting. Postsecondary school requires a copious degree of time management, advance planning, problem-solving, effective study habits, and scheduling; and many college students with ASD need explicit training in these areas to increase their likelihood of success (Adreon & Durocher, 2007).

The remainder of this chapter discusses ways in which some of the challenges for students with ASD, represented in Figure 13.2, can be addressed. Different strategies, resources, and behavioral supports can be helpful for increasing the likelihood of success in higher education.

METHODS FOR ADDRESSING CHALLENGES

Although the challenges facing college students with ASD may sound daunting, they are manageable. Professionals working with students with ASD can provide assistance to help these young adults make the transition to higher education and get the most out of the experience. Specific areas of assistance—choosing a college, implementing academic support strategies at college, and implementing supports to increase social integration—are discussed in the following sections.

Barriers to success in higher education

- Decrease in individualized supports
- Difficulty with social integration
- Challenges with executive functioning and daily living skills

Figure 13.2. Barriers to success in higher education.

Choosing a College

When working with students with ASD, it is important to spend time choosing a college that will be a good fit. Several factors should be considered (Adreon & Durocher, 2007; Graetz & Spampinato, 2008; Van Bergeik et al., 2008). Key factors are the size of the college, options for living arrangements, majors offered, academic accommodations provided, and available social support resources (Adreon & Durocher, 2007). Other important factors are the school's location, its proximity to the student's home, and the availability of community resources (e.g. Department of Rehabilitation, state and regional centers). Throughout the process of choosing a college, consider the unique individual and his or her particular strengths and weaknesses. It is common for students with ASD to initially enroll in a local community college to transition into the demands and structure of higher education, and then determine if their career goals can be met with a certificate or an associate's degree, or if they would like to transfer to a 4-year university. Starting at a community college often gives students an opportunity to receive more individualized attention, and it can be an easier setting to navigate (Adreon & Durocher, 2007; Graetz & Spampinato, 2008). Many students have found that they can earn a technical certificate or associate's degree and then obtain employment in their area of interest, while others choose to go on and pursue a bachelor's degree after gaining some experience at a community college.

Size of School For students with ASD, large and small colleges each have pros and cons (Adreon & Durocher, 2007; Van Bergeik et al., 2008). Large colleges can offer a more diverse student population, which may make it easier to find other students with similar interests (Adreon & Durocher, 2007). Larger campuses also typically offer a broader curriculum, so students with ASD may have a greater opportunity to excel in a specific academic area or strength (Van Bergeik et al., 2008); a larger choice of faculty; and access to more courses in their area of interest. However, smaller campuses may be easier to navigate and less overwhelming (Adreon & Durocher, 2007). Students with ASD may want to consider smaller campuses if they prefer smaller class sizes or get easily overstimulated by large groups of people (Van Bergeik et al., 2008). Consider the benefits and challenges of both small and large schools when determining the best fit for each individual student with ASD.

Living Arrangements In addition to the university's size, students should consider the types of living arrangements available, paying attention to options for living with or without roommates, having a meal plan, using transportation, living on or off campus, the style of off-campus apartments, and so forth (Adreon & Durocher, 2007). It may be helpful to contact the school's housing office to inquire about the options for food, lodging, and transportation. In addition, identifying a student's particular strengths and weaknesses related to living environments is helpful. For example, if a student finds it difficult to study in a noisy environment, a dorm or living situation designated for quieter, more studious students may be desirable. It is possible to place undergraduate students in apartments that primarily house graduate students, thus providing a quieter environment with generally more mature students. Similarly, some students prefer a private room in an apartment with a few other students so that they can mingle when they desire, but they also have a place to retreat when overstimulated. Most colleges provide early selection of living accommodations for students with disabilities, which can be very helpful for finding a good fit. It is worth contacting a school's office of residential life to inquire about early enrollment for housing and discuss the different options.

Majors Offered It is important to support students in choosing a major that matches well with their interests, abilities, and long-term goals. Many students may need extra support from career services, professors, parents, or counselors to choose realistic majors that fit their strengths. (The authors' professional experience includes students who chose to major in one of the most challenging subjects without understanding the rigor or requirements, who then had to change majors after failing several courses.) Requirements for each major may also depend on the size or nature of the college. Pre-requisite courses for a competitive major at a large university (e.g., business, biology) will likely be graded on a curve in which a student's grade is determined exclusively through two or three multiple-choice exams. A major with smaller class sizes (e.g., classics, Spanish) may be more likely to offer courses in which instructors determine a student's grade through a combination of homework assignments, research papers, class participation, and/or exams with written responses. Understanding the major's curriculum and course requirements in advance is helpful. In addition, many students have specific interests, such as video game design or exercise science, which are only available at certain schools. If a student knows that he or she may want to pursue a certain major, check with potential schools to make sure they offer that area of study.

Academic Supports Available academic supports and accommodations offered are important factors when selecting a college (Van Bergeik et al., 2008). Students should inquire about the academic modifications provided through the university's office of student disabilities (Graetz & Spampinato, 2008). Individuals should consider the level of accommodations that they can expect, such as whether the school offers early registration; encourages students to meet individually with professors, allows using laptop computers on exams, taking exams in separate rooms, extra time on tests and assignments, having a note-taker, using audio or electronic textbooks, or using assistive technology (Van Bergeik et al., 2008). Most professors are flexible once they understand a student with ASD's challenges. For example, we worked with one student who found it difficult to use the i-Clicker during class quizzes, so the professor assessed his knowledge using an alternative method. Another student had difficulty engaging in a group project, so the professor modified the assignment and allowed him to complete it individually. A different student had difficulty giving a presentation to the class, so the professor allowed her to present to him separately. Individuals can contact the school's support services for students with disabilities (e.g., Disabled Students program or DSP; Accessibility and Disability Services) to learn more about available services and to inquire about advocates for students with ASD. As previously mentioned, many college students find it difficult to advocate for themselves or describe their disability and how it may affect their schoolwork; therefore, having an advocate to help them access resources can be extremely helpful. If such individualized attention for students with ASD is not available, the student and his/her family may want to consider another college.

Social Support Resources Social support resources should also be a significant factor in assessing a college campus's "fit" for a student with ASD. Individuals should take note of the counseling services, campus clubs and organizations, and level of social support offered by staff when deciding which college to attend. Although colleges may not offer specific social supports unique to individuals with ASD, it is beneficial for potential students to have information about the general level of social support provided (Van Bergeik et al., 2008). It may be helpful to contact the offices of student life, counseling and psychological services, student health, and specific departments that interest the student with ASD to learn more about the resources for social support. If social support is not available, some parents choose to hire a fellow student, similar to a peer mentor, to attend social events with their child, study with him or her, and oversee other areas that the student with ASD may find challenging. In addition, most colleges have some type of access to community programs such as Independent Living Services (ILS) or Department of Rehabilitation (DOR) services that may be able to provide specialized social support if it is unavailable on the campus. It would be worthwhile to research community services and resources, and the university's relationship with those services, in addition to the supports provided on campus.

CASE HISTORY
Jack's Transition to College

Jack earned a high grade-point average in high school and wanted to pursue higher education in computer programming. In high school, he had an IEP, and his school counselors, teachers, and parents were all very involved in helping Jack with his assignments, reminding him to turn in his work, prompting him to complete his daily living activities, and assisting him to get ready for school and participate in activities. Jack and his family recognized that transitioning to a college environment was going to be overwhelming, and they began to consider different options to determine which setting would be a good match for Jack's unique challenges and strengths. Jack's goal was to obtain a bachelor's degree, but he decided to first enroll in a 2-year community college so that he could learn more about the requirements of different majors, have smaller classes, get used to living independently, and adjust to the workload and structure of college. He chose to attend a local community college close to home but opted to live in on-campus housing to integrate more in the campus community. He contacted the office of residential life and self-advocated to receive priority enrollment due to his disability. Jack was able to live in a single dorm room on a floor with other students who also were interested in computers and engineering. Although Jack did not have an IEP at the community college, he met with a counselor at the DSP before the year began to learn more about the academic accommodations he could receive. He received priority registration and was able to sign up for his first choice in classes. His counselor at DSP informed him that he was also eligible to receive a note taker for his classes, extra time on exams, and a laptop computer to take his exams. Jack was thankful he had these accommodations, but he had no experience signing up to receive help or initiate getting supports. The DSP counselor had to explicitly teach him how to navigate the web sites, communicate with professors, and access his notes and laptops. Jack also contacted his resident adviser in the dorm and disclosed that he had a disability and would benefit from some social support. Jack described that he had some challenges communicating with others and it was difficult for him to make friends; and the resident adviser agreed to go with Jack to dorm events and introduce him to other students on the floor. Jack visited the campus several times before school started to find his classes, locate different offices and buildings, and buy his textbooks.

Jack also contacted the DOR to gather information about available adult supports for him as a college student with autism. Jack's DOR counselor created an individualized plan for employment that included authorization for him to receive Personal, Vocational, and Social Adjustment (PVSA) services through the authors' autism center. Participating in higher education is a stepping stone toward obtaining employment, and DOR is often a very valuable resource for college students with ASD. Jack met with a clinician at the autism center on a weekly basis, and he received an individualized treatment program to help improve his social, academic, and behavioral skills. His clinician (an advanced graduate student in clinical psychology) provided intervention to help him appropriately groom, self-advocate, interact with peers and professors, regulate his emotions, engage in appropriate behavior on campus, and develop organization and planning skills. Jack's clinician also frequently attended meetings with the Disabled Students Program, Office of Residential Life, Academic Advising, and other campus departments to support Jack and help others understand his unique needs and learning style. Several times staff and professors were uncertain how to manage Jack and even considered disciplinary action for some of his behaviors (e.g., yelling out in the dining hall, looking at notes during an exam). However, Jack's clinician and faculty in the program were able to educate them about Jack's disability and work with staff to develop appropriate behavioral plans that would help Jack learn appropriate behaviors, rather than simply implementing consequences that may have been unhelpful in his goal to graduate. Although Jack was in a new environment and experienced the typical stress associated with transitioning to college, he had a strong support team to help him adjust and learn the skills necessary to succeed in higher education. He graduated with a bachelor of arts degree and is now employed.

Once an individual with ASD has been accepted to a higher education setting that is a good fit with his or her unique needs, certain supports can help the student to graduate successfully with a degree (Van Bergeik et al., 2008; White, Ollendick, & Bray, 2011; Zager & Alpern, 2010). The following are strategies that can help students to increase their academic success, social integration, executive functioning and daily living skills, and ability to navigate a college campus. Chapter 14 on employment also provides some suggestions related to these areas.

Strategies to Increase Academic Success

Several techniques can increase academic success for postsecondary students with ASD, including priming, attending faculty office hours, using study buddies, and utilizing accommodations offered by university programs for students with disabilities.

Priming Adjusting to the class structure and academic demands in a higher education setting can be challenging for any student. Becoming accustomed to spending fewer hours in the classroom and many hours of self-initiated studying outside of class can be an adjustment from high school, where the bulk of the day is spent in the classroom. Research shows that priming during periods outside of class times is an effective strategy to help improve students' academic success (Koegel, Koegel, Frea, & Green-Hopkins, 2003). Specifically, priming is a PRT strategy that involves previewing activities prior to instruction in a relaxed atmosphere and reinforces individuals for attempting the activity. Familiarizing students with the materials and activities in advance allows them to approach these in a low-demand context and prepares them to be "ahead of the game" and motivated when they enter the classroom or engage in the academic activity in real time.

To prime for the overall college experience, it may be helpful for students to visit campus several times before school starts and become familiar with the buildings and offices; meet faculty, support staff, and their advisers; and browse the book store for coursework. Many schools also offer a freshman summer start program or the opportunity to take one or two classes during the summer prior to beginning as a full-time student. Summer start and summer school, in which there are typically fewer students and sometimes fewer demands, are often helpful for students to get acquainted with the university, learn how to navigate campus, and gain experience in a college classroom before beginning the academic year. In addition, students may want to talk with the staff from the college or university's program for students with disabilities to explore supports and discuss the possibility of taking a reduced class load during their first few terms while they are adjusting to their new environment. Again, all of these strategies are designed with the goal of maximizing success and reinforcement, decreasing demands, and improving motivation.

Priming can also be used to help students prepare for academic courses, maximizing the probability of reinforcement both before and after the actual classes begin. Before the term begins, students can ask professors for a copy of the syllabus to preview the required assignments and the class format. Students may then realize that they wish to drop the class because it does not appeal to them or seems too challenging. If the class looks interesting, getting the textbooks ahead of time to become familiar with general course material is helpful. Students can look at section headings, highlight unfamiliar words, get a basic outline of the course, and perhaps even read some chapters. Also, many professors will provide lecture notes (e.g., slides) before the class so that students can become familiar with the content. Other examples of priming include practicing multiple-choice tests (e.g., filling out electronic forms), walking to each classroom before the first day of class, and practicing test-taking etiquette (e.g., take off hat, put all notes away, turn off phone).

Utilizing Office Hours and Study Buddies Students with ASD come from a more protective environment in high school in which they see the same teachers and peers daily and receive regular support from parents, school counselors, and others to help manage their workload. In higher education settings, it is often very valuable for students to participate in smaller study groups through campus tutoring services. These groups can help students receive additional support in a more relaxed and personal environment, which can help increase their understanding of the material and assignments. In addition, students with ASD seem to benefit from regularly attending office hours with professors and teaching assistants. If a professor can put a face to the name, the professor is often more accommodating. However, the student has to initiate accessing these services. Although students can visit the school's program for students with disabilities for information on available supports, many students we have worked with do not actively participate in these programs. Having someone available – a peer, clinician, or friend – to accompany the individual is often helpful. In addition, students may need explicit teaching on how to sign up for tutoring groups or attend office hours. For example, students with ASD may need assistance to look up when and where a professor's office hours are located, and an adult may need to prompt the student to put a specific office hour in his/her schedule. Some students with ASD also need assistance planning for what to ask during office hours or tutoring, and it can be helpful for a clinician to develop a list of questions or areas that the student would like to discuss. Another helpful strategy is to secure a "study buddy" in each academic course who can meet with the student to review and study after each class. This can be arranged by a clinician or staff member at the university, the professor if requested by the parent/clinician or staff member, or by the student. The study buddy can also serve as a point-person if a student has to miss class, is confused about the content, and/or needs to catch up on notes or assignments. All of these strategies maximize the probability that the educational experience will be both academically and socially rewarding.

Without such support, we have seen some college students with ASD quickly end up on academic probation, after earning a very high grade-point average in high school. Students with ASD often have difficulty managing a consistent study schedule, keeping up with reading, organizing major assignments, and preparing for mid-term and final exams. These issues parallel the issues related to full inclusion in elementary school, and similarly, it is not advisable to just place a student with ASD in college and hope for the best. It is important to plan ahead systematically. Study buddies can be helpful to plan out a study schedule, teach good study techniques (e.g., making outlines or flashcards), alert students to available review sessions or quiet places to study on campus, inform them of additional campus resources (e.g., writing centers, open lab hours), and help review lecture notes.

In our own work arranging a study buddy for college students with ASD, we first ask if the professor is willing to help coordinate this by asking if anyone is willing to tutor a student right after class or by sending out an email to students. If confidentiality is not a problem, the professor may even mention that the student has ASD. However, the professor will never share the name or other personal information that would identify the student. Alternatively, a teaching assistant can approach students in the class to request a study buddy. Sometimes study buddies are given academic units or course credits for their assistance, and some families have opted to pay the study buddy by the hour or provide a stipend at the end of the quarter or semester. Study buddies can be taught to arrange the study session, or they can email a teaching assistant for assistance in forming a study group. These regular study sessions provide an opportunity for students with ASD to review the reading materials and class lectures and also create an occasion for peer socialization. We have found that many students are willing and excited to help a peer with ASD, often reporting that being a study buddy also improved their own academic performance.

Accommodations Through Programs for Students With Disabilities
When a college or university offers programs or services for students with disabilities, the majority of students with ASD benefit from enrolling in these programs prior to arriving on their college campus. This can be accomplished in person during orientation, during a special visit, or online. Familiarizing the student with the location of services, specifics on how to access services, and locations where tutoring and test sessions are held is also helpful. Without support, some students are reluctant to seek out these services, thinking that they will not need accommodations. Others may worry about whether their participation in the program will affect their relationships with professors, teaching associates, and other students. In our experience, however, the most common effects are positive. Both students and faculty have been overwhelmingly positive when they see that there is a systematic program aimed at helping a student in their class. Objections are very rare, especially when the program has been explained properly.

Relatedly, it is important to remember that beginning college is a new experience. Students may not seek out needed supports right away. By the time help arrives, some students have not achieved passing grades due to preventable issues such as misunderstandings, poor time management, incomplete assignments, or insufficient time on exams. We have found that once a professor understands a student's disability, he or she will work with the student to help the student succeed in the course. Furthermore, when students are enrolled in programs for students with disabilities by the start of the quarter or semester, then they can request supports and accommodations *before* any issues arise. We highly recommend arranging accommodations prior to the student's first day of courses. Helpful accommodations may include any of the following:

- *Note taking:* Students can be provided a copy of notes taken by another classmate during each lecture, allowing them to focus on what the professor is saying with fewer distractions. Some electronic devices allow the student to listen to the notes if an auditory modality is more helpful.
- *Adaptive technology resources:* Students can receive e-textbooks that allow them to read or listen to scanned text. In addition, some software programs can record lectures or dictate writing for papers and assignments.
- *Test-taking accommodations*: Students can request extended time for exams, including mid-terms and finals. They can also request alternative testing conditions such as a quiet/private room, oral exam administration, or a laptop to type (rather than hand-write) answers.
- *Priority registration:* In addition to receiving priority for living accommodations, students with disabilities can enroll in classes before the usual registration date. This is particularly helpful for students with ASD who are taking fewer units per quarter/semester and may therefore end up with a late registration date (registration date is often determined by the number of units the student has accumulated). Early enrollment ensures that students with disabilities will be able to enroll in any classes they desire or need to complete.

Strategies to Increase Social Integration

Support for social integration is critical for increasing students' abilities to successfully participate in higher education and graduate (Adreon & Durocher, 2007, Jobe & White, 2007; Van Bergeik et al., 2008). Research shows that individuals with ASD do not prefer to be alone, but they experience increased isolation in college due to a lack of social skills and understanding (Jobe & White, 2007; Koegel & LaZebnik, 2009).

Peer mentors are a very effective support strategy to help students with ASD socially integrate into the campus community (Ashbaugh et al., 2017). Empirical studies show that if students with ASD are paired with peer mentors to attend social events, they engage in more campus/community events, increase their peer interactions, and report improved satisfaction with their overall college experience (Ashbaugh et al., 2017). Peer mentors can serve as social coaches that help the student with ASD identify potential activities of interest; learn the necessary details to attend the activity (e.g., how to enroll, where it is held); and accompany the student to the social activity where they can provide support, model appropriate interactions, and, afterward, provide feedback to the student on their social skills at the event. Students with ASD report that peer mentors are great resources for questions about appropriate social behavior and provide helpful information about activities offered on campus. When students with ASD are asked about what they feel were the most valuable aspects of their support plan, the peer mentors are always prominently listed.

When selecting social activities to attend, it is important for the student with ASD to find activities with groups of peers who share common interests. It is challenging for all students to find a niche and social group when they begin college, but it is especially difficult for students with ASD to join activities and form friendships. They often need extra support to identify activities that relate to their interests. A myriad of opportunities exists on college campuses, and students can explore clubs, dorm activities, recreational activities, department groups, internships, and other organizations that involve their motivational interests. For example, if a student has interests in art and dance, the student can explore art clubs, dance classes, or other groups in which they could meet peers who share a similar interest. Getting students involved in social activities around their personal interests is a key factor in increasing their social integration in higher education. Occasionally in our work with young adults, a parent will ask why we place so much value on social aspects of college when academics should be the primary objective. When students are happy with their campus social life, they tend to perform better academically; when they are unsuccessful in their social relations, they tend to experience symptoms of depression, which negatively affects their studies. Thus, when social interactions are handled appropriately and systematically, they enhance the academic experience in many important ways. As well, college students with ASD who have supported social activities to attend around their interests demonstrate improvements in their grade point averages (Koegel, Ashbaugh, Koegel, Detar, & Regester, 2013).

It is also important that students with ASD receive individualized support to improve their social communication skills with other students, roommates, staff, and professors. They may need help learning how to interact with others in new contexts, such as living with roommates, being in a lecture hall or dining hall, and simply meeting new people. Properly trained university personnel can help target individual social communication areas by explicitly teaching students appropriate social etiquette, modelling social skills, using role-play to practice social situations, and having peer mentors assist with socialization in the natural environment (Van Bergeik et al., 2008). Adam's story illustrates how targeted interventions can help students with ASD navigate the challenges of college social life. See Chapter 12 for more details on social interventions that can be used with young adults with ASD.

CASE HISTORY
Adam's Social Life at College

Adam entered a 4-year university and moved into the dormitory with one roommate. After a few weeks of fairly smooth sailing, his roommate brought a beer into the dorm room. Alcohol was prohibited in the dorms, and Adam was well aware of this. Upon seeing the beer, Adam screamed at his roommate, slammed the door, and ran to the residential assistant (RA). While confiding to his RA was probably the right thing to do, a number of the other students heard him and began referring to him as a "tattle tale." Adam's roommate refused to talk with Adam, as did the other students in the dorm.

In our practice, we were able to work with Adam and provide social skills training about steps to handle a conflict with a roommate or other peer. For example, the first step is to politely discuss the problem. For that age group, the conversation might start with the student saying, "I'm uncomfortable with you having alcohol in our room. Would you mind drinking in another room?" After explicit teaching, Adam understood, but he had now become "persona non grata" around the dorm, even among former companions. Therefore, we arranged for him to have a peer mentor so that he had support in meeting peers and forming positive relationships with other students. We offered this peer academic units for accompanying Adam to social events and clubs. Adam had an interest in dance and chose to attend the ballroom dancing club. His peer mentor also ate lunch with him several times a week at the dining hall, and together they would work on identifying peers who looked approachable and practice initiating greetings.

During our weekly supervision meeting with the peer mentor, she mentioned that Adam was often very negative in his communication with others. For example, when someone said, "Hi Adam, how are you?" he would begin a lengthy diatribe about everything that was not going well in his life and catastrophize things that most college students stress about, such as tests, papers, an early morning course, and so on. Therefore, during our one-to-one sessions with Adam, we taught him how to self-manage his responses and reframe his social conversation to be positive. For example, instead of saying, "I had the worst weekend ever. My computer crashed, and I could not use it all day Saturday," he could say "Luckily I was able to get my computer repaired at the bookstore on the weekend after it crashed so I could use it on Sunday."

With the peer mentor support and the weekly one-to-one meetings, Adam succeeded in graduating, forming positive relationships with roommates and peers, and securing a full-time job after graduation. He also met a girl he started dating during his junior year. Adam reported that the social skills training and peer mentor were extremely valuable in teaching him how to appropriately interact with others and providing him with the comfort level he needed to participate in social activities. Without support, it is likely he would have struggled socially and constantly come across as "Mr. Negative," which interfered with his ability to make friends and likely would have interfered with obtaining and maintaining employment. ▮▮▮

Strategies to Improve Executive Functioning and Daily Living Skills

Many individuals with ASD have the cognitive abilities to perform well in higher education but require support to improve their executive functioning and daily living skills (Duncan & Bishop, 2015). Koegel and LaZebnik (2009) pointed out that the change in structure alone is an enormous transition for most college students; while they might have spent 75% of their high school hours in the classroom and 25% studying at home, they experience the opposite pattern in college. First-year college students may struggle because "they just don't know how to manage their time, no one is checking on them, and it's human nature to procrastinate" (Koegel & LaZebnik, 2009, p. 225). Many first-year students with ASD struggle even more without the routine, rules, and prompting that enabled them to succeed in high school. However, planners and visual checklists can be helpful by providing them with another form of structure, one that they can self-manage and continue to use throughout their adult lives. Strategies to help students learn how to develop daily living routines are discussed in the following sections.

Daily Planners Many busy adults have joked that we would never remember anything if it was not in our telephone calendar or planner. In contrast, many incoming college students have never used a planner, relying instead on reminders from teachers and parents about upcoming deadlines, activities, and assignments. In college, professors may only provide this information on the syllabus or on-line and expect students to manage their own study schedule and remember assignments and exam dates. While many new college students struggle with time management and planning ahead for tests and assignments, those with ASD are particularly likely to struggle. These students may also be overconfident about their ability to remember something, whether it is a standing weekly appointment, course material, or the due date of a homework assignment.

An effective strategy is to teach students with ASD to use either a telephone or paper planner. Many campuses offer a free paper planner during orientation week that includes such important dates as school holidays, breaks, and registration deadlines. The important thing is to make sure that the students will use it consistently and have it with them at all times. At the beginning of each semester/quarter, students with ASD should take time to input all exam dates and assignment due dates (preferably with a reminder before important due dates). Most important, they can use this planner to schedule *daily* study time for each course. Many students with ASD have difficulty with executive functioning skills such as planning and prioritizing, organization, and task initiations. Regularly using a planner can assist in improving skills that will in turn improve academic performance. Planners can also be used for scheduling recurring weekly nonacademic tasks, such as going to the gym, doing laundry, grocery shopping, and attending office hours.

Checklists Checklists are also effective in improving organization and daily living skills in a college setting. A checklist can serve as a visual support to help individuals with ASD follow daily routines; organize their assignments; and break down larger, potentially overwhelming tasks (e.g., papers) into smaller steps. As Mesibov, Shea, and Shopler (2005) stated, structure is essential to the functioning of individuals with ASD, and visual methods are the most effective for helping individuals with ASD function more independently and successfully. (In Chapter 14, we describe how checklists can be used as a visual support in employment settings. Similar checklists can be used in college.)

Many students with whom we work use checklists in the form of weekly self-management charts. Students can use these charts to target several goals, such as behaviors related to hygiene, socialization, study time, office hours, organization, and living skills. Examples of items on these weekly charts include the following:

- Going to office hours
- Going to bed by a certain time/waking up by a certain time
- Showering
- Doing laundry
- Going to the library to study
- Attending a social activity
- Checking planner
- Exercising

Weekly charts can be tailored to the specific individual, updated regularly, and include a personalized reinforcer to help increase motivation to use the chart. Figure 13.3 shows an example of an individually tailored weekly chart used by a college student with ASD. Note that all targeted goals focused on his specific challenges in self-help, social, and academic areas.

Checklists may also be used to assist with routines and specific tasks (Mesibov et al., 2005). We have discussed how these can be used for daily tasks, but visual checklists can also be used in college to help improve skills with multiple steps. Following are some examples of routines and activities in which a visual checklist may be helpful:

	Sunday	Monday	Tuesday	Wednesday	Thursday	Friday	Saturday	Total	Weekly GOAL
MORNING									
Brush teeth	X		X	X	X			4	5
Deodorant		X	X	X	X		X	5	5
Appropriate clothes					X	X		2	3
EVENING									
Brought phone all day		X					X	2	3
Healthy dinner	X			X	X	X		4	3
Wash hair in the shower	X		X		X			3	2
Shave	X							1	1
Brush teeth		X	X	X		X	X	5	5
Social activities		X		X	X			3	3
Bedtime before 1:00 AM	X		X	X	X			4	4
WEEKLY									
Grocery shopping	X							1	1
Laundry							X	1	1
E-mail advisor						X		1	1
30–37 points: Board game on Tuesday								35	37

Figure 13.3. Sample weekly self-management chart.

- Morning and evening hygiene routine
- Items to put in backpack
- Steps for doing laundry
- Steps for writing a paper
- Process to prepare for an exam

Figures 13.4 and 13.5 show examples of visual checklists college students with ASD can use for completing a morning routine and for writing a paper. The student can check off each item as he or she completes the activity. These checklists increase structure, provide routine, and include visual prompts of steps to complete. These may be helpful if steps need to be broken down into smaller components or when a student needs more support in skill building relative to a specific routine or activity. In addition, having a visual checklist is helpful because students do not need to rely on a verbal prompt from another person.

Morning routine

- ☐ Brush teeth
- ☐ Shower
- ☐ Put on deodorant
- ☐ Take medications
- ☐ Eat breakfast
- ☐ Check planner

Figure 13.4. Sample checklist for completing a morning routine.

While most individuals with ASD are very responsive to visual supports and checklists, some can be less motivated. When this occurs, it can be helpful to adjust the number of items on the checklist, change the reinforcer, or provide reminders to complete the checklist via text, email, or telephone calls throughout the week.

Strategies to Help Navigate the University

In addition to the strategies to improve academic success, social integration, and organizational skills, it is important to consider supports to help students with

Writing a Paper*

- ☐ Read instructions from professor
- ☐ Choose a topic or thesis
- ☐ Make an outline of paper
- ☐ Take outline to give professor or teaching assistant (TA) for feedback
- ☐ Write a rough draft of paper
- ☐ Edit paper (check formatting guidelines)
- ☐ Turn in paper by deadline

*Due dates can be added if desired

Figure 13.5. Sample checklist for writing a paper.

ASD navigate the college environment. First, it may be helpful to provide explicit teaching to students to help them navigate the college campus. Higher education settings can be overwhelming with the many different departments, offices, and resources, and it may be helpful for students to have a visual cue that outlines common concerns and where/who to contact. For example, visual cues could look like these:

- If you are sick → call or visit student health services [list phone number, web site, and address],
- If you have questions about class accommodations → call or go into the disabled students' office [list phone number, web site, and address],
- If you have problems with your dorm room → talk to your Resident Adviser [list name and contact information]

Individuals with ASD often have strong visual skills, and visual cues like this can be very helpful.

Second, although universities may not have specific service providers trained in dealing with autism, students may benefit from supports provided by the school's counseling and psychological services. Students with ASD can inquire if any psychologists provide behavioral therapy or cognitive behavioral therapy; these psychologists may be a good fit for students with ASD. Of primary importance is that a service provider can actively assist with arranging peer mentors and study buddies and ensure that the student with ASD receives support for social outings and studying each week. It is sometimes helpful if students are seen by a university psychologist or other professional on a regular basis to make sure they are keeping up with their activities of daily living (e.g., self-care activities), check in on their academic performance, provide information on additional resources that may be helpful, and provide treatment for any co-morbid diagnoses. However, many individuals with ASD report that "talk therapy" is not helpful if their social needs are not addressed. Most know when they do not have friends. Therefore, specialized practice and feedback relating to specific social behaviors that interfere with developing friendships is more effective than simply discussing the problem. In short, carefully choosing providers on the campus who can provide the right support is critical. Many students with ASD do not receive treatment until a negative event occurs, such as failing a class or having a conflict with a peer. Proactively seeking support from counseling and psychology services may help prevent these events.

Although empirical research and clinical experience indicate these strategies can help improve outcomes for postsecondary students with ASD, it is important to note that higher education may not be the best option for all individuals with ASD. Many adults with ASD may not desire to continue their education, or they may find employment that is better suited to their strengths and abilities. It is important to assess if individuals with ASD want to attend college before pursuing this path and determine whether higher education is realistic and a good fit for their long-term goals. Figure 13.6 provides an overview of helpful strategies to support students with ASD in college settings.

Academics

- Connect with Office of Disabilities
- Priming
- Summer classes
- Reduced course load
- Support in choosing a major
- Campus tutoring programs
- Office hours
- Study buddy/groups

Social

- Peer mentors
- Campus clubs
- Recreational classes
- Dorm activities
- Social skills training

Organization and daily living

- Planners
- Visual checklists

Navigate campus

- Visual supports
- Counseling and psychological services

Figure 13.6. Strategies to increase success in higher education.

Key Insights ||| Helping College Students With ASD Succeed

When working with young adults with ASD who plan to attend college or are attending college, keep the following insights in mind:

- Many individuals with ASD desire a postsecondary education but without proper help find it too challenging to successfully participate in college or obtain a degree.
- Several common challenges can be addressed for these students. These include 1) a decrease in individualized supports, 2) difficulty with social integration, and 3) challenges with daily living and organization skills.
- It is important to consider different factors when selecting a college that is a good fit. These include 1) the size of the college, 2) options for living arrangements, 3) majors and academic accommodations offered, and 4) available social support resources.
- Research shows that there are effective strategies to help college students with ASD improve in the following areas: 1) academic success, 2) social integration, 3) executive functioning skills, 4) organization, and 5) the ability to navigate campus.
- Helpful strategies to increase academic performance include 1) priming, 2) study buddies, and 3) accessing accommodations through programs created for students with disabilities.

- Peer mentor relationships can be arranged to provide social support during activities related to the interests of the individual with ASD. Combined with intervention targeting specific communicative areas, these relationships often lead to substantial improvements in socialization, self-confidence, and general well-being.
- Study buddies can be a great resource for improving academics and social interaction.
- Visual checklists and self-management can be helpful to create prompts and appropriate levels of structure in academics, social areas, daily routines, and independent living skills.
- Organizational skills are difficult for many college students, but may be particularly challenging for the student with ASD. Using a planner or electronic device to help develop a calendar, create and manage schedules, and set reminders will be very helpful.
- Comprehensive programs for students with ASD are critical for success in higher education settings.

SUMMARY

College can be a wonderful experience for individuals with ASD and may provide opportunities for peer socialization, increase independence, and improve self-confidence. Acquiring a college education or even gaining skills from college courses can lead to higher pay, increased career and job opportunities, and improved job satisfaction. However, specific steps are important to ensure success. Too often, individuals with ASD report that they desire higher education but are not provided with the necessary supports to succeed. Effective programs are available, but there are too few, and not all colleges provide specialized support. With large numbers of individuals with ASD reaching adulthood, additional attention to this area is highly warranted.

STUDY QUESTIONS

1. Discuss the benefits of higher education for individuals with ASD.
2. Describe common challenges for college students and adults with ASD, specifically in the areas of accessing supports, social integration, executive functioning, and daily living skills.
3. Discuss various factors to consider when choosing a college for students with ASD.
4. Describes strategies to increase academic success for students with ASD in higher education.
5. Describe strategies to increase social integration for individuals with ASD in higher education.
6. Discuss interventions to improve organizational and daily living skills for students with ASD in higher education.

7. Describe supports to help students with ASD navigate the college environment.
8. Discuss campus and community resources that may be beneficial for college students with ASD.

REFERENCES

Adreon, D., & Durocher, J. (2007). Evaluating the college transition needs of individuals with high-functioning autism spectrum disorders. *Intervention in School and Clinic, 42*(5), 271–279.

Americans with Disabilities Act (ADA) of 1990, PL 101-336, 42 U.S.C. §§ 12101 *et seq.*

Ashbaugh, K., Koegel, R., & Koegel, L. (2017). Increasing social integration for college students with autism spectrum disorder. *Behavioral Development Bulletin, 22*(1), 183.

Bal, V. H., Kim, S., Cheong, D., & Lord, C. (2015). Daily living skills in individuals with autism spectrum disorder from 2 to 21 years of age. *Autism, 19*(7), 774–784.

Barnhill, G. P. (2014). Supporting students with Asperger syndrome on college campuses: Current practices. *Focus on Autism and Other Developmental Disabilities, 31*(1), 3–15.

Cimera, R. E., & Cowan, R. J. (2009). The costs of services and employment outcomes achieved by adults with autism in the US. *Autism, 13*(3), 285–302.

Dales, L., Hammer, S. J., & Smith, N. J. (2001). Time trends in autism and in MMR immunization coverage in California. *Jama, 285*(9), 1183–1185.

Dillon, M. R. (2007). Creating supports for college students with Asperger syndrome through collaboration. *College Student Journal, 41*(2), 499–505.

Dowrick, P., Anderson, J., Heyer, K., & Acosta, J. (2005). Postsecondary education across the USA: Experiences of adults with disabilities. *Journal of Vocational Rehabilitation, 22*, 41–47.

Duncan, A. W., & Bishop, S. L. (2015). Understanding the gap between cognitive abilities and daily living skills in adolescents with autism spectrum disorders with average intelligence. *Autism, 19*(1), 64–72.

Graetz, J. E., & Spampinato, K. (2008). Asperger's syndrome and the voyage through high school: Not the final frontier. *Journal of College Admission, 198*, 19–24.

Grigal, M., Neubert, D., & Moon, M. (2001). Public school programs for students with significant disabilities in post-secondary settings. *Education and Training in Mental Retardation and Developmental Disabilities, 36*(3), 244–254.

Hart, D., Grigal, M., & Weir, C. (2010). Expanding the paradigm: Postsecondary education options for individuals with autism spectrum disorder and intellectual disabilities. *Focus on Autism and Other Developmental Disabilities, 25*(3), 134–150.

Hendricks, D. R., & Wehman, P. (2009). Transition from school to adulthood for youth with autism spectrum disorders: Review and recommendations. *Focus on Autism and Other Developmental Disabilities, 24*(2), 77–88.

Individuals with Disabilities Education Improvement Act (IDEA) of 2004, PL 101-476, 20 U.S.C., §§ 1400 *et seq.*

Jobe, L. E., & White, S. W. (2007). Loneliness, social relationships, and a broader autism phenotype in college students. *Personality and Individual Differences, 42*(8), 1479–1489.

Kring, S., Greenberg, J., & Seltzer, M. (2008). Adolescents and adults with autism with and without co-morbid psychiatric disorders: Differences in maternal well-being. *Journal of Mental Health Research in Intellectual Disabilities, 1*(2), 53–74.

Koegel, L. K., Ashbaugh, K., Koegel, R. L., Detar, W. J., & Regester, A. (2013). Increasing socialization in adults with Asperger's syndrome. *Psychology in the Schools, 50*(9), 899–909.

Koegel, L. K., Koegel, R. L., Frea, W., & Green-Hopkins, I. (2003). Priming as a method of coordinating educational services for students with autism. *Language, Speech, and Hearing Services in Schools, 34*(3), 228–235.

Koegel, L. K., & LaZebnik, C. (2009). *Growing up on the spectrum: A guide to life, love, and learning for teens and young adults with autism and Asperger's.* New York, NY: Viking.

Matthews, N. L., Smith, C. J., Pollard, E., Ober-Reynolds, S., Kirwan, J., & Malligo, A. (2015). Adaptive functioning in autism spectrum disorder during the transition to adulthood. *Journal of Autism and Developmental Disorders, 45*(8), 2349–2360.

Mesibov, G. B., Shea, V., & Schopler, E. (2005). *The TEACCH approach to autism spectrum disorders.* New York, NY: Springer Science + Business Media.
Muller, E., Schuler, A., & Yates, G. (2008). Social challenges and supports from the perspective of individuals with Asperger syndrome and other autism spectrum disabilities. *Autism, 12*(2), 173–190.
Nevill, R., & White, S. (2011). College students' openness toward autism spectrum disorders: Improving peer acceptance. *Journal of Autism and Developmental Disabilities, 41*(12), 1619–1628.
Stewart, M. E., Barnard, L., Pearson, J., Hasan, R., & O'Brien, G. (2006). Presentation of depression in autism and Asperger syndrome: A review. *Autism, 10*(1), 103-116.
Stodden, R., & Mruzek, D. (2010). An introduction to postsecondary education and employment of persons with autism and developmental disabilities. *Focus on Autism and Other Developmental Disabilities, 25*(3), 131–133.
Van Bergeijk, E., Klin, A., & Volkmar, F. (2008). Supporting more able students on the autism spectrum: College and beyond. *Journal of Autism and Developmental Disorders, 38*(7), 1359–1370.
Webb, K., Patterson, K., Syverud, S., & Seabrooks-Blackmore, J. (2008). Evidence based practices that promote transition to postsecondary education: Listening to a decade of expert voices. *Exceptionality, 16*, 192–206.
Wenzel, C., & Rowley, L. (2010). Teaching social skills and academic strategies to college students with Asperger's syndrome. *TEACHING Exceptional Children, 42*(5), 44–50.
White, S. W., Ollendick, T. H., & Bray, B. C. (2011). College students on the autism spectrum: Prevalence and associated problems. *Autism, 15*(6), 683–701.
Zafft, C., Hart, D., & Zimbrich, K. (2004). College career connection: A study of youth with intellectual disabilities and the impact of postsecondary education. *Education and Training in Developmental Disabilities, 39*(1), 45–53.
Zager, D., & Alpern, C. S. (2010). College-based inclusion programming for transition-age students with autism. *Focus on Autism and Other Developmental Disabilities, 25*(3), 151–157.

14

Supporting Individuals With ASD in Employment Settings

Erin Engstrom, Kristen Ashbaugh, Lynn Kern Koegel, and Katarina Ford

CHAPTER GOALS

Goal 1. The reader will understand the importance of targeting employment as a realistic goal for individuals with autism spectrum disorders (ASD).

Goal 2. The reader will discuss the advantages of employment for individuals with disabilities and society at large.

Goal 3. The reader will discuss barriers to employment and potential ways to ameliorate these barriers.

Goal 4. The reader will describe interventions to target behaviors and job tasks in work settings.

Goal 5. The reader will describe areas relating to employment of individuals with ASD that are in need of future research.

Many members of society who have not had education or experience related to ASD think the future is bleak for children with ASD. It might seem impossible that a child with a significant disability might be able to be gainfully employed. Yet, as research advances show, some type of meaningful employment is actually a very appropriate goal for virtually all individuals with ASD.

Once one begins to think in terms of employment goals, a number of important issues become apparent. Seeking and obtaining stable employment is a critical transition area following secondary or postsecondary education for all individuals, including those with ASD (Hendricks, 2010). The benefits of employment, summarized in Figure 14.1, are considerable as they relate to both economic independence and improved mental health. That is, in addition to financial stability, working individuals are less reliant on government or other third-party support,

Figure 14.1. Benefits of employment.

and the favorable tax revenue from individuals with ASD who are employed benefits the public at large. Individuals with ASD become contributing members to society rather than being viewed as a financial burden. In addition, employment results in improved cognitive performance (Garcia-Villamisar, Ross, & Wehman, 2000). Employment also promotes human dignity and improves overall quality of life in individuals with ASD (Garcia-Villamisar et al., 2000; Hendricks, 2010). It is also notable that employers report high satisfaction with the unique strengths of their employees with ASD (Hagner & Cooney, 2005; Hendricks, 2010).

Unfortunately, ASD has often been viewed largely as a disorder of deficits (Graetz & Spampinato, 2008), a perspective that overlooks the fact that most individuals with ASD offer strengths in various domains that would benefit employment settings. For example, individuals with ASD often have a strong attention to detail, intense focus, enjoyment of specific tasks others may find tedious (Hillier et al., 2007), and strengths in visual areas (Kaldy, Giserman, Carter, & Blaser, 2016; Keehn, Shih, Brenner, Townsend, & Müller, 2013; Mayes & Calhoun, 2003; Samson, Mottron, Soulieres, & Zeffiro, 2012). When combined with noted increased long-term memory and a high degree of accuracy (that is often superior to neurotypical peers), individuals with ASD are highly desirable for many types of specific vocational positions (Hagner & Cooney, 2005). In addition, these individuals are more likely to exhibit personality and character strengths such as authenticity, fairness, kindness, and a love of learning that make them desirable additions to a workplace environment (Kirchner, Ruch, & Dziobek, 2016). This chapter explores the potential barriers to employment faced by adults with ASD, along with options for vocational rehabilitation and specific types of support that can be offered in the workplace.

BARRIERS TO EMPLOYMENT

Despite the benefits of hiring individuals with ASD, employment outcomes for this population are consistently low, and those who work do so for fewer hours and for lower wages than any other group of people with a specific disability (Burgess & Cimera, 2014; Cimera & Cowan, 2009). In fact, the National High School Longitudinal Transition Survey (Institute of Education Sciences, 2009) showed that only about 32.5% of young adults with ASD were working for pay, versus about 59% of participants receiving other special education services after completing high school. In addition, research examining the 2 years after completing high school found that more than 50% of young adults with ASD did not participate in employment or higher education, which is the lowest rate of any disability category (Roux et al., 2013; Shattuck et al., 2012). Further, for graduates from lower-income households, the odds of having a job were even poorer, particularly among individuals with lower conversational and cognitive abilities (Roux et al., 2013; Shattuck et al., 2012). This gap in employment success is in part due to the unique challenges that individuals with ASD face, including social communicative and behavioral difficulties. Potential barriers to employment are listed in Figure 14.2. These potential barriers include having no single point of coordination of services, stigma against hiring people with disabilities, and lack of awareness of services to support employment of people with disabilities, as well as the social-communication and behavioral challenges discussed in the sections that follow.

Social Communication Challenges

To start, individuals with ASD seeking employment must first communicate their skills and experience in a written resume and then navigate sophisticated social interactions in an interview setting. Unfortunately, due to communication difficulties inherent to the disability, many struggle to give positive first impressions and have difficulty responding to interview questions appropriately (Hagner & Cooney, 2005). Furthermore, it appears that adults with ASD who are employed often struggle to maintain employment due to their social communication challenges, as many are fired due to problems with social issues rather than poor job performance (Müller, Schuler, A. & Yates, 2008).

Some of the social challenges may include difficulties with reciprocal conversation, or the natural sustained "to and fro" pattern of conversation (Capps, Kehrs, & Sigman, 1998; Landa et al., 1992); difficulties with communicating the "gist" of a

Barriers to success in employment settings

- Lack of single point of coordination of services
- Difficulty with social communication and behavioral challenges
- Challenges with executive functioning and daily living skills
- Stigma against hiring workers with disabilities
- Lack of awareness of existing services to support workers with disabilities and their employers

Figure 14.2. Barriers to success in employment settings.

story, and difficulties with monitoring the type of information they give (Eales, 1993; Landa, Klin, Volkmar, & Sparrow, 2000). This can result in issues such as frequent and excessive discussion relating to preferred topics (Zager & Alpern, 2010) or sharing excessively detailed facts that may appear to lack cohesion and impact their communicative intent during conversation (Landa et al., 2000). As such, these individuals' conversational exchanges may seem confusing or unusual to conversation partners (Eales, 1993; Landa et al., 2000), affecting their ability to communicate effectively with co-workers and supervisors.

In addition, individuals with ASD often have difficulty with question asking, which can persist across the lifespan if not addressed (Howlin, Alcock, & Burkin, 2000; Koegel, 2000). Consequently, if a person with ASD does not demonstrate mutual interest during a conversation, typically developing individuals may perceive that person as uninterested or off-putting (Chambres, Auxiette, Vansingle, & Gil, 2008). Relatedly, many workers with ASD do not ask for help when it would be beneficial (Burt, Fuller, & Lewis, 1991). In combination with the challenge of learning how to respond positively to feedback and communicate politely (Burt et al.,1991; Sperry & Mesibov, 2005), these characteristics may make it much more difficult for this population to develop positive, professional relationships in the workplace and engage in the inquisitive behaviors needed to understand instructions or duties. Thus, competent and consistent intervention in these areas is essential.

Behavioral Challenges

In addition to social communicative challenges, some individuals with ASD also exhibit behavioral difficulties that can hinder their success in obtaining and maintaining employment. Daily living skills (e.g., personal hygiene, attending appointments on time), appear to be common areas of difficulty for this population that directly impact their ability to make positive first impressions and obtain employment (Burt et al., 1991). In addition, ritualistic and repetitive behavior and limited flexibility may impact job performance and social success (Hillier et al., 2007). For example, an individual with ASD may have rigid daily routines, such that they offer limited availability (e.g., available only in the mornings, not willing to work on weekends) or resist an adjustment of routine or schedule. Even repetitive motor behaviors or vocalizations may interfere with workplace success. Similarly, any disruptive behavior such as tantrums, aggression, or verbal outbursts may limit success (Burt et al., 1991). These challenges may be partly attributed to deficits in executive functioning, decreases in parent involvement in adulthood, and transitions into new living environments (Adreon & Durocher, 2007). However, with support and intervention, these challenges in social communication and appropriate behavior can be greatly reduced to make it easier for individuals with ASD to succeed in the workplace.

VOCATIONAL REHABILITATION AND RELATED PROGRAMS

Nationally, there are not enough state-of-the-art programs available to help individuals with ASD find and succeed in employment, and existing programs often struggle with knowing exactly what to do. Nevertheless, federal, state, and community programs attempt to mitigate the challenges relating to successful employment of adults with ASD. For example, organizations and programs that serve as resources for individuals with ASD include state Vocational Rehabilitation (VRs) Programs, Community Rehabilitation Programs (CRPs), state and local developmental disabilities agencies, One Stop Career Centers, and Work Incentives Planning and Assistance Projects (McDonough & Revell, 2010).

State VRs, administered by the U.S. Department of Education, offer employment services to individuals with ASD across the nation. The primary goals of VR programs are to provide an array of services—including assessment, diagnosis, job coaching, job search support, and on-the-job training—in order to maximize employment outcomes for individuals with disabilities (Lawer, Brusilovskiy, Salzer, & Mandell, 2009). VRs are the largest support system for adults with ASD, with more than 600,000 case closures annually (U.S. Department of Education, 2012), meaning that 600,000 individuals successfully acquire some type of employment after receiving these services. However, while the number of case closures for individuals with ASD in VR programs is growing (Cimera & Cowan, 2009; Migliore & Butterworth, 2008), it is still much smaller when compared with other groups of individuals with various disabilities (Migliore, Butterworth, & Zaleska, 2014). Furthermore, despite an enormous increase in access to VRs, employment outcomes for individuals with ASD are still low and employers report mixed satisfaction with the value of VR programs in their workplace (Alverson & Yamamoto, 2018; Gilbride, Stensrud, Ehlers, Evans, & Peterson, 2000), suggesting that these services may need further review and analysis to improve their effectiveness for this population. Further compounding the issue is the fact that employers express reservations about hiring individuals with disabilities and report not knowing about VR programs and their support for disabled workers (Gilbride et al., 2000). It is also important to consider that states have varying policies and practices to support individuals with disabilities; therefore, VR program success may be in part determined by geographical location (Migliore et al., 2014) as well as the skill level of the staff.

CRPs are nonprofit or for-profit agencies that offer vocational support to individuals with disabilities (McDonough & Revell, 2010). CRPs often work cooperatively with VR programs or secondary school settings to provide services that are more disability-specific and may address different areas such as job coaching, career counseling, job preparation, or job placement. In addition, state and local developmental disabilities agencies and One Stop Career Centers can help with transition planning and acquiring employment, though the latter are typically geared toward young adults. Work Incentives Planning and Assistance (WIPA) projects assist beneficiaries of the Social Security Administration to be better equipped in making informed choices about work in relation to their Social Security benefits (McDonough & Revell, 2010).

As a whole, these programs can be highly complex. Unlike elementary and secondary school systems, these programs do not have any single point of coordination of services. Instead, adults with ASD must navigate this multidimensional system to access the specific services and supports they need for successful employment.

BEHAVIORAL INTERVENTIONS THAT SUPPORT EMPLOYMENT

Despite the challenge of accessing quality services, promising research shows that specific behavioral interventions can help minimize barriers to employment and improve the social communication, organization, and daily living skills that are crucial for success in the workplace. A growing body of research demonstrates that behavior modification techniques can improve employment outcomes for adults with ASD (Burt et al., 1991; Cimera, 2012; Hagner & Cooney, 2005; Hendricks, 2010; Schaller & Yang, 2005). Some effective intervention procedures include modeling, teaching functionally equivalent replacement behaviors (FERBs), self-management, shaping, reinforcement, and video feedback (Burt et al., 1991; Hendricks, 2010). Previous chapters of this book describe how to use these behavioral techniques with children and adolescents and for improving social conversation for adults with ASD. The following sections describe how the techniques can be applied in the workplace specifically to social communication and daily living skills within employment contexts.

Improving Social Communication in the Workplace

In all employment positions or settings, employees are expected to communicate appropriately with co-workers and supervisors. Further, as communication in work settings shifts from face-to-face and verbal communication to emails and text messages, proficient written communication skills are becoming more necessary for employment positions. However, many individuals with ASD report social interaction problems in work domains (Schmidt et al., 2015). Kirchner and Dziobek (2014) found that interactions with clients, colleagues, and superiors were one of the primary factors interfering with work performance for adults with ASD.

Multiple interventions may be needed to target the areas, such as written and verbal social communication skills, that may be challenging for these employees. For example, if the employee needs to greet others appropriately, staff members can model an appropriate greeting for the adult, role-play a greeting, use video feedback to evaluate the differences between appropriate and inappropriate greetings, set up a self-management program, and positively reinforce appropriate greetings (Burt et al., 1991). Regardless of how or where these skills are taught, employees can learn to generalize social communication skills to new job sites, co-workers, customers, and situations that may arise at work; use of self-management assists employees with this generalization. This adaptability across settings and contexts is crucial for gaining and maintaining independent employment. Intervention for employment skills needs to be carefully coordinated across environments, as constant involvement of new adults in residential and home settings can create difficulties for adults with ASD, who are often dependent on the proximity of their parents or support staff and may struggle greatly when staff members are not available (Hume, Loftin, & Lantz, 2009).

Selection of Target Social Communication Skills While a variety of complex functional assessment procedures can be used to identify target skills, it is noteworthy that appropriate target behavior(s) often can be determined by a clinician or job coach relatively easily through direct observations in an informal functional analysis at work. If an individual with ASD is not yet employed, target skills might be chosen based on observations of social conversation, conversation probes with unfamiliar individuals, or even observations of employees who are employed in a position and workplace similar to the adult with ASD's desired position and workplace. Very likely, more than one social communication area will need to be targeted, as most workplaces require competence with a variety of complex social skills.

For example, an engineer may need to work cooperatively with co-workers when developing projects and considering each team member's unique contribution. Similarly, a grocery bagger uses multiple social techniques when interacting with a customer; the employee must make eye contact, display a positive affect, ask if the customer has brought any reusable bags, and respond appropriately to requests for how different items should be bagged. Likewise, an employee stocking shelves will need to communicate with co-workers in the back of the store, ask shoppers if they need help finding anything, and communicate concise directions to the appropriate aisle. Regardless of the exact position or job site, many social communication skills will be required. First areas to target might include greeting others politely, asking for help, engaging in small talk, using appropriate detail in conversation, responding appropriately to negative statements or facial expressions from a customer, reacting calmly to constructive criticism, and much more.

Skill Instruction Within Specific Settings Social communication skills can be targeted in clinical, community, or employment settings. Role-play and practice within a clinic setting can sometimes be helpful for navigating problematic situations at work, such as handling criticism or conflict with other co-workers. These role-plays may be based on the individual's own work experience or simulated examples. However, because naturalistic methods are more likely to lead to generalizability (e.g., Koegel, O'Dell, & Koegel, 1987), it is important to strive to implement behavioral programs within the natural employment setting when possible. In natural settings it is helpful if the treatment materials are nonintrusive but still accessible or visible to the employee at work. For example, an employee could keep a wrist counter in his or her pocket while greeting customers to track behaviors such as smiling and eye contact, asking if customers need help with anything, or providing appropriate detail in response to a question. In addition, community settings may provide opportunities for further practice of workplace skills. For example, if the behavior needs to be practiced with multiple people or unfamiliar individuals (e.g., appropriate greetings), one can walk around an area where there are likely to be opportunities for greetings, such as vendors in a university center, stores, or restaurants.

Self-Management Self-management is a discrete and effective strategy that can be used to improve a variety of target behaviors in adults with ASD. (See Chapter 10 for details on the procedures.) It teaches them to independently evaluate, record, and reinforce their own appropriate behaviors and has been shown to increase generalization and maintenance of target goals when they learn to use self-management in community settings (Boettcher, 1977; Koegel, Koegel, Hurley, & Frea, 1992; Koegel, Koegel, & Parks, 1995). Self-management is especially useful in employment settings where the employee is expected to demonstrate appropriate behaviors in the absence of constant vigilance by a treatment provider. For instance, to practice self-management in just one domain, an individual could use a checklist to self-manage multiple social communication skills at work. The following example demonstrates a self-management program the authors of this chapter set up for improving on-task behavior and social conversation at the workplace.

CASE HISTORY
Mike's Self-Management System at the Bike Repair Shop

The self-management checklist shown in Figure 14.3 was created for Mike, who worked at a community bike repair shop. When Mike began working there, his boss noted that he rarely spoke to customers and co-workers and spent quite a bit of his shift engaging in off-task behaviors, such as staring into space, pacing outside of the bike shop, and playing on his smartphone. Unfortunately, Mike's job coaches did not have experience with individuals with ASD; therefore, an experienced clinician was needed to provide the job coaches with weekly training. Target behaviors were individualized based on Mike's identified needs during baseline observations and the reports from his employers. Target social communication goals were clearly defined and written at the bottom of his checklist, which was

	Monday			**Tuesday**			**Wednesday**		
	Hour 1	Hour 2	Hour 3	Hour 1	Hour 2	Hour 3	Hour 1	Hour 2	Hour 3
Greet co-workers appropriately									
Use full and complete sentences									
Speak loudly and clearly									
Ask a co-worker one question									
Focus on work									
Ask for help if needed									

6 checks/hour = 5-minute break; 18 checks/day = coffee at the end day

Total points for week:

Appropriate greeting: Say "Hi, how are you?" or "Good morning!"; make eye contact; smile.

Full and complete sentence: Give a full response to a question. (Do not say "No," or "I don't know.")

Speak loudly and clearly: Use appropriate volume and speak slowly enough for the other person to understand you.

Focus on work: Remain on-task, looking at the computer screen or paper or at the bike parts.

Figure 14.3. Self-management checklist used by an employee at a bike-repair shop to improve his social communication skills at work.

placed on the wall above his desk. To start the self-management intervention, the experienced clinician met individually with Mike and described each behavior, then practiced during short intervals to ensure that Mike was able to engage in and monitor the appropriate behaviors at work. Once Mike was proficient at engaging in the target behaviors and independently monitored his behavior in the one-to-one setting, he was ready to use the self-management procedures at the workplace. Mike's job coaches were taught to help him set a target number of points for the day and select reinforcers before each shift that could be delivered at the scheduled times during the day. Reinforcers included smaller rewards that could be obtained throughout the day and a larger one at the end of his shift. Mike chose to reward himself with an extra 5-minute break every hour upon successful completion of his goals and coffee at the end of his shift if he had accumulated his target number of points for the day. The reward system was coordinated with Mike, his employers, and job coaches to ensure that he would have access to his reinforcing activities at time intervals that would not interfere with his completion of work duties. Mike then set a timer on his phone and filled out his checklist at the end of each hour interval and at the end of the day. The use of the self-management program was helpful in ensuring that Mike stayed on task and interacted appropriately throughout his shift. Following the self-management and regular monitoring by the job coaches, his productivity and social interaction improved greatly, and his employers expressed satisfaction with his performance. (For more about this intervention, see the section on job coaching for the instructions that were written for Mike's support staff at the bike shop.)

Video Modeling A fairly new intervention that is showing promise in improving social communication in adults with ASD is video modeling. Video modeling, when combined with self-management, has been shown to improve a variety of skills in adults with ASD, including eye gaze, positive statements, empathic expression, greetings, response latency, and socialization (Ayres & Langone, 2005; Bellini & Akullian, 2007; Koegel, Ashabugh, Navab, & Koegel, 2016; Koegel, Navab, Ashbaugh, & Koegel, 2016;). Because video modeling is described in Chapter 11, descriptions of specific methods in this chapter are brief.

This intervention can be implemented in several ways to target desired workplace behaviors. Often, when the authors of this book work with an adult, we begin by video recording him or her to identify target behaviors—discreetly, so as to avoid singling out or stigmatizing these adults. Once the recordings are completed, we select segments in which the target behavior occurred and places in which it would have been appropriate but was not observed. In a later session with a clinician, both the clinician and the person receiving intervention observe video clips that demonstrate the behaviors that are successful or may need improvement. The target behavior can then be discussed and practiced. This is repeated until the adult reaches a desired criterion for using the behavior.

Video modeling can also be used in conjunction with self-management. This way, the employee with ASD can engage in the target behavior, get feedback during the video modeling sessions, and monitor his or her successes. The self-management of the desired behaviors can be programmed to occur in other settings, such as the workplace. This combination of interventions is helpful because the individual can observe him- or herself during real-life situations and practice using the self-management procedures to monitor the use of the target behavior. Once the adult is proficient with self-management during the video modeling sessions, it can be generalized to occur in natural settings. Often this can be accomplished very simply—for example, by merely explaining to the person that he or she can now use the procedures to earn points in the community. Sometimes it's helpful to verify that the individual is actually engaging in the desired behaviors and monitoring in the natural settings, but for the most part this can be accomplished independently. The fact that intervention can be programmed in the absence of an interventionist is one of the benefits of self-management programs.

Improving Task Performance and Daily Living Skills

In addition to improving social interactions on the job, self-management can be helpful for teaching a variety of work duties (Burt et al., 1991; Wehman et al., 2017). When new to a job, employees are expected to memorize a fair amount of information in a short period of time, such as what to do when a customer walks in or how to package shipments for delivery. Often, these routines will vary slightly in different contexts or be revised periodically, increasing the challenge for those who have difficulty with understanding or accepting the changes in routine or context. Breaking up large tasks into smaller ones and allowing the individual to self-manage his or her duties helps the individual with ASD reduce mistakes and increase productivity (Burt et al., 1991). As noted, when using self-management as an intervention, checklists should be readily available for the individual with ASD and should be updated or faded based on changes in needs, behaviors, and improvements.

Figure 14.4 shows a self-management program for an adult with ASD who assisted with dissemination of printed manuals at work. This checklist also served as a reminder for the many steps involved in his employment.

Manual Orders Checklist

- ☑ Sign in.
- ☑ Get the orders out of the manual orders folder, and collect the books required for each order.
- ☑ Separate the orders into two stacks: 1) one that has all the orders you will be paying for at the post office and 2) one that has manuals to be paid for online.
- ☑ For one or two manuals, use the smallest envelope; for three to five manuals, use the next size up envelope or priority bubble mailers; and for more than five, use either the largest one or a box.
- ☑ Once you fill out all the orders, double-check your own work before having your supervisor check your work.
- ☑ Finish the orders, and print the labels.
- ☑ Build the packages, and make sure to put the correct labels on the top of the packages.
- ☑ Clean up the office, and fill up the bookracks. If getting low on manuals, write down how many are left.
- ☑ Take picture of sign-in sheet once all of these boxes are checked off and you're about to walk out the door, as insurance that you have as accurate information as possible about what time you started and left for the timesheet.
- ☑ Take the packages to the post office and pay for postage before putting them in the package drop-off.
- ☑ Mark the time you are walking out of the doors on your phone so that you know how long you worked for your timesheet.

Figure 14.4. Self-management checklist used by an employee who assisted with dissemination of printed material to improve his task performance at work.

Self-management strategies can also be used to improve daily living skills, which are also necessary for independence and success in employment settings (Smith, Maenner, & Seltzer, 2012). In adulthood, challenges with time management, decreases in parent involvement, and transitions into new living environments may contribute to difficulties with independence (Adreon & Durocher, 2007), which may in turn affect acquisition and maintenance of employment. It is critical that service providers pay attention to their client with ASD's daily living skills, because success in this area is one of the biggest predictors of positive outcomes in employment settings (Adreon & Durocher, 2007).

The use of daily living checklists and other behavioral interventions that integrate visual schedules and self-management show considerable promise (Wilkinson, 2008). As with work tasks and communication, items on a self-management program for daily living skills can be adjusted based on the current needs of the individual and his or her skill level, and specific tasks may be broken down into multiple parts for ease of training. For example, one individual may need the multiple components of showering broken out on his checklist (e.g., washing hair, washing body with soap, drying off with a towel), while another individual may simply require the general category "showering." See Figure 14.5 for an example of a daily living checklist developed for a young adult living independently. Interestingly, this young man did not have challenges in any of the targeted areas when he lived at home and his parents could regularly remind him to shower, brush his teeth, and complete household tasks. However, challenges emerged once his parents were not able to remind him. During baseline measures, consisting of observations, discussions with the individual, and input from his employer, several self-help needs were determined. Understanding of the individual's performance during baseline measures helped in developing behavioral goals (number of times per week the behavior would be completed). Goals were listed in the final column and represented small incremental steps that would improve each targeted behavior. The individual brought the checklist to weekly meetings with his clinician, at which time they discussed his performance in each target area. When he met his goals, the time increment or number of behaviors he needed for a reward was gradually and systematically increased. Challenging areas could be broken down into smaller tasks, or the goals could be reduced. The individual who used this checklist was fairly consistent about recording data for each area on a daily basis; others with whom the authors have worked, however, have needed additional support, especially initially, such as a text message reminder or providing on-site visits until regular monitoring occurred.

Functional Behavior Assessment in the Workplace

It is often simple to conduct informal assessments through direct observation of the client in the target environment. However, sometimes more formal procedures are necessary, such as conducting a systematic functional behavior assessment (FBA) and developing appropriate replacement behaviors for the workplace (Hendricks, 2010). If the function of an employee's inappropriate behavior (e.g., arriving late, disrupting the work environment, not completing tasks) is identified, then supervisors and job coaches can develop an intervention to improve the behavior by focusing on appropriate replacement behaviors (Hendricks, 2010). For example, one adult with whom the authors worked arrived to work late on a

	Monday	Tuesday	Wednesday	Thursday	Friday	Saturday	Sunday	GOALS
Shower	X	X		X	X	X		*5x per week*
Brush teeth	X	X	X	X	X	X	X	*7x per week*
Laundry		X						*1x per month*
Take out trash/ recycling			X					*Recycling- 1x per week* *Trash- every other week*
Wash and dry dishes				X				*2x per week*
Job search								*3x per week*
Apply for job			X					*3x per week*
Check e-mail	X		X		X			*2x per week*
Bring planner to meetings	X							*1x per week*
Social activities							X	*1x per week*
							TOTAL:	*21 points*
							THIS WEEK'S GOAL	*20 points*

Figure 14.5. Daily-living skills checklist for a young adult living independently.

daily basis because he stayed up all night working on his computer and was too exhausted to get up in the morning. Once we helped him get to bed at a reasonable hour, he could wake up earlier and arrive on time. In another example, an adult was spending excessive amounts of time in the bathroom because he didn't want to complete some of his job duties. Once we set up a self-management program for completing small amounts of work, his time in the bathroom decreased dramatically. Again, understanding the function of the behavior can help with developing the appropriate intervention.

Addressing Severe Behavioral Challenges

As discussed by Manente, Maraventano, LaRue, Delmolino, and Sloan (2010), it can be extremely challenging and labor intensive to intervene with severe behavior problems in adults. Severe behavior problems in adulthood that are resistant to change might be due to a variety of reasons, including a longer history of the individual's engaging in the behavior, multiple functions of the behavior, or multiple features of the behavior (e.g., screaming, throwing objects, crying to avoid a task [Manente et al., 2010]). It is most helpful to use FBA to understand all aspects of a certain behavior or pattern of behaviors so that clinicians and/or job coaches can intervene accordingly and so that the employee has an appropriate way of communicating, other than attempting to communicate through disruptive behavior.

In addition, FBA may be a useful tool for individuals with ASD who exhibit milder disruptive or inappropriate behaviors but have a difficult time identifying a solution to a problem. In one example, Daniel, a client with ASD who had been fired from three jobs in 3 years, was confused and frustrated by his negative interactions with his co-workers and supervisors but was unable to identify why he was having conflicts with co-workers. Following an FBA, his clinician determined that in an attempt to do what he perceived as a very high-quality job, Daniel created excessively detailed to-do lists, wrote emails with erroneous and excessive detail to his supervisor, and often talked to co-workers in a tone that was perceived as rude. It was noted that his work productivity decreased while he spent time creating his to-do lists, and his co-workers and supervisors were frustrated by the time his emails took away from their own productivity. Interventions included showing Daniel how his behaviors were negatively affecting his performance and relationships with co-workers; practicing creating to-do lists and emails of appropriate length; and improving his voice tone through intervention, practice, and self-management. Through these interventions, Daniel was able to reduce disruptive or unproductive behaviors and increase his use of appropriate communication and email. It is important to note that interventions for this population can be extremely successful, and that fewer individuals who receive support with job placement leave their job because of behavioral or work-related difficulties (Mawhood & Howlin, 1999). Therefore, developing a comprehensive intervention plan is not only valuable but may also be critical if long-term successful employment is to be realized.

INTEGRATING STRENGTHS INTO THE WORKPLACE

It is highly desirable to focus on the strengths of individuals with ASD, even though, historically, focusing on deficits has been the more common practice. For these individuals, it is valuable to consider idiosyncratic and special strengths when identifying job placement or assigning specific job tasks. The literature has long demonstrated that focusing on strengths results in the most positive outcomes relating to employment in this population (Hendricks, 2010; Howlin et al., 2005; Koegel & LaZebnik, 2009). In addition, practitioners should consider the individual's intellectual and educational background, as well as social skills, to ensure the job matches his or her skill level (Hendricks, 2010). Matching the adult to a position that is suited to his or her abilities has been shown to increase job satisfaction. This does not necessarily mean the individual needs to be cognitively functioning at a very high level. For example, we worked with a young woman who exhibited very few appropriate behaviors and spent most of her day playing with water in the sink. We attempted to use her strength, playing with water, to identify a job for her. We found a job advertisement for a dishwasher and tested to see if she would be able to handle the job. It turned out that she loved using the water on the dishes and, following a very brief intervention, was delighted to wash dishes for hours on end. As such, she was hired for the job, and due to her tireless and thorough work (completed with relatively minimal supervision), she earned a decent income.

SUPPORTED EMPLOYMENT

Supported employment is a major route to success at work for individuals with ASD and often necessary (Baker-Ericzén et al., 2016; Hedley, Dissanayake, Richdale, Spoor, & Uljarević, 2016; Hendricks, 2010; Howlin et al., 2005; Mawhood & Howlin, 1999; Migliore, Timmons, Butterworth, & Lugas, 2012). The supported employment model was developed in the United States in the early 1980s as "the process of enabling a person with a disability to secure and maintain a paid job in a regular work environment, by supplying all appropriate training support to them in the workplace where they will be doing the job" (Mawhood & Howlin, 1999, p. 231). It is not desirable to place the individual with ASD in a work setting without any supervision and/or support. Research suggests that with appropriate, specialized support, individuals with ASD are more likely to find and maintain suitable employment (Mawhood & Howlin, 1999). Key components of supported employment services include job placement, job coaching, workplace modifications, and education of employers and co-workers.

Job Placement

Fortunately, there is an increasing emphasis on placing individuals with ASD into appropriate jobs that match their skill level, strengths, and interests (Griffin, Hammis, Geary, & Sullivan, 2008; Hendricks, 2010). A study by Howlin et al. (2005) found that identifying the types of jobs that were appropriate for the client and capitalizing on his or her personal strengths resulted in higher rates of employment. This line of research seems logical; ideally, many typically developing individuals consider their own intellectual and educational background, social skills, and abilities when selecting a line of work. However, it may be particularly important with individuals with ASD who have restricted interests. Considering these restricted interests may not only help but may also even result in their excelling and sometimes outperforming their typically developing counterparts. In addition, matching adults with ASD to positions suited to their abilities has been shown to increase job satisfaction (Mawhood & Howlin, 1999) and decrease the likelihood that an individual with a disability would leave his or her job because of behavioral or work-related difficulties (Mawhood & Howlin, 1999).

Job Coaching

Appropriate placement is one way to help individuals with ASD be successful employees. However, it important to appreciate the fact that the majority will require on-the-job support (Hendricks, 2010). Job coaches can provide specialized training, helping their clients with actual job responsibilities, acclimation to the job site, and social integration (Hendricks, 2010). In addition, job coaches can help employees with disabilities understand workplace rules, manage their time, complete their job tasks, secure transportation to and from the work site, and appropriately communicate with co-workers and supervisors (Hendricks, 2010). Some of these goals may be targeted using behavioral interventions such as self-management checklists or video feedback and by helping to facilitate coordination of services with the employee's other clinicians or service providers. An example is Mike's checklist for appropriate social communication, shown in Figure 14.3. A clinician can provide checklists like these for job coaches. In addition, job coaches can be a great asset with their inherently naturalistic intervention; evidence shows that training is most beneficial when provided on the actual job site (Certo et al., 2003). However, it is also important to realize that job coaches typically do not need to stay forever. Much like other intervention programs, use of job coaches should be gradually and systematically faded so that the employee can increase his or her ability to independently perform job responsibilities (Burt et al., 1991).

Workplace Modifications

Workplace modifications can also be an important form of supported employment for individuals with ASD (Hagner & Cooney, 2005; Hendricks, 2010). Analogous to how a person in a wheelchair may need a ramp to access a higher-level station, some individuals with ASD may need modifications to the work environment, scheduling, and/or tasks. For example, if an individual has sensory issues in environments with loud or busy stimuli (Hendricks, 2010), systematic programs can be developed for desensitization or self-control. Further, modifications may be needed to ensure that the workplace is not distracting or disorienting; and adjustments in the noise level, crowding, interruptions and lighting might be necessary to improve outcomes (Hendricks, 2010). This may mean allowing the individual to be in a quieter room away from customers or other co-workers or to wear ear protection to guard against loud or disturbing noises. In addition, the employee with ASD may benefit from a consistent and predictable job schedule (Hagner & Cooney, 2005; Hendricks, 2010). Also, for some individuals it can be effective to restructure job duties to provide a consistent routine with minimal downtime or unstructured breaks (Hagner & Cooney, 2005). The routine can be complemented with instruction sheets or checklists for self-management and alternatives to downtime such as taking a walk (Burt et al., 1991).

Education of Employers and Co-workers

Education of employers and co-workers can also help increase the likelihood of success. An autism awareness training for employers who hire individuals with ASD can help employers learn how to best modify any work tasks, socially interact with the employee, and make any adjustments to the routine or environment. Most co-workers find increasing their level of knowledge about disabilities to be a very positive experience. Some supported employment programs work with supervisors and other employees to educate the staff about the autism spectrum (Hagner & Cooney, 2005; Hendricks, 2010). Research shows that if supervisors have knowledge and understanding about the disorder, then they can provide a more supportive and successful environment for a positive employment outcome (Hendricks, 2010). For example, it can be helpful for supervisors to learn that being direct, literal, and specific with directions often helps the individual with ASD deal with changes in the workplace and assists with reading social cues from others (Hagner & Cooney, 2005). A successful employment outcome is more likely if supervisors and co-workers understand and learn how to effectively work with employees with ASD.

Another approach to improving employment outcomes for individuals with ASD is through sheltered workshops (Cimera, Wehman, West, & Burgess, 2012). Sheltered workshops have been controversial, and society has clearly not developed a perfect model for employment. Sheltered workshops were designed to assist individuals who may not be considered by some to be capable of working in a competitive employment setting in their community; they provide training and experience in a separate work environment to assist individuals in acquiring the necessary skills for employment (Kregel & Dean, 2002). Unfortunately, sheltered workshops are common applications of subminimum wage work, which involves paying individuals according to their productivity level, with the assumption that work productivity by individuals with disabilities is severely impaired (Butterworth, Hall, Hoff, & Migliore, 2007; Soffer, Tal-Katz, Rimmerman, 2011). In addition, studies have found that sheltered workshop programs cost more than programs for individuals who do not engage in sheltered workshops prior to supported employment, in part due to their failure to produce meaningful employment outcomes (Cimera, 2012; Cimera et al., 2012; Kregel & Dean, 2002). Outside of the economic considerations, sheltered workshop programs separate individuals from their community and are argued to perpetuate stereotypes and stigma against this population (Perkins, Raines, Tschopp, & Warner, 2009). Conversely, work integration has been shown to evoke less stigma concerning individuals with disabilities, promoting higher levels of success and overall life satisfaction (Griffin et al., 2008; Perkins et al., 2009). The lack of financial and social benefits associated with sheltered workshops suggests that providing vocational support in the natural work environment may be more beneficial than working with individuals in a sheltered setting.

Key Insights ||| Fostering Successful Employment

The following points are important for practitioners to keep in mind when they work with adults with ASD who are transitioning into the work world or who are already employed and seek assistance in managing workplace expectations.

- Employment is an important area to address: Many adults with ASD are unemployed or earn low wages.
- There are several (solvable) barriers to success in employment: These include a lack of a single point of coordination of services, difficulty with social communication and behavior, and challenges with daily living and organization skills.
- Research shows that there are effective strategies to improve social communication and address behavioral challenges in the workplace, improve daily living and organization skills, and increase access to supported employment settings.
- Training both supervisors and co-workers is important for successful employment.
- Coordinating services across settings is helpful for targeting and addressing areas that may need intervention in the work setting.
- Sheltered workshops have few advantages: They are costly and exclude individuals with disabilities from integrated work settings.
- Focusing on the strengths of the individual can result in the most successful employment outcomes.
- Customized employment will likely become more common in the future: Customized employment focuses on the strengths of the employee, as well as the employer's needs, for successful long-term employment.

SUMMARY

Current literature on successful interventions for people with ASD indicates that the field appears to be changing in a positive direction. However, it is imperative that we understand that changes are still desperately needed to maximize the benefit to adults with ASD entering employment settings. Future research should help develop and improve behavioral interventions to improve this transition and foster workplace success. Integrating strength-based positive behavior support programs can make it more likely that individuals with ASD receive, and benefit from, effective long-term support. In addition, collaborative efforts between employers and specialized support staff appear to be helpful to ensure the continuity, consistency, and uniformity of support services. This chapter discusses multiple strategies for supporting employment of adults with ASD; these strategies are summarized in Figure 14.6.

Taken together, future research and job development services should focus on customized employment models, which have been shown to not only be effective but also to decrease state and federal costs compared to traditional supported employment (Griffin et al., 2008). According to the U.S. Department of Labor, Office of Disability & Employment Policy, customized employment means

> *"[I]ndividualizing the employment relationship between employees and employers in ways that meet the needs of both. It is based on an individualized determination of the strengths, needs, and interests of the person with a disability, and is also designed to meet the specific needs of the employer."* (Federal Register, June 26, 2002, pp. 43154– 43149).

Customized employment differs from supported employment in that it involves engaging the employer through interest-based negotiation to establish the benefits

Behavior modification for social communication

- Self-management
- Video modeling
- Functional behavior assessment

Supported employment

- Integration of personal strengths into workplace duties
- Job coaches
- Individualized workplace modifications
- Staff education
- Customized employment settings

Organization and daily living

- Daily living checklist
- Job coaches
- Visual support

Figure 14.6. Strategies to increase success in employment settings.

of hiring the individual with a disability for both parties (Griffin et al., 2008). It requires more effort be made to place individuals in higher-level employment settings and focus on deep-job development, which the research demonstrates will lead to increased skill development and longer-held job positions (Griffin et al., 2008). This approach to supported employment aligns well with our values and goals to mitigate employment gaps and increase quality of life of individuals with ASD.

STUDY QUESTIONS

1. Discuss the benefits of employment of adults with ASD.
2. Identify the barriers to success for individuals with ASD, specifically in the areas of obtaining employment, social communication, behavioral difficulties, and support for employment.
3. List interventions that may be needed to effectively improve social communication skills in the workplace.
4. Describes two ways in which self-management can be used to target areas for improvement in employment settings.
5. List supported employment strategies utilized by supported employment programs.
6. Compare and contrast sheltered workshops and customized employment models and identify the pros and cons of both approaches.

7. Discuss areas of need in the research related to employment of individuals with ASD.

8. Discuss the advantages of job coaches.

9. Describe ways in which society may be able to improve the transition to employment, acquisition of work, and job maintenance for individuals with ASD.

REFERENCES

Adreon, D., & Durocher, J. (2007). Evaluating the college transition needs of individuals with high-functioning autism spectrum disorders. *Intervention in School and Clinic, 42*(5), 271–279.

Alverson, C. Y., & Yamamoto, S. H. (2018). VR employment outcomes of individuals with autism spectrum disorders: A decade in the making. *Journal of Autism and Developmental Disorders, 48*(1), 151–162.

Ayres, K. M., & Langone, J. (2005). Intervention and instruction with video for students with autism: A review of the literature. *Education and Training in Developmental Disabilities,* 183–196.

Baker-Ericzén, M. J., Fitch, M. A., Kinnear, M., Jenkins, M. M., Twamley, E. W., Smith, L., Montano, G., Feder, J., Crooke, P. J., Winner, M. G., & Leon, J. (2018). Development of the Supported Employment, Comprehensive Cognitive Enhancement, and Social Skills program for adults on the autism spectrum: Results of initial study. *Autism, 22*(1), 6–19.

Bellini, S., & Akullian, J. (2007). A meta-analysis of video modeling and video self-modeling interventions for children and adolescents with autism spectrum disorders. *Exceptional Children, 73*(3), 264–287.

Boettcher, M. A. (1977). *Teaching social conversation skills to children with autism through self-management: An analysis of treatment gains and meaningful outcomes* (Doctoral dissertation), e-library, 3135.

Burgess, S., & Cimera, R. E. (2014). Employment outcomes of transition-aged adults with autism spectrum disorders: A state of the states report. *American Journal on Intellectual and Developmental Disabilities, 119*(1), 64–83.

Burt, D. B., Fuller, S. P., & Lewis, K. R. (1991). Competitive employment of adults with autism. *Journal of Autism and Developmental Disorders, 21*(2), 237–242.

Butterworth, J., Hall, A., Hoff, D., & Migliore, A. (2007). State and international efforts to reform or eliminate the use of sub-minimum wage for persons with disabilities. Boston, MA: Institute for Community Inclusion, University of Massachusetts.

Certo, N. J., Mautz, D., Smalley, K., Wade, H. A., Luecking, R., Pumpian, I., Sax, C., Noyes, D., Weschler, J., & Batterman, N. (2003). Review and discussion of a model for seamless transition to adulthood. *Education and Training in Developmental Disabilities, 38*(1), 3–17.

Capps, L., Kehres, J., & Sigman, M. (1998). Conversational abilities among children with autism and children with developmental delays. *Autism, 2*(4), 325–344.

Chambres, P., Auxiette, C., Vansingle, C., & Gil, S. (2008). Adult attitudes toward behaviors of a six-year-old boy with autism. *Journal of Autism and Developmental Disorders, 38*(7), 1320–1327.

Cimera, R. E. (2012). The economics of supported employment: What new data tell us. *Journal of Vocational Rehabilitation, 37*(2), 109–117.

Cimera, R. E., & Cowan, R. J. (2009). The costs of services and employment outcomes achieved by adults with autism in the US. *Autism, 13*(3), 285–302. doi:http://dx.doi.org/10.1177/1362361309103791.

Cimera, R. E., Wehman, P., West, M., & Burgess, S. (2012). Do sheltered workshops enhance employment outcomes for adults with autism spectrum disorder? *Autism, 16*(1), 87–94. doi:http://dx.doi.org/10.1177/1362361311408129

Eales, M. J. (1993). Pragmatic impairments in adults with childhood diagnoses of autism or developmental receptive language disorder. *Journal of Autism and Developmental Disorders, 23*(4), 593–617.

Federal Register. (June 26, 2002). *67*(123), 43154–43149.

Garcia-Villamisar, D., Ross, D., & Wehman, P. (2000). Clinical differential analysis of persons with autism in a work setting: A follow-up study. *Journal of Vocational Rehabilitation, 14*, 183–185.

Gilbride, D., Stensrud, R., Ehlers, C., Evans, E., & Peterson, C. (2000). Employers' attitudes toward hiring persons with disabilities and vocational rehabilitation services. *Journal of Rehabilitation, 66*(4), 17.

Graetz, J. E., & Spampinato, K. (2008). Asperger's Syndrome and the voyage through high school: Not the final frontier. *Journal of College Admission, 198*, 19–24.

Griffin, C., Hammis, D., Geary, T., & Sullivan, M. (2008). Customized employment: Where we are; where we're headed. *Journal of Vocational Rehabilitation, 28*(3), 135–139.

Hagner, D., & Cooney, B. F. (2005). "I do that for everybody": Supervising employees with autism. *Focus on Autism and Other Developmental Disabilities, 20*(2), 91–97.

Hedley, D., Dissanayake, C., Richdale, A., Spoor, J., & Uljarević, M. (2016). Long-term benefits of supported employment for adults with autism spectrum disorder. *Journal of Intellectual Disability Research, 60*(7), 679.

Hendricks, D. (2010). Employment and adults with autism spectrum disorders: Challenges and strategies for success. *Journal of Vocational Rehabilitation, 32*(2), 125–134.

Hillier, A., Campbell, H., Mastriani, K., Izzo, M. V., Kool-Tucker, A., Cherry, L., & Beversdorf, D. O. (2007). Two-year evaluation of a vocational support program for adults on the autism spectrum. *Career Development for Exceptional Individuals, 30*(1), 35–47.

Howlin, P., Alcock, J., & Burkin, C. (2005). An 8 year follow-up of a specialist supported employment service for high-ability adults with autism or Asperger syndrome. *Autism, 9*(5), 533–549.

Hume, K., Loftin, R., & Lantz, J. (2009). Increasing independence in autism spectrum disorders: A review of three focused interventions. *Journal of Autism and Developmental Disorders, 39*(9), 1329–1338.

Institute of Education Sciences. (2009). National Longitudinal Transition Study-2. https://nlts2.sri.com/index.html

Kaldy, Z., Giserman, I., Carter, A. S., & Blaser, E. (2016). The mechanisms underlying the ASD advantage in visual search. *Journal of Autism and Developmental Disorders, 46*(5), 1513–1527.

Keehn, B., Shih, P., Brenner, L. A., Townsend, J., & Müller, R. A. (2013). Functional connectivity for an "island of sparing" in autism spectrum disorder: An fMRI study of visual search. *Human Brain Mapping, 34*(10), 2524–2537.

Kirchner, J. C., & Dziobek, I. (2014). Towards successful employment of adults with autism: A first analysis of special interests and factors deemed important for vocational performance. *Scandinavian Journal of Child and Adolescent Psychiatry and Psychology, 2*(2), 77–85.

Kirchner, J., Ruch, W., & Dziobek, I. (2016). Brief report: Character strengths in adults with autism spectrum disorder without intellectual impairment. *Journal of Autism and Developmental Disorders, 46*(10), 3330–3337.

Koegel, L. K. (2000). Interventions to facilitate communication in autism. *Journal of Autism and Developmental Disorders, 30*(5), 383–391.

Koegel, L. K., Ashbaugh, K., Navab, A., & Koegel, R. L. (2016). Improving empathic communication skills in adults with autism spectrum disorder. *Journal of Autism and Developmental Disorders, 46*(3), 921–933.

Koegel, L. K., Koegel, R. L., Hurley, C., & Frea, W. D. (1992). Improving social skills and disruptive behavior in children with autism through self-management. *Journal of Applied Behavior Analysis, 25*(2), 341–353.

Koegel, R. L., Koegel, L. K., & Parks, D. R. (1995). *A guide to self-management: A training manual*. Santa Barbara: University of California.

Koegel, L. K., & LaZebnik, C. (2009). *Growing up on the spectrum: A guide to life, love, and learning for teens and young adults with autism and Asperger's*. New York, NY: Viking.

Koegel, L. K., Navab, A., Ashbaugh, K., & Koegel, R. L. (2016). Using reframing to reduce negative statements in social conversation for adults with autism spectrum disorder. *Journal of Positive Behavior Interventions, 18*(3), 133–144.

Koegel, R. L., O'dell, M. C., & Koegel, L. K. (1987). A natural language teaching paradigm for nonverbal autistic children. *Journal of Autism and Developmental Disorders, 17*(2), 187–200.
Kregel, J., & Dean, D. (2002). Sheltered vs. supported employment: A direct comparison of long-term earnings outcomes for individuals with cognitive disabilities. In *Achievements and challenges in employment services for people with disabilities: The longitudinal impact of workplace supports*. Monograph.
Landa, R., Klin, A., Volkmar, F., & Sparrow, S. (2000). Social language use in Asperger syndrome and high-functioning autism. *Asperger Syndrome*, 125–155.
Landa, R., Piven, J., Wzorek, M. M., Gayle, J. O., Chase, G. A., & Folstein, S. E. (1992). Social language use in parents of autistic individuals. *Psychological Medicine, 22*(01), 245–254.
Lawer, L., Brusilovskiy, E., Salzer, M. S., & Mandell, D. S. (2009). Use of vocational rehabilitative services among adults with autism. *Journal of Autism and Developmental Disorders, 39*(3), 487–494.
Manente, C. J., Maraventano, J. C., LaRue, R. H., Delmolino, L., & Sloan, D. (2010). Effective behavioral intervention for adults on the autism spectrum: Best practices in functional assessment and treatment development. *The Behavior Analyst Today, 11*(1), 36.
Mayes, S. D., & Calhoun, S. L. (2003). Ability profiles in children with autism: Influence of age and IQ. *Autism, 7*(1), 65–80.
Mawhood, L., & Howlin, P. (1999). The outcome of a supported employment scheme for high-functioning adults with autism or Asperger syndrome. *Autism, 3*(3), 229–254.
McDonough, J. T., & Revell, G. (2010). Accessing employment supports in the adult system for transitioning youth with autism spectrum disorders. *Journal of Vocational Rehabilitation, 32*(2), 89–100.
Migliore, A., & Butterworth, J. (2008). Trends in outcomes of the vocational rehabilitation program for adults with developmental disabilities: 1995–2005. *Rehabilitation Counseling Bulletin, 52*(1), 35–44.
Migliore, A., Butterworth, J., & Zalewska, A. (2014). Trends in vocational rehabilitation services and outcomes of youth with autism: 2006–2010. *Rehabilitation Counseling Bulletin, 57*(2), 80–89.
Migliore, A., Timmons, J., Butterworth, J., & Lugas, J. (2012). Predictors of employment and postsecondary education of youth with autism. *Rehabilitation Counseling Bulletin, 55*(3), 176–184.
Müller, E., Schuler, A., & Yates, G. B. (2008). Social challenges and supports from the perspective of individuals with Asperger syndrome and other autism spectrum disabilities. *Autism, 12*(2), 173–190.
Perkins, D. V., Raines, J. A., Tschopp, M. K., & Warner, T. C. (2009). Gainful employment reduces stigma toward people recovering from schizophrenia. *Community Mental Health Journal, 45*(3), 158.
Roux, A. M., Shattuck, P. T., Cooper, B. P., Anderson, K. A., Wagner, M., & Narendorf, S. C. (2013). Postsecondary employment experiences among young adults with an autism spectrum disorder. *Journal of the American Academy of Child & Adolescent Psychiatry, 52*(9), 931–939.
Samson, F., Mottron, L., Soulieres, I., & Zeffiro, T. A. (2012). Enhanced visual functioning in autism: An ALE meta-analysis. *Human Brain Mapping, 33*(7), 1553–1581.
Schaller, J., & Yang, N. K. (2005). Competitive employment for people with autism: Correlates of successful closure in competitive and supported employment. *Rehabilitation Counseling Bulletin, 49*(1), 4–16.
Schmidt, L., Kirchner, J., Strunz, S., Broźus, J., Ritter, K., Roepke, S., & Dziobek, I. (2015). Psychosocial functioning and life satisfaction in adults with autism spectrum disorder without intellectual impairment. *Journal of Clinical Psychology, 71*(12), 1259–1268.
Shattuck, P. T., Narendorf, S. C., Cooper, B., Sterzing, P. R., Wagner, M., & Taylor, J. L. (2012). Postsecondary education and employment among youth with an autism spectrum disorder. *Pediatrics,129*(6), 1042–1049.
Smith, L. E., Maenner, M. J., & Seltzer, M. M. (2012). Developmental trajectories in adolescents and adults with autism: The case of daily living skills. *Journal of the American Academy of Child & Adolescent Psychiatry, 51*(6), 622–631.
Soffer, M., Tal-Katz, P., & Rimmerman, A. (2011). Sub minimum wage for persons with severe disabilities: Comparative perspectives. *Journal of Comparative Policy Analysis: Research and Practice, 13*(3), 265–286.

Sperry, L. A., & Mesibov, G. B. (2005). Perceptions of social challenges of adults with autism spectrum disorder. *Autism, 9*(4), 362–376.

U.S. Department of Education. (2012). Institute of Education Sciences, National Center for Education Statistics, High School Longitudinal Study, 2009-2013 [United States]. Ann Arbor, MI: Inter-university Consortium for Political and Social Research. 2016-05-12. https://doi.org/10.3886/ICPSR36423.v1.

Wehman, P., Schall, C.M., McDonough, J., Graham, C., Brooke, V., Riehle, J.E., Brooke, A., Ham, W., Lau, S., Allen, J., & Avellone, L. (2017). Effects of an employer-based intervention on employment outcomes for youth with significant support needs due to autism. *Autism, 21*(3), 276–290.

Wilkinson, L. A. (2008). Self-management for children with high-functioning autism spectrum disorders. *Intervention in School and Clinic, 43*(3), 150–157.

Zager, D., & Alpern, C. S. (2010). College-based inclusion programming for transition-age students with autism. *Focus on Autism and Other Developmental Disabilities, 25*(3), 151–157.

Index

Note: Tables and figures are indicated by *t* and *f* respectively.

ABA, *see* Applied behavior analysis
Academics
  applying PRT to, 13–14
  and behavioral issues, 148–150
  in higher education, success strategies, 231–234
  supports, 229
Accommodations
  in higher education, 225–226, 228, 229, 234
  in inclusive education, 129, 136, 139
  for students with disabilities, 234
  workplace, 261
Acquisition tasks, 112
Activities
  after-school, 86
  child-preferred, 55–56
  cooperative, 92, 93–96
  extracurricular, 86–87, 99–100
  group, 99
  neutral, 56
  for play dates, 90–93
  social, 206, 210–215
ADA, *see* Americans with Disabilities Act
Adaptive technology resources, 234
Adolescents with ASD
  see also Individuals with ASD
  improving communication skills in, 185–199
  improving socialization in, 203–217
  interest-based social opportunities for, 207–209
ADOS-T, *see* Autism Diagnostic Observation Schedule-Toddler Module
Adults with ASD
  see also Individuals with ASD
  addressing severe behavioral challenges in, 259
  co-morbid disorders in, 204–205, 226
  employment opportunities for, 185–186, 204, 247–265
  higher education outcomes for, 223–244
  improving communication skills in, 185–199
  improving socialization in, 203–217
  interest-based social opportunities for, 207–209
  structured social planning for, 210–215
Affect
  assessment of child's, 26
  infant, 50
After-school activities, 86
Age, for play dates, 89
Americans with Disabilities Act (ADA), 225
Anxiety, 205, 226
Applied behavior analysis (ABA), 3–5, 69
ASD, *see* Autism spectrum disorders
Asian cultures, 37, 40
Asperger syndrome, xxi, 205
Assessment
  assessor's input in, 30–31
  behavioral, 24–26, 50
  of child's affect, 26
  cognitive, 50
  functional behavior, 162, 163–167, 257, 259
  key insights for, 32–33
  parent input in, 31–32
  preference, 27–28
  role of, 21–22
  of social opportunities, 85–87
  standardized testing, 22–24, 30
  strength-based, 26–28, 31–32, 55
  and treatment, 19–20, 29
Attribution, and learned helplessness, 6
Autism Diagnostic Observation Schedule-Toddler Module (ADOS-T), 56, 76
Autism Observation Scale for Infants, 50
Autism spectrum disorders (ASD)
  see also Adolescents with ASD; Adults with ASD; Children with ASD; Individuals with ASD
  across cultures, 37–39
  diagnosis of, 20, 22, 30–31, 49–53
  pivotal treatment areas for, xxi
  red flags for, 52*f*
  symptoms of, 22, 30, 49–50
  terminology, xxi
  trajectory of, 53*f*
Autonomy, 170
Aversive stimulation, 162
Avoidance behaviors, 152

Babbling, 50, 66
Bayley Scales of Infant and Toddler Development, 50

Behavioral assessments, 24–26, 50
Behavioral interventions
  history of, 162–169
  key insights for, 179–180
  positive behavior support, 162–163
  self-management, 169–173
  to support employment, 251–259
Behavioral momentum, power of, 74
Behavior(s)
  see also Challenging behaviors
  and academics, 148–150
  addressing severe challenges in, 259
  analyzing function of, 163–167
  avoidance, 152
  concerns, 21
  disruptive, 148, 161–162
  escape, 152
  recording (monitoring), 176–177
  replacement, 163–169
  target, 174–175
  teaching discrimination between, 176
  typical, 25–26
Bullying, 134

Caregivers
  see also Families; Parents
  social interventions by, 83–85
  as treatment mediators, 73–74
Carrier phrases, 75–76
Case histories
  college transition, 230–231
  cultural considerations, 42–43
  early intervention with infant, 59–60
  expressive communication skills, 11
  learned helplessness, 6–7
  mercy killing tragedy, 124
  parent education, 117–119
  priming, 154
  self-management, 254–255
  social communication skills, 196–197
  social integration in college, 236–237
  social interactions, 13–14
  teaching first words, 76–77
  teaching replacement behaviors, 166
CE, *see* Cognitive empathy
Chaining procedures, 4
Challenging behaviors
  during academic activities, 147–156
  addressing severe, 259
  and employment, 250
  interventions for, 162–179
  naturalistic observations of, 25–26
  preventing, 161–162
  providing choices to reduce, 7–8
  punishment of, 162
  reasons for, 148, 163
  replacement behaviors for, 163–169
Checklists, 238, 240, 240*f*, 257, 258*f*
Child attention, 111
Child choice
  for improved academic engagement and behavior, 150–153
  and motivation, 7–8
  and parent education, 111
  providing, 70, 150–153
Child-preferred activities, 55–56
Children with ASD
  see also Individuals with ASD
  appealing to interests of, 84–85
  applied behavior analysis for, 3–5
  assessment of, *see* Assessment
  challenges facing parents of, 20–22
  characteristics of social communication in, 51
  early language development in, 67–68
  friendship opportunities for, 81–102
  heterogeneity among, 20–21, 126–127
  inclusive education for, 123–141, 148–150
  isolation of, 191
  learned helplessness in, 5–7
  motivational academics for, 147–157
  nonresponsive, 74–76
  nonverbal, 67
  prognosis for, 31–32, 53
  with restricted interests, 13–14
  testing of, 22–24
Choice
  see also Child choice
  of college, 228–231
  and motivation, 7–8
  vs. preference, 8
  providing, 70, 150–153
Classroom curriculum, 152
Class sizes, 83
Cognitive assessment, 50
Cognitive empathy (CE), 191–192
Collaborative partnership approach, 110
Collectivistic cultures, 37–39
College
  choosing a, 228–231
  majors, 229
  navigating environment in, 240–241
College education, *see* Higher education
Communication
  see also Communication skills; Social communication
  nonverbal, 67, 68
  overall frequency of, 57*f*
  verbal, 10–12, 51–54, 65–79
  written, 252
Communication and Symbolic Behavior Scales, 50
Communication skills
  case history, 196–197
  empathy, 191–195

improving, in adolescents and adults with ASD, 185–199
key insights for, 198
question asking, 195–196
and self-management, 196
social, 252–256
teaching expressive, 10–12
video modeling of, 187–191
visual frameworks for, 186–187, 187*f*, 193–195
Community, social opportunities in, 85, 86–87
Community colleges, 228
Community rehabilitation programs (CRPs), 251
Co-morbid disorders, 204–205, 226
Contextual supports, for social interactions, 84
Contingent reinforcement, 111
Cooperative activities, 92, 93–96
Co-teaching, 133
Counseling services, 241
Co-workers, 262
Cues, child orientation to, 74–75
Cultural competence, 41–42
Culturally and linguistically diverse (CLD) individuals, 35
considerations and sensitivity for, 36–39
culturally competent service providers for, 41–42
key insights for, 43–44
positive behavior support with, 40–41
Cultural sensitivity, 36–39
Culture
ecocultural theory, 36
and treatment, 40–41
Customized employment, 263–264

Daily living skills, 227, 237–240, 250, 256–257, 258*f*
Daily planners, 237–238, 239
Depression
as co-morbid disorder, 205, 226
and learned helplessness, 6
Diagnosis
of ASD, 20, 22, 30–31
guidelines for early, 49–53
importance of early, 52–53
median age of, 50
parental stress and, 20–21
prognosis following, 31–32
standardized testing for, 22–24
Diagnostic and Statistical Manual of Mental Disorders (DSM-5), 22, 30–31
Direct observation, preference assessment through, 28
Direct rewards, 71
Disability, cultural differences in approaches to, 38–39
Disciplinary practices, cultural differences in, 40
Discrete trial training (DTT), 4, 68, 69
Disruptive behaviors, 148, 161–162
see also Challenging behaviors

Early diagnosis
guidelines for, 49–53
importance of, 52–53
Early intervention
see also Interventions
discrete trial training, 4, 68, 69
importance of, 52–53
with infants and toddlers, 49–62
key insights for, 60–61
positive outcomes of, xxiii
teaching first words, 65–79
for verbal communication, 11–12
Echolalia, 51
Ecocultural theory, 36, 40
Education
see also Parent education; School
cultural differences in approaches to, 38–39
of employers and co-workers, 262
higher, 223–244
inclusive, 123–141
motivational academics, 147–157
as top priority for children with ASD, 124–127
Emotional empathy (EE), 191–192
Empathy
cognitive, 191–192
defined, 191–192
emotional, 191–192
instruction in, 191–195
research on teaching, 192–195
Empathy Quotient (EQ), 192
Employers, 262
Employment
barriers to, 249–250
behavioral interventions to support, 251–259
benefits of, 247–248, 248*f*
customized, 263–264
and daily living skills, 256–257
functional behavior assessment for, 257, 259
goals, 247
and higher education, 228
of individuals with ASD, 247–265
integrating strengths into, 259–260
job coaching, 261
job placement, 260–261
key insights for, 262–263
levels of, 185–186

Employment—*continued*
and self-management, 253–255
sheltered workshops, 262
and socialization deficits, 204
statistics, 249
strategies to increase success in, 264*f*
supported, 260–262
video modeling of, 255–256
vocational rehabilitation programs, 250–251
workplace modifications, 261
Escape behaviors, 152
Ethics, of full inclusion, 136
Executive functioning skills, 212–213, 227, 237–240
Extracurricular activities, 86–87, 99–100
Eye contact
cultural differences in, 37
infants, 50

Families
see also Parents
culturally competent service providers for, 41–42
geographically distant, parent education for, 116–117
involvement of, in interventions, xxiii
Family Empowerment Scale (FES), 115
Family interactions, parental stress during, 12–13
Fear, of unknown, 20–21
Fidelity of implementation, of PRT, 108, 111–112
First words
case history, 76–77
delay in, 67–68
emergence of, 50, 53–54
key insights for, 77–78
rewarding attempts at, 71–73
teaching, 58, 65–79
working with nonresponsive children, 74–76
Friendship opportunities, 81–102
across settings, 97–100
benefits of intervention for, 82–85
for college students, 226
key insights for, 100–101
play dates, 87–97
Full inclusion, 136–139
see also Inclusive education
Functional behavior assessment (FBA), 162, 163–167
form for, 168*f*
home example, 164–166
school example, 166–167
in workplace, 257, 259

Gender, and play dates, 89
General education (GE) classrooms, 123, 127, 128, 149
see also Inclusive education
Genetic testing, 22
Guilt, felt by parents, 21

Higher education
academic success strategies for, 231–234
academic supports in, 229
accommodations in, 234
benefits of, 224, 224*f*
case history, 230–231
college choice, 228–231
common challenges, 225–227, 227*f*
improving outcomes in, 223–244
key insights for, 242–243
living arrangements, 228–229
majors, 229
navigation strategies for, 240–241
services in, 225–226
social integration strategies for, 235–237
social support resources, 230
supporting individuals with ASD in, 224
Hispanic families, 39
Home, social opportunities in, 85, 87
Homework assignments, 151

IDEA, *see* Individuals with Disabilities Education Act
IEP, *see* Individualized education program
Inclusive education, 123–141
benefits of, 149
cost of, vs. segregation, 138
co-teaching model, 133
debate over, 136–139
early arguments against, 136–137
efficacy of, vs. segregation, 138–139
improving socialization in, 134–135
key insights for, 139–140
meaning of, 128
paraprofessional support in, 132–133
parents' anxieties and desires about, 130–131
and partial participation, 148–150
perceptions and attitudes toward, 128–130
research supporting, 137–139
school culture and leadership for, 133
teacher training, support, and resources, 131–133
Inclusive environments, 83
Individualistic cultures, 37–39
Individualized education program (IEP), 86, 225

Individuals with ASD
  see also Adolescents with ASD; Adults with ASD; Children with ASD
  cultural considerations with, 35–44
  employment of, 185–186, 205, 247–265
  heterogeneity among, 185–186
  higher education outcomes for, 223–244
  improving communication skills in, 185–199
  improving socialization in, 203–217
  motivation to learn of, xxii
  self-advocacy by, 225–226, 229
  self-management with, 169–173, 171–179, 253–256
  strengths of, 248, 259–260
  transitioning to adulthood by, 185–186
Individuals with Disabilities Education Act (IDEA), 137, 225
Infant Autism Diagnostic Observation Schedule, 50
Infants
  see also Children with ASD
  diagnosis of, 49–53
  emerging social communication in typically developing, 50–51
  interventions for, 53–60
  key insights for, 60–61
  restricted interests and repetitive behaviors in, 51–52
  using PRT with, 55–56, 76
Intervention agents, xxii
Interventions
  ABA, 4–5
  academic, 150–155
  behavioral, 162–173, 251, 259
  early, 11–12, 49–62, 52–53, 65–79
  environment for, xxiii
  family involvement in, xxiii
  for first words, 68–72
  for friendship opportunities, 81–102
  for infants and toddlers, 49–62
  parent-mediated, 54
  peer-mediated, 135
  for socialization, 195–196, 205–215
  to teach expressive communication skills, 10–12
  and treatment goals, 29
Interviews, preference assessment through, 28
Isolation, 191, 205, 226
Item labeling, 70–71

Job coaching, 261
Job placement, 260–261

Korean culture, 38–39

Language
  see also Communication; Communication skills
  echolalia, 51
  samples, 26
  scripted speech, 51
Language development
  early, 66
  infants and toddlers, 51
  vocabulary burst, 66
Latency, 152
Latino families, 39
Learned helplessness, 5–7, 205
Learning
  see also Education
  role of motivation in, xxii, 5
Least restrictive environment (LRE), 128, 137, 148–149
  see also Inclusive education

Mainstreaming, 128, 136
  see also Inclusive education
Maintenance tasks, 112
Modeling, item labeling, 70–71
Models
  of inclusive education, 133
  of parent education, 112–117
Modified PRT interventions
  with infants, 55–56, 61*f*
  with toddlers, 56–59
Motivation
  and interspersing tasks, 8
  and learned helplessness, 5–7
  natural rewards to increase, 9
  and providing choice, 7–8
  and rewarding attempts, 9–10
  role of, in learning, xxii, 5
  and varied tasks, 8–9
Motivational academics, 147–157
  background on, 148–150
  key insights for, 155–156
  key strategies for, 150–154
  parent involvement, 154–155
  and priming, 153–155
Motivational components
  applying to other target behaviors, 13–14
  combining to teach expressive communication skills, 10–12
  effectiveness of, 12–13
  to elicit first words, 69–73, 70*f*
  for improved academic engagement and behavior, 150–154

Motivational components—*continued*
key insights for, 14–15
of PRT, xxii–xxiii, 7–15
research support for, 72–73
Mullen Scales of Early Learning, 50
Multiculturalism, 37
see also Culturally and linguistically diverse (CLD) individuals

National Education Association of the United States (PL 94-142), 137
National High School Longitudinal Transition Survey, 249
Natural environment, xxiii, 54
Naturalistic interventions, as basis for PRT, 69
Naturalistic observations, of behavior, 25–26
Natural Language Paradigm (NLP), 12
Natural reinforcers, 112
Natural rewards, 9, 71, 150–153
Navajo culture, 37
Needs-based perspective, on inclusion, 136–137
Negative enthusiasm, 26
Neutral activities, 56
Neutral enthusiasm, 26
NLP, *see* Natural Language Paradigm
Nonverbal communication, 67, 68*f*
Note taking, 234

Office hours, of professors, 232–233
One Stop Career Centers, 251
Opportunities
providing clear, 111
social, *see* Social opportunities

Paraprofessionals
co-teaching by, 133
culturally competent, 41–42
as one-to-one aides, 132–133
social program implementation by, 209–210
support from, in GE classrooms, 132–133
training for, 132–133, 209–210
Parental stress
and diagnosis of ASD, 20–21, 58
during family interactions, 12–13
and parent education, 109
Parent–child interactions, 55–56, 108, 110
Parent education, 107–120
case history, 117–119
collaborative approach to, 110
and fidelity of PRT implementation, 111–112
for geographically distant families, 116–117
How To issues in, 109–110
importance of, 108–111
key insights for, 119–120
models of, 112–117
and parent stress, 109
research on, 109, 113–116
strategies for, 110–111
strength-based approach to, 110
understanding of, 108
Parent-infant interactions, 53
Parenting Stress Index/Short Form, 115
Parent-mediated interventions, 54
Parents
advising, about behavioral assessments, 24–25
anxieties and desires about inclusive education of, 130–131
behavioral concerns of, 21
challenges facing, 20–22
of children with ASD, 4, 20–22
emotions of, 20–21
involvement of, in academics, 154–155
lack of social support for, 21
as primary intervention agents, xxii
social concerns of, 81–82
social interventions by, 83–85
as treatment mediators, 73–74
Partial participation
examples, 149–150
in inclusive classrooms, 148–150
PBIS, *see* Positive behavior intervention and support
Peer-mediated interventions, 135
Peer mentorship, 213–214, 235
Peer-peer relationships, 24
friendships, 81–102
importance of, 82
in inclusive schools, 134–135
Peer rejection, 134
Performance deficits, 83–84
Personal computers, for self-management, 173
Pervasive developmental disorder-not otherwise specified (PDD-NOS), xxi
Pivotal areas, xxi–xxii
Pivotal Response Treatment (PRT)
see also Interventions; Motivational components
applying to other target behaviors, 13–14
core principles, xxii–xxiii
development of, 12
fidelity of implementation of, 111–112
for first words, 69–77
goals of, xxii
history of, 3–5
and inclusive education, 123–141

introduction to, xxi–xxii
modified, with infants, 55–56, 61*f*, 76
modified, with toddlers, 56–59
motivational components of, 7–15
naturalist interventions as basis for, 69
and parental stress during family interactions, 12–13
parent education in, 107–120
training paraprofessionals to implement, 209–210
video modeling in, 187–191
working with nonresponsive children, 74–76
PL 94-142, *see* National Education Association of the United States
Planners, 237–238, 239
Play, infants and toddlers, 51
Play dates, 84, 87–97
activities for, 90–93
cooperative arrangements at, 93–96
length of, 93
picking right peers for, 88–90
potential obstacles to, 89–90
preparation for, 90–93
reflecting on, 96–97
structure and organization of, 91–92
Playgroups, 97–99
Point of view, in video modeling, 190
Positive behavior intervention and support (PBIS)
with culturally diverse families, 40–41
development of, 162–163
key insights for, 179–180
replacement behaviors, 163–169
self-management, 169–179
Positive enthusiasm, 26
Postsecondary education, *see* Higher education
"Practice-with-feedback" model, 54
Preference, vs. choice, 8
Preference assessments, 27–28
Preferred interests
as motivators, 152
and socialization, 206–207
Pre-service teachers, perceptions and attitudes toward inclusion of, 129
Priming, 153–155, 195, 232
Principals, perceptions and attitudes toward inclusion of, 129–130
Priority registration, 234
Professors, office hours of, 232–233
PRT, *see* Pivotal Response Treatment
Psychologists, 241
Punishment
as behavioral intervention, 162
cultural differences in, 40
use of, in ABA, 4

Question asking, 195–196, 250
Question banks, 195–196

Reframing, 188–189
Reinforcement
of attempts, 112
contingent, 111
natural, 112
role of, in maintaining replacement behaviors, 167–169
use of, in ABA, 4
Reinforcer Assessment for Individuals with Severe Disability (RAISD), 28
"Remaking Recess" program, 82
Replacement behaviors
role of reinforcement in maintaining, 167–169
teaching, 163–167
Representative samples, 24–25
Restricted and repetitive patterns of behavior (RRBs), 22, 30, 50–52
Restricted interests, 13–14, 22, 51–52, 206–207
Rewards
for attempts, 9–10, 71–72, 112
natural, 9, 71, 150–153
in self-management, 172, 175, 177–178
Rights-based approach
to disabilities, 38
to inclusion, 136
RRBs, *see* Restricted and repetitive patterns of behavior

SBA, *see* Strength-based assessment
School
see also Education
culture, 133
group activities in, 99
leadership, 133
social opportunities in, 85, 86
School administrators, perceptions and attitudes toward inclusion of, 129–130
School-based treatment model
to address children's heterogeneity, 126–127
development of, 125–126
Scripted speech, 51
Segregation
cost of, 138
efficacy of, vs. full inclusion, 138–139
negative effects of, 135
Self-advocacy, 225–226, 229
Self-management, xxiii
in additional settings, 178
applicability of, 178–179

Self-management—*continued*
as behavioral intervention, 169–173
benefits and versatility of, 170–171
case history, 254–255
cautions when using, 179
and daily living skills, 256–257
with individuals with ASD, 171–173
for individuals with greater support needs, 172–173
initial goals for, 175–176
plans for, 172*t*
program development, 174–178
and replacement behaviors, 167, 169
and social skills, 196, 253–255
and video modeling, 255–256
Service providers
culturally competent, 41–42
social interventions by, 83–85
Services, lack of, 21
Shaping procedures, 4
Sheltered workshops, 262
Skills
academic, 13–14
communication, *see* Communication skills
daily living, 227, 237–240, 250, 256–257, 258*f*
executive functioning, 212–213, 227, 237–240
self-management, *see* Self-management
social, *see* Social skills
video modeling of, 187–191
Social activities, 206, 235
Social clubs, 207–209
Social communication
see also Socialization; Social skills
case history, 196–197
challenges with, 186, 249–250
characteristics associated with ASD, 51
deficits in, 49–50, 204
defined, 50
early language development, 66–79
and empathy, 191–195
improving, in adolescents and adults with ASD, 185–199
individualized support in, 235–236
key insights for, 198
and self-management, 196, 253, 255
in typically developing infants and toddlers, 50–51
in the workplace, 252–256
Social (Pragmatic) Communication Disorder, 31
Social conversations, 195–196, 249–250
Social integration, strategies to increase, 235–237
Socialization
see also Social communication; Social skills
in adolescents and adults with ASD, 203–217
in colleges and universities, 226–227
deficits in, 205
impact of difficulties with, 204–205
interventions for improving, 205–209
key insights for, 215–216
restricted and preferred interests to improve, 206–207
structured social planning, 210–215
Social learning, 187
Social opportunities, 81–102
across settings, 97–100
assessment of child's, 85–87
benefits of intervention for, 82–85
in community, 85, 86–87
at home, 85, 87
in inclusive schools, 134–135
play dates, 87–97
at school, 85, 86
Social programs, training paraprofessionals to implement, 209–210
Social responsivity, 53
Social skills
see also Socialization
appealing to child's interests to motivate use of, 84–85
applying PRT to, 13–14
deficits in, 204
groups, 99
individualized training in, 214–215, 235–236
interventions for, 82–84, 195–196
performance deficits in, 83–84
and play dates, 88
supporting, 134
video modeling of, 187–191
Social support
lack of, 21
resources, in college, 230
Software training, for teaching empathic skills, 192–193
Sounds, in child's repertoire, 75–76
Speech-language pathologists (SLPs), 26
Standardized testing, 22–24, 30
Stereotypy, 22
Stimulus-response-consequence paradigm, 4
Strength-based assessment (SBA)
in infants, 55
parent input in, 31–32
preference assessments as component of, 27–28
specific applications of, 27
value of, 26–28

Stress, parental, 12–13, 20–21, 58, 109
Structured social planning, 210–215
  benefits of, 215, 217*f*
  create menu of social activities, 211, 212*t*
  identify motivational interests for social activities, 211
  implement individualized social skills training, 214–215
  provide peer mentorship, 213–214
  train in executive functioning skills, 212–213
  underlying PRT strategies of, 210*t*
Students
  see also Education; Higher education; Inclusive education
  academic supports for, 229
  accommodations for, 129, 136, 139, 225–226, 228, 229, 234
  challenges for higher education, 225–227
  with disabilities, accommodations for, 234
  individualized supports for, 225–226
Study buddies, 232–233
Summer camps, 99–100
Supported employment, 260–262
Surveys, preference assessment through, 28

Tactile prompts, for self-management, 173
Target behaviors, 174–175
Tasks
  acquisition, 112
  improving performance on, 256
  interspersing, 8, 150–153
  maintenance, 112
  varying, 8–9, 55–56, 71, 112
Teachers
  inclusion training and resources for, 131–133
  perceptions and attitudes toward inclusion of, 128–129
  training in self-management, 178–179
Test-taking accommodations, 234
Toddlers
  see also Children with ASD
  diagnosis of, 49–53
  emerging social communication in typically developing, 50–51
  group play, 97–99
  interventions for, 49–62
  key insights for, 60–61
  modified PRT with, 56–59
Treatment
  see also Interventions
  and assessment, 19–20, 29
  cultural differences in approaches to, 38–41
  goals, 29
Typical behavior, 25–26

Universities, *see* Higher education

Values, cultural, 37–38, 40–41
Verbal communication
  see also Communication; Communication skills; Language
  carrier phrases, 75–76
  concerns with, as early sign of ASD, 51
  creating opportunities for, 73–74
  interventions for, 10–12, 53–54
  rewarding attempts at, 71–73
  teaching first words, 65–79
  working with nonresponsive children, 74–76
Video modeling
  additional variables in, 190–191
  combined with visual frameworks, 193–195
  for employment settings, 255–256
  featuring oneself, peer, or adult, 188–190
  point of view, 190
  in PRT, 187–191
  for teaching empathic skills, 193–195
Video self-modeling (VSM), 188–190
Vignettes, for teaching empathic skills, 193
Vineland Adaptive Behavior Scales-II, 113
Visual frameworks, 186–187, 187*f*, 193–195, 194*f*
Vocabulary, expressive, 66
Vocational rehabilitation programs, 250–251

Wait lists, 21
Western cultures, 39
Work Incentives Planning and Assistance (WIPA) projects, 251
Workplace settings
  see also Employment
  education of employers and co-workers in, 262
  functional behavior assessment in, 257, 259
  integrating strengths into, 259–260
  modifications in, 261
  social communication in, 252–256
  strategies to increase success in, 264*f*
  supporting individuals with ASD in, 247–265
Written communication, 252